FROMMER'S

COMPREHENSIVE TRAVEL GUIDE

ACAPULCO, IXTAPA & TAXCO

2nd EDITION

by Marita Adair

MACMILLAN TRAVEL • USA

About the Author: Marita Adair's lifelong passion for Mexico's culture, people, and history began at age 11 on her first trip across the border to Nogales. An award-winning travel writer, she specializes in writing about Mexico and is the author of four Frommer guides to that country. Her freelance articles and photographs about Mexico have appeared in numerous newspapers and magazines, including the *Fort Worth Star-Telegram*, *Dallas Morning News*, *Houston Post*, *Los Angeles Times*, and *Newsday*.

Macmillan Travel
A Prentice Hall Macmillan Company
15 Columbus Circle
New York, NY 10023

Copyright © 1993, 1995 by Simon & Schuster Inc.

Macmillan is a registered trademark of Macmillan, Inc.

ISBN 0-671-88364-X
ISSN 1066-4939

Design by Robert Bull Design
Maps by Geografix Inc.

SPECIAL SALES

Bulk purchases (10+ copies) of Frommer's Travel Guides are available to corporations at special discounts. The Special Sales Department can produce custom editions to be used as premiums and/or for sales promotion to suit individual needs. Existing editions can be produced with custom cover imprints such as corporate logos. For more information write to: Special Sales, Prentice Hall, 15 Columbus Circle, New York, NY 10023.

Manufactured in the United States of America

CONTENTS

LIST OF MAPS

WHAT THE SYMBOLS MEAN

FROMMER'S FAVORITES—hotels, restaurants, attractions, and entertainments you should not miss

SUPER-SPECIAL VALUES—really exceptional values

FROMMER'S SMART TRAVELLER TIPS—hints on how to secure the best value for your money

IN HOTEL AND OTHER LISTINGS

The following symbols refer to the standard amentities available in all rooms:

A/C air conditioning   TEL telephone
FAN fan   TV television
MINIBAR refrigerator stocked with beverages and snacks

TRIP PLANNING WITH THIS GUIDE

Use the following features:

What Things Cost In . . . to help you plan your daily budget

Calendar of Events . . . to plan for or avoid

Suggested Itineraries . . . for seeing the cities and regions

What's Special About Checklist . . . a summary of each destination's highlights—which lets you check off those that appeal most to you

Easy-to-Read Maps . . . regional attractions, city sights, hotel and restaurant locations—all referring to or keyed to the text

Distances and Transportation Information . . . at the beginning of each town section

Fast Facts . . . all the essentials at a glance: climate, currency, embassies, emergencies, safety, taxes, tipping and more

OTHER SPECIAL FROMMER FEATURES

Did You Know . . . ?—offbeat, fun facts

Famous People—the region's greats

Impressions—what others have said

AN INVITATION TO THE READER

In researching this book, I have come across many wonderful establishments, the best of which are included here. I am sure that many of you will also come across wonderful hotels, inns, restaurants, guesthouses, shops, and attractions. Please don't keep them to yourself. Share your experiences, especially if you want to comment on places that have been included in this edition that have changed for the worse. You can address your letters to:

Marita Adair
Frommer's Acapulco, Ixtapa & Taxco
Macmillan Travel
15 Columbus Circle
New York, NY 10023

A DISCLAIMER

Readers are advised that prices fluctuate in the course of time and that travel information changes under the impact of the varied and volatile factors that affect the travel industry. Neither the author nor the publisher can be held responsible for the experiences of readers while traveling. Readers are invited to write to the publisher with ideas, comments, and suggestions for future editions.

A WORD ABOUT PRICES

Mexico has a value-added tax (Impuesto de Valor Agregado, or "IVA," pronounced "*ee*-bah") of 10% on almost everything, including hotel rooms, restaurant meals, bus tickets, tours, and souvenirs. Due to a change in the law, this tax will not necessarily be included in prices quoted to you. In addition, prices charged by hotels and restaurants have been deregulated. Mexico's new pricing freedom may cause some variations from the rates quoted in this book; always ask to see a printed price sheet and ask if the tax is included. *All prices given in this book already include the tax.*

In this book, I've listed only dollar prices, which are a more reliable guide than peso prices.

In this age of inflation, prices may change by the time you reach Mexico. Mexico's officially reported inflation rate is around 8%; however, hotel and restaurant prices have been going up 15% to 40% annually for the last several years.

Important note: In 1993, Mexico introduced the New Peso, which knocks three zeros off the old currency. The value remains the same—just over 3 New Pesos to each U.S. dollar. Old peso notes will be accepted until 1996; there's no announced time limit yet on coins.

CHAPTER 1

GETTING TO KNOW MEXICO & THE TRIANGLE OF THE SUN

This book encompasses a trio of cities known in Mexico as "The Triangle of the Sun"— Acapulco, Ixtapa/Zihuatanejo, and Taxco, all in the state of Guerrero. Near Taxco we'll take a look at Cuernavaca, in the state of Morelos. A trip through the region covered in this book is the opportunity to brush shoulders with Mexico's resort present and its pre-Hispanic and colonial past.

Acapulco was born in the mid-1500s when trade linked Mexico with China. When that trade ended, Acapulco languished until the 1930s, when a highway was built linking it to Mexico City. Acapulco quickly became a jet-age resort and began the coastal tourism boom that swept through Mexico in the 1970s.

Ixtapa, born in the late 1970s, and Zihuatanejo, an age-old fishing village, have become a resort pair only four hours north of Acapulco by car.

For a taste of colonial Mexico, Taxco and Cuernavaca are a three- to four-hour drive from Acapulco. Towns in the hinterland between Acapulco and Taxco (Chilpancingo and Iguala) came into being as way stations for 16th- through 19th-century travelers making the long journey over the mountains on foot to Mexico City.

Today this hinterland area is full of craft villages with rich craft traditions, excellent markets, and unusual festivals that date from before the Conquest through colonial times. Yet millions of travelers who have discovered the relaxing and modern amenities of the area's Pacific coastal resorts never venture off the beaten track and miss these villages entirely. So even here, where tourists have been coming for decades, are new discoveries to be made.

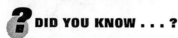

DID YOU KNOW . . . ?

- More than 20% of the population of Guerrero State lives in Acapulco.
- Of Guerrero's population, 60% speak an indigenous language.
- In 1823 the first Mexican Congress was held in Chilpancingo, Gro.
- Mexico's independence from Spain was first proclaimed in Iguala, Gro., in 1821.
- Chilpancingo and Iguala were founded as safe layovers on the way to Mexico City for the shipments of riches brought from the Orient to Acapulco, Mexico City, and Veracruz.

1. GEOGRAPHY, HISTORY & POLITICS

GEOGRAPHY

The region covered by this book includes the state of Guerrero, which encompasses the coastal resorts of Acapulco and Ixtapa/Zihuatanejo, the valley and mountain region from Chilpancingo to Tlapa, and the colonial mountain city of Taxco, as well as a portion of Morelos State and the colonial-era city of Cuernavaca.

Guerrero's 25,720 square miles are divided into **75 municipios** (counties) and **six geographic regions.** Since locals frequently use the regional names, it's useful to know them. The **Sierras del Norte** (Northern Sierras) include the forested regions in the highlands north of Iguala around Taxco and Ixcateopán, extending to Cuernavaca in the state of Morelos. The highest mountains are the Cerro de la Tentación at 10,495 feet and the Cerro Huizteco at 8,215 feet. Besides a timber and furniture-making industry, farmers raise peanuts, corn, tomatoes, avocado, watermelon, and mango. Where there are wide valleys and less rain you'll see fields of beans, sugarcane, sesame, and a variety of fruits. The **Tierra Caliente** (Hot Country) more or less follows Highway 140 west of Iguala to Ciudad Altamirano where it meets the Río Balsas, which marks the Guerrero/Michoacán state boundary. Heat burns off humidity after torrential rains, which come only in the rainy season (May through September). Sesame seed (*ajonjoli*) is the crop of choice, with one-third of Mexico's production coming from the Tierra Caliente.

Mexico lacks an extensive river system, but the longest is the Río Balsas, which starts its twisty path in the rugged mountains of Guerrero near Mezcala, and empties near Lázaro Cárdenas on the Pacific. The Río Balsas actually begins in the state of Tlaxcala, where it's known as the Zahuapan. As it passes through Puebla State, it's the Río Atoyac until it enters Guerrero, where it's called the Mezcala and then becomes the Balsas. Three major hydroelectric dams use the Balsas to produce energy for the region.

Each year at the end of October and beginning of November is the Río Balsas riverboat race, which begins at Mezcala, charges over thrilling rapids, and ends where the Balsas empties into the Pacific just above Zihuatanejo.

The **Valles Centrales** (Central Valleys), with top elevations of around 4,000 feet, include the area around Chilpancingo, a bit south to Mochitlán, Quechultenango, and Colotlipa, and east to Tixtla and Chilapa. This fertile area of oak and pine trees, with plenty of rain all year, also produces fruits and vegetables.

Continuing east of Chilpancingo from Chilapa to Tlapa and including Olinalá, is the region called **La Montaña** (The Mountain), with mountain elevations of at least 10,000 feet separated by valleys and river-cut canyons. The climb is so gradual, however, that nothing seems as high as it is; the changing vegetation from oak and pine to cactus, close to Tlapa, is a better indication of elevation difference. In the center of the region there's less rain, so coaxing plants from the earth is more difficult than it is in the valleys. Nevertheless, because of the region's diverse climates, sugarcane, avocado, guayaba, watermelon, papaya, and rice are cultivated, with Tlapa being the regional commercial center.

Better known to most visitors is the **Costa Grande** (Big Coast), which stretches northward along the Pacific from Acapulco to Ixtapa/Zihuatanejo. All along the two-lane coastal highway are vast banana and coconut-palm plantations. South of Acapulco along the Pacific to the state line with Oaxaca is the **Costa Chica** (Small Coast), with its many mangroves, small lakes, lagoons, and hundreds of birds. Coconut, mango, and cacao (chocolate) plantations are seen along the route, and inland are fields of sugarcane, corn, chile, tomatoes, beans, and squash. Guerrero is cave-filled, with two of the most famous being the Cacahuamilpa Caves near Taxco and the Juxtlahuaca Caves southeast of Chilpancingo.

HISTORY

The earliest "Mexicans" were Stone Age men and women, descendants of the race that had crossed the Bering Strait and reached North America before 10,000 B.C. These were Homo sapiens who hunted mastodons and bison, and gathered other food as they could. Later (Archaic Period, 5200–1500 B.C.), signs of agriculture and domestication appeared: baskets were woven; corn, beans, squash, and tomatoes were grown; turkeys and dogs were kept for food. By 2400 B.C. the art of pot making had been discovered (the use of pottery was a significant advance). Life in these times was still very primitive, of course, but there were "artists" who made clay figurines for use as votive offerings or household "gods." Actually, "goddesses" is a better term, for most of the figurines found so far have been female, and are supposed to symbolize Mother Earth or fertility. (Use of these figurines predates any belief in well-defined gods.)

THE PRECLASSIC PERIOD It was in the Preclassic Period (1500 B.C.–A.D. 300) that the area known by archeologists as Mesoamerica (from the northern Mexico Valley to Costa Rica) began to show signs of a farming culture. Farming used either the "slash-and-burn" method of cutting grass and trees, then setting fire to the area to clear it for planting, or else terraces and irrigation ducts were constructed, this latter method being the one used principally in the highlands around Mexico City where the first large towns developed. At some time during this period, religion became an institution, as certain men took the role of shaman, or guardian of magical and religious secrets. These were the predecessors of the folk healers and nature priests still found in modern Mexico.

The most highly developed culture of this Preclassic Period was that of the Olmecs, which flourished from 1500 to 100 B.C. They lived in what are today the states of Veracruz and Tabasco, where they used river rafts to transport the colossal multiton blocks of basalt, used to carve roundish heads. All have the peculiar "jaguar mouth," a high-arched upper lip that is the identifying

DATELINE

- **10,000–2,300 B.C.** Prehistoric Period.
- **1500 B.C.–A.D. 300** Preclassic Period: Olmec culture develops and spreads.
- **1000–900 B.C.** Olmecs' San Lorenzo center is destroyed; they begin anew at La Venta.
- **600 B.C.** Olmec cultural zenith. Cholula begins a 2,000-year history as a ceremonial center.
- **500–100 B.C.** Zapotecs flourish: Olmec culture disintegrates.
- **A.D. 100** Building begins on sun and moon pyramids at Teotihuacán, which eventually becomes largest in the world.
- **300–900** Classic Period: Xochicalco established in 300. Maya civilization develops in Yucatán and Chiapas. Teotihuacán burns and is deserted by 700. Zapotecs conquer Valley of Oaxaca in 750.
- **900–1500** Postclassic Period: Toltec culture emerges at Tula and

(continues)

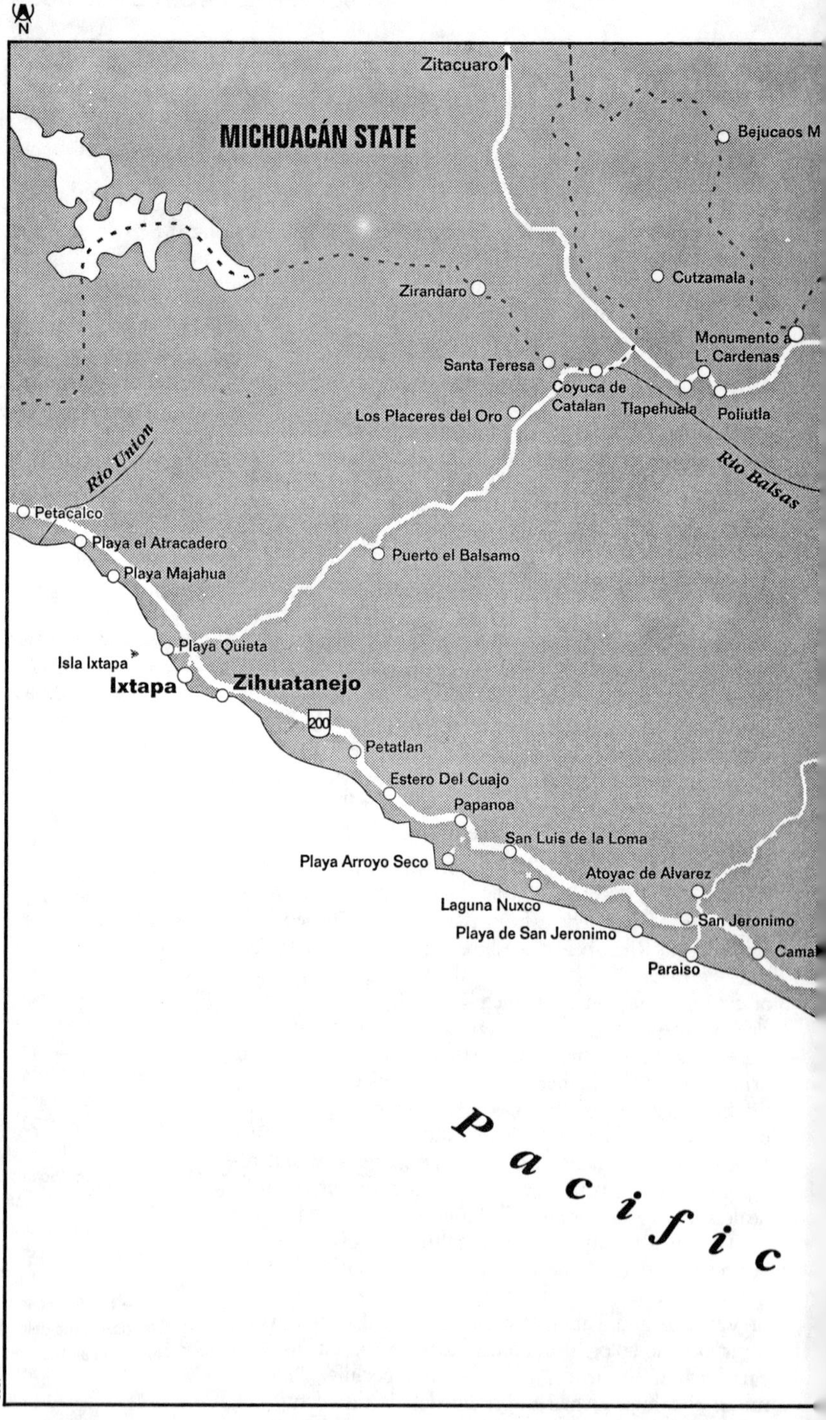

Zitacuaro↑

MICHOACÁN STATE

Bejucaos M

Cutzamala

Zirandaro

Monumento a
L. Cardenas

Santa Teresa

Coyuca de
Catalan   Tlapehuala   Poliutla

Los Placeres del Oro

Rio Balsas

Rio Union

Petacalco

Playa el Atracadero

Puerto el Balsamo

Playa Majahua

Isla Ixtapa

Playa Quieta

Ixtapa   Zihuatanejo

200

Petatlan

Estero Del Cuajo

Papanoa

San Luis de la Loma

Playa Arroyo Seco

Atoyac de Alvarez

Laguna Nuxco

San Jeronimo

Playa de San Jeronimo

Cama

Paraiso

Pacific

N

6997

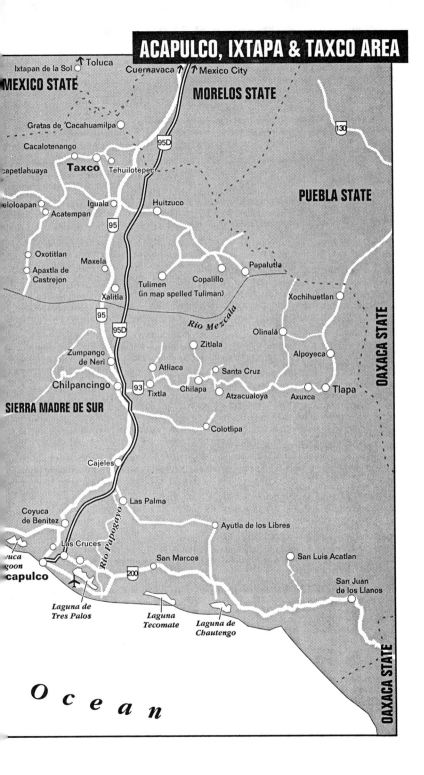

ACAPULCO, IXTAPA & TAXCO AREA

Ixtapan de la Sol ○ ↑ Toluca
Cuernavaca ↑ / ↑ Mexico City

MEXICO STATE

MORELOS STATE

Gratas de Cacahuamilpa ○

130

Cacalotenango ○

95D

apetlahuaya   **Taxco** ○ Tehuilotepec ○

PUEBLA STATE

eloloapan ○   Iguala ○   Huitzuco ○
○ Acatempan

95

○ Oxotitlan   Maxela   ○ Papalutla
○ Apaxtla de   ○   ○
Castrejon   Tulimen   Copalillo
         ○ Xalitla   (in map spelled Tuliman)   Xochihuetlan ○

95

95D   *Rio Mezcala*

Olinalá ○

○ Zitlala   Alpoyeca ○

Zumpango
de Neri ○

○ Atliaca   ○ Santa Cruz

OAXACA STATE

Chilpancingo ○   93   Chilapa ○   ○ Tlapa
         Tixtla   ○ Atzacualoya   Axuxca

SIERRA MADRE DE SUR

○ Colotlipa

Cajeles ○

○ Las Palma

Coyuca
de Benitez ○   ○ Ayutla de los Libres

○ Las Cruces
uca   *Rio Papagayo*
goon   San Marcos ○   ○ San Luis Acatlan
capulco

200   San Juan
de los Llanos ○

*Laguna de
Tres Palos*   *Laguna
Tecomate*   *Laguna de
Chautengo*

OAXACA STATE

O c e a n

DATELINE

spreads to Chichén-Itzá by 978.

- **1290** Zapotecs decline and Mixtecs emerge at Monte Alban.
- **1325–1521** Aztec capital, Tenochtitlán, founded. Aztecs dominate Mexico, including Guerrero and Morelos.
- **1519–21** Conquest of Mexico: Cortés and troops arrive near present-day Veracruz; Conquest is complete when Cortés defeats Aztecs at Tlaltelolco near Tenochtitlán in 1521.
- **1521–24** Hernán Cortés organizes Spanish empire in Mexico and builds Mexico City on ruins of Tenochtitlán.
- **1524–35** Cortés removed from leadership. Spanish king sends officials, judges, and finally an audiencia to govern.
- **1532** Cortés begins first road leading from Mexico City to Acapulco.
- **1534** In Taxco first silver is extracted by Spaniards.
- **1535–1821** Viceregal Period: Mexico governed by 61 viceroys appointed by king of Spain. Landed aristocracy emerges with huge portions of land (haciendas) owned by few.

(continues)

mark of the Olmecs, which was borrowed and adapted by many later cultures. Besides their achievements in sculpture, the Olmecs were the first in Mexico to use a calendar and to develop writing, both to be later perfected by the Maya.

Evidence of Olmec occupation in the area covered in this book exists near Chilapa, Zitlala, Juxtlahuaca, and Mezcala. In the Juxtlahuaca Cave, an Olmec pictograph shows the merger of land (represented by the jaguar) and water (symbolized by the serpent). The most significant Olmec-inspired cave paintings are in three caves near Oxtototitlán, close to Chilapa. Paintings here show figures fused together with jaguars, sometimes part jaguar and part human, as well as geometric designs. Near Iguala, the discovery of a wooden mask showing Olmec features sparked more speculation about the early Olmec presence on the west coast.

Some scholars believe that the Olmec culture actually began in the area encompassing the states of Guerrero, Morelos, and Puebla and spread to the east coast, including their centers in the state of Veracruz. This puts in question the long-held theory that the Olmecs originated on Mexico's east coast. An earthen pyramidal site near Teopantecuanitlán, which means "place of the temple of the jaguar," at the confluence of the Balsas and Amacuzac rivers in western Guerrero, is dated around 1460 B.C. A stone quarry there was used to sculpt figures and make ceramics. An excavated tomb at this site revealed human remains and a sculpted head similar to those found at La Venta. Nearby, archeologists unearthed two ball courts and a ceremonial plaza with pyramidal structures. According to recent studies, the demise of Teopantecuanitlán coincided with that of the Olmec site of La Venta, on the east coast in the state of Tabasco.

Other evidence of Guerrero's pre-Hispanic past includes the discovery of traces of cinnabar (a red dust used to dress entombed bodies) near Puerto Marqués (near Acapulco), dating from around 2500 B.C. Rock-etched figures of humans and animals, about the same age as the cinnabar, have been identified near Acapulco at Palma Sola and La Sabana.

Just as the link between the Olmecs of Guerrero and those of the east coast has not been clearly established, neither has the link between the Olmecs and the Maya. But Izapa (400 B.C.–A.D. 400), a ceremonial site in the Chiapan cacao-growing region near the Pacific coast, appears to be one of several transitional sites between the two cultures. When it was discovered, the monuments and stelae were in place, not having undergone the destruction that erased so many sites. El Pital, a large site being excavated in northern Veracruz state, may provide additional clues about links between the Olmecs and other cultures.

THE CLASSIC PERIOD Most artistic and cultural achievement in pre-Hispanic Mexico came about during the Classic Period (A.D. 300 to 900), when life began to center in cities. Class distinctions arose as the military and religious aristocracy took control; a class of merchants and artisans grew, with the independent farmer falling under a landlord's control. The cultural centers of the Classic Period were the Yucatán and Guatemala (also home of the Maya), the Mexican Highlands at Teotihuacán, the Zapotec cities of Monte Alban and Mitla (near Oaxaca), and the cities of El Tajín and Zempoala on the Gulf coast.

Who exactly inhabited Teotihuacán (100 B.C.–A.D. 700—near present-day Mexico City) isn't known, but it is thought to have been a city of 200,000 or more inhabitants covering nine square miles. At its height, Teotihuacán was the greatest cultural center in Mexico, with its influence extending as far southeast as Guatemala. Its layout has religious significance; on the tops of its pyramids consecrated to the sun and moon, high priest's rituals were carried out, attended but not observed by the masses of the people, who remained below at the foot of the pyramid. Some of the magnificent reliefs and frescoes that decorated religious monuments can be seen in Mexico City's museums. Teotihuacán's cultural influence spread to Guerrero as well, as evidenced by pottery found around Chilpancingo, Taxco, Tixtla, Acapulco, and Tecpan. One of the most famous pieces is a mosaic mask found near Mezcala, and made of turquoise and coral with a handsome coral necklace.

The Zapotecs, influenced by the Olmecs, raised an impressive culture around Oaxaca, just southeast of the region covered in this book. Their two principal cities were Monte Alban (500 B.C.–A.D. 800), inhabited by an elite of merchants and artisans, and Mitla, reserved for the high priests. Both cities exhibit the artistic and mathematical genius of the people: characteristic geometric designs, long-nosed gods with feathered masks, hieroglyph stelae, a bar-and-dot numerical system, and a 52-cycle calendar. Like the Olmecs, the Zapotecs favored grotesque art, of which the frieze of the "Danzantes" at Monte Alban—naked figures of distorted form and contorted position—is an outstanding example.

El Tajín (A.D. 300–1100), covering at least 2,600 acres on the upper Gulf coast of Veracruz, continues to stump scholars. The Pyramid of the Niches there is unique and recent excavations have uncovered a total of

DATELINE

1537 Mexico's first printing press installed in Mexico City.
1562 Friar Diego de Landa destroys 5,000 Maya religious stone figures and burns 27 hieroglyphic painted manuscripts at Maní, Yucatán.
1565 The first ship to sail successfully from Manila, Philippines, arrives in Acapulco, beginning 250 years of Mexican trade with Asia.
1573 The first Spanish galleon laden with riches from Asia arrives in Acupulco.
1575 Felipe II of Spain declares that Acapulco is the only commercial port between America and Asia.
1578 Pirates begin stalking the Manila galleons.
1595 First hospital for Indians established in Acapulco.
1617 In Acapulco the first part of the Fort of San Diego is completed to protect the city from pirates.
1751 After bonanza mine discovery in Taxco, José de la Borda obtains permission to build the opulent Santa Prisca y San Sebastián Church.
1758 Completion of Taxco's Santa Prisca y San Sebastián Church, one of the finest examples of baroque architecture in Mexico.

(continues)

DATELINE

- **1764** José de la Borda, having financial difficulties, leaves Taxco.
- **1767** Jesuits expelled from New Spain.
- **1769** José de la Borda again strikes it rich in the mines of Zacatecas.
- **1783** Vicente Guerrero, distinguished independence war hero and Mexico's second president, is born in Tixtla, Guerrero.
- **1810–21** Independence War: Father Miguel Hidalgo starts movement for Mexico's independence from Spain, leading eventually to a compromise between monarchy and a republic, outlined by Agustín de Iturbide.
- **1815** The last Spanish galleon arrives from Manila after 250 years of trade linking two continents.
- **1821** Independence from Spain achieved, and declared in Iguala, Guerrero.
- **1822** First Empire: Agustín de Iturbide, independence leader, orchestrates his ascendancy to throne as emperor of Mexico.
- **1823** First Mexican Congress held in Chilpancingo.
- **1824** Iturbide is expelled, returns, and is executed by firing squad.
- **1824–55** Federal Republic Period:

(continues)

17 ball courts and Teotihuacán-influenced murals. Although Huastec Indians inhabited the region, who built the site and occupied it remains a mystery. Death and sacrifice are reoccurring themes depicted in relief carvings. Pulque (pre-Hispanic fermented drink), cacao (chocolate) growing, and the ball game figured heavily into Tajín society.

THE POSTCLASSIC PERIOD In the Postclassic Period (A.D. 900–1500), warlike cultures developed impressive societies of their own, although they never surpassed the Classic peoples. All paintings and hieroglyphs of this period show war, migration, and disruption. Somehow the glue of society became unstuck, people wandered from their homes, and the religious hierarchy lost influence. Finally, in the 1300s, the warlike Aztecs settled in the Mexico Valley on Lake Texcoco (site of Mexico City), with the island city of Tenochtitlán as their capital. Legend has it that as the wandering Aztecs were passing the lake they saw a sign predicted by their prophets: an eagle perched on a cactus plant with a snake in its mouth. They built their city there and it became a huge (pop. 300,000) and impressive capital. The Aztec empire was a more or less loosely united territory of great size. The high lords of the capital became fabulously rich in gold, stores of food, cotton, and perfumes; skilled artisans were prosperous; events of state were elaborately ceremonial. Victorious Aztecs returning from battle sacrificed thousands of captives on the altars atop the pyramids, cutting their chests open with stone knives and ripping out their still living hearts to offer to the gods.

In pre-Hispanic times, what is now Guerrero attracted many indigenous groups, among them Chontales, better known in the Yucatán, and Mixtecos, generally recognized as a Oaxaca group. Others include Nahua, or Nahuatl-speaking people found in a large part of Mexico, and the Olmec, whose remains we associate with Veracruz, Yucatán, and Oaxaca, but who left pictographs on cave walls in Guerrero. By the time the Spanish conquerors arrived, these groups were vassals of the Aztecs. Their cotton weaving was prized by the Aztecs, who used it to replace clothing woven of henequin and ixtle. Those who showed up at the grand Tlatelolco market in Mexico City (colorfully described by Bernal Díaz de Castillo, in his *True History of the Conquest of New Spain*) brought turkeys, rabbits, turtles, ducks, deer, chocolate, salt, and feathers to sell. Forced tribute to the Aztecs included honey, corn, carved wood vessels, copal (an incense), cotton clothing, gold, feathers, and iron-oxide paint, all sent on a regular basis for fear of retribution by the Aztecs.

QUETZALCOATL The legend of Quetzalcoatl, a holy man who appeared during the time of troubles at the end of the Classic Period, is one of the most important tales in Mexican history and folklore, and contributed to the overthrow of the Aztec empire by the Spaniards. Quetzalcoatl means "feathered serpent." Learned beyond his years, he became the high priest and leader of the Toltecs at Tula, and put an end to human sacrifice. His influence completely changed the Toltecs from a group of warriors to peaceful and productive farmers, artisans, and craftsmen. But his success upset the old priests who wanted human sacrifice, and they called upon their ancient god of darkness, Texcatlipoca, to degrade Quetzalcoatl in the eyes of the people. One night the priests conspired to dress Quetzalcoatl in ridiculous garb, get him drunk, and tempt him to break his vow of chastity. The next morning, shame of this night of debauchery drove him out of his own land and into the wilderness, where he lived for 20 years. He emerged in Coatzacoalcos, in the isthmus of Tehuantepec, bade his few followers farewell, and sailed away, having promised to return in a future age. But artistic influences noted at Chichén-Itzá in the Yucatán suggest that in fact he landed there and began his "ministry" again, this time called Kukulkán, with much success among the Maya. He died there, but the legend of his return in a future age remained.

SPANISH CONQUISTADORES When Hernán Cortés and his men landed in 1519, in what would become Veracruz, the Aztec empire was ruled by Moctezuma (often misspelled Montezuma) in great splendor. The emperor was not certain what course to pursue. If the strangers were Quetzalcoatl and his followers, returning at last, no resistance must be offered. On the other hand, if the strangers were not Quetzalcoatl, they might be a threat to his empire. Moctezuma tried to bribe them with gold to go away, but this only whetted their appetites. Despite the fact that Moctezuma and his ministers received the conquistadores with full pomp and glory when they reached Mexico City, Cortés eventually took Moctezuma captive.

Though the Spaniards were no match for the hundreds of thousands of Aztecs, they skillfully kept things under their control until a revolt threatened Cortés's entire enterprise. He retreated to the countryside, made alliances with non-Aztec tribes, and finally marched on the empire, now governed by the last Aztec emperor, Cuauhtémoc. Cuauhtémoc defended himself and his people valiantly for almost three months, but was finally captured, tortured, and executed.

DATELINE

Guadalupe Victoria is elected first president of Mexico.

- **1829** President Vicente Guerrero abolishes slavery, expels all Spaniards, and repels a Spanish reinvasion of Mexico.
- **1834** Ignacio Manuel Altamirano, father of Mexican literature, is born in Tixtla, Guerrero.
- **1835** Texas declares independence from Mexico.
- **1836** Santa Anna defeats Texans at Battle of the Alamo, at San Antonio, Texas, but is later defeated and captured.
- **1838** France invades Mexico at Veracruz.
- **1845** U.S. annexes Texas.
- **1846–48** War with U.S.: U.S. pays Mexico $15 million and Mexico relinquishes half of its national territory to the U.S. in Treaty of Guadalupe Hidalgo.
- **1849** Guerrero State is formed and named after Vicente Guerrero.
- **1855–67** Reform Years: Country wages three-year war on itself in a search for ideology, stability, and political leadership.
- **1855–72** President Benito Juárez nationalizes church property and declares separation of church and state.
- **1857** Morelos State is created.

(continues)

DATELINE

- **1864–67** Second Empire: French Emperor Napoleon Bonaparte III sends Ferdinand Maximilian Joseph of Hapsburg, 32, and his wife, Marie Charlotte Amélie Léopoldine, 24, to be emperor and empress of Mexico.

- **1867** Juárez orders execution of Maximilian at Querétaro and resumes presidency in Mexico City until his death in 1872.

- **1872–84** Post-Reform Period: Only four presidents hold office but country is nearly bankrupt.

- **1876–1911** Porfiriato: With one four-year exception, Porfirio Díaz is president/dictator of Mexico for 35 years, leading the country in tremendous modernization at the expense of human rights.

- **1911–17** Mexican Revolution: Francisco Madero drafts revolutionary plan, Díaz resigns, and country is thrown into revolution. Pancho Villa, Emiliano Zapata, Venustiano Carranza, Francisco Madero, Alvaro Obregón, Lázaro Cárdenas, and others jockey for power during period of great violence.

- **1913** President Madero assassinated.

(continues)

The Spanish Conquest had started out as an adventure by Cortés and his men, unauthorized by the Spanish crown or its governor in Cuba. Soon Christianity was being spread through "New Spain." Guatemala and Honduras were explored and conquered, and by 1540 the territory of New Spain included Spanish possessions from Vancouver to Panama. In the two centuries that followed, Franciscan and Augustinian friars converted great numbers of Indians to Christianity, and the Spanish lords built up huge fuedal estates on which the Indian farmers were little more than serfs. The silver and gold that Cortés had sought made Spain the richest country in Europe.

Guerrero's history is inextricably linked with the trail of riches developed by the Spanish conquerors that ran from China to Manila in the Philippines, to Acapulco, Mexico City, Veracruz, and Spain.

Though it had been discovered earlier, the state's post-Conquest history really begins in 1573 in Acapulco when the first Spanish galleon arrived loaded with treasures from China via Manila—porcelain, ivory, silk, inlaid furniture, spices, gold jewelry, pearls, precious stones, bricks of silver and gold, and more. This newly discovered trade route linked three continents (Asia, America, and Europe), and for the next 250 years, merchants in both Manila and Acapulco eagerly awaited the annual arrival of the magnificent sailing ships. The ships grew larger and carried more each year, despite Spain's pronouncements limiting size and weight. Acapulco was insect-infested in those days, so few people lived there. However, arrival of the long-awaited vessel was the occasion of a grand fair and a temporary population of nearly 10,000 people showed up, sometimes waiting for months for the moment when the galleon's white sails appeared on the horizon. One can only imagine what the beaches of Acapulco Bay must have looked like with makeshift sunshades billowing over valuable foreign cargo spread out on the sand, with thousands of eager merchants making deals. Ships arrived from Peru to cart back their portion, but even more merchandise went over the treacherous mountains, carried by mules and led by valiant and valuable *arrieros* (mule drivers), to Mexico City and Jalapa, Veracruz, Guadalajara, Puebla, Oaxaca, and Morelia. The king of Spain's portion left from Veracruz. On land, bandits appeared all along the way to wrest the treasure from those charged with transporting it. Ships returned from Acapulco to the Philippines loaded with silver in payment for the cargo, as well as cochinil (a natural dye), cacao (chocolate), and wool, all prized trade items. Both coming and going, pirates dogged the galleons' watery trails. Almost four dozen ships were lost either by shipwreck or pirate attack during the 250 years of trade. To defend against pirate attack, Fort San Diego was designed in 1617, by a Dutch engineer, but was not completed until 1783. Cargo of another kind, colonists, left in 1602 bound for California. Though it was one of the most important ports in the world, and the only one authorized by Spain in the Americas, it wasn't until 1799 that the king of Spain officially named it Acapulco and recognized it as a city. Only 11 years later Mexico began its fight for independence from Spain. The turmoil of Mexico's independence war and changes in world trade diminished Mexico and Spain's influence and the famed Manila galleons stopped coming in 1815.

INDEPENDENCE Spain ruled Mexico until 1821, when Mexico finally gained its independence after a decade of upheaval. The independence movement had begun in 1810 when a priest, Father Miguel Hidalgo, gave the cry for independence from his pulpit in the town of Dolores, Guanajuato. The revolt soon became a revolution, and Hidalgo, Ignacio Allende, and another priest, José María Morelos, gathered an "army" of citizens and threatened Mexico City. Ultimately Hidalgo was executed, but he is honored as "the Father of Mexican Independence." Morelos kept the revolt alive until 1815, when he was executed. Guerrero State, with its important port of Acapulco, figured prominently in the fight for independence. Out of its ranks came Vicente Guerrero, who later became president, and Nicolás Bravo, a key leader and military strategist.

When independence finally came, Agustín de Iturbide was ready to take over. Iturbide founded a short-lived "empire" with himself as emporer in 1822. The next year it fell and was followed by the proclamation of a republic with Gen. Guadalupe Victoria as first president. A succession of presidents and military dictators followed Guadalupe Victoria until one of the most bizarre and extraordinary episodes in modern times: the French intervention. In the 1860s, Mexican factions offered the Archduke Maximilian of Hapsburg the crown of Mexico, and with the support of the ambitious French emperor, Napoléon III, the young Austrian actually came to Mexico and "ruled" for three years (1864–67), while the country was in a state of civil war. This European interference in New World affairs was not welcomed by the United States, and the French emperor finally withdrew his troops, leaving misguided Maximilian to be captured and executed by firing squad in Querétaro. His adversary and successor (as president of Mexico) was Benito Juárez, a Zapotec lawyer and one of the most heroic figures in Mexican history. After victory over

DATELINE

- **1914–1916** Two U.S. invasions of Mexico.
- **1917–40** Reconstruction: Present constitution of Mexico signed, land and education reforms initiated, and labor unions strengthened. Mexico expels U.S. oil companies and nationalizes all natural resources and railroads. Presidents Obregón and Carranza are assassinated, as are Pancho Villa and Emiliano Zapata.
- **1940–Present** Mexico enters period of political stability and makes tremendous economic progress, though not without continued problems of corruption, inflation, national health, and unresolved land and agricultural issues.
- **1955** Women given full voting rights.
- **1982** Nationalization of Mexican banks.
- **1985** Mexico's first astronaut, Rodolfo Meri Vela of Guerrero, joins U.S. astronauts and goes into space aboard the U.S. Atlantis spaceship.
- **1988** Mexico enters the General Agreement on Tariffs and Trade (GATT).
- **1991** Mexico, Canada, and the United States begin Free Trade Agreement negotiations.

(continues)

DATELINE

1992 The U.S. declares its legal right to kidnap Mexicans and bring them to the U.S. for trial. Mexico retaliates by refusing all U.S. funds in the war against drugs and by limiting U.S. drug-agent activity in Mexico. Mexico allows *ejido* land (peasant communal property) to be sold. Mexico and the Vatican establish diplomatic relations after an interruption of 100 years; clergy allowed to vote and wear religious garments in public.

1993 Mexico deregulates hotel and restaurant prices; New Peso currency begins circulation. The North American Free Trade agreement is approved by Mexico, Canada, and the U.S.

1994 A January Indian uprising in Chiapas sparks protests countrywide over land distribution, bank loans, health care, education, voting, and human rights. In an apparently unrelated incident, PRI candidate Luis Donaldo Colosio is assassinated five months before the presidential election, and replacement candidate Ernesto Zedillo Ponce de León takes over.

Maximilian, Juárez did his best to unify and strengthen his country before dying of a heart attack in 1872. His effect on Mexico's future was profound, however, and his plans and visions bore fruit for decades.

THE PORFIRIATO From 1877 to 1911, a period now called the "Porfiriato," the prime role in Mexico was played by Porfirio Díaz, a Juárez general. Recognized as a modernizer, he was a terror to his enemies and to challengers of his absolute power. He was forced to abdicate in 1911 by Francisco Madero and public opinion.

Foreigners were given opportunities to buy land and become involved in businesses in Guerrero and throughout Mexico during the Porfiriato. The policy had mixed blessings; on the one hand, large hunks of land bought by foreigners for agricultural purposes produced more food for the state and country but took profits and control away from local citizens. Foreign capital began construction of the Mexico City–to-Acapulco railroad in 1892 and the first leg of the journey as far as Iguala was finished in 1898. During the Porfiriato, exploration of and production in Guerrero's mines more than doubled, with foreign companies responsible for much of the mining progress. Besides silver and gold, other minerals were mined that were needed by growing industrialized countries. These years of growth were also years of long hours and harsh treatment for those who actually did the work. Peasants who lost their land to outsiders were displaced, disease cost many lives, and only 13 in 100 children went to school, usually children of the privileged and professionals. Because of lack of a good communication and transportation network (except between Acapulco, Chilpancingo, and Iguala) most of Guerrero remained out of the mainstream. Towards the end of the Porfiriato, citizens of Guerrero and Morelos joined the rest of Mexico in rowdy social protests. In the end, soldiers from both states were among the strongest and most recognized supporters of the revolution.

After the fall of the Porfirist dictatorship, several factions split the country, including those led by "Pancho Villa" (whose real name was Doroteo Arango), Alvaro Obregón, Venustiano Carranza, and Emiliano Zapata. The decade that followed is referred to as the Mexican Revolution. Drastic reforms occurred in this period, and the surge of vitality and progress from this exciting if turbulent time has inspired Mexicans up to the present. Succeeding presidents have invoked the spirit of the revolution, which is still studied and discussed.

THE 20TH CENTURY After the turmoil of the revolution, Mexico sought stability in the form of the Partido Revolucionario Institucional (el PRI), the country's dominant political party. With the aim of "institutionalizing the revolution," el PRI (pronounced ell-*pree*) literally engulfed Mexican society, leaving little room for vigorous, independent opposition. For over half a century the monolithic party has had control of the government, labor unions, trade organizations, and other centers of power in Mexican society.

The most outstanding Mexican president of the century was Gen. Lázaro Cárdenas (1934–40). An effective leader, Cárdenas broke up vast tracts of agricultural land and distributed parcels to small cooperative farms called *ejidos*, reorganized the labor unions along democratic lines, and provided funding for village schools. His most famous action was the expropriation of Mexico's oil industry from U.S. and European interests. It became Petroleros Mexicanos (Pemex), the government petroleum monopoly.

Since that time, the PRI has selected Mexico's president (and, in fact, virtually everyone else on the government payroll) from its own ranks, the national election being only a confirmation of the choice. Among these men have been Avila Camacho, who continued many of Cárdenas's policies; Miguel Alamán, who expanded national industrial and infrastructural development; Adolfo López Mateos, who expanded the highway system and increased hydroelectric power sources; and Gustavo Díaz Ordaz, who provided credit and technical help to the agricultural sector.

In 1970 Luís Echeverria came to power, followed in 1976 by José López Portillo. During their presidencies there emerged a studied coolness in relations with the United States and an activist role in international affairs. This period also saw an increase in charges of large-scale corruption in the upper echelons of Mexican society. The corruption, though endemic to the system, was encouraged by a river of money from the rise in oil prices. When oil income skyrocketed, Mexican borrowing and spending did likewise. The drop in oil prices in the 1980s left Mexico with an enormous foreign bank debt and serious infrastructure deficiencies.

MEXICO TODAY Without king oil, Mexico must rebuild agriculture and industry, cut expenditures, tame corruption, and keep creditors at bay. Pres. Miguel de la Madrid Hurtado, who assumed the presidency in 1982, struggled with these problems and made important progress. President Carlos Salinas de Gortari managed to slow inflation from 200% annually to between 10% and 15%. In January 1994, under Salinas de Gortari's leadership, Mexico joined with the United States and Canada in the North American Free Trade Agreement, which will be phased in over a 15-year period, and which will eliminate many trade barriers between the three countries. But the economy and society are still under tremendous economic pressure, and charges of government corruption still abound, although the situation has improved.

Peasant revolts erupted in Chiapas in January 1994, and soon spread to other areas of the country. The protesters' grievances over land, voting, human rights, and access to loans mimics the same unresolved ills that led to Mexico's revolution early this century. Careful handling by governmental leaders could diffuse this powder keg, but it remains to be seen how this and successive governments will handle the disputes.

Mexico's current economic difficulties have led to a newly vigorous and open political life with opposition parties gaining strength. The traditionally victorious PRI party won the hotly contested presidential election in 1988, but its candidate, Carlos Salinas de Gortari, only managed to claim a historically low 50.36% of the vote amid claims of fraud by his chief rival, Cuauhtémoc Cárdenas of the newly formed National Democratic Front (FDN). Ironically, Cárdenas is the son of the beloved

Mexican president who founded the PRI. However, opposition parties managed to win a few Senate seats for the first time since the PRI came to power, and recent local elections produced strong opposition candidates.

Mexico's new president was to be elected as this book went to press. The campaign for president was doubly troubled by the assassination in Tijuana of PRI candidate Luis Donaldo Colosio and the replacement candidacy of Ernesto Zedillo Ponce de León, his campaign manager, just five months before the election. The main opposition candidate was Diego Fernandez de Cevallos.

POLITICS

The Republic of Mexico today is headed by an elected president and a bicameral legislature. It is divided into 31 states, plus the Federal District (Mexico City). Economically, Mexico is not by any means a poor country. Only about a sixth of the economy is in agriculture. Mining is still fairly important. Gold and silver and many other important minerals are still mined, but the big industry today is oil. Mexico is also well industrialized, manufacturing textiles, food products, and everything from tape cassettes to automobiles.

In short, Mexico is well into the 20th century, with all the benefits and problems of contemporary life, and although vast sums are spent on education and public welfare, a high birthrate, high unemployment, and unequal distribution of wealth show that much remains to be done.

2. MEXICO'S FAMOUS PEOPLE

Juan Ruiz de Alarcón y Mendoza (1581–1639) Born in Taxco, he began his studies in Mexico City and continued in Salamanca, Spain. He returned to Mexico to practice law before the Royal Audiencia until he returned to Spain in 1614. However, writing, not law, brought him fame. Partly because he was not Spanish born, his comedies and poetry were criticized by his peers (Lope de Vega and Tirso de Molina among them), although revered by the Spanish people. Today Spain recognizes him as a Spanish dramatist born in Mexico. His comedies were natural and colorful and had ethical themes, combating immorality, vice, and social corruption. Among his most famous dramas is *Las Paredes Oyen* (The Walls Have Ears). Alarcón's dramas are in the forefront of Taxco's Jornadas Alarconianas, a week-long literary and musical festival held there each May.

Ignacio Manuel Altamirano (1834–93) The community of his birth, Tixtla, Guerrero, proudly proclaims Altamirano "Hijo de Tixtla" (son of Tixtla) because of his widely acclaimed contributions to Mexican literature as poet, novelist, critic, historian, and politician. As a young writer he started Mexico's most important 19th-century literary movement when he balked at imitating Spanish and French writers and began creating Mexican characters and themes, incorporating the language, history, and customs of his country. His leadership influenced others in the arts and among his contemporaries were Riva Palacio (grandson of Vicente Guerrero), Manuel Payano, and José Peón Contreras. Among his famous works are *El Zarco, Episodios de la Vida Mexicano*, covering the years 1861–63, and *Paisajes y Leyendas Tradicones y Costumbres*, published in 1884.

José de la Borda (1699–1778) Taxco's most famous citizen was born Joseph Borde in France, and came to Taxco in 1716 at age 17 to work with his brother,

Francisco, in the mines of nearby Tehuilotepec. As the years passed he became known as José de la Borda. Twenty-eight years later he inherited the Tehuilotepec mines from his brother, but his own San Ignacio mines provided the bonanza of riches for which he is best known. With his newfound wealth he asked permission to construct the Santa Prisca y San Sebastián Church to his specifications. The church was begun in 1751 when he was 50 years old and finished in 1758; his son Manuel became its first parish priest. But within five years of this joyous occasion José's personal finances were low, and by 1772 he was forced to sell a monstrance from the Santa Prisca to the Metropolitan Cathedral in Mexico City. He left Taxco for Zacatecas where, at over 70 years of age, he again struck it rich in the Quebradilla mine. He died in Cuernavaca on May 30, 1778, at age 79. He was considered a mining genius in his time, and for all his wealth he lived simply. His burial place is unknown although a funerary piece thought to be from his funeral was found in a secret room in the Santa Prisca during its recent restoration.

Hernán Cortés (1485–1547) Brash, bold, greedy, and a brilliant military leader, 34-year-old Hernán Cortés conquered Mexico in the name of Spain without the knowledge of that country's king. He sank his ships to prevent desertion and with only 550 men and 16 horses, conquered a nation of 400,000 and a territory larger than his native country. He became governor and captain-general of New Spain immediately after the Conquest and later he was given title of marqués of the Valley of Oaxaca and substantial landholdings from Mexico City to Oaxaca. He built and lived in both the National Palace on the Zócalo in Mexico City and the Cuernavaca Palace facing the Jardín de los Héroes, now the Museum de Cuauhnáhuac. He sent Spaniards to Taxco in search of tin and introduced sugarcane cultivation around Cuernavaca. Later his son, Martín, oversaw a silver mine in Taxco and continued sugarcane cultivation in the region. But by 1528 Cortés was removed from governorship and the king sent others to take charge. Cortés died in Spain while seeking his proper recognition and a more significant title from the Spanish court, which shunned him. Mexicans regard him as the destroyer of a nation and no monuments honor him. His remains are in a vault at the Church of the Hospital of Jésus Nazareño, Mexico City.

Cuauhtémoc (late 1400s–1521?) Cousin of Moctezuma II, and last ruler of the Aztec empire, Cuauhtémoc is revered for his valiant leadership. Though only in his twenties, he assumed control of the endangered Aztec empire after Cuitlahuac, successor of Moctezuma II, succumbed to smallpox, a disease brought by the Spaniards. He led his people nobly during the final three-month Spanish siege that brought an end to the Aztec Empire. Legend tells us that after the battle he was tortured to reveal the whereabouts of Aztec gold but would not give in. Another legend has him buried at Ixcateopán, near Taxco, where indigenous groups from all over the Americas come to pay him homage each February 28. It is he, not Moctezuma, whom Mexicans hold up as an example of courage and strength and honor with a statue on Reforma Avenue in Mexico City.

Porfirio Díaz (1830–1915) Born in Oaxaca and schooled in law, at age 32 he distinguished himself at the famous Puebla battle. Within 14 years he became president of Mexico and remained as dictator for the next 34 years, with one four-year interruption. His contributions were enormous: He moved the country from turmoil and bankruptcy into peace and stability through improvements in communication, railroads, agriculture, manufacturing, mining, port enlargement, oil exploration, and foreign investment. He built lavish public buildings and sent promising art students to Europe on full scholarships. He achieved these successes, however, by disregarding the law and at the expense of the poor, the Indians, and all intellectuals who opposed his methods, which brought about his downfall in 1911 and began the Mexican Revolution, which lasted until 1917. He died in exile in Paris and is buried in the Père Lachaise Cemetery there.

Josefa Ortiz de Dominguez   (1768–1829) Known as La Corregidora, wife of the corregidor (mayor) of Quéretaro, she assured her place in history the night she sent a messenger to warn the other conspirators, notably Miguel Hidalgo, that their plot to push for independence from Spain had been discovered by government officials. For her role she was imprisoned several times between 1810 and 1817. She died impoverished and forgotten, but today she is much revered. She was the first woman to appear on a Mexican coin, the 5-centavo piece, minted from 1942 to 1946.

Vicente Guerrero Saldaña   (1783–1831) In 1849, the state of Guerrero was named after this humble hero of Mexican independence, who for a brief time 20 years earlier was the second president of the new republic. Peasant born, of Indian, Spanish, and African heritage, he was recruited by independence leader José María Morelos, and assumed leadership when Morelos was killed. He was known for his sheer devotion to the cause and determination to see it through. He knew the area between Mexico City and Acapulco intimately, having been an *arriero* (mule driver) over the then-roadless route. His knowledge of the rugged terrain stood him well during the independence war. During the tumultuous years following independence he was the second to attempt leadership following the hapless empire of Agustín de Iturbide. Though in office less than a year, he abolished slavery, expelled all Spaniards, and successfully fought off a Spanish reinvasion. In 1831, betrayed by his vice president, Antonio Bustamante, he was kidnapped in Acapulco and put aboard a ship headed south to Santa Cruz Huatulco (now part of the Bays of Huatulco resort), sentenced, and later executed by a firing squad in Cuilapa, Oaxaca.

Miguel Hidalgo y Costilla   (1753–1811) A small-town priest in Dolores, Guanajuato, before his fame as Father of Mexican Independence, he was better known for his anticelibacy beliefs and disbelief in papal supremacy. As priest he taught parishioners to grow mulberry trees for silkworms (for silk making) and grapes (for wine making, prohibited by the crown), and he also taught them ceramic making; the latter two skills still thrive in the region. He was among those who secretly conspired to free Mexico from Spanish domination. On the morning of September 16, 1810, a messenger from Josefa Ortiz de Dominguez brought Hidalgo word that the conspiracy was uncovered. He quickly decided to publicly call for independence (known today as the *grito* or "cry") from his parish church, after which he galloped from village to village spreading the news and gathering troops. Executed in 1811, his remains are in the Independence Monument in Mexico City.

Agustín de Iturbide   (1783–1824) After Mexico's long fight for independence was accomplished, Agustín de Iturbide set himself up as emperor. He was crowned in an elaborate ceremony that took months to plan, and he went on to create an elaborate imperial monarchy with titles and right of succession by his children. He lived in an 18th-century palace in Mexico City, built for the Counts of San Mateo de Valparaiso; it's a Banamex branch today. But he reigned only briefly from 1822 to 1824, when General Santa Anna led a successful rebellion to dethrone him. He returned surreptitiously from exile but was captured and shot by a firing squad in Padilla, Tamaulipas. For years he was regarded as a usurper and self-interested politician, but in a rare move, public sentiment recognized his role in gaining Mexico's independence from Spain and his remains were fittingly interred in the Metropolitan Cathedral in Mexico City.

Benito Juárez   (1806–72) A full-blooded Zapotec, he was orphaned at the age of 3. He became governor of Oaxaca in 1847 but was exiled to New Orleans by grudge-holding president Santa Anna because Juárez had refused to grant Santa Anna asylum in Oaxaca years before. On becoming president of Mexico, first in 1858, his terms were interrupted once during the Reform Wars and again during the French intervention. During his presidency he occupied part of the north wing of the National Palace in Mexico City, now the Juárez Museum. Juárez cast the deciding vote favoring the execution of Maximilian. He died from a heart attack before completing his fourth term. Devoid of personal excesses, Juárez had a clear vision for Mexico that included honest leadership, separation of church and state, imposition of civilian rule, reduction of the military, and education reform. He is buried in the San Fernando Cemetery in Mexico City.

Doña Marina [La Malinche]   (early 1500s) Born to Nahuatl-speaking parents in Veracruz, but sold into slavery in the Maya-speaking Yucatán when her mother remarried, this young Indian girl knew two languages when she met Cortés in 1519. With Jerónimo de Aguilar, a Spaniard who had been shipwrecked off the coast of the Yucatán and knew Maya, she translated conversations for Cortés to Nahuatl speakers of central Mexico while also becoming Cortés's mistress and bearing him a son, Martín. Later she married a Spaniard, Juan Jaramillo. To Mexicans her name, Malinche (*malinchismo*), means traitor and a preference for foreign people and their customs. Her burial place is unknown.

Moctezuma II   (1468–1520) At age 52, after consolidating an empire that included all the territory surrounding his magnificent capital, Tenochtitlán, plus today's Veracruz, Chiapas, Oaxaca, and Guerrero, Moctezuma (misspelled Montezuma) may have fallen victim to a belief about the return of the white-skinned god Quetzalcoatl that cost him his life and his empire. Though so exalted that no one was allowed to look at him or sit in his presence, Moctezuma went out to meet Cortés when he arrived in Tenochtitlán, hosted him lavishly, and toured the city with him. Eventually the Spaniards made Moctezuma a prisoner. During one confusing night, the Aztecs rebelled; Moctezuma, sent to the rooftop to quell the rebellion, was accidentally hit by a stone and died a few days later.

José María Morelos y Pavón   (1765–1815) Like Miguel Hidalgo, he was an undistinguished parish priest before the independence movement. After Hidalgo's execution in 1811, Morelos took over leadership of the rebel cause and distinguished himself militarily for several years before being executed. Cuautla, Morelos, near Cuernavaca, became his headquarters for resistance for a time. Like Hidalgo, he is buried in the Independence Monument in Mexico City.

Diego Rivera   (1886–1957) Considered the most outstanding of Mexico's famous "Big Three" muralists, Rivera began his artistic training at age 10 at the San Carlos Academy in Mexico City and continued in Europe off and on until 1922. He adopted a Marxist political philosophy, and his grand and often controversial murals present Mexico's history through romanticized Communist eyes. Some of his greatest murals are at the National Palace in Mexico City and the Palacio de Cortés in Cuernavaca. His mural painted for New York City's Rockefeller Center was destroyed because Lenin appeared in it. He later re-created it in the Palacio de Bellas Artes in Mexico City. At his insistence the Mexican government gave Communist leader Leon Trotsky refuge in Mexico City. He married, divorced, and remarried artist Frida Kahlo. Museums of his work and his pre-Hispanic art collections are in Mexico City and Guanajuato. He is buried in the Rotunda of the Illustrious in the Dolores Cemetery in Mexico City's Chapultepec Park.

Antonio López de Santa Anna (1794–1876) One of the most scorned characters in Mexican history, he was president of Mexico 11 times between 1833 and 1855. Audacious, pompous, and self-absorbed, his outrageous exploits disgust and infuriate Mexicans even today, but none more than his role in losing half the territory of Mexico to the United States—still a very sore point among Mexicans. Defeated and captured at the Battle of San Jacinto outside Houston, Texas, in 1836, he agreed to allow Texas to be a separate republic and to mark the boundary at the Río Grande. When the U.S. voted to annex Texas, it sparked the Mexican-American War, which the U.S. won in 1848. In the Treaty of Guadalupe Hidalgo that followed between the two nations, the U.S. paid Mexico $15 million for Texas, New Mexico, California, Arizona, Nevada, Utah, and part of Colorado. Eventually Santa Anna was exiled, but returned two years before he died, poor, alone, and forgotten. He is interred in the Guadalupe Cemetery behind the Basílica de Guadalupe in Mexico City.

David Alfaro Siquieros (1896–1974) Born in Chihuahua, and enrolled at age 15 in the San Carlos Academy, he became one of the "Big Three" Mexican muralists. Early influenced by Communist thought, he spent a lifetime passionately fighting for his political ideals, even interrupting his painting career from 1925 to 1930 to work for trade unionization, and again in 1937 when he fought in the Spanish civil war. Siquieros wound up on probation in Taxco after imprisonment in Mexico City in 1930, forbidden to leave the village. There he became friends with William Spratling and other intellectuals and artists who joined together to organize his first one-man show in Mexico City. The show was of works completed during his imprisonment as well as Taxco subjects during his probation, about which Spratling had also published a book. His criticism of the Mexican government again landed him in prison for almost four years, where he continued to paint. In 1966, two years after release, he received the government's prize for art.

Pancho Villa (1877–1923) Born Doroteo Arango, he was a noted cattle rustler until effectively leading the northern forces (*División del Norte*) against the dictatorship of Porfirio Díaz. History remembers him as a bandit, a colorful hero, and a notoriously unfaithful husband—he allegedly had at least 23 wives. After the end of the revolution, he took up residence at Quinta Luz, in Chihuahua. He was assassinated, and his bullet-riddled car is on display in the Museum of the Revolution in Chihuahua. He is buried in the Monument to the Revolution in Mexico City.

IMPRESSIONS

It is impossible for Mexicans to produce the humblest thing without form and design. A donkey wears a load of palm leaves arranged on either flank in great green sunbursts. Merchants hang candles by their wicks to make patterns in both line and colour. . . . Sarapes are thrown with just the right line over the shoulders of ragged peons, muffling them to the eyes. Merchants in the market will compose their tomatoes, oranges, red seeds and even peanuts into little geometric piles. Bundles of husks will be tied in a manner suitable for suspension on an artist's studio. To the traveller . . . this is a matter of perpetual wonder and delight.
—STUART CHASE, *MEXICO: A STUDY OF TWO AMERICAS*, 1931

No other race that I can call to mind allowed so wide a disparity between the simple bread with which they fed their bodies and the arts by which they nourished their souls. . . . Even today, Mexican Indians have only a rudimentary development of the so-called instinct of acquisition, and a very sophisticated development of artistic appreciation as reflected in their craftsmanship.
—STUART CHASE, *MEXICO: A STUDY OF TWO AMERICAS*, 1931

3. ART, ARCHITECTURE & LITERATURE

ART & ARCHITECTURE

Mexico's artistic and architectural legacy began more than 3,000 years ago. Until the fall of the Aztec empire after the Spanish Conquest of Mexico in A.D. 1521, art, architecture, politics, and religion in Mexico were inextricably intertwined and remained so to an extent throughout the colonial period.

World-famous archeological sites in Mexico—more than 15,000 of them—have individual characteristics even when built by the same group of people. Each year scholars decipher more information about the ancients who built these cities, using information they left behind in bas-relief carvings, sculptures, murals, and hieroglyphics.

Mexico's pyramids are truncated platforms, not true pyramids, and come in many different shapes. At Tzintzuntzan, near Lake Pátzcuaro, the buildings, called *yacatas,* are distinguished by semicircular structures attached to rectangular ones. Many sites have circular buildings, usually called the observatory and dedicated to Ehécatl, god of the wind. At El Tajín, the Temple of the Niches has 365 niches, one for every day of the year, while El Castillo at Chichén-Itzá has 365 steps. The Temple of the Magicians at Uxmal has beautifully rounded and sloping sides. The Huastecas of northern Veracruz and Tamaulipas State were known for their many circular ceremonial platforms. Evidence of building one pyramidal structure on top of another, a widely accepted practice, has been found throughout Mesoamerica.

The largest pyramid by volume is the Tepanapa pyramid at Cholula. The Temple of the Inscriptions at Palenque is the only pyramid built specifically as a tomb, although tombs have been found in many other pyramids. Cobá has the longest road (*sacbe*), stretching 62 miles. Numerous sites in Mesoamerica had ball courts. In Mexico the longest is at Chichén-Itzá—nearly the length of a football field. El Tajín, with 17 ball courts, has the greatest number.

Architects of many of these edifices used a sloping panel (*tablud*) alternating with a vertical panel (*tablero*). Good examples of this are found at Teotihuacán and Cholula.

The true arch was unknown in Mesoamerica, so the Maya made multiple use of the **corbeled arch,** in which a keystone juts out over the others and is used to build a modified, inverted V-shaped arch.

The Olmecs, considered the parent culture in Mexico, built earthen pyramids, so little remains to tell us what their buildings looked like. The Olmecs, however, left an enormous sculptural legacy, from small, intricately carved pieces of jade to 40-ton basalt rock heads that they carved with stone tools and, incredibly, shipped to their homesites by river raft. And in Guerrero, a state which seems to have been a crossroads for many pre-Hispanic cultures, the Olmecs left behind them extensive cave paintings.

○ **The Olmecs, considered Mexico's parent culture, left behind extensive cave paintings in Guerrero.**

Throughout Mexico, the pyramids were embellished with carved stone or mural art, not for the purpose of pure adornment, but for religious and historic reasons. **Hieroglyphs,** picture symbols etched on stone or painted on walls or pottery, function as the written language of the ancient peoples, particularly the Maya. By deciphering the glyphs, scholars allow the ancients to speak again, giving us specific names to attach to rulers and their families, demystifying the great dynastic histories of the Maya.

Carving important historic figures on freestanding stone slabs, *stelae,* was a common Maya commemorative device. Several are in place at Cobá, and good examples are in the Museum of Anthropology in Mexico City and the Carlos Pellicer Museum in Villahermosa.

Pottery played an important role, and different indigenous groups are distinguished by their use of color and style in pottery. The Cholulans had distinctive red-clay pottery decorated in cream, red, and black; Teotihuacán was noted for its three-legged painted orangeware; Tenochtitlán, for its use of brilliant blue and red; Casas Grandes, for anthropomorphic and zoomorphic images on clay vessels; and the Maya, for pottery painted with scenes from daily and historic life. Besides those in regional museums, the best collection of all this work is in the Museum of Anthropology in Mexico City.

Pre-Hispanic cultures left some fantastic painted murals, some of which are remarkably preserved, such as those at Bonampak and Cacaxtla, and others which are fragmentary, such as those at Teotihuacán, Cholula, El Tajín, and in the caves of Guerrero. Amazing stone murals or mosaics, using thousands of pieces of fitted stone to form figures of warriors, snakes, or geometric designs, decorate pyramid facades at Xochicalco, Mitla, Uxmal, and Chichén-Itzá.

With the arrival of the Spaniards a new form of architecture came to Mexico; it proliferated for the next 300 years, which are known as the Viceregal era, when Spain's appointed viceroys ruled Mexico. Many sites that were occupied by indigenous groups at the time of the Conquest were razed, and in their place appeared Catholic churches, public buildings, and palaces for conquerors and the king's bureaucrats. Indian artisans, who formerly worked on pyramidal structures, were recruited to give life to these structures, often guided by drawings of European buildings the Spanish architects tried to emulate. Frequently left on their own, the indigenous artisans sometimes implanted their symbolism on the buildings. They might sculpt a plaster angel swaddled in feathers reminiscent of the god Quetzalcoatl or the face of an ancient god surrounded by corn leaves, or use the pre-Hispanic calendar counts or the thirteen steps to heaven or the nine levels of the underworld to determine how many flowerettes to carve around the church doorway. Good examples of native symbolism are at the church in Xochimilco near Mexico City and Santa María Tonanzintla near Puebla. Native muralists had a hand in painting a knight in tiger skin on the Augustinian monastery in Ixmiquilpan, Hidalgo.

To convert the native populations, New World Spanish priests and architects altered their normal ways of building and reaching. Often before the church was built, an open-air atrium was first constructed so that large numbers of parishioners could be accommodated for services. *Posas* (shelters) at the four corners of churchyards were another architectural technique unique to Mexico, again for the purpose of accommodating crowds during holy sacraments. Because of the language barrier between the Spanish and natives, church adornment became more graphic. Biblical tales came to life in frescoes splashed across church walls and Christian symbolism in stone and stucco supplanted that of pre-Hispanic times. Out went the eagle (sun symbol), feathered serpent (symbol of fertility, rain, earth, and sky), and jaguar (power symbol), and in came Christ on a cross, saintly statues, and Franciscan, Dominican, and Augustinian symbolism on church facades. The talents of native master stone- and wood-carvers were turned to Christian subjects. It must have been a confusing time for the indigenous peoples, which accounts for the continued intermingling of Christian and pre-Hispanic ideas as they tried to make sense of it all by mixing preexisting ideas with new ones. The convenient apparition of the Virgin Mary on former pre-Hispanic religious turf made it "legal" to return there to worship and build a "Christian" shrine. Baroque became even more baroque in Mexico and was dubbed *churrigueresque*. Excellent Mexican baroque examples are Santa Prisca in Taxco and San Cayetano de la Valencia near Guanajuato. The term *plateresque* was given to facade ornamentation resembling silver design, which seemed to be planted on a structure rather than a part of it. Acolman convent near the ruins of Teotihuacán has one of the best plateresque facades in Mexico. The Viceregal Museum in Tepozotlán, north of Mexico City, holds a wealth of artwork from Mexican churches during this period. The new Museo Virreynal in Taxco holds colonial-era art recently found in a hidden room during the restoration of the Santa Prisca y San Sebastián church in Taxco.

✪ In religious art, there was a continual mingling of Christian and pre-Hispanic ideas.

Concurrently with the building of religious structures, public buildings took shape, modeled after those in European capitals. Especially around Puebla, locally made, colorful tile, a fusion of local art and Talavera style from Spain, decorated public walls and church domes. Dome tiles on Santa Prisca y San Sebastián in Taxco came from Puebla. The hacienda architecture sprang up in the countryside, resulting in often massive, thick-walled, fortresslike structures built around a central patio. Remains of haciendas, some of them still operating, can be seen in almost all parts of Mexico including Taxco, where Martín Cortés's silver-processing hacienda has been converted into Taxco's Convention Center. The San Carlos Academy of Art was founded in Mexico City in 1785, modeled after the renowned academies of Europe. Though the emphasis was on a Europeanized Mexico, by the end of the 19th century, the subject matter of easel artists was becoming Mexican: Still lifes with Mexican fruit and pottery and clearly Mexican landscapes with cactus and volcanoes appeared, as did portraits, whose subjects wore Mexican regional clothing. José María Velasco (1840–1912), the father of Mexican landscape painting, emerged during this time. His work and that of others of this period are at the National Museum of Art in Mexico City.

✪ By the end of the 19th century, the subject matter of Mexican art had become clearly Mexican.

With the late-19th-century entry of Porfirio Díaz into the presidency came another European infusion. Díaz idolized Europe and during this time he lavished on the country a number of striking European-style public buildings, among them opera houses still used today. He provided European scholarships to promising young artists who later returned to Mexico to produce Mexican subject paintings using techniques learned abroad. While the Mexican Revolution, following the resignation and exile of Díaz, ripped the country apart between 1911 and 1917, the result was the birth of Mexico, a claiming and appreciation of it by all Mexicans.

In 1923, Minister of Education José Vasconcelos was charged with educating the illiterate masses. As one means of reaching many people, he started the muralist movement when he invited Diego Rivera and several other budding artists to paint Mexican history on the walls of the Ministry of Education building and the National Preparatory School in Mexico City. From then on, the "Big Three" muralists, David Siquieros, José Clemente Orozco, and Rivera, were joined by others in bringing Mexico's history in art to the walls of public buildings throughout the country for all to see and interpret. The years that followed eventually brought about a return to easel art, and exploration of Mexico's culture, and a new generation of artists and architects who are free to invent and draw upon subjects and styles from around the world.

Among the 20th-century greats are the "Big Three" muralists, as well as Rufino Tamayo, Gerardo Murillo, José Guadalupe Posada, Saturnino Herrán, Francisco Goitia, Frida Kahlo, José María Velasco, Pedro and Rafael Coronel, Miguel Covarrubias, Olga Costa, and José Chávez Morado. Among the important architects during this period is Luis Barragán, who incorporated design elements from haciendas, and Mexican textiles, pottery, and furniture, into sleek, marble-floored structures splashed with the vivid colors of Mexico. His ideas are used by Mexican architects all over Mexico today.

LITERATURE

By the time Cortés arrived in Mexico, the inhabitants of Mexico were already masters of literature, recording their poems and histories by painting in fanfold books (codices) made of deerskin and bark paper or carving on stone. To record history, gifted students were taught the art of bookmaking, drawing, painting, reading, and writing, abilities the general public didn't have. The ancient Maya produced two important epic works, the *Book of Popol Vuh* and the *Chilam Balam*. After the Conquest the Spaniards deliberately destroyed native books. However, several Catholic priests, among them Bernardo de Sahugun and Diego de Landa (who was one of the book destroyers), encouraged the Indians to record their customs and history. These records are among the best we have to document life before the Conquest.

During the Conquest Cortés wrote his now-famous five letters to Charles V, which give us the first printed Conquest literature, but it was spare by contrast to the work of Díaz de Castillo. Enraged by an inaccurate account of the Conquest written by a flattering friend of Cortés, 40 years after the Conquest Bernal Díaz de Castillo, one of the conquerors, wrote his lively and very readable version of the event, *True History of the Conquest of Mexico*: it's regarded as the most accurate.

The first printing press appeared in Mexico in 1537 and was followed by a proliferation of printing, mostly on subjects about science, nature, and getting along in Mexico. The most important literary figure during the 16th century was Sor Juana Inés de la Cruz, child prodigy and later poet-nun whose works are still treasured.

The first Spanish novel written in Mexico was *The Itching Parrot* by José Joaquin Fernández de Lizardi, about 19th-century Mexican life. In the mid-1800s, Guerrero writer and novelist Ignacio Manuel Altamirano, known as the father of Mexican literature, filled his writing with Mexican characters and themes that began a similar movement in all the arts.

Nineteenth-century writers produced a plethora of political fiction and nonfiction. Among the more explosive was *The Presidential Succession of 1910* by Francisco

---

IMPRESSIONS

Considering the variety of nations, tongues, cultures, and artistic styles, the unity of these peoples comes as a surprise. They all share certain ideas and beliefs. Thus it is not inaccurate to call this group of nations and cultures a Mexoamerican civilization. Unity in space and continuity in time; from the first millennium before Christ to the sixteenth century, these distinct Mexoamerican peoples evolve, reelaborate, and re-create a nucleus of basic concepts as well as social and political techniques and institutions. There were changes and variations . . . but never was the continuity broken.
—OCTAVIO PAZ, 1990

Madero (who later became president), which contributed to the downfall of Porfirio Díaz, and *Regeneración,* a weekly anti-Díaz magazine published by the Flores Mignon brothers.

Among 20th-century writers of note are Octavio Paz, author of *The Labyrinth of Solitude* and winner of the 1991 Nobel Prize for literature, and Carlos Fuentes, who wrote *Where the Air Is Clear.*

Books in Mexico are relatively inexpensive to purchase but editions are not produced in great quantity. Newspapers and magazines proliferate, but the majority of those who read devour comic book novels, the most visible form of literature.

4. RELIGION, MYTH & FOLKLORE

Mexico is a predominantly Catholic country, a religion brought by the Spaniards during the Conquest of Mexico. Despite the preponderance of the Catholic faith, in many places (Chiapas, Oaxaca, and Guerrero, for example) Catholicism has assumed pre-Hispanic overtones. One need only visit the *curandero* (folk healing) section of a Mexican market, or attend a village festivity featuring pre-Hispanic dancers, to understand that supernatural beliefs often run parallel to Christian ones.

Mexico's complicated mythological heritage from pre-Hispanic literature is jammed with images derived from nature—the wind, jaguars, eagles, snakes, flowers, and more, all intertwined with elaborate mythological stories to explain the universe, climate, seasons, and geography. So strong were the ancient beliefs in their mythological deities that Mexico's indigenous peoples built their cities according to the cardinal points, with each direction assigned a particular color (the colors might vary from group to group). The sun, moon, and stars took on godlike meaning and religious, ceremonial, and secular calendars were arranged to show tribute to these omnipotent gods.

Most groups believed in an underworld (not a hell), usually of nine levels, and a heaven of 13 levels, so the numbers 9 and 13 become mythologically significant. The solar calendar count of 365 days and the ceremonial calendar of 260 days are numerically significant.

How one died determined where one wound up after death, in the underworld, heaven, or at one of the four cardinal points. Everyone had to first make the journey through the underworld.

One of the richest sources of mythological tales is the *Popol Vuh,* a Maya bible of sorts, that was recorded after the Conquest. The *Chilam Balam,* another such book existed in hieroglyphic form at the Conquest and was recorded, using the Spanish alphabet, into Mayan words that could be understood by the Spaniards. The *Chilam Balam* differs from the *Popol Vuh* in that it is the collected histories of many Maya communities.

Each of the ancient cultures had its set of gods and goddesses and while the names might not cross cultures, their characteristics or purpose often did. Chac, the hook-nosed rain god of the Maya, was Tláloc, the mighty-figured rain god of the Aztecs; Quetzalcoatl, the plumed-serpent god/man of the Toltecs, became Kukulkán of the Maya. The tales of the powers and creation of these deified personages make up Mexico's rich mythology. Sorting out the pre-Hispanic pantheon and mythological beliefs in ancient Mexico can become an all-consuming study (the Maya alone had 166 deities), so below is a list of some of the most important gods.

Coatlíque	Huitzilopochtli's mother, whose name means "she of serpent skirt," goddess of death and earth.
Ehécatl	Wind god whose temple is usually round; another aspect of Quetzalcoatl.
Huitzilopochtli	War god and primary Aztec god, son of Coatlíque.
Kukulkán	Quetzalcoatl's name in the Yucatán.
Mayahuel	Goddess of pulque.
Ometeotl	God/goddess, all-powerful creator of the universe, ruler of heaven, earth, and underworld.
Quetzalcoatl	A mortal who took on legendary characteristics as a god (or vice versa). When he left Tula in shame after a night succumbing to temptations, he promised to return; he reappeared in the Yucatán. He is also symbolized as Venus, the morning star, and Ehécatl, the wind god. He is said to have introduced Mexico to cacao and taught the people how to grow, ferment, roast, and grind it into what we know as chocolate.
Tezcaltipoca	Aztec sun god known as "Smoking Mirror."
Tláloc	Aztec rain god.
Tonant	Aztec motherhood goddess.
Xochipill	Aztec god of dance, flowers, and music.
Xochiquetzal	Flower and love goddess.

5. CULTURAL & SOCIAL LIFE

PEOPLE

The population of Mexico is 85 million, with 15% of Spanish descent, 60% mestizo (mixed Spanish and Indian), and 25% pure Indian (descendants of the Maya, Aztecs, Huastecs, Otomies, Totonacs, and other peoples). Added to this ethnic mix are Africans brought as slaves from the Caribbean islands more than 200 years ago, when it was illegal to enslave the Indians—they are completely assimilated into the population today. Their descendants are often seen along the Pacific Costa Chica south of Acapulco, and are employed in all aspects of Guerrero's tourist industry. Included also in Mexico's ethnic mix are European merchants and soldiers of fortune, and the lingering French influence from the time of Maximilian's abortive empire in the New World.

Although Spanish is the official language, about 50 Indian languages are still spoken, mostly in the Yucatán peninsula, Oaxaca, Chiapas, Chihuahua, Nayarit, Puebla, Sonora, Veracruz, Michocán, and Guerrero. At least 25% of Mexico's population speaks Nahuatl, the language of the Aztecs. And in Guerrero as much as 60% of the population speaks only a native language.

Despite its fame as a state with two important coastal resorts (Acapulco and Ixtapa/Zihuatanejo), Guerrero is still very close to its pre-Hispanic roots. That's partly because there was no road linking the coast with the capital until 1928 and partly because portions of the state still remain isolated due to lack of adequate roads. Thus, indigenous groups present at the Conquest, and their attendant beliefs and customs, are still found in large numbers in Guerrero. Nahua Indians from the Sierras del Norte, Valles Centrales, and La Montaña are part of the Acapulco and

Ixtapa/Zihuatanejo backdrop. They arrive to sell their crafts, often with the women dressed in satin and ruffles, usually protected by an apron. Many move easily between their native tongue and Spanish and sometimes into English as well. Mixtec and Amuzgo Indians live in La Montaña region bordering Oaxaca, and while they weave and embroider beautiful cotton huipiles, of pre-Hispanic origin and design that are sold all over Mexico, they are rarely seen in populated areas.

In most of the region's out-of-the-way places, as well as in Acapulco or Zihuatanejo, it isn't unusual to see members of Guerrero's indigenous groups wearing clothing that was adopted after the Conquest. In Tlapehuala, in northern Guerrero, the women wear long, brilliantly colored skirts to mid-calf, with skirt, blouse, and hair adorned with ribbons. They wear gold or colorful jewelry and sandals. Men are still seen in the traditional homespun white cotton clothing and handmade leather sandals. The women of Acatlán (the Central Valleys) weave and embroider unusual skirts and traditional blouses for the women of nearby Zitlala, but Acatlán women no longer wear the traditional garb (see Chapter 7 for details). Near Coyuca de Catalán (on the Costa Grande) women use brightly colored skirts and blouses and wear gold filigree jewelry. In Mochitlán (southeast of Chilpancingo), women don colorful slips as well as multicolored skirts bordered in flowers, adopted in post-Conquest times.

Modern Mexico clings to its identity while embracing outside cultures, so Mexicans enjoy the Bolshoi Ballet as easily as a family picnic or village festival. Mexicans have a knack for knowing how to enjoy life, and families, weekends, holidays, and festivities are given priority. They also enjoy stretching a weekend holiday into four days called a *puente* (bridge) and with the whole family in tow flee the cities en masse to visit relatives in the country, picnic, or relax at resorts.

The Mexican workday is a long one; laborers begin around 7am and get off at dusk; office workers go in around 9am and, not counting the two- to three-hour lunch, get off at 7 or 8pm. Once a working career is started, there is little time for additional study. School is supposedly mandatory and free through the sixth grade, but many youngsters quit long before that, or never go at all.

Sociologists and others have written volumes trying to explain the Mexican's special relationship with death. It is at once mocked and mourned. Day of the Dead (November 1 and 2), a cross between our Halloween and Memorial Day, is a good opportunity to see Mexico's relationship to the concept of death.

MUSIC & DANCE

One has only to walk down almost any street or attend any festival to understand that Mexico's vast musical tradition is inborn; it predates the Conquest. Musical instruments were made from almost anything that could be made to rattle, produce a rhythm, or a sound—conch-shell trumpets, high-sounding antler horns, rattlers from seashells and rattlesnake rattlers, drums of turtle shell as well as upright leather-covered wood (*tlalpanhuéhuetl*), and horizontal hollowed logs (*teponaztli*), bells of gold and copper, wind instruments of hollow reeds or fired clay, and soundmakers from leather-topped armadillo shells and gourds. Many were elaborately carved or decorated befitting the important ceremonies they accompanied.

So important was music that one of Moctezuma's palaces, the Mixcoacalli, was devoted to the care and housing of musical instruments, which were guarded around the clock. In Aztec times, music, dance, and religion were tied together with literature. Music was usually intended to accompany poems that were written for religious ceremonies. Children with talent were separated and trained to adulthood, especially as musicians and poets, two exacting professions in which mistakes carried extreme consequences. The dead were buried with musical instruments for the journey into the afterlife.

Music and dance in Mexico today is divided into three kinds, pre- and post-Hispanic and secular. Besides regional village fiestas, two of the best places to see pre-Hispanic dancing are the Ballet Folklórico de Mexico in Mexico City and the summer Guelaguetza in Oaxaca. Among pre-Hispanic dances still performed there or elsewhere in Mexico are "The Flying Pole Dance," "Dance of the Quetzales" (the sacred quetzal bird), "Deer Dance," and dances of the Huicholes and Coras of Jalisco and Nayarit. Post-Hispanic music and dance evolved first in order to teach the native inhabitants about Christianity with such dances as "Los Santiagos," with St. James battling heathens, and "Los Moros," with Moors battling Christians. Others, such as "Los Jardineros," were spoofs on pretentious Spanish life. Secular dances are variations of Spanish dances performed by both men and women characterized by lots of foot tapping, skirt-swishing, and flirtatious gestures.

✪ Mexico's musical tradition is inborn; it predates the Conquest.

No Mexican fiesta night would be complete without the "Jarabe Tapatío," the national folk dance of Mexico. The "Huapango," accompanied by violins and guitars, is a native dance of Veracruz, Tamaulipas, and San Luis Potosí. "Jaranas" are folk dances of the Yucatán danced to the lively beat of a ukulele-like instrument and drums. Some of the most unusual and authentic dances can be seen at village festivals in Guerrero State. (For more on Guerrero's village festivals, see Chapter 7.)

Besides the native music and dances, there are regional, state, and national orchestras. On weekends state bands often perform free in central plazas. Mexicans have a sophisticated enjoyment of the performing arts from around the world and world-class auditoriums in which they are presented. It's possible to find national as well as international groups touring most of the year but especially in conjunction with the Cervantino Festival, which takes place in Guanajuato in October and November. Invited groups perform throughout the country before and after the festival.

6. SPORTS & RECREATION

The precise rules of the ball game played by pre-Hispanic Mexicans aren't known, but it is fairly well established that some of the players were put to death when the game was over. Stone carvings of the game left on the walls of ball courts throughout Mesoamerica depict heavily padded players elaborately decked out. With that interesting beginning, team sports are still popular in Mexico.

Bullfighting, introduced by the Spaniards, is countrywide today. Jai alai, a Spanish game, is played in arenas in Mexico City and Tijuana. By the 18th century the Mexican gentleman cowboy, the charro, displayed skillful horsemanship during the "charreada," a Mexican-style rodeo. Today charro associations countrywide compete all year, usually on Sunday mornings. It is sometimes easier to rent a horse in Mexico than a car, since it is a pastime enjoyed by many people at beach resorts as well as in the countryside. Although supposedly illegal, in many places cockfights are held in specially built arenas.

Probably the most popular spectator team sport today is soccer; turn on the TV almost anytime to catch a game. Mexico has numerous golf courses, especially in the resort areas. Sport bicycling has grown in popularity, so it isn't unusual to see young men making the grind of steep mountain passes during cycling club marathons.

Tennis, racquetball, squash, waterskiing, surfing, and scuba diving are all sports visitors can enjoy in Mexico. While it's possible to scuba dive on the Pacific, the best place for that sport is Mexico's Yucatán Caribbean coast. Mountain climbing and hiking volcanoes are rugged sports in which you'll meet like-minded folks from around the world.

7. FOOD & DRINK

Mexican food served in the United States isn't really Mexican food, it's a transported variation that gets less Mexican the farther you get from the border. True Mexican food usually isn't fiery hot; hot spices are added from sauces and garnishes at the table. While there are certain staples like tortillas and beans that appear almost universally, Mexican food and drink varies considerably from region to region; even the beans and tortillas sidestep the usual in some areas just to keep you on your toes.

DINING CUSTOMS

If you are a businessperson you may grab a cup of coffee or *atole* and a piece of sweet bread just before heading for work around 8am. Around 10 or 11am it's time for a real breakfast and that's when restaurants fill with men (usually) eating hearty breakfasts that may look more like lunch with steak, eggs, beans, and tortillas. Between 1 and 5pm patrons again converge for lunch, the main meal of the day. Lunch begins with soup, then rice, then the main course with beans and tortillas and maybe a meager helping of a vegetable, followed by dessert and coffee. Workers return to their jobs until 7 or 8pm. Dinner is late, usually around 9 or 10pm. Although you may see many Mexicans eating in restaurants at night, big evening meals aren't traditional; a typical meal at home would be a light one with leftovers from breakfast or lunch, perhaps soup, or tortillas and jam, or a little meat and rice.

Foreigners searching for an early breakfast will often find that nothing gets going in restaurants until around 9am; that's a hint to bring your own portable coffeepot and coffee and buy bakery goodies the night before to make breakfast yourself. Markets, however, are bustling by 7am and that's the best place to get an early breakfast. Though Mexico grows flavorful coffee in Chiapas, Veracruz, and Oaxaca, a jar of instant coffee is often all that's offered, especially in budget restaurants.

Some of the foreigner's greatest frustrations in Mexico have to do with attracting and retaining the waiter and receiving the final bill. If the waiter arrives to take your order before you are ready, you may have trouble getting him again when you are ready. Once an order is in, ordinarily the food arrives in steady sequence. Once your meal is before you, and you're close to savoring your last morsel, an eager waiter often appears to whisk away your plate before you're even finished! "¿Puedo retirar?" ("Can I take your plate away?") he asks, nearly clicking his heels with efficiency. At this point guard your plate, for at any moment it could disappear midfork. Finding him to get the check, however, is another matter. It's considered rude for the waiter to bring it before it's requested, so you have to ask for it (sometimes more than once, when at last you've found the waiter). To summon the waiter, wave or raise your hand, but don't motion with your index finger, a demeaning gesture that may cause the waiter to ignore you. Or if it's the check you want, a smile and a scribbling motion into the palm of your hand can send the message across the room. In many budget restaurants, waiters don't clear the table of finished plates or soft-drink bottles because they use them to figure the tab. Always double-check the addition.

REGIONAL CUISINE

Mexico's regional foods are a mixture of pre-Hispanic, Spanish, and French cuisines and at their best are among the most delicious in the world. Recipes developed by nuns during colonial times to please priests and visiting dignitaries have become part of the national patrimony, but much of Mexico's cuisine is derived from pre-Hispanic times. For the visitor, finding hearty, filling meals is fairly easy on a budget, but finding truly delicious food is not as easy. However, some of the best food is found in small inexpensive restaurants where regional specialties are made to please discerning locals. Explanations of specific dishes are found in the Appendix.

Tamales are one of Mexico's traditional foods, but regional differences make trying them as you travel a treat. In northern Mexico they are small and thin with only a tiny sliver of meat inside. Chiapas has many tamal types but all are plump and usually come with a sizable hunk of meat and sauce inside. A *corunda* in Michoacán is a triangular-shaped tamal wrapped in a corn leaf rather than the traditional corn husk. In Oaxaca traditional tamales come steaming in a banana leaf. The *zacahuil* of coastal Veracruz is the size of a pig's leg (which is in the center) and pit baked in a banana leaf. *Molote*, a tiny football-shaped tamal, is a specialty around Papantla, Veracruz.

Tortillas, another Mexican basic, are not made in the same way everywhere. In northern Mexico flour tortillas are served more often than corn tortillas. Blue-corn tortillas, once a market food, have found their way to gourmet tables throughout the country. Oaxaca state boasts a large assortment of tortillas, including a hard, thick one with holes used like a cracker, and the huge tlayuda that holds an entire meal. Tortillas are fried and used as garnish in tortilla and Tarascan soup. Filled with meat, they become tacos. A tortilla stuffed, rolled, or covered in a sauce and garnished results in an enchilada. A tortilla filled with cheese and lightly fried is a quesadilla. Rolled into a narrow tube, stuffed with chicken, then deep-fried, it's known as a flauta. Soft tortillas become *tacos* when filled with any number of meats; however, in some places in Mexico what's called a taco on the menu may be more like a flauta elsewhere. Leftover tortillas cut in wedges and crispy fried are called totopos and used to scoop beans and guacamole salad. Yesterday's tortillas mixed with eggs, chicken, peppers, and other spices are called chilaquiles. Small fried corn tortillas are delicious with ceviche; when topped with fresh lettuce, tomatoes, sauce, onions, and chicken, they become tostadas. Each region has a variation of these tortilla-based dishes.

Regional drinks are almost as varied as food in Mexico. Tequila comes only from the blue agave grown near Guadalajara. Hot *ponche* (punch) is found often at festivals and is usually made with fresh fruit and spiked with tequila or rum. Baja California and the region around Querétaro is prime grape-growing land for Mexico's wine production. The best pulque supposedly comes from Hidalgo State. Beer is produced in Monterrey, the Yucatán, and Veracruz. Delicious fruit-flavored waters appear on tables countrywide, made from hibiscus flowers, ground rice and melon seeds, watermelon, and other fresh fruits. Sangría is a spicy tomato, orange juice, and pepper-based chaser for tequila shots.

8. RECOMMENDED BOOKS, FILMS & RECORDINGS

BOOKS

There is an endless supply of books written on the history, culture, and archeology of Mexico and Central America. I have listed those that I especially enjoyed.

HISTORY *A Short History of Mexico* (Doubleday, 1962), by J. Patrick McHenry, is a concise historical account. A remarkably readable and thorough college textbook is *The Course of Mexican History* (Oxford University Press, 1987), by Michael C. Meyer and William L. Sherman. *The Conquest of New Spain* (Shoe String, 1988), by Bernal Díaz de Castillo, is the famous story of the Mexican Conquest written by Cortés's lieutenant. *The Crown of Mexico* (Holt Rinehart & Winston, 1971), by Joan Haslip, a biography of Maximilian and Carlota, reads like a novel. *Ancient Mexico: An Overview* (University of New Mexico, 1985), by Jaime Litvak, is a short, very readable history of pre-Hispanic Mexico. *The Wind That Swept Mexico* (University of Texas Press, 1971), by Anita Brenner, is a classic illustrated account of the Mexican Revolution. Charles Flandrau wrote the classic *Viva Mexico: A Traveller's Account of Life in Mexico* (Eland Books, 1985) early this century, a blunt and humorous description of Mexico. Most people can't put down Gary Jenning's *Aztec* (Avon, 1981), a superbly researched and colorfully written fictionalized account of Aztec life before and after the Conquest. Good bookstores in Mexico often carry a copy of the special edition of *Taxco* (Artes de Mexico), which gives a detailed history of the town, its customs, and Santa Prisca y San Sebastián. The fascinating history of Mexico's 250 years of trade with Asia appears in the September 1990 issue of *National Geographic* magazine.

CULTURE *Five Families* (Basic Books, 1959) and *Children of Sanchez* (Random House, 1979), by Oscar Lewis, are sociological studies written in the late 1950s and early 1960s about typical Mexican families. *Mexican and Central American Mythology* (Peter Bedrick Books, 1983), by Irene Nicholson, is a concise illustrated book that simplifies the subject.

A good, but controversial, all-around introduction to contemporary Mexico and its people is *Distant Neighbors: A Portrait of the Mexicans* (Random House, 1984), by Alan Riding. Another such book is Patrick Oster's *The Mexicans: A Personal Portrait of the Mexican People* (Harper & Row, 1989), a reporter's insightful account of ordinary Mexican people. Another book with valuable insights into the Mexican character is *The Labyrinth of Solitude* (Grove Press, 1985), by Octavio Paz.

The best single source of information on Mexican music, dance, festivals, customs, and mythology is Frances Toor's *A Treasury of Mexican Folkways* (Crown, 1967). *Life in Mexico: Letters of Fanny Calderón de la Barca* (Doubleday, 1966), edited and annotated by Howard T. Fisher and Marion Hall Fisher, is as lively and entertaining today as when it first appeared in 1843, but the editors' illustrated and annotated update makes it even more contemporary. Scottish-born Fanny was married to the Spanish ambassador assigned to Mexico and the letters are the accounts of her experiences in Mexico written to relatives. Her colorful account of riding to Cuernavaca and the Cacahuamilpa Caves and staying in surrounding haciendas is worth reading.

ART, ARCHEOLOGY & ARCHITECTURE   The most important recent book (in Spanish only) published on Taxco's Santa Prisca Church, *Santa Prisca Restaurada* (Gobierno del Estado de Guerrero, 1990) is a magnificently illustrated book detailing not only the restoration of the 18th-century church, but the history of its construction down to the discovery of the contents of a secret room. The *Mexican Codices and Their Extraordinary History* (Ediciones Lara, 1985) by María Sten tells the story of the Indians' "painted books." *Mexico Splendors of Thirty Centuries* (Metropolitan Museum of Art, 1990), the catalog of the 1991 traveling exhibition, is a wonderful resource on Mexico's art from 1500 B.C. through the 1950s. Another superb catalog, *Images of Mexico: The Contribution of Mexico to 20th Century Art* (Dallas Museum of Art, 1987), is a fabulously illustrated and detailed account of Mexican art gathered from collections around the world. *Art and Time in Mexico: From the Conquest to the Revolution* (Harper & Row, 1985), by Elizabeth Wilder Weismann, illustrated with 351 photographs, covers Mexican religious, public, and private architecture with excellent photos and text. *Casa Mexicana* (Stewart, Tabori & Chang, 1989), by Tim Street-Porter, takes readers through the interiors of some of Mexico's finest homes-turned-museums or public buildings and private homes using color photographs. *Mexican Interiors* (Architectural Book Publishing Co., 1962), by Verna Cook Shipway and Warren Shipway, uses black-and-white photographs to highlight architectural details from homes all over Mexico.

FOLK ART   Chloë Sayer's *Costumes of Mexico* (University of Texas Press, 1985), is a beautifully illustrated and written work. *Mexican Masks* (University of Texas Press, 1980), by Donald Cordry, remains a definitive work on Mexican masks based on the author's collection and travels. Cordry's *Mexican Indian Costumes* (University of Texas Press, 1968) is another classic on that subject. The two-volume *Lo Efímero y Eterno del Arte Popular Mexicano* (Fondo Editorial de la Plastica Mexicana, 1974), produced during the Echeverria presidency, is out of print, but it's one of the most complete works ever produced on Mexican folk art and customs. Carlos Espejel wrote both *Mexican Folk Ceramics* and *Mexican Folk Crafts* (Editorial Blume, 1975 and 1978), two comprehensive books that explore crafts state by state. *Folk Treasures of Mexico* (Harry N. Abrams, 1990), by Marion Oettinger, curator of folk art and Latin American art at the San Antonio Museum of Art, is the fascinating illustrated story behind the 3,000-piece Mexican folk-art collection amassed by Nelson Rockefeller over a 50-year period, and contains much information about individual folk artists. All of these books carry important information on the crafts of Guerrero.

NATURE   *A Field Guide to Mexican Birds* (Houghton Mifflin, 1973), by Roger Tory Peterson and Edward L. Chalif, is an excellent guide to the country's birds. *A Guide to Mexican Mammals & Reptiles* (Minutiae Mexicana, 1989), by Normal Pelham Wright and Dr. Bernardo Villa Ramírez, is a small but useful guide to some of the country's wildlife.

FILMS

Mexico's first movie theater opened in 1887 in Mexico City. Almost immediately men with movie cameras began capturing everyday life in Mexico as well as what later became news, including both sides of the Mexican Revolution. All these early films are safe in Mexican archives. The movies got their Mexican start as an entertainment industry with the 1918 film *The Gray Automobile Gang* (La Banda del Automóvil Gris) by Enrique Rosas Priego, based on an actual cops-and-robbers event in Mexico, but the industry's heyday really began in the 1930s and lasted only until the 1950s. Themes revolved around the Mexican Revolution, handsome but luckless singing cowboys, and helpless, poor-but-beautiful maidens, all against a classic Mexican backdrop, at first rural or village (*rancho*) settings and later in city neighborhoods. While many of the stories followed a typical problem, solution, all-ends-well storyline, some were touching tearjerkers with sad endings. Classic films and directors from that era are *Alla en el Rancho Grande* and *Vamonos Con Pancho Villa*, both by Fernando de Fuentes; *Champion Without a Crown* (*Campeón sin Corona*), a true-life boxing drama, by Alejandro Galindo; *The Pearl* (*La Perla*), by Emilio Fernández, based on John Steinbeck's novel; *Yanco*, by Servando Gonzalez, about a poor, young boy of Xochimilco who learned to play a violin; and the sad tale of María Candelaria, also set in Xochimilco, another Fernández film starring Dolores del Río. Comedian Cantinflas starred in many Mexican films, and became known in the U.S. for his role in *Around the World in Eighty Days*.

If Mexico's golden age of cinema didn't last long, Mexico as subject matter and location has had a long life. The Durango mountains have become the film-backdrop capital of Mexico. *The Night of the Iguana* was filmed in Puerto Vallarta, putting that seaside village on the map. *Old Gringo* was filmed in Zacatecas, and *Viva Zapata!* and *Under the Volcano* were both set in Cuernavaca.

The most recent well-known film produced in Mexico is *Like Water for Chocolate*, which is a wonderfully done movie based on the best-selling novel by Laura Esquivel (Doubleday, 1992). Lusty and intimate, the story intertwines the secrets of traditional Mexican food preparation with a magical and surrealistic yet believable account of Mexican hacienda family life along the Río Grande/Río Bravo at the turn of the century.

RECORDINGS

While Mexico's homegrown cinema may have hit a snag, its recording industry has not. Mexicans take their music very seriously—just notice tapes for sale almost everywhere, nearly ceaseless music in the streets, and bus drivers' collections of tapes to entertain passengers.

For the collector there are numerous choices, from contemporary rock to ballads from the revolution, ranchero, salsa, and sones, and romantic trios. For trio music, some of the best is by Los Tres Diamantes, Los Tres Reyes, and Trio Los Soberanos. If you're requesting songs of a trio, good ones to ask for are "Sin Ti," "Usted," "Adios Mi Chaparita," "Amor de la Calle," and "Cielito Lindo." Traditional ranchero songs to request, which can be sung by soloists or trios, is "Tu Solo Tu," "No Volveré," and "Adios Mi Chaparita." Heartthrob soloists from years past include Pedro Vargas, Hector Cabrera, Lucho Gatica, Pepe Jara, and Alberto Vazquez. Marimba music is popular in Veracruz, Chiapas, and the Yucatán. Peña Ríos makes excellent marimba recordings. Though marimba musicians seldom ask for requests, some typical renditions would include "Huapango de Moncayo" and "El Bolero de Ravel." Mariachi music is played and sold all over Mexico. Among the top recording artists is Mariachi Vargas. No mariachi performance is complete without "Guadalajara," "Las Mañanitas," and "Jarabe Tapatío." One of the best recordings of recent times is the Royal Philharmonic Orchestra's rendition of classic Mexican music titled *Mexicano;* it's one purchase you must make.

CHAPTER 2

PLANNING A TRIP TO MEXICO

In this chapter, the where, when, and how of your trip is discussed—the advance planning that gets your trip together and takes it on the road.

After they decide where to go, most people have two fundamental questions: What will it cost? and How do I get there? This chapter not only answers those questions, but addresses such important issues as when to go, whether or not to take a tour, what pretrip health precautions should be taken, what insurance coverage to investigate, where to obtain additional information, and more.

1. INFORMATION, ENTRY REQUIREMENTS & MONEY

SOURCES OF INFORMATION

TOURIST OFFICES

In the United States Tourist offices are located at 70 E. Lake St., Suite 1413, Chicago, IL 60601 (tel. 312/565-2778); 2702 N. Loop W., Suite 450, Houston, TX 77008 (tel. 713/880-5153); 10100 Santa Monica Blvd., Suite 224, Los Angeles, CA 90067 (tel. 310/203-8191); 233 Ponce de Leon Blvd., Suite 710, Coral Gables, FL 33134 (tel. 305/443-9160); 405 Park Ave., Suite 1401, New York, NY 10022 (tel. 212/755-7261); and 1911 Pennsylvania Ave. NW, Washington, DC 20006 (tel. 202/728-1750).

In Canada Information is available at One Place Ville-Marie, Suite 1526, Montréal, PQ H3B 2B5 (tel. 514/871-1052); and 2 Bloor St. W., Suite 1801, Toronto, ON M4W 3E2 (tel. 416/925-0704).

In Great Britain There's a Mexican tourist office at 60-61 Trafalgar Sq., London WC 2N 5DS (tel. 44/071-839-3177).

In Europe Information is available at Weisenhüttenplatz 26, 6000 Frankfurt-am-Main 1, Germany (tel. 4969/25-3413); Calle de Velázquez 126, Madrid 28006, Spain (tel. 341/261-1827); 4 rue Notre-Dame-des-Victoires, 75002 Paris, France (tel. 331/40-20-07-34); and via Barberini 3, 00187 Roma, Italy (tel. 396/482-7160).

In Asia Contact 2.15.1 Nagata-Cho, Chiyoda-Ku, Tokyo 100, Japan (tel. 813/580-2962).

OTHER SOURCES

The following newsletters may be of interest to readers:

Mexico Meanderings, P.O. Box 33057, Austin, TX 78764, is a six- to eight-page newsletter with photographs featuring off-the-beaten-track destinations in Mexico. It's aimed at readers who travel by car, bus, or train, and is published six times annually. A subscription costs $18.

Travel Mexico, Apdo. Postal 6-1007, Mexico, DF 06600, is published six times a year by the publishers of *Traveler's Guide to Mexico*—the book frequently found in hotel rooms in Mexico. The newsletter covers a variety of topics from news about archeology, to hotel packages, new resorts, and hotels, and the economy. A subscription costs $15.

ENTRY REQUIREMENTS

DOCUMENTS All travelers are required to:

1. Present proof of citizenship such as an original birth certificate with a raised seal, or valid passport, or naturalization papers. This proof of citizenship may also be requested to reenter both the U.S. and Mexico. Photocopies are not acceptable.
2. Carry a Mexican Tourist Permit, which is issued free of charge by Mexican border officials after proof of citizenship is accepted. The Tourist Permit is more important than a passport in Mexico, so guard it carefully—if you lose it, you may not be permitted to leave the country until you can replace it; that bureaucratic hassle takes several days or a week at least.

A Tourist Permit can be issued for up to 180 days, and although your stay south of the border may be less than that, you should get the card for the maximum time, just in case. Sometimes the officials don't ask, they just stamp a time limit, so be sure and say "six months," or at least twice as long as you think you'll stay. You may decide to stay, and you'll eliminate hassle by not needing to renew your papers. This is especially important for those who take cars into Mexico.

Other requirements:

1. Children under age 18 traveling without parents or with only one parent must have a notarized letter from the absent parent or parents authorizing the travel.
2. Additional documentation is required for driving a personal vehicle to Mexico. (See Section 7, "Getting There.")

Lost Documents To replace a lost passport, contact your embassy or nearest consular agent, listed below in "Fast Facts: Mexico." You must establish a record of your citizenship, and also fill out a form requesting another Mexican Tourist Permit. Without the Tourist Permit, you can't leave the country; and without an affidavit regarding your passport and citizenship, you may have hassles at Customs when you get home. You'll need them also to get a new passport later. So you must get everything cleared up before trying to leave.

CUSTOMS When you enter Mexico, Customs officials are tolerant as long as you have no drugs (marijuana, cocaine, etc.) or firearms. You're allowed to bring two cartons of cigarettes, or 50 cigars, plus 1 kilogram (2.2 lb.) of smoking tobacco; the liquor allowance is two bottles of anything, wine or hard liquor.

When you reenter the U.S., federal law allows duty-free, up to $400 in purchases every 30 days. The first $1,000 over the $400 allowance is taxed at 10%. You may bring in a carton (200) of cigarettes, or 50 cigars, or 2 kilograms (4.4 lb.) of smoking tobacco, or proportional amounts of these items, plus 1 liter of an alcoholic beverage (wine, beer, or spirits). If you bring larger amounts of these things, you will have to pay federal duty and internal revenue tax. You will also be subject to state laws which may not allow you to bring back any liquor.

Canadian citizens are allowed $20 in purchases after a 24-hour absence from the country or $100 after a stay of 48 hours.

MONEY

CASH/CURRENCY In 1993 the Mexican government dropped three zeros from its currency. The new unit of currency is called the Nuevo Peso or New Peso. The change doesn't devalue the peso; it simplifies accounting—all those zeros were becoming too difficult to manage. Old Peso notes will be valid until 1996; no date for last use of old coins has been announced. Paper currency comes in denominations of 2, 5, 10, 20, 50, and 100 New Pesos. Coins come in denominations of 1, 2, 5, and 10 pesos and 20 and 50 centavos (100 centavos equals 1 New Peso). The coins are somewhat confusing because different denominations have a similar appearance. New Peso prices appear written with an N or NP beside them; and for a while the Old Peso prices will appear as well. Currently the U.S. dollar equals just over NP$3; an item costing NP$5, for example, would be equivalent to U.S. $1.66.

These changes are likely to cause confusion among U.S. and Canadian travelers to Mexico in several ways. First, Nuevo Peso prices are close enough to those in the U.S. and Canada to ensure some confusion; some people will take advantage of the similarity. Then, for the first time in years, everyone must become accustomed to making small change and seeing it on restaurant bills and credit cards. On restaurant bills that you pay in cash, for example, the change is rounded up or down to the nearest 5-centavo multiple. But credit-card bills show the exact amount and will have N or NP written before the amount to denote that the bill is in New Pesos. Be sure to double-check any credit-card vouchers to be sure the N or NP appears on the total line.

Getting change continues to be a problem in Mexico. Small-denomination bills and coins are hard to come by, so start collecting them as soon as you cross the border and continue as you travel. Shopkeepers everywhere seem always to be out of change and small bills; that's doubly true in a market.

Take stock of your cash needs before a weekend, when banks are closed. Once you're away from a major tourist center, such as Acapulco or Ixtapa, banks are hard to come by; credit cards and even traveler's checks can be virtually useless. Even banks in Taxco sometimes cannot change foreign currency to pesos. See also "Wire Funds" in "Fast Facts: Mexico," below.

The official inflation rate in Mexico is 8%, but prices for hotels and restaurants have been increasing between 10% and 40% annually in most parts of the country. Every effort is made to provide the most accurate and up-to-date information in this book, but price changes are inevitable.

The following is a sample of costs in three of the major areas covered in this book. Keep in mind that inflation will increase these costs by the second year of this edition's lifetime.

WHAT THINGS COST IN ACAPULCO   U.S. $

Collectivo van from the airport to downtown	$7.50
Local bus ride	.35
Local telephone call	.50–$1
Double at the Acapulco Princess (very expensive)	$320–$600
Double at the Acapulco Sheraton (expensive)	$160–$190
Double at the Acapulco Dolphins Hotel (moderate)	$90
Double at the Hotel Sand's (budget)	$58
Three-course dinner for one at Miramar (very expensive)	$60
Three-course dinner for one at Madeiras (expensive)	$40
Three-course dinner for one at Su Casa (expensive)	$30
Three-course dinner for one at Cocula (moderate)	$20
Three-course lunch for one at El Cabrito (moderate)	$15
Three-course lunch for one at San Carlos (budget)	$6
Beer	$1.50
Margarita	$2.50–$4
Full day of deep-sea fishing	$100–$150
Half-day bay cruise	$20–$60
Round of golf	$70–$115
Disco cover charge	$15–$30

WHAT THINGS COST IN IXTAPA/ZIHUATANEJO   U.S. $

Collectivo van from the airport to downtown	$15
Local bus ride	.50
Local telephone call	.50–$1
Double at La Casa Que Canta (very expensive)	$260–$400
Double at the Sheraton Ixtapa (expensive)	$165–$265
Double at the Villas Miramar (moderate)	$80–$90
Double at the Posada Citlali (budget)	$35
Three-course dinner for one at Villa de la Selva (very expensive)	$60
Three-course dinner for one at Becco Fino (expensive)	$30
Three-course lunch for one at La Bocana (moderate)	$15–$20
Three-course lunch for one at La Sirena Gorda (budget)	$8
Beer	$1.50
Margarita	$2–$4
Day of deep-sea fishing	$120–$180
Scuba diving	$70
Round of golf	$35–$70
Hour of tennis	$10–$15
Sunset cruise	$35
Fiesta night	$30–$40
Disco cover charge	$14–$20

WHAT THINGS COST IN TAXCO — U.S. $

Local telephone call	.50–$1
Double at the Hotel Montetaxco (expensive)	$108–$120
Double at the Hotel Taxco Victoria (moderate)	$40–$54
Double at the Posada de los Castillo (budget)	$30
Three-course dinner for one at Toni's (very expensive)	$40–$50
Three-course lunch for one at La Taberna (moderate)	$15
Three-course lunch for one at La Hamburguesa (budget)	$8
Beer	$1.50–$2
Margarita	$2–$3
Disco cover charge	$8
Half-day city tour	$50

EXCHANGING MONEY   Cash can sometimes be difficult to exchange because counterfeit U.S. dollars have been circulating recently in Mexico; merchants and banks are wary, and many, especially in small towns, refuse to accept dollars in cash.

Banks in Mexico often give a rate of exchange below the official daily rate, and hotels usually exchange below the bank's daily rate. Personal checks may be cashed, but will delay you for weeks since a bank will wait for your check to clear before giving you your money. Canadian dollars seem to be most easily exchanged for pesos at branches of Banamex and Bancomer.

Banks are open Monday through Friday from 9am to 1:30pm; a few banks in large cities offer extended afternoon hours. Although they open earlier, you'll save time at the bank or currency-exchange booths by arriving no earlier than 10am. Generally they don't receive the official rate for that day until shortly before then and they won't exchange your money until they have the daily rate.

Large airports have currency-exchange counters that sometimes stay open as long as flights are arriving or departing.

TRAVELER'S CHECKS   For the fastest and least complicated service, you should carry traveler's checks, which are readily accepted nearly everywhere. Mexican banks pay more for traveler's checks than for dollars in cash—but *casas de cambio* (exchange houses) pay more for cash than for traveler's checks. Some banks, but not all, charge a service fee, as high as 5%, to cash both dollars and traveler's checks. Sometimes banks post the service charge amount so you can see it, but they might not, so it pays to ask first and shop around for a bank without a fee.

CREDIT CARDS   You'll be able to charge some hotel and restaurant bills, almost all airline tickets, and many store purchases. You can get cash advances of several hundred dollars on your card, but you may have to wait anywhere from 20 minutes to two hours. However, you can't charge gasoline purchases in Mexico.

VISA (Bancomer in Mexico), MasterCard (which is Carnet in Mexico), and less widely American Express, are the most accepted cards. The Mexican bank named Bancomer, with branches throughout the country, has inaugurated a system of Automatic Teller Machines linked to VISA International's network. If you are a VISA customer, you *may* be able to get peso cash from one of these Bancomer ATMs.

But I must warn you not to depend too heavily on your credit cards if you plan to venture beyond Acapulco or Ixtapa/Zihuatanejo. Pesos are a must. In addition, for some unknown reason, some places don't accept credit cards on Sunday.

BRIBES Called a *propina* (tip), *mordida* (bite), or worse, the custom is probably almost as old as mankind. Bribes exist everywhere, but in developing countries the amounts tend to be smaller and collected more often. You will meet with bribery, so you should know how to deal with it.

With the administration of President Salinas de Gortari, border officials have become more courteous, less bureaucratic, and less inclined to ask/hint for a bribe. I'm still wary, however, so just so you're prepared here are a few hints based on the past. If you don't offer a tip of a few dollars to the man who inspects your car (if you're driving), he may ask for it, as in "Give me a tip *(propina)*." Some border officials will do what they're supposed to do (stamp your passport or birth certificate and inspect your luggage) and then wave you on through. If you're charged for it, ask for a receipt. If you get no receipt, you've paid a bribe.

Officials don't ask for bribes from everybody. Travelers dressed formally, with pitch-black sunglasses and a scowl on the face, are rarely asked to pay a bribe. Those who are dressed for vacation fun and seem good-natured and accommodating are charged every time. You may not want the bother of dressing up for border crossings, but you should at least act formal, rather cold, dignified, and businesslike, perhaps preoccupied with "important affairs" on your mind. Wear those dark sunglasses. Scowl. Ignore the request. Pretend not to understand. Don't speak Spanish. But whatever you do, avoid impoliteness, and absolutely never insult a Latin American official! When an official's sense of machismo is roused, he can and will throw the book at you, and you may be in trouble. Stand your ground—politely.

SCAMS As you travel in Mexico, you may encounter several types of scams. The **shoeshine scam** is an old trick. Here's how it works. A tourist agrees to a shine for, say, 3 pesos. When the work is complete the vendor says, "That'll be 30" and insists the shocked tourist misunderstood. A big brouhaha ensues, involving bystanders who side with the shoeshine vendor. The object is to get the bewildered tourist to succumb to the howling crowd and embarrassing scene and fork over the money. A variation of the scam has the vendor saying the price quoted is per shoe. To avoid this scam, ask around about the price of a shine, and when the vendor quotes his price, write it down and show it to him *before* the shine.

Tourists are suckered daily into the **iguana scam**—look out for it anywhere there are iguanas. Someone, often a child, strolls by carrying a huge iguana and says, "Wanna take my peekchur." Photo-happy tourists seize the opportunity. Just as the camera is angled properly, the holder of the iguana says (more like mumbles), "One dollar." That means a dollar per shot. Sometimes they wait until the shutter clicks to mention money.

Because hotel desk clerks are usually so helpful, I hesitate to mention the **lost objects scam** for fear of tainting them all. But here's how it works. You "lose" your wallet after cashing money at the desk, or you leave something valuable such as a purse or camera in the lobby. You report it. The clerk has it, but instead of telling you that he does, he says he will see what he can do; meanwhile, he suggests that you offer a high reward. This one has all kinds of variations. In one story a reader wrote about, a desk clerk in Los Mochis was in cahoots with a bystander in the lobby who lifted her wallet in the elevator.

Another scam readers have written about might be called the **infraction scam.** Officials, or men presenting themselves as officials, demand money for some supposed infraction. Never get into a car with them. I avoided one with a bona fide policeman-on-the-take in Chetumal when my traveling companion feigned illness and began writhing, moaning, and pretending to have the dry heaves. It was more than the policeman could handle.

Legal and necessary car searches by military personnel looking for drugs are mentioned elsewhere. But every now and then there are police-controlled yet illegal roadblocks where motorists are allowed to continue after paying, usually to some protest or striking group.

Along these lines, if you are stopped by the police, I also suggest that you avoid handing your driver's license to a policeman. Hold it, *firmly*, so that it can be read, but don't give it up.

My advice is to be aware of potential hazards and how to deal with them. I log thousands of miles and many months in Mexico each year without serious incident, and I feel safer there than at home. (See also "Emergencies" and "Safety" in "Fast Facts: Mexico," below).

2. WHEN TO GO—CLIMATE, HOLIDAYS & EVENTS

CLIMATE From Puerto Vallarta south to Ixtapa/Zihuatanejo, Acapulco, and Huatulco, Mexico offers one of the world's most perfect winter climates—dry, balmy, with temperatures ranging from the 80s by day to the 60s at night. Rains come usually at night in Acapulco and Ixtapa/Zihuatanejo and both places rightfully boast of one of the sunniest climates in the country. Inland, however, the area around Chilapa and Taxco can have unseasonal rains, and the temperatures in both places will be cooler all around. From Puerto Vallarta south you can swim year-round.

In summer the west coast area becomes warm and rainy. There is a handy temperature conversion chart in the Appendix to this book.

HOLIDAYS Banks, stores, and businesses are closed on national holidays, so plan accordingly. Remember that hotels fill up quickly, so you'll need to make reservations well in advance. You should also expect airports, trains, and buses to be unusually crowded.

January 1	New Year's Day
February 5	Constitution Day
March 21	Birthday of Benito Juárez
March–April (movable)	Holy Week (Good Friday through Easter Sunday)
May 1	Labor Day
May 5	Battle of Puebla, 1862 (Cinco de Mayo)
September 1	President's Message to Congress
September 6	Independence Day
October 12	Columbus Day (Mexico: Day of the Race)
November 1–2	All Saints' and All Souls' Days (Day of the Dead)
November 20	Mexican Revolution Anniversary
December 11–12	Day of the Virgin of Guadalupe (Mexico's patron saint)
December 24–25	Christmas Eve (evening); Christmas Day

MEXICO
CALENDAR OF EVENTS

JANUARY

☐ **Three Kings Day.** Commemorates the Three Kings' bringing of gifts to the Christ Child. On this day the Three Kings "bring" gifts to children. January 6.

FEBRUARY

☐ **Candlemas Day.** On January 6, Rosca de Reyes, a round cake with a hole in the middle is baked with a tiny doll inside representing the Christ Child. Whoever gets the slice with the doll must give a party on February 2.

☐ **Ash Wednesday.** The start of Lent and time of abstinence. It's a day of reverence nationwide, but some towns honor it with folk dancing and fairs. Movable date.

✪ *CARNAVAL* *Three days before Ash Wednesday. In some towns there will be no special celebration, in others a few parades.*
Where: Especially celebrated in Tepoztlán, Mor.; Huejotzingo, Pue.; Chamula, Chi.; Veracruz, Ver.; Cozumel, Q. Roo; and Mazatlán, Sin. When: Date variable, but always the three days preceding Ash Wednesday. How: Transportation and hotels will be clogged, so it's best to make reservations six months in advance and arrive a couple of days ahead of the beginning of celebrations. On Tuesday before Ash Wednesday, in Tepoztlán and Huejotzingo, masked and brilliantly clad dancers fill the streets.

MARCH

☐ **Benito Juaréz's Birthday.** Celebrated with small hometown celebrations countrywide, but especially in Juaréz's birthplace, Gelatao, Oaxaca. March 21.

✪ *HOLY WEEK* *Celebrates the last week in the life of Christ from Good Friday through Easter Sunday with almost nightly somber religious processions, spoofing of Judas, and reenactments of specific biblical events, plus food and craft fairs. Businesses close and Mexicans travel far and wide during this week.*
Where: Special in Pátzcuaro, Taxco, Malinalco, and among Tarahumara villages in the Copper Canyon. When: March or April. How: Reserve early with a deposit. Airlines into and out of the country will be reserved months in advance. Buses to these towns or almost anywhere in Mexico will be full, so try arriving on the Wednesday or Thursday before Good Friday. Easter Sunday is quiet.

MAY

☐ **Labor Day.** Workers' parades countrywide and everything closes. May 1.

☐ **Holy Cross Day** (Día de la Santa Cruz). Workers place crosses atop unfinished buildings and have feasts, bands, folk dancing, and fireworks around the worksite. Celebrations are particularly colorful in Valle de Bravo, State of Mexico; Tehuilotepec, Guerrero; and Paracho, Michoacán. May 3.

☐ **Cinco de Mayo.** A national holiday that celebrates the defeat of the French at the Battle of Puebla. May 5.

☐ **Feast of San Isidro.** The patron saint of farmers is honored with a blessing of seeds and work animals. May 15.

☐ **Jornadas Alarconianas.** In Taxco, honors the dramatist Juan Ruíz de Alarcón, with plays, music, and literary events.

JUNE

☐ **Navy Day.** Celebrated by all port cities. June 1.

☐ **Corpus Christi Day.** Honors the Body of Christ—the Eucharist—with religious processions, masses, and food. Celebrated nationwide, about 66 days after Easter.

☐ **St. Peter** (Día de San Pedro). Celebrated wherever St. Peter is the patron saint and honors anyone named Pedro or Peter. It's especially festive at San Pedro Tlaquepaque, near Guadalajara, with numerous mariachi bands, folk dancers, and parades with floats. June 29.

JULY

☐ **Virgin of Carmen.** A nationally celebrated religious festival centered at churches nationwide. July 16.

☐ **St. James Day** (Día de Santiago). Observed countrywide wherever St. James is the patron saint, and for anyone named Jaime or James, or any village with Santiago in the name, often with rodeos, fireworks, dancing, and food celebrations. July 25.

AUGUST

❂ *ASSUMPTION OF THE VIRGIN MARY* Venerated throughout the country with special masses and in some places processions.
Where: Special in Huamantla, Tlaxcala, and Santa Clara del Cobre, Michoacán. **When:** August 15 and 16. **How:** Buses to Huamantla from Puebla or Mexico City will be full and there are few hotels in Huamantla. Plan to stay in Puebla and commute for the festivities. Streets are carpeted in flower petals and colored sawdust. At midnight on the 15th a statue of the Virgin is carried through the streets. August 16 is a running of the bulls. On August 15, in Santa Clara del Cobre, the copper capital of Mexico, near Pátzcuaro, Our Lady of the Cibary is honored with a parade of floats, dancers on the main square, and an exposition of area crafts, especially copper.

SEPTEMBER

☐ **Independence Day.** Celebrates Mexico's independence from Spain. A day of parades, picnics, and family reunions throughout the country. At 11pm on September 15, the president of Mexico gives the famous independence *grito* (shout) from the National Palace in Mexico City. It's also elaborately celebrated in Querétaro and San Miguel de Allende where independence conspirators lived and met. September 16 (parade day).

OCTOBER

☐ **Feast of San Francisco de Asis** (Día de San Francisco). Anyone named Frances or Francis or Francisco and towns whose patron saint is San Francisco will be celebrating with barbecue parties, regional dancing, and religious observances. October 4.

☐ **Día de la Raza.** Day of the Race, or Columbus Day (the day Columbus discovered America) commemorates the fusion of two races—Spanish and Mexican. October 12.

NOVEMBER

○ *DAY OF THE DEAD* *What's commonly called Day of the Dead is actually two days. November 1 is All Saints' Day, honoring saints and children. November 2 is All Souls' Day, honoring adults. Relatives gather at cemeteries countrywide, carrying candles and food, often spending the night beside graves of loved ones. It resembles a combination of our Memorial Day and Halloween. Weeks before, bakers begin producing bread formed in the shape of mummies or round loaves decorated with bread in the shape of bones. Decorated sugar skulls emblazoned with glittery names are sold everywhere. Many days ahead homes and churches erect special altars laden with Day of the Dead bread, fruit, flowers, candles, and favorite foods and photographs of saints and of the deceased. On the two nights of Day of the Dead, children dress in costumes and masks, often carrying mock coffins through the streets and pumpkin lanterns into which they expect money will be dropped. The most famous celebration is on Janitzio, an island on Lake Pátzcuaro, Michoacán, west of Mexico City, but it's become almost too well known. Mixquic, a mountain village south of Mexico City, hosts an elaborate street fair, and around 11pm on both nights, solemn processions lead to the cemetery in the center of town where villagers are already settled in with candles, flowers, and food.*

☐ **Revolution Day.** Commemorates the start of the Mexican Revolution in 1910, with parades, speeches, rodeos, and patriotic events. November 20.

DECEMBER

☐ **Day of Guadalupe.** Throughout Mexico, the patroness of Mexico is honored, with religious processions, street fairs, dancing, fireworks, and mass. The Virgin of Guadalupe appeared to a small boy, Juan Diego, in December 1531 on a hill near Mexico City. He convinced the bishop that the apparition had appeared by revealing his cloak upon which the Virgin was emblazoned. It's customary for children to dress up as Juan Diego, wearing mustaches and red bandanas. The most famous and elaborate celebration takes place at the Basilica of Guadalupe, north of Mexico City, where the Virgin appeared. But every village celebrates this day, often with processions of children carrying banners of the Virgin, and with charreadas, bicycle races, dancing, and fireworks. December 12.

☐ **Christmas Posadas.** Each night for 12 days before Christmas it's customary to reenact the Holy Family's search for an inn, with door-to-door candlelit processions in cities and villages nationwide. You may see them especially in Querétaro and Taxco.

☐ **Christmas.** Mexicans extend this celebration and leave their jobs, often beginning two weeks before Christmas all the way through New Year's. Many businesses close and resorts and hotels fill up. December 23 there are significant celebrations.

☐ **New Year's Eve.** As in the U.S., New Year's Eve is the time to gather for private parties of celebration and to explode fireworks and sound off noisemakers. Places with special festivities include Santa Clara del Cobre, with its candlelit procession of Christs, and Tlacolula near Oaxaca, with commemorative mock battles for good luck in the new year.

3. HEALTH & INSURANCE

HEALTH PREPARATIONS

Of course, the very best ways to avoid illness or to mitigate its effects are to make sure that you're in top health and that you don't overdo it. Travel tends to take more of your energy than a normal working day, and missed meals mean that you get less nutrition than you need. Make sure you have three good, wholesome meals a day, get more rest than you normally do, and don't push yourself if you're not feeling in top form.

TURISTA *Turista*, "Moctezuma's Revenge," or the "Aztec Two-Step" are names given to the pervasive diarrhea, often accompanied by fever, nausea, and vomiting, that attacks so many travelers to Mexico on their first trip. Doctors, who call it "travelers' diarrhea," say it's not just one "bug," or factor, but a combination of different food and water, upset schedules, overtiring, and the stresses that accompany travel. Being tired and careless about food and drink is a sure ticket to turista. A good high-potency (or "therapeutic") vitamin supplement, and even extra vitamin C, is a help; yogurt is good for healthy digestion, but it is not available everywhere in Mexico.

Preventing Turista The U.S. Public Health Service recommends the following measures for prevention of travelers' diarrhea:

- Drink only purified water. This means tea, coffee, and other beverages made with boiled water; canned or bottled carbonated beverages, including carbonated water; beer and wine; or water that you yourself have brought to a rolling boil or otherwise purified. Avoid ice, which may be made with untreated water. First-class restaurants, however, generally serve purified water and ice.
- Choose food carefully. In general, avoid salads, uncooked vegetables, and unpasteurized milk or milk products (including cheese). Choose food that is freshly cooked and still hot. Peel fruit yourself. Don't eat undercooked meat, fish, or shellfish.

The Public Health Service does not recommend that you take any medicines as preventatives. All the applicable medicines can have nasty side effects if taken for several weeks.

How to Get Well If you get sick, there are lots of medicines available in Mexico that can harm more than help. You should ask your doctor before you leave home what medicine he or she recommends for travelers' diarrhea, and follow his or her advice.

Public Health Service guidelines are these: If there are three or more loose stools in an eight-hour period, especially with other symptoms such as nausea, vomiting, abdominal cramps, and fever, it's time to go to a doctor.

The first thing to do is go to bed and don't move until it runs its course. Traveling makes it last longer. Drink lots of liquids: tea without milk or sugar, or the Mexican *té de manzanilla* (chamomile tea), is best. Eat only *pan tostada* (dry toast). Keep to this diet for at least 24 hours, and you'll be well over the worst of it. If you fool yourself into thinking that a plate of enchiladas can't hurt, or that beer or liquor will kill the germs, you'll have a total relapse.

The Public Health Service advises that you be especially careful to replace fluids and electrolytes (potassium, sodium, etc.) during a bout of diarrhea. Do this by drinking glasses of fruit juice (high in potassium) with honey and a pinch of salt added, and also a glass of pure water with ¼ teaspoon of sodium bicarbonate (baking soda) added.

ALTITUDE SICKNESS   At high altitudes (5,000 ft./1,500m or more) it takes about 10 days or so to acquire the extra red blood corpuscles you need to adjust to the scarcity of oxygen. Lack of oxygen and decrease in barometric pressure may mean that your car won't run very well, and you yourself may suffer from sleeplessness. Symptoms may also include shortness of breath, fatigue, headache, and even nausea.

Avoid altitude sickness by taking it easy for the first few days after you arrive at high altitude. Drink extra fluids, but avoid alcoholic beverages, which not only tend to dehydrate you, but also are more potent in a low-oxygen environment. (If you have heart or lung problems, talk to your doctor before going above 8,000 feet.)

BUGS & BITES   Mosquitoes and gnats are prevalent in coastal areas (especially between the big coastal resorts). Insect repellent (*repellante contra insectos*) is a must, and it's not always available in Mexico. If you're sensitive to bites, pick up some antihistamine cream from a drugstore at home. Rubbed on a fresh mosquito bite, the cream keeps down the swelling and reduces the itch. In Mexico, ask for "Camfo-Fenicol" (Camphophenique), the second-best remedy.

Most readers won't ever see a scorpion, but if you're stung, it's best to go to a doctor.

SUNBURN   Be aware that the sun is more intense at this latitude and therefore more likely to cause sunburn in a short time. Use sunscreen lavishly at the beach and archeological sites. At the ruins wear a hat and carry water, or stop for nonalcoholic refreshment often.

MORE SERIOUS DISEASES   You don't have to worry about tropical diseases too much if you stay on the normal tourist routes. You can also protect yourself by taking some simple precautions. Besides being careful about what you eat and drink, do not go swimming in polluted waters. This includes any stagnant water such as ponds and slow-moving rivers. Mosquitoes can carry malaria, dengue fever, and other serious illnesses. Cover up, avoid going out when mosquitoes are active, use repellent, sleep under mosquito netting, and stay away from places that seem to have a lot of mosquitoes. The most dangerous areas seem to be on Mexico's west coast, away from the big resorts (which are relatively safe).

To prevent malaria if you go to a malarial area, you must get a prescription for antimalarial drugs, and begin taking them before you enter the area. You must also continue to take them for a certain amount of time after you leave the malarial area. Talk to your doctor about this. It's a good idea to be inoculated against tetanus, typhoid, and diptheria, but this isn't a guarantee against contracting disease.

The following list of diseases should not alarm you, as their incidence is rare among tourists. But if you become ill with something more virulent than travelers' diarrhea, I want you to have this information ready at hand:

Cholera   Cholera comes from sewage-contaminated water and it's transmitted by using the contaminated water to drink, cook, or wash food. Thus raw fish and raw or lightly cooked vegetables are good candidates for transmitting the disease. Outbreaks of cholera in Mexico have been isolated and contained immediately and have not occurred in any major tourist area. Symptoms are extreme diarrhea, vomiting, abdominal pain, and rapid incapacitation. Dehydration can be immediate, dangerous, even deadly, so drink plenty of nonalcoholic liquids and go to a hospital immediately.

Dengue Fever Transmitted by mosquitoes, it comes on fast with high fever, severe headache, and joint and muscle pain. Three or four days after the onset of the disease, there's a skin rash. Highest risk is during July, August, and September. Risk for tourists is normally low.

Dysentery Caused by contaminated food or water, either amoebic or bacillary in form, it is somewhat like travelers' diarrhea, but more severe. Risk for tourists is normally low.

Hepatitis, Viral This virus is spread through contaminated food and water (often in rural areas), and through intimate contact with infected persons. Risk for tourists is normally low.

Malaria Spread by mosquito bites, malaria can be effectively treated if caught soon after the disease is contracted. Malaria symptoms are headache, malaise, fever, chills, sweats, anemia, and jaundice.

Rabies This virus is almost always passed by bites from infected animals or bats, rarely through broken skin or the mucous membranes (as from breathing rabid-bat-contaminated air in a cave). If you are bitten, wash the wound at once with large amounts of soap and water—this is important! Retain the animal, alive if possible, for rabies quarantine. Contact local health authorities to get rabies immunization. This is essential, as rabies is a fatal disease that may be prevented by prompt treatment.

Schistosomiasis This is a parasitic worm, passed by a freshwater snail larva which can penetrate unbroken human skin. You get it by wading or swimming in fresh water where the snails are, such as in stagnant pools, streams, or cenotes. Two or three weeks after exposure, there's fever, lack of appetite, weight loss, abdominal pain, weakness, headaches, joint and muscle pain, diarrhea, nausea, and coughing. Six to eight weeks after infection, the microscopic snail eggs can be found in the stools. Once diagnosed (after a very unpleasant month or two), treatment is fast, safe, effective, and cheap. If you think you've accidentally been exposed to schistosomiasis-infected water, rub yourself vigorously with a towel, and/or spread rubbing alcohol on the exposed skin.

Typhoid Fever You can protect yourself by having a typhoid vaccination (or booster, as needed), but protection is not total; you can still get this very serious disease from contaminated food and water. Symptoms are similar to those for travelers' diarrhea, but much worse. If you get typhoid fever, you'll need close attention by a doctor, perhaps hospitalization for a short period.

Typhus Fever You should see a doctor for treatment of this disease, which is spread by lice. Risk to tourists is normally very low.

EMERGENCY EVACUATION For extreme medical emergencies there's a service from the United States that will fly people to American hospitals: **Air-Evac,** 24-hour air ambulance (tel. collect 24 hours 713/880-9767 in Houston, 619/278-3822 in San Diego, or 305/772-0003 in Miami).

INSURANCE

HEALTH/ACCIDENT/LOSS It can happen anywhere in the world—you discover you've lost your wallet, your passport, your airline ticket, and your Tourist Permit. Always keep a photocopy of these documents in your luggage—it makes replacing them easier. To be reimbursed for insured items once you return, you'll need to report the loss to the Mexican police and get a written report. If you don't speak

Spanish, take along someone who does. If you lose official documents, you'll need to contact both Mexican and U.S. officials in Mexico before you leave the country.

Before leaving home ask your insurance agent what health coverage is in force while you are out of the country. Several credit-card companies include accident and trip-cancellation insurance coverage as a benefit for charging airline tickets on a charge card.

For additional coverage you may want to consider policies from the following companies:

Health Care Abroad, 107 Federal St. (P.O. Box 480), Middleburg, VA 22117 (tel. 703/687-3166, or toll free 800/237-6615); and **Access America, Inc.,** 6600 W. Broad St., Richmond, VA 23230 (tel. 804/285-3300, or toll free 800/628-4908), offers medical and accident insurance as well as coverage for luggage loss and trip cancellations. But always read the fine print to be sure that you're getting the coverage that you want.

For British Travelers   Most big travel agents offer their own insurance, and will probably try to sell you their package when you book a holiday. Think before you sign. Britain's Consumers' Association recommends that you insist on seeing the policy and reading the fine print before buying travel insurance.

You should also shop around for better deals. Try **Columbus Travel Insurance Ltd.** (tel. 071/375-0011) or, for students, **Campus Travel** (tel. 071/730-3402). If you're unsure about who can give you the best deal, contact the **Association of British Insurers,** 51 Gresham St., London EC2V 7HQ (tel. 071/600-333).

4. WHAT TO PACK

CLOTHING   In summer, it gets warm during the day and cool, but not cold, at night. In the central valleys of Guerrero and in the mornings in Taxco it can be chilly any time of year. Generally speaking, throughout Mexico it rains almost every afternoon or evening between May and October—so take rain gear. Instead of an umbrella or raincoat, an easily packable rain poncho is most handy, since it fits in a purse or backpack and is ready for use in an instant.

Mexico tends to be a bit more conservative in dress, so shorts and halter tops are generally frowned on except at seaside resorts. Lightweight cotton clothes are preferable for coastal areas. For dining out in a nice restaurant in a city, a jacket and tie for men and nice dress or suit for women is appropriate. For dressing up at a coastal resort, cool cotton slacks and shirt for men and a nice cool dress or slacks outfit is fine for women.

GADGETS   I never leave home without a luggage cart, which saves much effort and money, and is especially useful in small towns where there are no porters at bus stations. Buy a sturdy one with at least four-inch wheels that can take the beating of cobblestone streets, stairs, and curbs.

A hot pot or heat-immersion coil, plastic cup, and spoon are handy for preparing coffee, tea, and instant soup and may come in very handy if you are ill and can only stomach herb tea. For power failures, and if you plan to visit archeological sites with dark interiors, a small flashlight is a help. A combo pocket knife (for peeling fruit) with screwdriver (for fixing cameras and eyeglasses), bottle opener, and corkscrew is a must.

5. TIPS FOR THE DISABLED, SENIORS, SINGLES, FAMILIES & STUDENTS

FOR THE DISABLED Travelers who are unable to walk, or those who are in wheelchairs or on crutches, discover quickly that Mexico is one giant obstacle course. Beginning at the airport on arrival you may encounter steep stairs before finding a well-hidden elevator or escalator—if one exists. Airlines will often arrange wheelchair assistance for passengers to the baggage area. Porters are generally available to help with luggage at airports and large bus stations. Escalators (and there aren't many in the country) are often not operating. Airports may have an escalator going up, but not one coming down. Few handicapped-equipped restrooms exist, or when one is available, access to it may be via a narrow passage that won't accommodate a wheelchair or someone on crutches. Many deluxe hotels (the most expensive) now have rooms with handicapped-equipped bathrooms and handicap access to the hotel. For those traveling on a budget, stick with one-story hotels, or those with elevators. Even so there will probably still be step obstacles somewhere. Stairs without handrails abound in Mexico. Intracity bus drivers generally don't bother with the courtesy step upon boarding or disembarking; on city buses the step up from the street to the bus can require considerable force to board. Generally speaking, no matter where you are, someone will lend a hand, although you may have to ask for it.

FOR SENIORS Handrails are often missing. Unmarked or unguarded holes in sidewalks countrywide present problems for all visitors.

Mexico is a popular country for retirees, although income doesn't go nearly as far as it once did. If you are interested in venturing south permanently, stay for several weeks in any place under consideration, rent before buying, and check on the availability and quality of health care, banking, transportation, and rental costs. How much it costs to live depends on your lifestyle and where you choose to live. Car upkeep and insurance, clothing and health costs are important variables to consider.

The Mexican government requires foreign residents to prove they have a specific amount of income before permanent residence is granted, but you can visit for six months on a tourist visa and renew it every six months without committing to a "legal" status. Mexican health care is surprisingly inexpensive. You can save money by living on the local economy: Buy food at the local market, not imported items from specialty stores; use local transportation and save the car for long-distance trips.

The following newsletters are written to inform the prospective retiree about Mexico: **AIM,** Apdo. Postal 31-70, Guadalajara 45050, Jal., is a well-written, plain-talk, and very informative newsletter on retirement in Mexico. Recent issues reported on retirement background and considerations for west coast beaches and Acapulco. It costs $16 in the U.S. and $19 in Canada. Back issues are available.

Retiring in Mexico, Apdo. Postal 5-409, Guadalajara, Jal. (tel. 36/21-2348 or 47-9924), comes in three editions—a large January edition and smaller spring and fall supplements—all for $12. Each newsletter is packed with useful information about retiring in Guadalajara. It's written by Fran and Judy Furton, who also sell other packets of information as well as host an open house in their home every Tuesday for $12.

Sanborn Tours, 1007 Main St., Bastrop, TX 78602 (tel. toll free 800/531-5440 in the U.S.), offers a "Retire in Mexico" Guadalajara orientation tour.

FOR SINGLE TRAVELERS Mexico may be the land for romantic honeymoons, but it's also a great place to travel on your own without really being or feeling alone. Although combined single and double rates is a slow-growing trend in Mexico, most of the budget hotels mentioned in this book offer singles at cheaper rates. Mexicans are very friendly and it's easy to meet other foreigners and take up with them for a day or two or meal along the way if you desire. Certain cities, such as Acapulco, Manzanillo, and Huatulco, have such a preponderance of twosomes that single travelers there may feel as though an appendage is missing. On the other hand, singles can feel quite comfortable in Puerto Vallarta, Zihuatanejo, Ixtapa, and Puerto Angel. In those places you'll find a good combination of beachlife, nightlife, and tranquillity, whichever is your pleasure. If you don't like the idea of traveling alone then you might try **Travel Companion Exchange,** P.O. Box 833, Amityville, NY 11701 (tel. 516/454-0880; fax 516/454-0170), which brings prospective travelers together. Members complete a profile, then place an anonymous listing of their travel interests in the newsletter. Prospective traveling companions then make contact through the exchange. Membership costs $36 to $66 for six months.

For Women As a frequent female traveler to Mexico, mostly traveling alone, I can tell you firsthand that I feel safer traveling in Mexico than in the U.S. Mexicans are a very warm and welcoming people and I'm not afraid to be friendly wherever I go. But I use the same common sense precautions I use traveling anywhere else in the world: I'm alert to what's going on around me.

Mexicans in general, and men in particular, are nosy about single travelers, especially women. They want to know with whom you're traveling, whether you're married or have a boyfriend, and how many children you have. My advice to anyone exchanging these details with taxi drivers or other people whose paths you'll never cross again or with whom you don't want to become friendly, is to make up a set of answers regardless of the truth: I'm married, traveling with friends, and I have three children. Being divorced may send out a wrong message about availability or imagined degree of loneliness.

Drunks are a particular nuisance to the lone female traveler. Don't try to be polite—just leave or duck into a public place.

Generally women alone will feel comfortable going to a hotel lobby bar, but may encounter trouble or hassles in a pulquería or cantina. In restaurants, as a general rule, single women are offered the worst table and service. You'll have to be vocal about your preference and insist on service. Service may improve (but don't count on it) if you dine at off-peak hours. Tip well if you plan to return. Don't tip at all if service is bad.

And finally, remember, Mexican men learn charm early. The chase is as important as the conquest (maybe more so). Despite whatever charms *you* may possess, think twice before taking personally or seriously all the adoring, admiring words you'll hear.

For Men I'm not sure why, but non-Spanish-speaking, foreign men seem to be special targets for scams and pickpockets. So if you fit this description, whether traveling alone or in a pair, exercise special vigilance.

FOR FAMILIES Mexicans travel extensively with their families, so your child will feel very welcome. Hotels will often arrange for a babysitter. Several hotels in the mid to upper range have small playgrounds for children and hire caretakers on weekends to oversee them and the children's pool so the parents can relax.

Before leaving for Mexico, you should check with your doctor and get advice on medicines to combat diarrhea and other ailments. Bring a supply, just to be sure. Disposable diapers are made and sold in Mexico (one popular brand is Kleen Bebé).

The price is about the same as at home, but the quality is poorer. Gerber's baby foods are sold in many stores. Dry cereals, powdered formulas, baby bottles, and purified water are all easily available in mid-size to large cities.

Cribs, however, may present a problem. Except for the largest and most luxurious hotels, few Mexican hotels provide cribs.

Many of the hotels we mention in the coastal areas have swimming pools, which can be dessert at the end of a day traveling with a child who has had it with sightseeing.

FOR STUDENTS   Students traveling on a budget may want to contact the student headquarters in the various cities that can supply information on student hostels. Maps and local tourist information are also available. The office in Mexico City is at Hamburgo 273 (tel. 5/514-4213).

6. EDUCATIONAL/ADVENTURE TRAVEL

EDUCATIONAL/STUDY TRAVEL

SPANISH LESSONS   Of the towns listed in this book, Cuernavaca and Taxco are the two with Spanish-language schools catering to foreign students. A dozen other towns south of the border are famous for their Spanish-language programs. Most of these are covered in *Frommer's Mexico on $45 a Day*. Enrolling is simple: Write to those in towns that interest you and ask for their course outline, prices, and recommended housing list. Some schools can arrange your stay with a host family. There's often no need to wait for a "semester" or course year to start. The Mexican Government Tourism Office nearest you may also have information about schools.

Don't expect the best and latest in terms of language texts and materials. Many are well out-of-date. Teachers tend to be underpaid and perhaps undertrained, but very friendly and extremely patient.

The National Registration Center for Studies Abroad (NRCSA), 823 N. 2nd St., Milwaukee, WI 53203 (tel. 414/278-0631), has a catalog ($7) of schools in Mexico. They will register you at the school of your choice, arrange for room and board with a Mexican family, and make your airline reservations. Contact them and ask for a (free) copy of their newsletter. Charges for their service are reflected in a fee that's included in the price quoted to you for the course you select.

HOMESTAYS   Spanish-language schools frequently provide lists of families who offer rooms to students. Often the experience is just like being one of the family. Pay in advance for only a week or 10 days, and if things are going well, continue. If your "family stay" ends up being little more than a room rental, feel free to go elsewhere. Family stays are not particularly cheap, by the way, so you should get your money's worth in terms of interaction and language practice.

World Learning Inc., The U.S. Experiment in International Living, Kipling Road, P.O. Box 676, Brattleboro, VT 05302-0676 (tel. 802/257-7751; fax 802/258-3248), offers a wide range of options for international experiences ranging from accredited programs to homestays and Elderhostel affiliation.

ADVENTURE/WILDERNESS

Mexico is behind in its awareness of tourists' interest in ecology-oriented adventure and wilderness travel. As a result, most of the national parks and nature reserves are understaffed and/or not staffed by knowledgeable persons. Most companies offering that kind of travel are U.S. operated and trips are specialist-led. The following companies offer a variety of off-the-beaten-path travel experiences.

Victor Emanuel Tours, P.O. Box 33008, Austin, TX 78764 (tel. 512/328-5221, or toll free 800/328-8368 in the U.S.), is an established leader in birding and natural-history tours.

The Foundation for Field Research, P.O. Box 771, Mornejaloux, St. George's, Grenada, West Indies (tel. 809/440-8854), accepts volunteers who contribute a tax-deductible share to project costs during scientific work.

Wings, Inc., P.O. Box 31930, Tucson, AZ (tel. 602/749-1967), has a wide assortment of trips.

7. GETTING THERE

BY PLANE

The airline situation is changing rapidly with many new regional carriers offering scheduled service to areas previously not served or underserved. Besides regularly scheduled service, charter service direct from U.S. cities to resorts is making Mexico much more accessible.

THE MAJOR INTERNATIONAL AIRLINES The main airlines operating direct or nonstop flights from the U.S. to points in Mexico include: **Aero California** (tel. toll free 800/237-6225), **Aeromexico** (tel. toll free 800/237-6639), **Air France** (tel. toll free 800/237-2747), **Alaska Airlines** (tel. toll free 800/426-0333), **American** (tel. toll free 800/433-7300), **Continental** (tel. toll free 800/231-0856), **Delta** (tel. toll free 800/221-1212), **Lacsa** (tel. toll free 800/225-2272), **Lufthansa** (tel. toll free 800/645-3880), **Mexicana** (tel. toll free 800/531-7921), **Northwest** (tel. toll free 800/225-2525), and **United** (tel. toll free 800/241-6522). **Southwest Airlines** serves the U.S. border (tel. toll free 800/435-9792). The main departure points for international airlines are Chicago, Dallas/Fort Worth, Denver, Houston, Los Angeles, Miami, New Orleans, New York, Orlando, Philadelphia, Raleigh/Durham, San Antonio, San Francisco, Seattle, Toronto, Tucson, and Washington, D.C.

Bargain hunters, rejoice! Excursion and package plans proliferate, especially in the off-season. A good travel agent will be able to give you all the latest schedules, details, and prices for all airlines, but the changes in regional airlines are ongoing, so you may have to sleuth those for yourself. The least expensive airline prices are midweek, in the off-season (after Easter to December 15).

Sample off-season, midweek, round-trip fares are as follows: A round-trip excursion fare from New York to Mexico City, $372; Guadalajara, $370. From Los Angeles to Guadalajara a typical fare runs from $283; to Cancún, $425; to Mexico City, $302. From Dallas/Fort Worth to Mexico City, the cost is $200; to Cancún, $286. From Denver, a round-trip fare to Mexico City runs $332; and to Guadalajara, $361.

CHARTERS Charter service is growing and usually is sold as a package combination of air and hotel. Charter airlines, however, may sell air only, without hotel. Charter airlines include **Taesa Airlines** with direct service from several U.S. cities. **Latur** offers charters from New York to Acapulco during the high season.

Tour companies operating charters include: Club America Vacations, Apple Vacations, and Friendly Holidays. Travel agents have information on these.

FLIGHTS FROM THE U.K.

British travelers should comparison-shop carefully to find the best airfare bargains. **British Airways** (tel. 081/897-4000 in London) offers nonstop service three times a week from London to Mexico City, where there are frequent daily flights to Acapulco and Ixtapa (but none to Taxco). Another option is to fly to a major hub in the United States, from which you will be able to connect with a flight to your Mexican destination.

Your best bet is to have a reputable travel agent, such as **Thomas Cook,** sort out the many possibilities and look for the best price available on your travel dates.

BY TRAIN

For getting to the border by train, call **Amtrak** (tel. toll free 800/872-7245 in the U.S.) for fares, information, and reservations. There are no passenger trains in the region covered in this book, but you can get from the border to Mexico City by train.

BY BUS

Greyhound-Trailways, or their affiliates, offers service from the U.S. to the border, where passengers disembark, cross the border, and buy a ticket for travel into the interior of Mexico. At many border crossings there are scheduled buses from the U.S. bus station to the Mexican bus station.

BY CAR

Driving is certainly not the cheapest way to get to Mexico, but it is the best way to see the country.

Unleaded gas (Magna Sin) costs around $1.60 a gallon, and regular gas (Nova) only slightly less.

Insurance costs are high (see below). Parking is a problem in the cities. Unless you have a full carload, the bus and train come out cheaper per person, and with public transport you don't have to undertake the tedious amount of driving needed to see a country this big.

If you want to drive to the Mexican border, but not into Mexico, border area chambers of commerce or convention and visitor's bureaus can supply names of secured parking lots. You can leave your car there while you see the country by rail, bus, or plane.

CAR DOCUMENTS   To drive a car into Mexico, you'll need a Temporary Car Importation Permit, granted upon presentation of a long and strictly required list of documents. The permit can be obtained through Mexican border officials at the time you cross the border, *or* before you travel, through Sanborns or American Automobile Association (AAA) offices. They may charge a fee for this service, but it may be worth it if it improves the uncertain prospects of traveling all the way to the border without proper car documents for crossing.   However, because these regulations are subject to frequent change, call your nearest Mexican consulate, Mexican National Tourist Council office, AAA, or Sanborn's for the latest information before setting out. Or call the Mexican Car Importation Office (tel. toll free 800/446-8277 in the U.S.). Then call again en route to the border—yes, folks, they've required compliance with rules that changed overnight. (It's a bit difficult to run back to Iowa for your car title when all you thought you needed was your car's registration.) At this time here is what is required:

1. A valid driver's license.
2. The car's current registration. (Carry a photocopy of the car title as well—but don't show it unless you're asked to.) If the registration is in more than one name, and that person on the registration is not traveling, then a notarized letter from the absent person(s) authorizing the use of the vehicle for the trip will be required.
3. A letter from the lien holder if your registration shows a lien, giving you permission to take the vehicle into Mexico.
4. A valid international credit card—only VISA, MasterCard, or American Express. Using only your credit card (no cash or checks) you are required to pay a $10 car-importation fee.
5. Those without credit cards to pay the $10 importation fee will be required to post a cash bond equal to the value of the car which will be determined by the Mexican border official; generally the bond is about 2% of the car's value. If you post a bond you must also leave your original car title with the bond, both of which are returned to you when you return with your car. This also requires coming and going through the same border entry.
6. You must sign a declaration promising to return to your country of origin with the vehicle.

RETURNING TO THE U.S. WITH YOUR CAR   The car papers obtained when you entered Mexico *must* be returned when you cross back with your car *or* within the time limit of 180 days. (You can cross as many times as you wish within 180 days.) If the documents aren't returned, heavy fines may be imposed ($250 for each 15 days late), and your car may be impounded and confiscated if you ever re-cross in the same car again. You can only return them to a Banjercito official, who is on duty at the Mexican Customs (Aduana) building immediately before you cross back into the United States. Some Mexican border cities have Banjercito officals on duty 24 hours; others are open fewer hours; and some don't have Sunday hours. Call the Mexican Vehicle Import Information office (tel. toll free 800/446-8277 in the U.S.) for current hours at each entry point. *Important note:* At presstime, Mexican authorities were only scolding people who failed to turn in car documents, but the mechanism was in place to begin charging fines, and it could happen at any time.

On the U.S. side customs agents may or may not inspect your car from stem to stern.

Other Rules   You must carry your vehicle permit, Tourist Permit, and proof of insurance in the car at all times. Remember too that the driver of the car will not be allowed to leave the country without the car (even if it's wrecked or stolen) unless he or she satisfies Customs that the import duty will be paid. In an emergency, if the driver of the car must leave the country without the car, the car must be put under Customs seal at the airport and the driver's Tourist Permit must be stamped to that effect. There may be storage fees.

The car-permit papers will be issued for the same length of time as your Tourist Permit was issued for. It's a good idea to greatly overestimate the time you'll spend in Mexico when applying for your permit, so that if something unforeseen happens and you have to (or want to) stay longer, you don't have to go through the long hassle of getting your papers renewed. Six months is the maximum length of a Tourist Permit and temporary vehicle-importation permit.

Other documentation is required for permission to enter the country (see "Entry Requirements," above).

MEXICAN AUTO INSURANCE   Although auto insurance is not legally required in Mexico, anyone who drives without it is foolish. U.S. and Canadian insurance is invalid in Mexico. To be insured there, you must purchase Mexican insurance. Any party involved in an accident who has no insurance is automatically sent to jail and the car is impounded until fault is determined and all claims are settled. This is true even if you just drive across the border to spend the day—and it may be true even if you're injured. Those with insurance are assumed to be good for claims and are released.

The agency will show you a full table of current rates and will recommend the coverage it thinks adequate. The policies are written along lines similar to those north of the border. It's best to overestimate the amount of time you plan to be in Mexico, because if you stay longer, it's a real runaround to get your policy term lengthened. Any part of the term unused will be prorated and that part of your premium refunded to you in cash at the office on the American side on return, or by mail to your home. Be sure the policy you buy will pay for repairs in either the U.S. or Mexico and that it will pay out in dollars, not pesos.

One of the best insurance companies for south of the border travel is **Sanborn's Mexico Insurance,** with offices at all of the border crossings in the U.S. I never drive across the border without Sanborn's insurance. It costs the same as the competition's, and you get a **Travelog** that's almost like a mile-by-mile guide along your proposed route. Information occasionally gets a bit dated, but for the most part it's like having a knowledgeable friend in the car telling you how to get in and out of town, where to buy gas (and which stations to avoid), highway conditions, and scams. It's especially helpful in remote places. Most of Sanborn's border offices are open Monday through Friday, and a few are staffed on Saturday and Sunday. You can purchase your auto liability and collision coverage by phone in advance and have it waiting at a 24-hour location if you are crossing when their office is closed. An annual policy for a car valued between $10,000 and $15,000 would be $397. For information contact Sanborn's Mexico Insurance, P.O. Box 310, Dept. FR, 2009 S. 10th, McAllen, TX 78502 (tel. 210/686-0711; fax 210/686-0732). AAA auto club also sells insurance.

PREPARING YOUR CAR Know the condition of your car before you cross the border. Parts made in Mexico may be inferior, but service generally is quite good and relatively inexpensive. (One of the bonuses of the Free Trade Agreement will be the availability of U.S.-made auto parts, but it won't be immediate.) Your cooling system should be in good condition, with the proper mixture of coolant and water. Be sure your car is in tune to handle Mexican gasoline. Carry a spare radiator hose and spare belts for the engine fan and air conditioner. Can your tires last a few thousand miles on Mexican roads?

Take simple tools along if you're handy with them, also a flashlight or spotlight, a cloth to wipe the windshield, toilet paper, and a tire gauge. Mexican filling stations generally have air to fill tires, but no gauge to check the pressure. If you don't carry your own gauge you'll have to find a tire repair shop to get your tires checked and filled with air. When driving I always bring along a combination gauge/air compressor sold at U.S. automotive stores. It plugs into the car cigarette lighter, making it a simple procedure to check the tires every morning and pump them up at the same time.

Not that many Mexican cars comply, but Mexican law requires that every car have **seat belts** and a **fire extinguisher.** Be prepared.

CROSSING THE BORDER WITH YOUR CAR After you cross the border into Mexico from the U.S., you'll stop to get your Tourist Permit and a permit for your car; a tourist decal will be affixed to a rear car window. After that you'll come to a Mexican Customs post somewhere between 12 and 16 miles down the road. Some motorists (chosen at random) will be stopped for inspection. If the light is green just present your permits. If it's red, stop for inspection. In the Baja Peninsula the procedures may differ—there may no inland Customs station. Theoretically, you should not be charged for your Tourist Permit, auto permit, and inspection, but the uniformed officer may try to extract a bribe from you (see "Bribes," above).

When you cross back into the U.S. after an extended trip in Mexico, the American Customs officials may inspect every nook and cranny of your car, your bags, even your person. They're looking for drugs, which includes illegal diet pills.

BY SHIP

Numerous cruise lines serve Mexico. There are trips to ports of call down the Pacific coast including Ixtapa/Zihuatanejo and Acapulco. These are expensive if you pay full price; however, if you don't mind taking off at the last minute several cruise tour specialists can arrange substantial discounts on unsold cabins. One such company is **The Cruise Line, Inc.,** 4770 Biscayne Blvd., Penthouse 1-3, Miami, FL 33137 (tel. 305/576-0036, or toll free 800/777-0707 in the U.S. and Canada, 800/327-3021 in the U.S.).

PACKAGE TOURS

Package tours offer some of the best values to the coastal resorts especially during high season from December until after Easter. Off-season packages can be real bargains. But to know for sure if the package is a cost saver you must price the package yourself by calling the airline for round-trip flight costs, and the hotel for rates. Add in the cost of transfers to and from the airport (which packages usually include) and see if it's a deal. Packages are usually per person, and single travelers pay extra. In the high season a package may be the only way of getting there because wholesalers have blocked airline seats. The airline may say there are not seats available when you call, but a travel agent can get you there through a package purchase. The cheapest package rates will be those in hotels in the lower range, always without as many amenities or as beautiful rooms as more costly hotels. But you can go to the public areas and beaches of any other hotel and spend the day without being a guest there. Use this book to read up on the hotels and make your selection.

Travel agents have information on specific packages.

TOUR OPERATORS IN GREAT BRITAIN

BA Holidays, Airtours, and Sunset Travel are three of the largest companies offering package tours to Mexico. I recommend you pay a visit to the Mexican Government Tourist Office in London at 60-61 Trafalgar Sq., London WC2N 5DS, U.K. (tel. 44/071-839-3177), or check with a reputable travel agent such as Thomas Cook.

8. GETTING AROUND

BY PLANE

U.S. and international airlines fly to and from Mexico, but to fly from point to point within the country, you must rely on Mexican airlines. Mexico has two privately owned, large national carriers, **Mexicana** (tel. toll free 800/531-7921 in the U.S.), and **Aeromexico** (tel. toll free 800/237-6639 in the U.S.), and several up-and-coming regional carriers. Mexicana is Latin America's largest air carrier, dating back to 1921. Mexicana offers extensive connections to the U.S. as well as within

Mexico. Aeromexico also has U.S. connections. Several of the new regional carriers are operated by, or can be booked through Mexicana. Regional carriers are **Aero Cancún** (see Mexicana); **Aero Caribe** (see Mexicana); **Aero Leo López** (tel. 915/778-1022 in El Paso; fax 915/779-3334); **Aerolitoral** (see Aeromexico); **AeroMar** (tel. toll free 800/950-0747 in the U.S., or see Mexicana); **Aero Monterrey** (see Mexicana); and **Aerovias Oaxaqueños** (tel. 951/6-3842 in Oaxaca). The regional carriers are expensive, but they go to places that are difficult to reach. Look for this trend to continue.

Because major airlines can book some regional carriers, read your ticket carefully to see if a connecting flight is on one of these smaller carriers since they may leave from a different airport or check in at a different counter.

AIRPORT TAXES Mexico charges an airport tax on all international departures. Passengers pay $12 in cash—dollars or the peso equivalent—to get out of the country. Each domestic departure you make within Mexico costs around $6 unless you are on a connecting flight and paid at the start of the flight—you won't be charged again when you change planes.

RECONFIRMING FLIGHTS Although airlines in Mexico say it is not necessary to reconfirm a flight, I always do. On several occasions I have arrived to check in with a valid ticket only to discover my reservation had been canceled. Now I leave nothing to chance. Also be aware that airlines routinely overbook. To avoid getting bumped, check in for an international flight the required 1½ hours in advance of travel. That will put you near the head of the line.

BY TRAIN

Special note: Mexico's train service is undergoing dramatic changes and more are in store. First-class service has been greatly curtailed (fewer Pullman cars and irregular or non-existent dining service) and several popular routes have been suspended. However, if you find a first-class train going your way, try it, although the closest passenger service to the territory covered in this book is to Mexico City. Train travel is safer and more comfortable than going by bus, but it is slower, costs more, and schedules are likely to be less convenient.

SERVICE CLASSES Traveling *segunda* (second class) anywhere is usually hot, overcrowded, dingy, and unpleasant. *Primera* (first class) can be the same way unless you are sure to ask for **primera especial** (first-class reserved seat), a day or so in advance, if possible. In primera especial there is rarely such crowding and disorder. The top-of-the-line accommodations on trains, cheaper than flying but more expensive than the bus, are Pullman compartments (*alcolba* or *camarín)* for overnight travel. Some first-class trains have a Pullman and diner, others have only a diner, and most will have comfortable reclining chairs.

Service and cleanliness may vary dramatically, but generally I've found first-class trains to be a delightful experience and a good value. This qualified statement means that the cars will be clean at the start of the journey, but little may be done en route to keep them that way. Trash may accumulate, toilet paper vanishes, the water cooler runs dry or has no paper cups, and the temperature may vary between freezing and sweltering. Conductors range from solicitous to totally indifferent.

Sleeping compartments, called a camarín for one person, and alcolba for two (with two beds) are available on some overnight journeys. These convert to private sitting rooms during the day. Cramming more people than this in either size compartment is very uncomfortable, and not recommended.

MAJOR TRAINS There are two major train hubs—Mexico City and Guadalajara. If you plan to get on and off before your final destination, you must tell the agent your exact on-off schedule at the time of your ticket purchase. First-class trains are often filled, especially on holidays or with tour groups.

TICKETS & RESERVATIONS If you purchase your ticket at the train station, do it as soon as your plans are firm. In cities served by first-class trains, you may find travel agents that will arrange your tickets, but they usually charge a service fee of up to 25% of the price of the ticket.

For advance planning using first-class trains, you might consider the services of **Mexico by Train** (not to be confused with Mexico by Rail), 3015 S. Main, Laredo, TX 78043 (tel. toll free 800/321-1699). Given 10 days' notice they will prepurchase your first-class service train ticket and mail it to you. For holiday travel, make plans 45 days ahead. If you leave from Nuevo Laredo, the company will arrange secured parking, a prestamped tourist card, and transfers across the border. They charge a high percentage on top of the regular price of the train ticket.

When deciding whether to use Mexico by Train or another agent, consider the cost of going to the train station yourself and the uncertainty of space if you wait until you get there to reserve a seat. Although they seldom reply to mail, for the latest train itinerary or other questions, you can try writing well in advance to Commercial Passenger Department, National Railways of Mexico, Buenavista Grand Central Station, Mexico, DF 06358, or call (tel. 5/547-1084, 547-1097, or 547-6593). For the Pacific Railroad Company write Tolsa 336, Guadalajara, Jal. Both companies have special personnel and divisions to handle group train travel. With enough lead time, they'll even put on extra cars.

TRAVEL TIME From Nuevo Laredo at the Texas border, it's a 25-hour, 735-mile ride to Mexico City. Other border towns are farther from the capital. The trip from Ciudad Juarez, across from El Paso, takes over 35 hours to Mexico City. There is a daily train from Matamoros, across from Brownsville, Texas, to Monterrey. This trip takes eight hours and then a change of trains is made. There is an overnight sleeper train daily between Monterrey and Mexico City. From Nogales, the trip takes 26 or 36 hours, depending on which train you take. From Mexicali, the train takes 25 hours to Guadalajara. Pacific coast trains are notorious for running as much as 24 hours behind time.

BY BUS

Buses are frequent, readily accessible, and can get you to almost anywhere you want to go. More than a dozen Mexican companies operate large air-conditioned Greyhound-type buses between most cities. The cost works out to around $1.75 an hour for first class or $3 per hour for deluxe class. Modern buses have replaced most of the legendary "village buses" that growled and wheezed along. Today it's best to buy your reserved-seat ticket, often via a computerized system, a day in advance on many long-distance routes. Schedules are fairly dependable, so be at the terminal on time for departure.

New buses are being added all over the country featuring large windows with an unobstructed view from every seat. Many companies have added **deluxe service** sometimes called *plus* (pronounced *ploos) or servicio de lujo* (luxury service) from several cities. Deluxe buses cost more than regular buses, carry half the number of passengers, have stewards, and include video movies and machine refreshments. They are worth every penny in comfort.

Many Mexican cities now have new central bus stations that are much like sophisticated airport terminals.

I've included information on bus routes along my suggested itineraries. Keep in mind that routes, times, and prices may change, and as there is no central directory of schedules for the whole country, current information must be obtained from local bus stations or travel offices.

For long trips, carry some food, water, toilet paper, and a sweater (in case the air conditioning is too strong).

See the Appendix for a list of helpful bus terms in Spanish.

BY CAR

Most Mexican roads are not up to northern standards of smoothness, hardness, width of curve, grade of hill, or safety marking. *Cardinal rule:* Never drive at night if you can avoid it. The roads aren't good enough; the trucks, carts, pedestrians, and bicycles usually have no lights; you can hit potholes, animals, rocks, dead ends, or bridges out with no warning. Enough said.

You will also have to get used to the spirited Latin driving styles, which tend to depend more on flair and good reflexes than on system and prudence. Be prepared for new procedures, as when a truck driver flips on his left-turn signal when there's not a crossroad for miles. He's probably telling you that the road's clear for you to pass—after all, he's in a better position to see than you are. It's difficult to judge, however, if he really means that he intends to pull over on the left-hand shoulder. Left turns are made by pulling off on the right shoulder, waiting until traffic clears, then making your turn. You may have to follow trucks without mufflers and pollution-control devices for miles. Under these conditions drop back and be patient, take a side road, or stop for a break when you feel tense or tired.

Take extra care not to endanger pedestrians. People in the countryside are not good at judging the speed of an approaching car, and often panic in the middle of the road even though they could easily have reached the shoulder.

Be prepared to pay tolls on some of Mexico's expressways and bridges. Tolls are outrageously high in this country. The word for "toll" in Spanish is *cuota*.

CAR RENTALS   With some trepidation I wander into the subject of car-rental rules, which change often in Mexico. The best prices are obtained by reserving your car a week in advance from the U.S. Acapulco and most other large Mexican cities have several rental offices representing the various big firms and some smaller ones. You'll find rental desks at the airports, at all major hotels, and at many travel agencies. The large firms such as Avis, Hertz, National, and Budget have rental offices on main streets as well.

Cars are easy to rent if you have a credit card (American Express, VISA, MasterCard, etc.), are 25 or over, and have a valid driver's license and passport with you. (Budget, however, will guarantee a car reservation only with an American Express or Diners Club card.) Without a credit card you must leave a cash deposit, usually a big one. Rent-here/leave-there arrangements are usually simple to make, but are very costly.

Costs   Don't underestimate the cost of renting a car. Daily charges are much higher than the per-day equivalent if you keep the car a week. Costs vary from city to city and during certain times of year. Mileage added rather than included in the rate can run up the cost of using a car considerably. When I checked in low season, Avis's *basic daily rates* for a manual-shift VW Beetle, with mileage included, were $29 in Acapulco, Ixtapa, and Mexico City (but I've paid much higher than this certain times of the year). Add to this 10% tax and $15.50 daily for insurance. *Basic weekly rates*, for a VW Beetle with mileage included, vary from $169 in Acapulco, and $199 in Mexico City and Ixtapa (but I've seen it as high as $200). Again, add tax and insurance. Cars with automatic transmission cost more.

As an example, at Avis, weekly cost of a manual-shift VW Beetle with unlimited mileage in Acapulco is:

Basic weekly charge	$169.00
Daily insurance at $15.50	108.50
10% IVA tax	27.75
	$305.25

Remember that unleaded gas (used by all new cars—the only used by rental agencies) costs $1.60 a gallon. Consider also the cost of the new toll road, if you plan to use it to go to Taxco or Acapulco. The price is $80 one way between Mexico City and Acapulco. A car is not really necessary in Acapulco, Ixtapa/Zihuatanejo, or Taxco. But if you plan to tour the hinterland between Acapulco and Taxco, or take several side trips from Taxco, then a car will enhance your experience. There are no car-rental agencies in Taxco, however, so Cuernavaca and Acapulco are your closest cities for rentals. But consider that in Taxco there are guides with cars who will also take you on excursions.

Rental Confirmation Make your reservation directly with the car-rental company using their toll-free 800 number. Write down your confirmation number and request that a copy of the confirmation be mailed to you (rent at least a week in advance so the confirmation has time to reach you). Present that confirmation slip when you appear to collect your car. If you're dealing with a U.S. company, the confirmation must be honored, even if they have to upgrade you to another class of car—don't allow them to send you to another agency. The rental confirmation also has the agreed-on price which prevents you from being charged more, in case there is a price change before you arrive. Insist on the rate printed on the confirmation.

Deductibles *Be careful:* Deductibles vary greatly; some are as high as $2,500, which comes out of your pocket immediately in case of car damage. So don't fail to get information about deductibles.

Insurance Car insurance isn't mandatory in Mexico, but you're inviting disaster if you don't buy it. Many credit-card companies offer their cardholders free rental-car insurance. *Don't use it in Mexico,* for several reasons. Even though rental-car insurance is supposedly optional in Mexico, there may be major consequences if you don't have it: First, if you buy insurance and you have an accident, you pay only the deductible, which limits your expense. Second, if you have an accident, or the car is vandalized or stolen, you'll have to pay for everything before you can leave the rental-car office. This includes full value of the car if it is unrepairable—a determination made only by the rental-car company. While your credit card company will eventually pay your costs, you will have to lay out the money in the meantime. Third, if an accident occurs, everyone may wind up in jail until guilt is determined. If you are the guilty party, you may not be released from jail until all restitution is paid to the rental-car owners and to injured persons—made doubly difficult if you have no rental-car insurance. Insurance is offered in two parts: **Collision and damage** insurance covers your car and others if the accident is your fault, and **personal accident** insurance covers you and anyone in your car. I always take both. Always ask about the deductible. If you don't purchase the insurance, you must pay a $2,500 deposit. Other companies have similar policies.

Damage Always inspect your car carefully before renting it, using this checklist:

- Hubcaps
- Windshield (for nicks and cracks that will grow larger)
- Body (for dents, nicks, etc.)

- Fenders (for dents, etc.)
- Muffler (is it smashed?)
- Trim (loose, damaged, or missing?)
- Head and tail lights
- Fire extinguisher (it should be under the driver's seat, required by law)
- Spare tire and tools (in the trunk)
- Seat belts (required by law)
- Gas cap
- Outside mirror
- Floor mats

Note every damaged or missing area, no matter how minute, on your rental agreement or you will be charged for all missing or damaged parts, including missing car tags, should the police confiscate your tags for a parking infraction (very costly). I can't stress enough how important it is to check your car carefully. Car companies have attempted to rent me cars with bald tires and tires with bulges, a car with a license plate that would expire before I returned the car, as well as cars with missing trim, floor mats, fire extinguisher, etc.

Fine Print   Read the fine print on the back of your rental agreement and note that insurance is invalid if you have an accident while driving on an unpaved road.

Trouble Number   One last recommendation. Before starting out with a rental car, be sure you know their trouble number. The large firms have toll-free numbers, which may not be well staffed on weekends.

Problems, Perils, Deals   At present, I find the best prices are through Avis and that's the company I use; generally I am a satisfied customer, though I sometimes have to dig in my heels and insist on proper service. I have had even more difficult problems with other agencies. Situations I have encountered within the past three years are: An attempt to push me off to a no-name company rather than upgrade me to a more expensive car when a VW Beetle wasn't available; poorly staffed offices with no extra cars, parts, or mechanics in case of a breakdown; a demand that I sign a credit-card voucher for 75% of the value of the car in case of an accident even though I had purchased insurance (I refused and still rented the car). Since potential problems are varied, I'd rather deal with a company based in the States so that at least I have recourse if I am not satisfied.

Signing the Rental Agreement   Once you've agreed on everything, the rental clerk will tally the bill before you leave and you will sign an open credit-card voucher that will be filled in when you return the car. Read the agreement and double-check all addition. The time to catch mistakes is before you leave, not when you return.

Picking Up/Returning the Car   When you rent the car, you agree to pick it up at a certain time and return it at a certain time. If you're late in picking it up or cancel, there are usually penalties—ask what they are when you make the reservation. If you return the car more than an hour late, an expensive hourly rate kicks in. Also, you must return the car with the same amount of gas in the tank that it had when you drove out. If you don't, the charge added to your bill for the difference is much more than for gas bought at a public station.

GASOLINE   There's one government-owned brand of gas and one gasoline station name throughout the country—Pemex (Petroleras Mexicanas). Each Pemex station has a franchise owner. There are two types of gas in Mexico—Nova, an 82-octane leaded gas, and Magna Sin, 87-octane unleaded gas. Magna Sin is sold from bright green pumps and costs around $1.60 a gallon. Nova costs almost the same. In Mexico, fuel and oil are sold by the liter, which is slightly more than a quart (40l equals about 10½ gal.). Nova is readily available. Magna Sin is now available in most areas of Mexico, along major highways and in the larger cities. Even in areas where it should be available, you may have to hunt around. The usual station may be out of Magna Sin for a couple of days—weekends and holidays especially. Or you may be told that none is available in the area, just to get your business. Plan ahead: Fill up every chance you get; keep your tank topped off. Pemex publishes a helpful *atlas de carreteras* (road atlas), which includes a list of filling stations with Magna Sin gas (there are some inaccuracies). No credit cards are accepted for gas purchases.

Here's what to do when you have to fuel up: Drive up to the pump, close enough so that you will be able to watch the pump run as your tank is being filled. Check that the pump is turned back to zero, go to your fuel filler cap and unlock it yourself, and watch the pump and the attendant as the gas goes in. Though many service station attendants are honest, many are not. It's good to ask for a specific peso amount rather than saying "full." This is because the attendants tend to over-fill, splashing gas on the car and anything within range.

As there are always lines at the gas pumps, attendants often finish fueling one ve-hicle, turn the pump back quickly (or don't turn it back at all), and start on another vehicle. You've got to be looking at the pump when the fueling is finished, because it may show the amount you owe for only a few seconds. This "quick draw" from car to car is another good reason to ask for a certain peso-amount of gas. If you've asked for 20 New Pesos' worth, the attendant can't charge you 22 New Pesos for it.

Once the fueling is complete, let the attendant check the oil, or radiator, or put air in the tires. Do only one thing at a time, be with him as he does it, and don't let him rush you. Get into these habits, or it'll cost you.

If you get oil, make sure that the can that is tipped into your engine is a full one. If in doubt, have the attendant check the dipstick again after the oil has sup-posedly been put in. Check your change, and again, don't let them rush you. Check that your locking gas cap is back in place.

DRIVING RULES If you park illegally, or commit some other infraction, and you are not around to discuss it, police are authorized to remove your license plates (*placas*). You must then trundle over to the police station and pay a fine to get them back. Mexican car-rental agencies have begun to weld the license tag to the tag frame; you may want to devise a method of your own to make the tags difficult to remove. Theoretically, this will make the policeman move on to another set of tags easier to confiscate. On the other hand, he could get his hackles up and decide to have your car towed. To weld or not to weld is up to you.

Be attentive to road signs. A drawing of a row of little bumps means that there are speed bumps (*topes*) across the road to warn you to reduce your speed while driving through towns or villages. Slow down when coming to a village whether you see the sign or not—sometimes they install the bumps but not the sign!

Kilometer stones on main highways register the distance from local population centers. There is always a shortage of directional signs, so check quite frequently that you are on the right road. Other common road signs include:

Camino en Reparación	Road Repairs
Conserva Su Derecha	Keep Right

Cuidado con el Ganado, el Tren	Watch Out for Cattle, Trains
Curva Peligrosa	Dangerous Curve
Derrumbes	Earthquake Zone
Deslave	Caved-in Roadbed
Despacio	Slow
Desviación	Detour
Disminuya Su Velocidad	Slow Down
Entronque	Highway Junction
Escuela	School (Zone)
Grava Suelta	Loose Gravel
Hombres Trabajando	Men Working
No Hay Paso	Road Closed
Peligro	Danger
Puente Angosto	Narrow Bridge
Raya Continua	Continuous (Solid) White Line
Tramo en Reparación	Road Under Construction
Un Solo Carril a 100 m.	One-lane Road 100 Meters Ahead
Zona Escolar	School Zone

MAPS Guía Roji and AAA have good maps of Mexico. In Mexico, maps are sold at large drugstores such as Sanborn's or bookstores and hotel gift shops.

BREAKDOWNS Your best guide to repair shops is the yellow pages. For specific makes and shops that repair them, look under *Automoviles y Camiones: Talleres de Reparación y Servicio*; auto-parts stores are listed under *Refacciones y Accesorios para Automoviles*. On the road often the sign of a mechanic simply says *Taller Mecánico*. Junkyards (and there are few of them in Mexico) are called *huesero* (boneyard).

I've found that the Ford and Volkswagen dealerships in Mexico give prompt, courteous attention to my car problems, and prices for repairs are, in general, much lower than in the U.S. or Canada. I suspect that other big-name dealerships—General Motors, Chrysler, etc.—give similar, very satisfactory service. Often they will take your car right away and make repairs in just a few hours, sometimes minutes.

If your car breaks down on the road, help might already be on the way. Green, radio-equipped repair trucks manned by uniformed, English-speaking officers patrol the major highways during daylight hours to aid motorists in trouble. The **"Green Angels"** will perform minor repairs and adjustments free, but you pay for parts and materials.

ACCIDENTS When possible, many Mexicans drive away from accidents to avoid hassles with police. Even people who have damages but are not at fault leave the scene, and people leave even when there are injuries. If the police arrive while the involved persons are still there, everyone may be locked in jail until blame is assessed. In any case you have to settle up immediately, which may take days of red tape. Foreigners without fluent Spanish are at a distinct disadvantage when trying to explain their side of the event. Three steps may help the foreigner who doesn't wish to do as the Mexicans do: If you're in your own car, notify your Mexican insurance company, whose job it is to intervene on your behalf. If you're in a rental car, notify the rental company immediately and ask how to contact the nearest adjuster. (You did buy insurance with the rental—right?) Finally, if all else fails, ask to contact the nearest Green Angels, who may be able to explain to officials that you are covered by insurance.

PARKING When you park your car on the street, lock up and leave nothing within view inside (day or night). I use guarded, gate-locked, parking lots, especially at night, to avoid vandalism and break-ins. This way you also avoid parking violations. When pay lots are not available, dozens of small boys will surround you as you stop, wanting to "watch your car for you." Pick the leader of the group, let him know you want him to guard it, and give him a peso or two when you leave. Kids may be very curious about the car and may look in, crawl underneath, or even climb on top, but they rarely do any damage.

BY RV

Touring Mexico by recreational vehicle is a popular way of seeing the country. Many hotels have hookups. RV parks, while not as plentiful as in the U.S., are available throughout the country.

HITCHHIKING

You see Mexicans hitching rides at crossroads after getting off a bus, for example, but as a general rule hitchhiking isn't done. It's especially unwise for foreigners, who may be suspected of carrying large amounts of cash.

SUGGESTED ITINERARIES

IF YOU HAVE 5 DAYS

Since each of the major cities in this book is a popular gateway to the region, I've included five-day suggested itineraries for each one—Acapulco, Ixtapa/Zihuatanejo, and Taxco.

A TOUR BASED IN ACAPULCO

Day 1: Arrive in Acapulco, unpack, don resort duds, head to the beach for the best breeze and view, and relax. Have dinner.

Day 2: Head for the beach, the pool, a golf course, or a tennis court. Have dinner at one of the beachside restaurants or make reservations for dinner on the terrace at La Perla on La Quebrada and watch the cliff divers at night.

Day 3: Go to the zócalo in Old Acapulco for breakfast, visit the Museo San Diego overlooking Old Acapulco, then spend the rest of the day relaxing. Find a panoramic-view restaurant, such as Su Casa, and arrive early for drinks before sunset followed by dinner and watching Acapulco Bay come alive with glittering lights. Or leave Acapulco behind and enjoy sunset at Pie de la Cuesta north of the city, followed by dinner at one of the beach restaurants there.

Day 4: Meet the deep-sea fishing boat early for half a day of fishing. Spend the afternoon relaxing. After dinner save some energy for one of Acapulco's famous discos or have late-night drinks at the El Olvido.

Day 5: Laze by the beach or pool, and do some last-minute shopping at the crafts market in Old Acapulco. For your last night pick a special restaurant for a splurge meal and enjoy the evening.

A TOUR BASED IN IXTAPA/ZIHUATANEJO

Day 1: Arrive at your hotel, unpack, settle in. Stroll on the beach or downtown Zihuatanajo in search of a good place to people-watch, have a snack and drink, and unwind. Have an early dinner and relax.

Day 2: Sleep in and have a late breakfast. Relax by the pool or on the beach. Have lunch at one of the restaurants in Ixtapa or downtown Zihuatanejo. Make reservations for deep-sea fishing, diving, or snorkeling for tomorrow. Have drinks in the lobby of the Westin Hotel and dinner with a view at Villa de la Selva.

Day 3: Rise early, spend the morning fishing, diving, or snorkeling. If you caught a fish, take it to a restaurant to prepare for your evening meal. Find a happy hour for sunset drinks. Eat your fish at the restaurant where it's prepared, or pick a restaurant for dinner in Zihuatanejo or a special one in Ixtapa such as Becco Fino, and finish off the evening with an ice cream and a stroll, or late-night drinks at Coconuts. Arrange for lunch on the beach at Casa de la Tortuga tomorrow.

Day 4: Be picked up for lunch and an afternoon at Casa de la Tortuga on a secluded beach north of Ixtapa. In the evening try one of the beachside restaurants on La Ropa Beach, and end with music at one of the hotel lobby bars in Ixtapa.

Day 5: Have breakfast at one of the umbrella-covered eateries on the streets of Zihuatanejo. Do some last-minute shopping. Go to La Ropa or Las Gatas Beach, spend the day and have lunch at one of the palapa restaurants on the beach. Try a new restaurant for your last night, perhaps the elegant Portofino at the Westin in Ixtapa, or something more casual such as La Mesa del Capitán or Garrobos in Zihuatanejo.

A TOUR BASED IN TAXCO

Day 1: Arrive, settle in at your hotel. Relax if you can, but you'll probably be too eager to see what this mountain colonial village and "Silver Capital of Mexico" is all about. Shop and wander the streets. Have dinner at one of the restaurants on the zócalo and early to bed. (Taxco doesn't stay up late anyway.)

Day 2: Have a leisurely breakfast and be ready for the silver shops and museums to open around 10am. Shop, stroll, and don't miss going inside the Santa Prisca y San Sebastián Church. Have lunch at La Taberna. Shop. Drop in at the other museums. Make reservations for dinner and drinks with a view at Toni's or La Taberna.

Day 3: Take a day-trip to Ixcateopan or head out to the Los Castillo Workshop and Spratling Ranch to see how silversmiths work. Have afternoon drinks at Paco's and dinner at Sr. Castilla's or Bora Bora Pizza overlooking the square. If you have energy for dancing there's always Windows disco overlooking the city.

Day 4: Rise early for a day-trip to Cuernavaca. See the Casa de Cortés/Museo de Cuauhnahuac, stroll through the downtown area, and have lunch. Hop on a bus at the central market for the short trip to the village of Tepoztlán, especially if it's Sunday (market day) or one of the village festival days. Return to Taxco and enjoy a leisurely dinner.

Day 5: Finish shopping and seeing the museums. Take a day-trip to the Cacahuamilpa Caves, or if you have a car, head to the ruins of Xochicalco. Have a Berta at Berta's (everyone must), dinner someplace special, then relax overlooking the square at Paco's until it closes.

9. WHERE TO STAY

Hotel prices are no longer regulated by the government in Mexico. Often desk clerks will quote a lower price if business is slack or if you suggest a slight reduction. Room rates are required to be posted in plain view near the reception desk, and as a rule they are; places like Acapulco are the exception. Ask the clerk to show you the *tarifa*.

Mexican hotels, like hotels throughout the world, have an assortment of rooms in a range of prices. Rooms with bath or air conditioning are always more expensive. In addition, rooms with a view of the street may be more expensive (and noisier) than those with windows opening onto an airshaft.

Remember also that the 10% IVA tax may be added to your bill, or it may be included in the quoted price. When you register, remember to ask if the tax has been included in the rate quoted to you.

HOLIDAY RESORTS In Acapulco or Ixtapa/Zihuatanejo, and in the inland cities of Taxco and Cuernavaca, write ahead for hotel reservations on major holidays (Mexican as well as international). Christmas, New Year's, and Easter week are the worst for crowding. If you discover it's a holiday when you're en route to the resort, and you have no reservations, plan to arrive early in the day to find a room.

Several readers have written to me about difficulties they encountered in making reservations by mail, and even by toll-free reservation numbers. Some report no answer or no record of their request (or deposit check) when they've arrived. Or they are quoted a higher price than one they might have paid by just arriving without a reservation. I've experienced the same frustrations. Here's a suggestion: Only make reservations during high season if you are going to a beach area. Off-season just arrive and find out what's available by calling when you arrive. If you truly want a reservation, write or fax well in advance, saying in your letter that you'll forward a deposit upon receipt of a confirmation. Or, instead, call the hotel, make the reservation, get the name of the person who takes the reservation, and then send your deposit by registered mail, return receipt requested—all of which can take a good deal of time. If the clerk asks where you are calling from, pick someplace nearby in Mexico; if you say the U.S. or some distant Mexican City, the quoted rate could be two to three times the current local price (especially true in Acapulco); if they think you are nearby they know you can easily find out the true rate. If in doubt about the price on arrival, ask the price as though you're just another tourist looking for a room. Don't tell them you've made a reservation. See what price they quote you. If it's a lot lower than the price quoted in the reservation, accept the lower price and register. If you've paid a deposit, make sure it's applied to your bill. You may have to debate the point with them a bit, but it's worth it.

For stays in first-class resorts, my best advice is to look for a packaged deal through a travel agent or tour operator. Sometimes packages, which may include airfare, some meals, or other amenities, work out to be much cheaper than what you'd pay if you book each component of your trip separately.

VILLAS & CONDOS Renting a private villa or condominium home is a popular vacation alternative. The difference between the two, of course, is that villas are usually freestanding and condos may be part of a large or small complex. Often the villas are true private homes, in exclusive neighborhoods and rented out seasonally by their owners. Condominiums, on the other hand, may seem more like a hotel, although the secluded ones feel more exclusive. Either accommodation ordinarily comes with private kitchen and dining area, maid service, and pool. Often a full-time cook, maid, or gardener/chauffeur is on duty. I've seen prices as low as $90 a night to a high of $1,500. Prices are seasonal, with the best deals between May and October. Of course, depending on the number of bedrooms, you can get a group together and share the cost. Two companies specializing in this type of vacation rental are: **Creative Leisure,** 951 Transport Way, Petaluma, CA 94954-1484 (tel. 707/778-1800, or toll free 800/426-6367); and **Mexico Condo Reservations,** 5801

Soledad Mountain Rd., La Jolla, CA 92037 (tel. 619/275-4500, or toll free 800/262-4500 in the U.S. and 800/654-5543 in Canada). Both have brochures with photographs of potential properties.

YOUTH HOSTELS Mexico has some clean, adequate, and low-priced hostels built and maintained by the government, although none is located in the areas covered in this book. For a list, write to **SETEJ**, Hamburgo 305, Mexico, D.F. The phone is 5/211-0743.

A source of information on inexpensive youth hostel tours is the **Agencia Nacional de Turismo Juvenil**, Glorieta del Metro Insurgentes, Local C-11, Mexico 6, D.F. The phone is 5/211-6636. It's at the Insurgentes Metro plaza, in case you are in Mexico City and want to stop in.

CAMPING It's easy and relatively cheap to camp south of the border if you have a recreational vehicle or trailer. It's more difficult if you only have a tent. Some agencies selling Mexican car insurance in the U.S. (including Sanborn's) will give you a free list of campsites if you ask. The AAA also has a list of sites.

Campgrounds here tend to be slightly below U.S. standards (with many attractive exceptions to this rule, though). Remember that campgrounds fill up just like hotels during the winter rush-to-the-sun and at holiday times. Get there early. And for safety's sake, don't camp alone. Always pick a campground where there are other campers.

10. SHOPPING

The charm of Mexico is no better expressed that in its arts and crafts. Hardly a tourist will leave this country without having bought at least one handcrafted item. Mexico is famous for textiles, ceramics, baskets, and onyx and silver jewelry, to mention only a few. The state of Guerrero, the main subject of this book, is especially noted for dance masks, pottery, basket weaving, bark paintings, and lacquerware.

This guide is designed to help the traveler know some of the crafts and the regions they come from. I have listed the cities or villages where the item is sold (and often crafted), the first place listed being the best place to buy. The larger cities, especially Acapulco, Ixtapa/Zihuatanejo, and Mexico City, will have many crafts from other regions but, in general, a greater variety and better prices are to be found in the areas where the items are made. Tables of metric conversions and clothing sizes are in the Appendix. I have not listed any prices for the crafts since this is really dependent on one's bargaining ability. I would add that it is very helpful to visit a government fixed-price shop (every Mexican city has one, usually called the Artes Populares or FONART) before attempting to bargain. This will give you an idea of the cost versus quality of the various crafts.

Following, now, are the various crafts, in alphabetical order.

Baskets: Woven of reed or straw—Taxco, Chilapa, Oaxaca, Cooper Canyon, Toluca, Yucatán, Puebla, Mexico City.

Blankets: Saltillo, Toluca, Santa Ana Chiautempan (north of Puebla), Oaxaca, and Mitla (made of soft wool with some synthetic dyes; they use a lot of bird and geometric motifs). Make sure that the blanket you pick out is in fact the one you take since often the "same" blanket in the wrapper is not the same.

Glass: Hand-blown and molded—Monterrey and Tlaquepaque; Mexico City at the Avalos Brothers glass factory, Carretones 5 (Metro: Pino Suarez).

Guitars: Made in Paracho, 25 miles north of Uruapan on Highway 37.

Hammocks and Mosquito Netting: Mérida, Campeche, Mazatlán.

Hats: Mérida has Panama hats made of sisal from the maguey cactus; finest-quality weaving; easy to pack and wash. San Cristóbal de las Casas, Chiapas, is a good place for varied regional hats.

Huaraches: Leather sandals often with rubber-tire soles—San Blas, Mérida, Mexico City, Guadalajara, Hermosillo, San Cristóbal de las Casas, and in fact most states.

Huipils: Handwoven, embroidered, or brocaded overblouses are indigenous to almost all Mexican states but are especially evident in Guerrero, Yucatán, Chiapas, Oaxaca, Puebla, and Veracruz. Most of the better huipils are in fact used ones that have been bought from the village women. Huipils can be distinguished by villages; look around before buying; you'll be amazed at the variety.

Lacquer Goods: Olinalá, Guerrero, northeast of Acapulco, is known for ornate lacquered chests and other lacquered decorative and furniture items. Pátzcuaro and Uruapan, west of Mexico City, are also known for gold-leafed lacquered trays.

Leather Goods: Monterrey, Saltillo, León, Mexico City, San Cristóbal de las Casas, and Oaxaca.

Masks: Wherever there is locally observed regional dancing you'll find maskmakers. The tradition is especially strong in the states of Guerrero, Chiapas, Puebla, Oaxaca, and Michoacán.

Onyx: Puebla (where onyx is carved), Querétaro, Matehuala, Mexico City.

Pottery: Chilapa and Tlapa, Guerrero; Tlaquepaque, Tonalá, and Oaxaca, Puebla; Michoacán; Coyotepec; Izúcar de Matamoras; Veracruz; Copper Canyon; Dolores Hidalgo; and Guanajuato.

Rebozos: Woman's or man's rectangular woven cloth to be worn around the shoulders, similar to a shawl—Guerrero, Oaxaca, Mitla, San Cristóbal de las Casas, Mexico City, and Pátzcuaro. Rebozos are generally made of wool or a blend of wool and cotton but synthetic fibers are creeping in, so check the material carefully before buying. Also, compare the weave from different cloths since the fineness of the weave is proportional to the cost.

Serapes: Heavy woolen or cotton blankets with a slit for the head, to be worn as a poncho—Santa Ana Chiautempán (30 miles north of Puebla near Tlaxcala), San Luis Potosí, Santa María del Río (25 miles south of San Luis Potosí), Chiconcoac (an hour's drive northeast from Mexico City, near Texcoco), Saltillo, Toluca, Mexico City.

Silver: Taxco, Mexico City, Zacatecas, Guadalajara. Sterling silver is indicated by "925" on the silver, which certifies that there are 925 grams of pure silver per kilogram, or that the silver is 92.5% pure. In Mexico City they also use a spread-eagle hallmark to indicate sterling. Look for these marks or otherwise you may be paying a high price for an inferior quality that is mostly nickel, or even silver plate called alpaca.

Stones: Chalcedony, turquoise, lapis lazuli, amethyst — Querétaro, San Miguel de Allende, Durango, Saltillo, San Luis Potosí. The cost of turquoise is computed by weight, so many pesos per carat.

Textiles: Guerrero, Oaxaca, Chiapas, Santa Ana near Puebla, and Nayarit are known for their excellent weaving, each culturally distinct and different.

Tortoiseshell: It's illegal to bring it into the U.S.

MEXICO

Abbreviations Dept.—apartments; Apdo.—post office box; Av.—Avenida; Blv.—Bulevar or Boulevard; Calz.—calzada: C on faucets stands for caliente (hot), and F stands for fría (cold). In elevators, PB (planta baja) means "ground floor."

American Express Wherever there is an office, I've mentioned it.

Business Hours In general Mexican businesses in larger cities are open between 9am and 7pm. Smaller towns may close between 2 and 4pm. Most are closed on Sunday. Bank hours are 9 or 9:30am to 1pm Monday to Friday. A few banks in large cities have extended hours. It's hard to reach anyone in an office between 3 and 5pm.

Camera and Film Both are more expensive in Mexico than in the U.S.; take full advantage of your 12-roll film allowance by bringing 36 exposures per roll, and bring extra batteries. AA batteries are generally available, but AAA and small disk batteries for cameras and watches are rarely found. A few places in resort areas advertise color-film developing, but it might be cheaper to wait until you get home.

If you're a serious photographer, bring an assortment of films at various speeds as you will be photographing against glaring sand and forested mountains. Proper filters are a help.

Cigarettes Cigarettes are much cheaper in Mexico, even U.S. brands, if you buy them at a grocery or drugstore and not a hotel tobacco shop.

Climate See Section 2, "When to Go," earlier in this chapter.

Crime See "Legal Aid" and "Safety," below, and "Bribes" and "Scams" in Section 1, "Information, Entry Requirements, and Money," earlier in this chapter.

Currency See Section 1, "Information, Entry Requirements, and Money," earlier in this chapter.

Customs Mexican Customs procedures have been streamlined. At most crossings entering tourists are requested to punch a button. If the resulting light is green you go through without inspection. If it's red your luggage or car may be inspected thoroughly or briefly.

Doctors and Dentists Every embassy and consulate is prepared to recommend local doctors and dentists with good training and modern equipment; some of the doctors and dentists even speak English. See the list of embassies and consulates under "Embassies and Consulates," below, and remember that at the larger ones a duty officer is on call at all times. Hotels with a high clientele of foreigners are often prepared to recommend English-speaking doctors. Almost all first-class hotels in Mexico have a doctor on call.

Documents Required See Section 1, "Information, Entry Requirements, and Money," earlier in this chapter.

Driving Rules See Section 8, "Getting Around," earlier in this chapter.

Drug Laws Briefly, don't use or possess illegal drugs in Mexico. Mexicans have no tolerance of drug users and jail is the solution, with very little hope of getting out until the sentence (usually a long one) is completed or heavy fines or bribes are paid. (*Important note:* It isn't uncommon to be befriended by a fellow user only to be turned in by that "friend," who then collects a bounty for turning you in. It's a no-win.) Bring prescription drugs in their original containers. If possible pack a copy of the original prescription with the generic name of the drug. I don't need to go into detail about the penalties for illegal drug possession upon return to the U.S. Customs officials are also on the lookout for diet drugs sold in Mexico that are illegal in the U.S., possession of which could also land you in jail. If you buy antibiotics over the counter (which you can do in Mexico), say, for a sinus infection, and still have some left, you probably won't be hassled by U.S. Customs.

Drugstores Drugstores (*farmacias*) will sell you just about anything you want, with prescription or without. Most are open Monday through Saturday from 8am to 8pm. If you need to buy medicines after normal hours, you'll have to search for the *farmacia de turno*—pharmacies take turns staying open during the off-hours. Find any drugstore, and in its window may be a card showing the schedule of which farmacia will be open at what time.

Electricity Current in Mexico is 110 volts, 60 cycles, as in the U.S. and Canada, with the same flat-prong plugs and sockets. Some light bulbs have bayonet bases.

Embassies and Consulates They provide valuable lists of doctors and lawyers, as well as regulations concerning marriages in Mexico. Contrary to popular belief, your embassy cannot get you out of a Mexican jail, provide postal or banking services, or fly you home when you run out of money. Consular officers can provide you with advice on most matters and problems, however. Most countries have a representative embassy in Mexico City and many have consular offices or representatives in the provinces.

The embassy of **Australia** in Mexico City is at Jaime Balmes 11, Plaza Polanco, Torre B (tel. 5/395-9988); open Monday through Friday from 8am to 1pm.

The embassy of **Canada** in Mexico City is at Schiller 529, in Polanco (tel. 5/724-7900); open Monday through Friday from 9am to 1pm and 2 to 5pm; at other times the name of a duty officer is posted on the embassy door. In Acapulco, the Canadian consulate is in the Hotel Club del Sol, Costera Miguel Alemán, at the corner of Reyes Catolicos (tel. 74/85-6621); open 8am to 3pm.

The embassy of **New Zealand** in Mexico City is on the eighth floor of the building at Homero 229 (tel. 5/250-5999); open Monday through Thursday from 9am to 2pm and 3 to 5pm, Friday 9am to 2pm.

The embassy of the **United Kingdom** in Mexico City is at Lerma 71, at Río Sena (tel. 5/207-2569 or 207-2593). Hours are 8:30am to 3:30pm Monday through Friday. There is an honorary consul in Acapulco at the Hotel Las Brisas, Carretera Escénica (tel. 74/84-6605 or 84-1580).

The embassy of the **United States** in Mexico City is right next to the Hotel María Isabel Sheraton at Paseo de la Reforma 305, corner of Río Danubío (tel. 5/211-0042, or for emergencies, 5/211-4536). A consular agent resides in Acapulco (tel. 74/85-6600).

Emergencies The 24-hour **Tourist Help Line** in Mexico City is 5/250-0151.

Etiquette As a general rule, Mexicans are very polite. Foreigners who ask questions politely and say "please" and "thank you" will be rewarded. On the other hand, Mexicans will brazenly step ahead of you in lines, especially at ticket counters. The corrective words are *"La cola está altras,"* which means "The end of the line is back there." Mexicans are also very formal; an invitation to a private home, no matter how humble, is an honor. And although many strangers will immediately begin using the familiar form *tu* for you, if you want to be correct, the formal *usted* is still preferred until a friendship is established. How long it takes to establish a friendship varies. I know neighbors in Mexico who are still on formal terms after 10 years. When in doubt use the formal and wait for the Mexican to change to the familiar. Mexicans are normally uncomfortable with our "Dutch treat" custom of dining and will usually insist on paying. It can be touchy, and you don't want to be insulting. But you might offer to get the drinks or insist on paying the tip. If you're invited to a home it's polite to bring a gift, perhaps a bottle of good wine or flowers.

Guides Most guides in Mexico are men. Many speak English (and occasionally other languages) and are formally trained in history and culture to qualify for a federally approved tourism license. Hiring a guide for a day at the ruins, or to squire you around Mexico City may be a worthwhile luxury *if* you establish boundaries in the beginning. Be specific about what you want to do, and how long you want the service. The guide will quote a price. Discussion may reduce the initial quote. If your guide is using his own car, is licensed (something he can prove with a credential), and speaks English, the price will be higher and is generally worth it. If you are together at lunch, it's customary to buy the guide's meal. When bus tours from the U.S. diminished a few years ago, many licensed English-speaking guides became taxi drivers, so it isn't unusual to find incredibly knowledgeable taxi drivers who are experienced guides. In Mexico City these licensed guides/taxi drivers often have a permanent spot outside the better hotels and are available for private duty. If the service has been out of the ordinary, a tip is in order—perhaps 10% of the daily rate. On tours, the recommended tip is $1.50 to $2 per day per person.

Hitchhiking Generally speaking hitchhiking is not a good idea in Mexico. Take a bus; they are cheap and go everywhere.

Holidays See Section 2, "When to Go," earlier in this chapter.

Information See Section 1, "Information, Entry Requirements, and Money," earlier in this chapter, and specific city chapters for local information offices.

Language The official language is Spanish, but there are at least 50 Indian languages spoken and more than four times that many Indian dialects. English is most widely spoken in resort cities and in better hotels. It's best to learn some basic phrases.

Legal Aid Procuraduría Federal de Consumedor (Proseco), Calle Doctor Navarro 210, 4 Piso, Col. de los Doctores, Mexico DF 06720 (tel. 5/761-4546; fax 5/761-3885), is a contact for tourists with legal problems. International Legal Defense Counsel, 111 S. 15th St., Packard Building, 24th floor, Philadelphia, PA 19102 (tel. 215/977-9982), is a law firm specializing in legal difficulties of Americans abroad. See also "Embassies and Consulates" and "Emergencies," above.

Mail Mail service south of the border tends to be slow (sometimes glacial in its movements) and erratic. If you're on a two-week vacation, it's not a bad idea to buy and mail your postcards in the arrivals lounge at the airport to give them maximum time to get home before you do.

For the most reliable and convenient mail service, have your letters sent to you c/o the American Express offices in major cities, which will receive and forward mail for you *if* you are one of their clients (a travel-club card or an American Express traveler's check is proof). They charge a fee if you wish them to forward your mail.

If you don't use American Express, have your mail sent to you care of *Lista de Correos,* followed by the city, state, and country. In Mexican post offices there may actually be a "lista" posted near the Lista de Correos window bearing the names of all those for whom mail has been received. If there's no list, ask, and show them your passport so they can riffle through and look for your letters. If the city has more than one office, you'll have to go to the central post office—not a branch—to get your mail. By the way, in many post offices they return your mail to sender if it has been there for more than 10 days. Make sure people don't send you letters too early. In major Mexican cities there are also branches of U.S. express mail companies such as Federal Express and DHL as well as private mailboxes such as Mail Boxes Etc.

Maps   AAA maps to Mexico are quite good and available free to members at any AAA office in the U.S.

Newspapers and Magazines   The English-language newspaper *The News*, published in Mexico City, carries world news and commentaries, and a calendar of the day's events including concerts, art shows, and plays. Newspaper kiosks in larger Mexican cities will carry a selection of English-language magazines.

Passports   See Section 1, "Information, Entry Requirements, and Money," earlier in this chapter.

Pets   Taking a pet into Mexico entails a lot of red tape. Consult the Mexican National Tourist Council office nearest you (see Section 1, "Information, Entry Requirements, and Money," earlier in this chapter).

Photography   All archeological sites and many museums have restrictions on the use of personal cameras. At archeological sites visitors using their own video cameras are charged $8.50. A similar charge may be levied at all sites for still cameras; some sites charge it while others do not. It's courteous to ask permission before photographing anyone.

Police   Police in Mexico are generally to be suspected rather than trusted; however, you'll find many who are quite helpful with directions, even going so far as to lead you where you want to go.

Prices   In 1993 the Mexican government began allowing hotels and restaurants the right to set their own prices. Previously each establishment was graded by the government and given an official price structure by which to operate. Now these businesses can charge what the traffic will bear. Businesses are still finding their way in this new, free environment; some took the opportunity to raise prices dramatically while others changed prices little or not at all. Some found out there were no takers for their raised rates and they reduced them. Some seem to have high posted rates, but when clients left without booking rooms at that price, they then offered lower, "promotional" rates, which seem more permanent than their posted rates. When in doubt at a hotel, ask to see their rate sheet, which is required to be posted within view. If prices are high, leave and go to another hotel—this sends the message that the hotel is charging too much. In the past, quoted prices were required to include the 10% IVA tax. Now a quoted price does not have to include tax, so be sure to ask before ordering a meal or taking a room. The deregulation of prices also affects taxis, tours, and car rentals.

Radio and TV   Many hotels now have antennae capable of bringing in U.S. TV channels. Large cities will have English-language stations and music.

Restrooms   The best bet in Mexico is to use restrooms in restaurants and hotel public areas. Always carry your own toilet paper and hand soap, neither of which is in great supply in Mexican restrooms. Public facilities, usually near the central market, vary in cleanliness and usually have an attendant who charges a few pesos for toilet use and a few squares of toilet paper. Pemex gas stations have improved the maintenance of their restrooms along major highways. No matter where you are, even if the toilet flushes with paper, there'll be a waste basket for paper disposal. Many people come from homes without plumbing and are not accustomed to toilets that will take paper, and will throw paper on the floor rather than put it in the toilet—thus you'll see the basket no matter what quality of place you are in. On the other hand the water pressure in many establishments is so low that paper won't go down. There's often a sign saying "don't" flush paper: "No tirar papel en toilet."

Safety   Whenever you're traveling in an unfamiliar city or country, stay alert. Be aware of your immediate surroundings. Wear a moneybelt and hold on to your camera or purse, and keep your valuables in the hotel safe. This will minimize the possibility of your becoming a victim of crime.

Crime is more of a problem in Mexico than it once was. Although you will feel physically safer in most Mexican cities than in comparable big cities at home, you must take some basic, sensible precautions.

First, remember that you're a tourist, and an obvious target for crime. Beware of pickpockets on crowded buses, the Metro, and in markets. Guard your possessions very carefully at all times; don't let packs or bags out of sight even for a second (the big first-class bus lines will store your bag in the luggage compartment under the bus, and that's generally all right, but keep your things with you on the less responsible second-class and village buses on country routes).

Next, if you have a car, park it in an enclosed or guarded lot at night. Vans are a special mark. Don't depend on "major downtown streets" to protect your car—park it in a private lot with a guard, or at least a fence with a locked gate.

Women must be careful in cities when walking alone, night or day. Busy streets are no problem, but empty streets (even if empty just for afternoon siesta) are lonely places.

Important warnings: Agreeing to carry a package back to the States for an acquaintance or a stranger could land you in jail for years and cost a lot of money to get you out. Never do it no matter how friendly, honest, or sincere the request. Perpetrators of this illegal activity prey on innocent-looking single travelers and especially senior citizens.

Allowing anyone into your room that you don't know could invite an instant robbery. This includes someone announcing him- or herself (by phone or at your hotel room door) as room service bringing a "free" meal or drinks as compliments of the house—or anything you didn't order. When you open the door expectantly, robbers burst in. Always use caution before opening your door to anyone. When in doubt, call hotel security or the reception desk.

Seasons and Booking   Those planning to be in popular cities such as Acapulco, Ixtapa, Cuernavaca, and the colonial village of Taxco on weekends and major holidays (Mexican as well as international) should make hotel reservations well in advance of the anticipated trip. Christmas, New Year's, and Easter week are the worst for crowding. Friday and Saturday nights are crowded in Cuernavaca, Taxco, and Acapulco. These cities begin to return to normal occupancy levels by 3pm each Sunday. If you discover it's a holiday when you're en route to the resort, plan to arrive early in the day to allow plenty of time for finding a room.

Taxes   There's a 10% IVA (value added) tax on goods and services in Mexico; always check whether it's included in the quoted and posted prices.

Telephone and Fax   Area codes and city exchanges are being changed all over the country. If you have difficulty reaching a number, ask an operator for assistance. Mexico does not have helpful recordings to inform you of changes or new numbers.

Most public pay phones in the country have been converted to Ladatel phones, many of which are both coin- and card-operated. Those that accept coins take the old 100 peso coins; at some yet unannounced point they may begin accepting New Peso coins. Instructions on the phones tell you how to use them. Local calls generally cost the peso equivalent of 75¢ per minute. At some point you'll hear three odd-sounding beeps, and then you'll be cut off unless you deposit more coins. Ladatel cards come in denominations of 10, 20, and 30 New Pesos. If you're planning to make many calls, purchase the 30–New Peso card; it takes no time at all to use up a 10-peso card (about $3.35). They're sold at pharmacies, bookstores, and grocery stores near Ladatel phones. You insert the card, dial your number, and start talking, all the while watching a digital counter tick away your money.

Next is the caseta de larga distancia (long-distance telephone office), found all over Mexico. Most bus stations and airports now have specially staffed rooms exclusively for making long-distance calls and sending faxes. Often they are efficient and inexpensive, providing the client with a computer printout of the time and charges. In other places, often pharmacies, the clerk will place the call for you, then you step into a private booth to take the call. Whether it's a special long-distance office or a pharmacy there's usually a service charge of around $3.50 to make the call, which you pay in addition to any call costs. If you call collect, you pay only the service charge.

For long-distance calls you can access an English-speaking AT&T operator by dialing the star button twice, then 09. If that fails, try dialing 09 for an international operator. To call the U.S. or Canada, tell the operator that you want a collect call (*una llamada por cobrar*), or station-to-station (*teléfono a teléfono*), or person-to-person (*persona a persona*). Collect calls are the least expensive of all, but sometimes caseta offices won't make them, so you'll have to pay on the spot.

To make a long-distance call from Mexico to another country, first dial 95 for the U.S. and Canada, or 98 for anywhere else in the world. Then dial the area code and number you are calling.

To call long-distance (abbreviated "lada") within Mexico, dial 91, the area code, then the number. Mexico's area codes (*claves*) may be one, two, or three numbers and are usually listed in the front of telephone directories. In this book the area code is listed under "Fast Facts" for each town. (Area codes, however, are changing throughout the country; see above).

To place a phone call to Mexico from your home country, dial the international service (011), Mexico's country code (52), then the Mexican area code (for Acapulco, for example, that would be 74), then the local number. Keep in mind that calls to Mexico are quite expensive, even if dialed direct from your home phone.

Better hotels, which have more sophisticated tracking equipment, may charge for each local call made from your room. Budget or moderately priced hotels often don't charge for local calls, since they don't have the sophisticated phone equipment to keep track of calls made from individual rooms. To avoid checkout shock, it's best to ask in advance if local calls are extra. Hotels with sophisticated telephone systems are charging between 50¢ and $1 per call. In addition, if you make a long-distance call from your hotel room, there is usually a hefty service charge added to the cost of the call.

Time   Central standard time prevails throughout most of Mexico. The west coast states of Sonora, Sinaloa, and parts of Nayarit are on mountain standard time. The state of Baja California Norte is on Pacific standard time, but Baja California Sur is on mountain time. Beginning in the spring of 1995, Mexico may adopt daylight saving time to save on energy costs. Baja California already uses it between late April and October.

Tipping   Throw out the ironclad 15% rule right away in budget restaurants south of the border, no matter what other travel literature may say. Do as the locals do: For meals costing under $3, leave the loose change; for meals costing from $4 to $5, leave 6% to 10%, depending on service. Above $5, you're into the 10% to 15% bracket. Some of the more crass high-priced restaurants will actually add a 15% "tip" to your bill. Leave nothing extra if they do.

Bellboys and porters will expect about 25¢ per bag. You needn't tip taxi drivers unless they've rendered some special service—carrying bags or trunks.

Tourist Offices See Section 1, "Information, Entry Requirements, and Money," earlier in this chapter, and also specific city chapters.

Visas See Section 1, "Information, Entry Requirements, and Money," earlier in this chapter.

Water Most hotels have decanters or bottles of purified water in the rooms and the better hotels have either purified water from regular taps or special taps marked AGUA PURIFICADA. In resort areas, hoteliers are beginning to charge for in-room bottled water. Virtually any hotel, restaurant, or bar will bring you purified water if you specifically request it, but you'll usually be charged for it.

Wire Funds If you need cash in a hurry, Dineros en Minutos (Money in Minutes) is affiliated with Western Union and makes wire cash transactions at Electrika furniture and electronic stores in Mexico. Your contact on the other end presents cash to Western Union, which is credited by Electrika, and presented (in pesos) to you. The service only recently began in Mexico, but 500 outlets are planned.

CHAPTER 3

GETTING TO KNOW ACAPULCO

- **WHAT'S SPECIAL ABOUT ACAPULCO**
1. **ORIENTATION**
2. **GETTING AROUND**
- **FAST FACTS: ACAPULCO**

The astounding thing about Acapulco (pop. 600,000) is its perennial romantic reputation and its jet-set image, though it's been attracting vacationers for almost 60 years. This city, spreading across foothills around a vast blue bay, is an exciting playground and a bustling commercial center. And it's still growing and adding sparkle to the nighttime hillside glitter: Condominium and time-share units are sprouting up all along the bay, up the verdant mountainsides, and along the beaches. Fabulous new villas continue to emerge behind exclusive rock walls in posh suburbs that wind from the shoreline to the mountaintops. The latest addition is the upscale **Acapulco Diamante.** An enormous development running along the coast from Puerto Marquéz almost to the airport, it will include several luxury hotels, including the Sheraton, Vidafel, and new Camino Real hotels.

A real city rather than simply a resort, Acapulco (which in Nahuatl means "place where they were destroyed") has its share of grit along with the glitz. There are slums as well as villas and some of the hotels could use a face-lift. But the Acapulco of a few years ago, with a well-used edge to it and annoying street vendors who dogged your steps and interrupted your pleasure at every turn, has all changed.

Acapulco has been working hard to regain some of the old glamour that originally put it on the map in the 1950s. Then many Hollywood stars hung out there (some still do, in private homes and rented villas). In the past the city's touted cleanup campaigns resulted in few visible changes, but improvement is apparent now. A program called "ACA-Limpia" (Clean Acapulco) has encompassed cleaning up the bay (where whales have been sighted recently for the first time in years), sprucing up the Costera, removing the shack eyesores on the road from the airport, and moving itinerant street vendors to newly created but still convenient market areas. Vendors are now prohibited from approaching anyone either on the street or beach (though a few are still at it around the zócalo). Beaches are groomed and swept every morning and vigilantly patrolled by special police. New city buses have been added and old ones have received new paint inside and out. Sturdy wooden blue-and-white beach chairs have replaced worn ones, and dot beaches all along the bay. All day city employees wielding brooms sweep up the dirt and accumulated trash along the Costera Alemán.

Acapulco has always been known for its restaurants, which are changing and improving their menus, and new eateries are opening. And of course when it comes to nightlife, the vibrant variety of this city's discos and clubs is hard to top in Mexico, just as the view of Acapulco Bay at night, spangled with twinkling lights, remains one of the most breathtaking views in the world.

WHAT'S SPECIAL ABOUT ACAPULCO

Nightlife
- ☐ Acapulco's vibrant and varied nightlife, unrivaled in all of Mexico.

Views
- ☐ The world-famous view of Acapulco Bay at night, glittering with lights.
- ☐ Stunning sunsets, especially from the beach at nearby Pie de la Cuesta.

Dining
- ☐ Acapulco's top restaurants offer some of Mexico's finest dining.
- ☐ Something for every budget.

Beaches
- ☐ Beaches all around the bay, offering swimming and water sports.

Accommodations
- ☐ From fabulous hotels offering rooms with private swimming pools to your own exclusive villa with spectacular bay views, a pool, and a cook, maid, and gardener.

All combined, Acapulco is once again an extremely pleasant resort city for a vacation, whether you want to sample its nightlife, go deep-sea fishing, or experience the thrill of parasailing, or simply to relax.

1. ORIENTATION

ARRIVING

BY PLANE The following major airlines have nonstop or direct service to Acapulco: **Aeromexico** from Houston, New York, Guadalajara, Mexico City, Toluca, and Tijuana; **American** from Dallas/Fort Worth; **Continental** from Houston and Newark; **Delta** from Dallas/Fort Worth and Los Angeles; **Mexicana** from Chicago, Los Angeles, and Mexico City; **Taesa** from Laredo, Mexico City, and Guadalajara. Regional carriers include **AeroLibertad** from Ixtapa/Zihuatanejo and Oaxaca; and **AeroMorelos** from Cuernavaca Puebla. Check with a travel agent about charter flights.

BY BUS Buses from Mexico City to Acapulco leave from the Terminal Central de Autobuses del Sur (Tasqueño Metro line) for the seven-hour trip. The bus line **Estrella de Oro** has hourly service from Mexico City to Acapulco, but try to reserve your seat a few days in advance. There's little difference between express and deluxe service. **Lineas Unidas del Sur/Flecha Roja** also runs 24 daily buses to Acapulco from Mexico City's south bus station. From Ixtapa/Zihuatanejo, **Estrella Blanca** has six direct buses daily and nine *de paso* buses to Acapulco.

BY CAR From Mexico City, take Highway 95 south—either the curvy toll-free highway (a seven-hour drive) or 95D, the toll highway, (which cuts the drive to 3½ to 4 hours but costs around $80 one way. From Taxco the free road is in good condition and it's worth taking to save around $40 in tolls from there through Chilpancingo to Acapulco. From points north or south along the coast, the only choice is Highway 200.

DEPARTING

BY PLANE   Airline offices are at the airport and/or downtown: **Aeromexico** (tel. 85-1600 for reservations, or at the airport 66-9104); **American** (tel. 84-1244 or 84-1179 for reservations, or at the airport 84-0372); **Aerocaribe** and **Aerocozumel,** at the airport (tel. 84-2521); **Continental,** at the airport (tel. 66-9063); **Delta,** at the airport (tel. 84-0716, 84-0717, or toll free 91-800/9-0221 in Mexico); **Mexicana** (tel. 84-6943, 84-6890, or at the airport 84-1815); **SARO** (tel. toll free 91-800/8-3224) in Mexico; **Taesa** (tel. 66-9067 for reservations, or at the airport 86-4576 or 81-1214).

Transportación Aeropuerto (tel. 85-2332, or 83-6500) has colectivo service to and from the airport. Call the day before your departure for a reservation. One-way costs $7.50 per person; children pay half price. The service picks you up 90 minutes (flights within Mexico) to two hours (international flights) before your departure time. Taxis from town to the airport cost $20.

BY BUS   From Acapulco, **Estrella de Oro** (tel. 85-8705 or 85-9360) has more than a dozen direct buses daily to Mexico City, three to Taxco at 7am, 9am, and 4:30pm, and several to Ixtapa/Zihuatanejo daily. **Lineas Unidas del Sur/Flecha Roja** (tel. 82-0351) also has frequent buses to Mexico City, Chilpancingo, and Taxco, but they are not as nice as those of Estrella de Oro. **Estrella Blanca** (tel. 83-0802) has service to Ixtapa/Zihuatanejo, Monterrey, Zacatecas, Guadalajara, and the region around San Luis Potosí.

The bus station for **Lineas Unidas del Sur/Flecha Roja** is in the market area at Cuauhtémoc 97, about six blocks from the zócalo, or main square (downtown), and close to many downtown budget hotels. The **Estrella de Oro** bus station is much farther from downtown at Cuauhtémoc 1490 and Massieu, but still within walking distance of some economical accommodations on the Costera. Local buses pass the terminal going in both directions on Cuauhtémoc. There's a hotel reservation service in the lobby there. The relatively new (1990) **Estrella Blanca** terminal at Ejido 47 is north of downtown and farthest from our hotel selections. This station also has a hotel reservation service, Sendetur, open 24 hours.

CITY LAYOUT

Acapulco stretches for more than four miles around the huge bay, so walking to see it all is impractical. The main boulevard, the Costera (Costera Miguel Alemán), follows the outline of the bay from downtown on the west side, where "Old Acapulco" began, to the Hyatt Regency Hotel on the east side. Most hotels are either on the Costera and the beach, or a block or two away; as you go east from downtown they become increasingly luxurious. Avenida Cuauhtémoc is the major artery inland and runs roughly parallel to the Costera.

Street names and numbers in this city can be confusing and hard to find—many streets are not well marked, or change names unexpectedly. Fortunately you're seldom far from the Costera, so it's hard to get really lost.

NEIGHBORHOODS IN BRIEF

The areas below begin in order from south of Acapulco to north around the bay.

Las Brisas   This cliffside area between the naval base and the airport is dotted with exclusive hotels, villas, and restaurants. The main thoroughfare from the airport, called the Carretera Escénica (Scenic Road), runs through it.

Acapulco Diamante and Punta Diamante   Acapulco Diamante is a massive resort development that stretches from just north of the airport beginning just before the Acapulco Princess Hotel and ending at Puerto Marquéz, south of the naval base. Punta Diamante is part of that project but refers to a mountaintop area overlooking Puerto Marquéz. Developers are carving streets there that will front even more villas, condominiums, and hotels.

The Costera Miguel Alemán This main artery connects with the Carretera Escénica coming south from the airport and runs north the length of the bay into "Old Acapulco," where it becomes the Gran Vía Tropical as it rises around the bay. It's lined with high-rise hotels and beaches, including Icacos, Condesa, and Hornos beaches.

Downtown, the Zócalo, and "Old Acapulco" Acapulco was located originally at the northern end of the bay around a small plaza (the zócalo) near the docks and fort. Between the mid-1930s to the late 1950s, fashionable Acapulco fanned out south up into the cliffside around the bay with hotels that overlooked the bay and beaches and the open ocean. This area became what is called today "Traditional" or "Old" Acapulco. Until the late 1950s these mountainside hotels were *the* place to stay. But in the mid- to late 1950s new, more modern hotels began to spring up on the beaches along the Costera. Even with their fabulous, palatial palm-shaded pools, and notorious, swanky ballroom nightlife, the beachless mountain hotels couldn't compete with the new hotels by the sand and ocean. But the older area still exudes the charm remaining from those famous days when Acapulco was a mecca for Hollywood stars, and constant fodder for tabloid news.

2. GETTING AROUND

BY BUS For a city with such a confusing street system, it's amazingly easy and inexpensive to use city buses. Two kinds of buses run along the Costera: pastel color-coded, air-conditioned buses for tourists and regular "school buses" for locals. As a rule, both types pick up tourists and nontourists alike. Covered bus stops are all along the Costera with handy maps on the walls showing tourist bus routes to major sights and hotels.

"Caleta Directo" or **"Base-Caleta"** buses run between the naval base (by the Hyatt Regency) and Caleta Beach and will take you to the zócalo, Hornos, Caleta, and Caletilla beaches along the Costera; some buses return along the same route, others go around the peninsula and return to the Costera. As for the restaurants and nightspots in the upscale hotel district on the north and east sides of the bay, catch either a **"Base-Caleta"** or **"Base-Cine Río-Caleta"** bus. The latter runs inland along Cuauhtémoc to the Estrella de Oro bus terminal, then heads back to the

IMPRESSIONS

That picturesque port of Acapulco has of late years fallen into disuse, since new ways have been opened across the continent, but in olden times it was a busy and a celebrated maritime city. To it went, and from it sailed, all those grand old galleons, which performed their portion of the voyage between the Indies and Spain, six months, sometimes on the voyage between Manilla and the Mexican coast.
— F.A. OBER, *TRAVELS IN MEXICO*, 1884

Acapulco today is a perfect blend of Riviera sunshine and South Sea glamour.
—BYRON STEEL, *LET'S VISIT MEXICO*, 1946

Costera and beach at the Ritz Hotel and continues east along the Costera to Icacos Beach near the Hyatt Recengy Hotel. **"Zócalo Directo"** and **"Caleta Directo"** buses follow the same route in the opposite direction. For longer expeditions there are buses to Puerto Marquéz and Las Brisas to the east (**"Puerto Marquéz–Base"** and **"Las Brisas"**) and Pie de la Cuesta to the west (**"Zócalo–Pie de la Cuesta"**). Pie de la Cuesta buses start from Sanborn's, a block from the zócalo. Be sure to verify the time and place of the last bus back if you hop one of these!

For a cheap way to get to the discos and restaurants south of town near Hotel Las Brisas, take a **"Base" bus** as far as the Hyatt Regency. Then take a **"Las Brisas" bus** the rest of the way. City buses stop at 10pm.

BY TAXI Taxis charge $2 to $8 for a ride within the city and more if you go farther out. For approximate prices, ask at your hotel or scan one of the taxi tariff lists found in most major hotel lobbies. Always establish the price with the driver before starting out. Report any trouble or overcharges to the *Focuruduría del Turista*—the Tourist Assistance Office on the Costera in front of the Convention Center (tel. 74/84-4583 or 84-7050, ext. 165 or 175).

 ACAPULCO

American Express The main office is at Costera Alemán 709, east of the Diana traffic circle (tel. 84-1095 travel services; 84-5200 financial services; 84-5550 customer service; 84-6060 tours); another branch is at the Hyatt Regency near the naval base (tel. 84-2888).

Area Code The area code is 74.

Climate Although June through October is the rainy season, June, September, and October are the wettest months, while July and August are relatively dry. Most rains occur at night and are seldom enough to spoil a vacation.

Consular Agents The **U.S.** has an agent at the Hotel Club del Sol (tel. 85-6600, ext. 7348), across from the Hotel Acapulco Plaza; open Monday to Friday 10am to 2pm. **Canada's** consular agent (tel. 85-6621) is also at the Hotel Club del Sol; open Monday to Friday 9am to 1pm. The agent for the **United Kingdom** (tel. 84-6605) is at Hotel Las Brisas, in the Las Brisas area; open Monday to Friday 9am to 6pm.

Currency Exchange Banks along the Costera are open Monday through Friday from 9am to 1 or 1:30pm (though hours for exchanging money may be shorter) and generally have the best rates. *Casas de cambio* (currency booths) along the street may have better exchange rates than hotels.

Information The State of Guerrero Tourism Office operates the Focuraduría del Turista at street level in front of the Convention Center (tel. 84-4583 or 84-7050, ext. 165 or 175). They offer maps and information about the city and state. It's open daily from 9am to 9pm.

Parking It is illegal to park on the Costera at any time.

Post Office The central post office is on the Costera near the zócalo and Sanborn's. Other branches are located in the Estrella de Oro bus station on Cuauhtémoc, inland from the Acapulco Ritz Hotel; and on the Costera near Caleta Beach.

Safety Pay careful attention to warning flags posted on Acapulco beaches! These alert you to the presence of riptides, which claim a few lives every year. Red or black flags mean stay out of the water, yellow signifies caution, and white or green flags mean it's safe to swim. Don't swim on any beach that fronts an open sea. But don't let down your guard on the bays either. It's difficult to imagine how powerful an undertow can be. Along Condesa Beach swimming areas are marked off by colored floating ropes, and lifeguards are on duty.

As always, tourists are vulnerable to thieves. This is especially true when you are shopping in a market, lying on the beach, wearing jewelry, or carrying a camera, purse, or bulging wallet. To remove temptation from would-be thieves, purchase one of those waterproof plastic tubes on a string to wear around your neck at the beach—it's big enough for a few bills and your room key. Street vendors and hotel variety shops sell them.

Tourist Police   If you see policemen in white and blue uniforms, they're from a special corps of English-speaking police who assist tourists.

Telephone Numbers   As mentioned above, the area code for Acapulco is 74, a recent change from the old one, which was 748. Be aware that now all Acapulco numbers begin with 8, but many people have not made the transition and still give their numbers without the 8, or still print the area code as 748.

CHAPTER 4

WHERE TO STAY IN ACAPULCO

The descriptions below begin with the very expensive resorts south of town (nearest the airport) and continue along the famous main avenue, Costera Miguel Alemán, to those less expensive hotels north of town in what is considered the zócalo, downtown, or "Old Acapulco" part of the city. Though many hotels charge well over $100 a day for a room, there are many very comfortable but much less expensive lodging choices in Acapulco. On the other end of the price scale, private, very secluded villas are available for rent all over the hills south of town; renting one of these luxurious and palatial homes makes an unforgettable Acapulco vacation alternative. See Chapter 2, Section 9 for U.S. companies handling Acapulco villa rentals.

1. SOUTH OF TOWN

The steep forested hillsides south of town between the naval base and Puerto Marquéz hold some of Acapulco's most exclusive hotels, restaurants, and villas for which Acapulco is justly famous. The new **Hotel Camino Real** on Playa Guitarrón and the enormous **Vidafel** resort, next to the Acapulco Princess Hotel, just opened as this book went to press.

VERY EXPENSIVE

ACAPULCO PRINCESS, El Revolcadero Beach, Acapulco, Gro. 39868. **Tel. 74/84-3100,** or toll free 800/223-1818 in the U.S. Fax 74/84-7185. 916 rms, 92 suites, 11 penthouses. A/C MINIBAR TV TEL
$ Rates: High season (including breakfast and dinner) $320–$600 single or double; low season (without meals) $120–$290 single or double. **Parking:** Free.
The first luxury hotel most people see on arriving in Acapulco is the 480-acre Acapulco Princess on El Revolcadero Beach just off the road to the airport. Set apart from the Manhattan of skyscraper hotels downtown, the Princess complex, framed by the fabulously groomed and palm-dotted golf course, reminds one of a great Aztec ceremonial center. Its pyramidlike buildings dominate the flat surrounding land.

To Pie de la Cuesta
Ixtapa - Zihuatanejo

Flecha
Roja Bus

Av. Cuauhtémoc

Parque Papagayo

Vasco Nuñez

Río Camarón

Playa Hornos

Playa Ho

La Quebrada

Fort
San Diego

Zócalo

Playa Langosta

Commercial Wharfs

Bahía de Acapulco

Costera M. Alemán

Playa Larga

La Pinzona

Gran Via Tropical

Av. de la Aguada

Av. A. López Mateos

Playa Caletilla

Playa Caleta

Playa Roqueta

Isla La Roqueta

Río Coyuca

Laguna de
Coyuca

Pie de la Cuesta

Acapulco

Puerto
Marqués

Laguna de
Tres Palos

Aeropuerto

Barra Vieja

Bahía de Acapulco

6998

ACCOMMODATIONS:

Acapulco Princess Hotel **31**
Acapulco Ritz Hotel **16**
Acapulco Sheraton Resort **27**
Belmar Hotel **4**
Calinda Acapulco
  Quality Inn **20**
Camino Real Diamante **26**

Continental Plaza Acapulco **14**
Fiesta Americana
  Condesa Acapulco **18**
Hotel Acapulco Tortuga **15**
Hotel Boca Chica **2**
Hotel El Cano **21**
Hotel Howard Johnson Maralisa **17**
Hotel Sinfonia del Mar **7**

Lindavista Hotel **4**
Hotel Westin Las Brisas **30**
Motel la Jolla **3**
Paraíso Radisson Hotel **13**
Plaza Las Glorias
  Hotel/El Mirador **12**
Villa Romana **8**
Villa Vera Raquet Club **22**

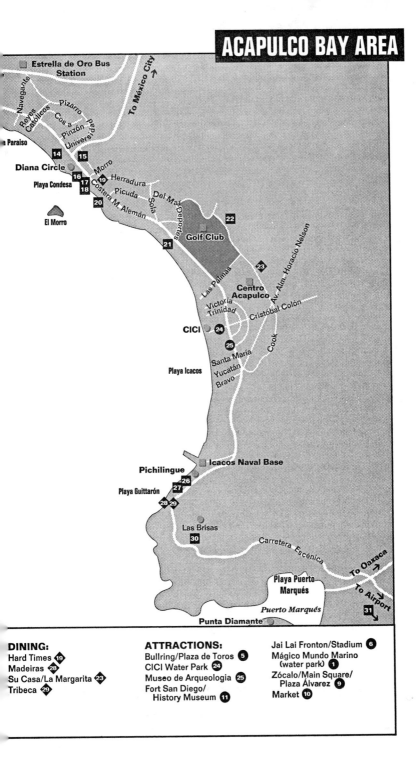

ACAPULCO BAY AREA

Estrella de Oro Bus Station

Navegante
Reyes Católicos
Pizarro
Cos a
Pinzón
Univers
Peppi

To México City →

a Paraiso

14 **15**

Diana Circle

Morro

16 **17** **19** Herradura
Playa Condesa **18**
Picuda
20 Del Mar
Costera M. Alemán
Sola
Deportes

El Morro

21

22

Golf Club

Las Palmas

23

Centro
Acapulco

Av. Alm. Horacio Nelson

Victoria
Trinidad
Cristóbal Colón

CICI **24**

Cook

25

Santa María
Yucatán
Bravo

Playa Icacos

Icacos Naval Base

Pichilingue
26
27
Playa Guittarón

28 **29**

Las Brisas

30

Carretera Escénica

To Oaxaca →

To Airport →

Playa Puerto
Marqués

31

Puerto Marqués

Punta Diamante

DINING:
Hard Times **19**
Madeiras **28**
Su Casa/La Margarita **23**
Tribeca **29**

ATTRACTIONS:
Bullring/Plaza de Toros **5**
CICI Water Park **24**
Museo de Arqueologia **25**
Fort San Diego/
 History Museum **11**

Jai Lai Fronton/Stadium **6**
Mágico Mundo Marino
 (water park) **1**
Zócalo/Main Square/
 Plaza Álvarez **9**
Market **10**

Within the spacious and gracious complex of buildings at the Acapulco Princess is a self-contained tropical-paradise world: a system of waterfalls, fountains, and pools set amid tropical trees, flowers, and shrubs, with swans, peacocks, and flamingos. Though the beach is long, inviting, and beautifully kept, there is no bay and therefore swimming in the open here is unsafe; look but don't go in. The dramatic lobby is enormous, and other public spaces are bold and striking in the best Mexican fashion. Guest rooms at the Acapulco Princess are big, bright, and luxurious, with marble floors and balconies. Room rates vary from selection of standard, superior, and deluxe rooms, and two types of suites, with the highest prices for the one- and two-bedroom penthouses.

During high season, when prices include two meals, children between ages 4 and 12 pay $33 each for meals. During low season children within these age groups may share a room with two adults at no extra charge. Ask about special packages which may include unlimited golf and daytime tennis, free use of the fitness center and other perks, and, during high season, perhaps a seven-night stay for the price of five nights.

Next door is the older, more sedate **Hotel Pierre Marqués,** open during high season only and offering Princess amenities and privileges at a fraction of Princess prices.

Dining/Entertainment: Restaurants are open seasonally and therefore all may not be open when you are there, but the lineup includes: Le Gourmet, the elegant French restaurant, and La Hacienda for excellent Mexican specialties, both open only for dinner; Chula Vista and La Posadita for buffets; and La Princesa and Veranda for international buffets. El Jardín serves casual snacks 24 hours daily, and there's a snack shop on the golf course. Bars include Laguna and La Cascada, where mariachis often entertain; La Palma and La Palapa by the beach; and Grotto, the swim-up bar. Tiffany's is the trendy disco that gets going late and stays open until the wee hours of the morning. Garden theme parties, with regional music and dancing, are often offered.

Services: Laundry and room service, travel agency, babysitter, cribs, wheelchairs.

Facilities: Five free-form swimming pools, a saltwater lagoon with water slide, two 18-hole golf courses, and nine outdoor tennis courts (all lit for night play) and two indoor courts with stadium seating. Fishing and other water sports can be arranged with the hotel's travel agency. There's also a barber and beauty shop with massage available, a fitness center with aerobic classes, boutiques, a flower shop, and an ice machine on each floor.

CAMINO REAL DIAMANTE, Carretera Escénica Km 14, Calle Bajacatitia 18, Pichilinque, Puerto Marquéz, Acapulco, Gro. 39887. Tel and fax 74/81-2010, or toll free 800/7-CAMINO in the U.S. and Canada. 156 rms. A/C MINIBAR TV TEL

$ Rates: High season $170–$240. Low season $155–$225. Ask about low season and midweek discounts.

One of Acapulco's finest, this hotel opened in 1993 in a secluded location on 81 acres as part of the enormous Acapulco Diamante project. From the Carretera Escénica, you wind down, down, down a handsome brick road to the hotel's location beside and overlooking Puerto Marquéz Bay. Reception is gracious in the expansive lobby, which offers a sitting area and an enormous terrace facing the water. Elevators whisk you to all but the outside terrace levels. The spacious rooms, each with a small sitting area, have cool marble floors, and are furnished in an elegantly austere way. Televisions and minibars are sequestered within lightly hued wooden armoires. Each room has a ceiling fan in addition to air conditioning and a safety deposit box in the closet.

It's secluded here in this relaxing, completely self-contained resort. And it's an ideal choice for accommodations if you already know Acapulco and don't need to explore much, since a taxi to town costs $6 one way.

Dining/Entertainment: La Vela is the outdoor seafood grill overlooking the bay. Cabo Diamante features both Mexican and international food. The open-air lobby bar facing the bay is the place to be for evening cocktails.

Services: Room and laundry service, travel agency, car rental.

Facilities: Tri-level pool, tennis courts, beauty and barber shops, and shopping arcade. The health club offers aerobics, massage, and complete workout equipment.

WESTIN LAS BRISAS, Apdo. Postal 281, Carretera Escénica, Las Brisas, Acapulco, Gro. 39868. Tel. 74/84-1580, or toll free 800/228-3000 in the U.S. Fax 74/84-2269. 300 units. A/C MINIBAR TV TEL

$ Rates (including continental breakfast): Nov–Apr $245–$1,125 double; $25 per day service charge extra (in lieu of all tips). May–Oct $190–$910 double plus service charge. Two children stay free in parents' room.

Some consider this the ultimate hostelry in Acapulco. Perched in tiers on a hillside overlooking the bay, it presents a pink stucco facade that is a traditional trademark in Acapulco. The pink theme is carried on to the 175 pink Jeeps rented exclusively to Las Brisas guests. The hotel is a community unto itself: The elegantly simple, marble-floored rooms are like separate little villas built into a terraced hillside, and each has a private (or semiprivate) swimming pool with a panoramic bay view. Spacious Regency Club rooms are at the top of the property and all have private pools and fabulous commanding views of the bay. Altogether, there are 300 casitas and 250 swimming pools. Although its location on the airport road southeast of the bay means that Las Brisas is a long way from the center of town, guests tend to find this an advantage rather than a drawback. Outsiders aren't permitted on the property without an invitation.

Prices for this luxury (wait till you see the lights of all Acapulco twinkling across the bay) depend on the number of bedrooms you want, whether you want a room with a private or shared pool, and whether you choose to be a Regency Club guest.

Dining/Entertainment: Complimentary breakfast of fruit, rolls, and coffee served to each room daily. Bella Vista is the reservation-only (and now open to the public) panoramic-view restaurant, open 7 to 11pm daily. El Mexicano Restaurant on a starlit terrace is open Saturday to Thursday evenings. La Concha Beach Club offers seafood daily from 12:30 to 4:30pm. The Deli Shop is open from 11am to 7pm daily.

Services: Travel agency and gas station, express checkout with advance notice, 24-hour shuttle transportation around the resort, laundry and room service, beauty and barber shops.

Facilities: Private or shared pools with each room with fresh floating flowers daily; private La Concha Beach Club at the bottom of the hill has both fresh and saltwater pools; five tennis courts; pink Jeeps rent for $85 each a day and include tax, gas, mileage, and insurance.

EXPENSIVE

ACAPULCO SHERATON RESORT, Costera Guitarrón 110, Acapulco, Gro. 39300. Tel. 74/84-3737, or toll free 800/325-3535 in the U.S. Fax 74/84-3760. 226 rms, 8 suites. A/C MINIBAR TV TEL

$ Rates: High season $160–$190 single or double; low season $115–$150 single or double. **Parking:** $5 daily.

Opened in 1992, this is one of the newest resort hotels north of town. Secluded and tranquil, and completely invisible from the scenic highway, it's nestled in a landscaped ravine with a waterfall and wonderful bay view. The 17 multistoried units descend to a small beach beside the pool. Each building unit has an elevator, making it possible to come and go from the lobby to the rooms without climbing stairs —though you may need a trail of rice to remember your route. Rooms have travertine tile floors and rattan furniture and come with a private or shared balcony, purified tap water, and in-room safety-deposit boxes. Some have separate living room and kitchenette. The 32 Sheraton Club rooms have extra amenities. All rooms have remote-control TV, alarm clocks, and tub/shower combinations. It's located between La Base and Las Brisas, off the Carretera Escénica at Playa Guitarrón at the eastern end of the bay. A small sign marks the turnoff.

Dining/Entertainment: La Bahía Restaurant, with a magnificent semicircular bay view, elegantly set tables, and international cuisine, is open for all three meals. El Jardín del Mar, the open-air restaurant overlooking the ocean and pool, also serves all three meals. The Deli Garden, open for lunch, has Kosher service. The Lobby Bar offers live piano music nightly and a bay view. The famous Jorongo Bar of the Sheraton María Cristina in Mexico City is re-created here with its cantina atmosphere, live trio music, and regional food specialties. Restaurants and bars are seasonal and all may not be open during low season.

Services: Laundry and room service, travel agency, car rental; scheduled shuttle service to and from town may be offered.

Facilities: Beach, two swimming pools, two handicapped-equipped rooms, 20 no-smoking guest rooms, boutiques, beauty shops, small gym with sauna, steam room, and massage. The hotel has a tennis membership at the Club Brittanica and provides guests with free transportation.

2. CONVENTION CENTER & ICACOS BEACH AREA

These hotels are all on the far eastern side of the bay, near the Convention Center (Centro Acapulco) and CICI *(Centro Internacional de Convivencia Infantil)*, Acapulco's fabulous children's water amusement park.

VERY EXPENSIVE

VILLA VERA RACQUET CLUB, Lomas del Mar 35, Acapulco, Gro. 39690. Tel. 74/84-0333, or toll free 800/223-6510 in the U.S. Fax 74/84-7479. 81 rms, suites, and villas. A/C MINIBAR TV TEL

$ Rates: Las Casas de Villa, high season $820–$1,700, low season $650–$1,400; two-bedroom villa, high season $575–$650, low season $390; one-bedroom villa, high season $485, low season $325; suite, high season $325, low season $234; superior deluxe suite, high season $280, low season $195; superior room, high season $235, low season $165. No children under age 16 are accepted. **Parking:** Free.

What began as a private home with villas for visiting friends in the 1950s has become one of Acapulco's most exclusive inns. Pat and Richard Nixon celebrated their 25th wedding anniversary here, and President Eisenhower and Elvis Presley were

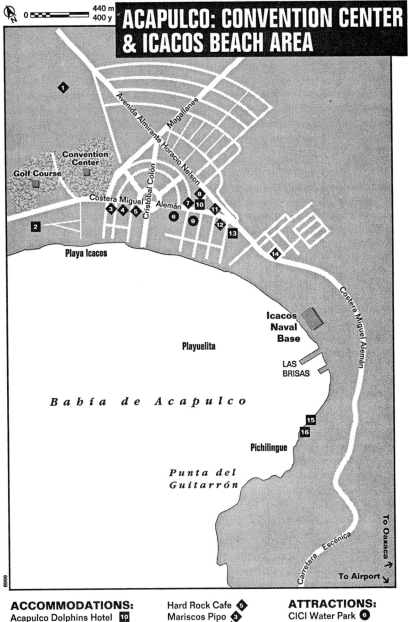

ACAPULCO: CONVENTION CENTER & ICACOS BEACH AREA

0 — 440 m / 400 y

Avenida Almirante Horacio Nelson

Magallanes

Convention Center

Golf Course

Costera Miguel Alemán

Cristóbal Colón

Playa Icacos

Icacos Naval Base

Playuelita

LAS BRISAS

Bahía de Acapulco

Pichilingue

Punta del Guitarrón

Carretera Escénica

To Oaxaca

To Airport

6669

ACCOMMODATIONS:
Acapulco Dolphins Hotel **10**
Acapulco Sheraton Resort **16**
Camino Real Diamante **15**
El Cano **2**
Hotel Sol-I-Mar **13**

DINING:
El Cabrito ◆**4**

Hard Rock Cafe ◆**5**
Mariscos Pipo ◆**3**
100% Natural ◆**12**
Restaurant Cocula ◆**8**
Restaurant Fersato's ◆**11**
Seraphino ◆**14**
Su Casa/La Magarita ◆**1**
Suntory ◆**7**

ATTRACTIONS:
CICI Water Park ●**6**
Cultural Center/
 Museo Antrolopolgía ●**9**

booked at the same time when Elvis filmed *Fun in Acapulco*. Elizabeth Taylor and Mike Todd tied the knot here with Debbie Reynolds and Eddie Fisher as attendants. The roster of who's who in guests doesn't stop even today, and the inn remains as captivating as ever for the rich and/or famous of our present era.

Spread out inland on a secluded 15-acre hillside with a spectacular view of Acapulco Bay, there's a range of choices in accommodations, all handsomely furnished. Private villas, called Las Casas de Villa Vera, include the Casa Lisa and Casa Alanda with four bedrooms. Both are sumptuously outfitted, luxury Mexican-style homes and come with 24-hour security, cook, servant, two maids, and gardeners. Casa Lisa, however, is not air-conditioned.

Spacious two-bedroom villas (there are three) include the Villa Laurel (the largest) with a private pool; Villa Teddy, also with private pool; and the Penthouse, with a spectacular view—but no private pool. Spacious one-bedroom villas (there are five of these) come with a private pool and terrace, separate living area, and huge bedrooms and baths. Suites (seven in all) have large living and bedroom areas and share a pool. Most of these have a terrace or patio and great bay views. Superior deluxe suites (there are eight of these), scattered throughout the grounds, have a large bedroom and sitting area and most have a shared pool. Most of the largish superior rooms (38 of these) are in one building and share a pool. Though there are many pools here, guests discover the place to see and be seen is at the main pool and other pools are practically empty during the day.

Dining/Entertainment: The dining terrace by the pool and overlooking the grounds and Acapulco Bay serves daily from 7:30am to 11pm.

Services: Room and laundry service, beauty shop with sauna and massage. Front desk will make car-rental and golf arrangements.

Facilities: One large pool by the outdoor dining terrace and 19 private pools; three lighted clay tennis courts with tennis pro and pro shop. Guests pay $17 per hour for tennis and nonguests pay $25.

EXPENSIVE

HOTEL EL CANO, Costera Alemán 75, Acapulco, Gro. 39690. Tel. 74/84-1950, or toll free 800/222-7692 in the U.S. Fax 74/84-2230. 144 rms. A/C TV TEL

$ Rates: $180 studio and standard room; $200 junior suite. Ask for promotional discount.

If you knew the old El Cano, you'll see that this completely new one is nothing like it. Completely gutted during two years of renovation, it reopened without showing even a hint of its former frumpy self. The lobby is a sea of Caribbean blue and white and the rooms are themed around trendy navy-and-white tile. All have tub/shower combinations, and ceiling fans in addition to the central air conditioning; all except studio rooms have balconies. The very large junior suites, all located on corners, have two queen-size beds and huge closets. Standard rooms are a little smaller than suites. Studios are quite small, with king-size beds and small sinks outside the

---

IMPRESSIONS

The original atmosphere of the old port exists no more. There are now broad paved streets, modern stores, and dozens of hotels, several of them huge luxury establishments. . . . There are, of course, compensations for the lost atmosphere: comfortable hotels, lively night clubs, a country club, and facilities for all known water sports. And the natural beauty of the place is such that no amount of modern construction could change it.
— G. M. BASHFORD, *TOURIST GUIDE TO MEXICO*, 1954.

FROMMER'S SMART TRAVELER: HOTELS

1. Absolutely never book a hotel listed in the Very Expensive, Expensive, or Moderate categories without first checking with hotels, travel agents, and airlines about packages. What you save from the hotel's advertised "rack" rate in a package can add days to your vacation.
2. When buying a package, be sure to note whether the hotel is on or near the beach or has a pool if these things are important to you.
3. Hotels in the lower end of package rates will not have the amenities of more expensive hotels.
4. May and June and September through December 15 is the low season, when room prices are cut substantially.
5. Now that Acapulco is only 3½ hours from Mexico City, it fills up on weekends, especially during school holidays, which includes July and August.
6. The higher up you are in high-rise hotels, the less adequate the air conditioning and the longer the wait for elevators. Request rooms on the first five or six floors.

bathroom area. In the studios a small portion of the TV armoire serves as a closet. The studios don't have balconies, but full sliding doors open to let in the breezes. All rooms have purified tap water and in-room safety-deposit boxes.

Dining/Entertainment: The informal Bambuco restaurant is by the pool and beach and is open from 9am to 11pm daily. The more formal Victoria is on an outdoor terrace overlooking the pool and beach and is open from 6 to 11pm daily.

Services: Room and laundry service, travel agency.

Facilities: One beachside pool, workout room, gift shop, boutiques, travel agency, beauty shop, massages, video-game room, an ice machine on each floor.

MODERATE

ACAPULCO DOLPHINS HOTEL, Costera Alemán 50, Acapulco, Gro. 39300. Tel. 74/84-4441 or 84-6678. Fax 74/84-3072. 255 rms. A/C TV TEL

$ Rates: High season $90 single or double. Low season $80 single or double.

A young and lively clientele that includes many French-speaking Canadians is attracted to this hotel. The rooms are tidy, modern, and comfortably furnished. There's a swimming pool in an interior courtyard. You'll find it south of CICI next to Fersato's restaurant.

HOTEL LA PALAPA, Playa Icacos, Fracc. Costa Azul, Fragata Yucatán 210, Acapulco, Gro. 39850. Tel. 74/84-5363, or toll free 91/800-10-9777 in Mexico. Fax 74/84-8399. 333 rms. A/C TEL

$ Rates (including breakfast): High season $110 single or double. Low season $105 single or double. Two children stay free in parents' room. **Parking:** Free.

Between the naval base and the Convention Center, you can't fail to see this hotel's 30 stories towering over the beach. While not in the luxury category, with white Formica furniture, every room has an ocean view and balcony. Some rooms are smaller than others but all are suites, with living area separate from the bedroom, many have small bars and a dining table, and all have in-room safety-deposit boxes. The palm-lined beachside pool is the hotel's relaxing focal point. Mariscos is the poolside restaurant, open 7:30am to 11pm daily. La Nouvell is off the lobby and open for all three meals. El Muelle Pizzaria, with seafood specialties, is open daily in high season only from 1 to 11pm. There's a travel agency in the lobby, and the hotel offers laundry and room service.

BUDGET

HOTEL SOL-I-MAR, Bravo 5, Acapulco, Gro. 39850. Tel. **74/84-1534.** Fax 74/84-1534. 70 rms. A/C (52 rms) FAN (18 rms)
$ Rates: High season $52 single, $68 double, $145 bungalow; Low season $35 single, $50 double, $127–$145 bungalow. **Parking:** Free.
Several two-story neocolonial buildings with lots of brick, tile, and wrought ironwork comprise this hotel complex just a block from the beach. It's a place wintering northerners call home year after year. Most of the rooms have kitchens and large private patios, and there are two small swimming pools. It's off the Costera behind the Romano Days Inn.

---

3. CONDESA BEACH & DIANA CIRCLE AREA

The row of gigantic hotels along the northern shore of Acapulco Bay has been photographed over and over for travel brochures and posters, and at dusk as the lights twinkle on, these giants certainly do offer a romantic vista.

EXPENSIVE

CALINDA ACAPULCO QUALITY INN, Costera Miguel Alemán 1260, Acapulco, Gro. 39300. Tel. **74/84-0410,** or toll free 800/228-5151 in the U.S. Fax 74/84-4676. 358 rms. A/C TV TEL
$ Rates: Year-round $80–$180 single, $85–$190 double.
You can't miss this tall cylindrical tower rising at the eastern edge of Condesa Beach. The design allows each room to have a view, usually of the bay. The guest rooms, though not strikingly furnished, are large and comfortable and most come with two double beds. Remodeling in recent years has given it a modern face-lift.

A package price will reduce the rates listed above, which otherwise are too high for the quality of accommodations. Numerous discount rates apply to senior citizens, government and military employees, corporations, and travel clubs such as AAA, Allstate, and Quest.

Dining/Entertainment: For snacks by the pool there's the Bergantin Snack Bar; El Delfín, the hotel's coffee shop, is open from 7am to 11pm. Las Palmeras on the mezzanine serves Mexican food nightly from 5:30pm to midnight. For cocktails, the Lobby Bar gets going around 6pm and stops at 1am, with a happy hour from 4 to 9pm when drinks are two for the price of one and live music between 9pm and 1am.

Services: Laundry and room service, travel agency.

Facilities: There's one swimming pool, several lobby boutiques, a pharmacy, beauty shop, ice machine on the third floor, two handicapped-equipped rooms, and four no-smoking floors.

CONTINENTAL PLAZA ACAPULCO, Costera Miguel Alemán, Acapulco, Gro. 39868. Tel. **74/84-0909,** or toll free 800/342-AMIGO in the U.S. Fax 74/ 84-2081. 370 rms, 12 suites. A/C MINIBAR TV TEL

$ Rates: High season $180–$211 standard single or double, $237 Continental Club. Low season $121–$145 standard single or double, $160 Continental Club.

The Continental Plaza Acapulco (formerly the Hyatt Continental) should be completely refurnished and remodeled when you travel. Rooms have purified tap water, and whitewashed rattan furniture against an oyster-white background, and all (except Lanai rooms) have balconies facing the ocean. Continental Club rooms, on the concierge floor, have complimentary continental breakfast as well as canapés and drinks in the early evening. The pride of the Continental and the focal point for relaxing is the swimming pool surrounding a "tropical island" luxuriously shaded by palms. It's the biggest pool in Acapulco. The island is filled with a bar, restaurant, and lounge chairs for sunning and sipping. The atmosphere around the pool is so sybaritic that you tend to forget the beach is right on the hotel's doorstep. Between the pool, beach, and numerous restaurants, the hotel is so well outfitted there's little need to venture off the property. A new condominium addition may be under way when you travel, which will have two tennis courts available to hotel guests.

Dining/Entertainment: The swim-up bar, Caracol, is open between 10am and 6pm, with two drinks for the price of one between 5 and 6pm. The Bar Marino, on the beach, is open between 10am and 10pm, with a happy hour between 4 and 5pm. The Lobby Bar Terraza serves between 10:30am and 1am, with a happy hour between 6 and 7pm and occasionally live music. La Margarita, with a view of the pool, is known for its breakfast buffet and taco and steak bar at night, and is open from 7am to 11pm. La Fontana serves Italian food between 6 and 11pm with room service for pizzas. El Varadero is the casual seafood specialty restaurant overlooking the water, and is open 10am to 10pm. The poolside snack bar, La Isla, is open during pool hours. Tony Roma Ribs is the hotel's focal point restaurant, cantilevered on the front of the hotel. Every Saturday evening there's a Mexican buffet in the garden; ask about other theme nights. The recreation director starts pool activities for all ages around noon daily.

Services: Laundry and room service, travel agency.

Facilities: Besides the one giant pool, there's a water slide. A playground for children with inner tubes and swings is in a grassy area separate from the pool. Lining the lobby area is a full range of shops, including a beauty shop. There are two handicapped-equipped rooms, and 35 rooms on two floors are no-smoking. The beauty shop has a sauna, and massages can be arranged.

FIESTA AMERICANA CONDESA ACAPULCO, Costera Miguel Alemán 1220, Acapulco, Gro. 39300. Tel. 74/84-2828, or toll free 800/223-2332 in the U.S. Fax 74/84-1828. 475 rms, 13 suites. A/C MINIBAR TV TEL

$ Rates: High season $225–$250 single or double. Low season $125–$162 single or double.

Once called the Condesa del Mar, the Fiesta Americana Condesa Acapulco is among Acapulco's long-standing favorite luxury hotels. The 18-story hotel towers above Condesa Beach, just east up the hill from the Glorieta Diana. The attractive and very comfortable rooms are furnished in soft pastels. Each has a private terrace with an ocean view. The more expensive rooms have the best bay views and all rooms have purified tap water.

Dining/Entertainment: The breezy lobby hosts live entertainment nightly beginning at 9:30pm, but it's open from 5pm to 2am. From the Techo del Mar (Roof of the Sea), the 18th-floor fine-dining restaurant, you have a marvelous panoramic view of the town and the bay and live (but soft) music for dining most evenings. The Chula Vista, by the children's pool, is open from 7am to 11pm.

Services: Laundry and room service, travel agency.

Facilities: The hotel's dramatic adult swimming pool is perched atop a hill with the land dropping off toward the bay, and this situation affords swimmers the best view of Acapulco from any pool in the city. Another smaller pool is reserved for children. There are two handicapped-equipped rooms, beauty shop, boutiques, and pharmacy.

MODERATE

HOTEL ACAPULCO TORTUGA, Costera Miguel Alemán 132, Acapulco, Gro. 39300. Tel. 74/84-8889, or toll free 800/832-7491 in the U.S. Fax 74/84-7385. 250 rms. A/C TV TEL
$ Rates: High season $91 single or double. Low season $66 single or double.

The Acapulco Tortuga is a modern eight-story hotel on the landward side of the Costera Alemán near Condesa Beach, almost across the street from the Fiesta Americana Condesa hotel and Beto's Safari Restaurant. You enter the hotel to find a cavernous atrium lobby, in the midst of which are the restaurants Los Portales and La Fonda. Despite its modern construction, the decor in the atrium is theatrical Spanish colonial, with lots of greenery. The reception desk is at the left-rear side of the cavernous atrium. The rooms have wall-to-wall carpeting, cable color TVs, and radios, though upkeep could be better. At the very back of the hotel is a nice little swimming pool with a shady palapa (thatched shelter). By the way, the toll-free number (which you dial in the U.S.) rings in Mexico and those who answer may not speak English if you call before 9am, midafternoon, or late evening.

BUDGET

HOTEL SAND'S, Costera Alemán 178, Acapulco, Gro. 39690. Tel. 74/84-2260. Fax 74/84-1053. 93 rms. A/C TV TEL
$ Rates: $58 single or double all year except Christmas, Easter, and other major Mexican holidays.

Nestled among the giant resort hotels and away from the din of Costera traffic is this unpretentious and comfortable hostelry, across the Costera from the Plaza. From the road, you enter the hotel lobby through a stand of umbrella palms and a pretty garden restaurant. The rooms are light and airy in the style of a good-quality modern motel, with fairly dressy furniture and wall-to-wall carpeting. The Sand's has four swimming pools (one of them for children), a squash court, as well as volleyball and Ping-Pong areas. The price here is more than reasonable, the accommodations satisfactory, and the location excellent.

4. PAPAGAYO PARK TO DIANA CIRCLE

MODERATE

ACAPULCO RITZ HOTEL, Costera Miguel Alemán, Acapulco, Gro. 39580. Tel. 74/85-7544 or 85-7336. Fax 74/85-0178. 252 rms. A/C TV TEL
$ Rates: High season $150 double, $130 single. Low season $110 single, $125 double.

The Acapulco Ritz is right on the beach near the Paraíso Radisson and Papagayo Park. Guest rooms in the older West Tower are more spacious than those in the newer East Tower. The hotel is not luxurious, though the public price suggests it. The comfortable rooms are done in modern white and pastels with Mexican art providing accents. The colorful lobby is splashed with color, interesting modern Mexican paintings, bits of sculpture and pottery, mod furniture, and a young and

ACAPULCO: PAPAGAYO PARK TO DIANA CIRCLE

N

Adolfo Ruiz Cortínez

Paseo del Farrallón

Avenida Cuauhtémoc

Costera Miguel Alemán

Estrella de Oro Bus Terminal

Diana Circle

10
9

8
7
6

5
1 **4**
3
2

11

13 **13**
14

Parque Papagayo

Río Camarón

Avenida Cuauhtémoc

Costera Miguel Alemán

Playa Hornitos

Playa Hornos

Bahía de Acapulco

Playa Tamarindo

Playa Dominguillo

7000

MEXICO CITY

Acapulco

ACCOMMODATIONS:
Acapulco Ritz Hotel **3**
Continental Plaza **8**
Hotel del Valle **5**
Fiesta Americana Condesa Hotel **11**
Hotel Howard Johnson Maralisa **4**
Paraíso Acapulco Radisson Hotel **2**

DINING:
Antojitos Mayab **1**
Da Rafaela **13**
Dino's **10**
Italianissimo **9**
Carlos 'n' Charlie's **12**
La Tortuga **14**

upbeat feel. The hotel is popular with tours and package travelers; so to save get a package to avoid paying for otherwise overpriced rooms.

Dining/Entertainment: La Estancia Bar, furnished in wicker and bamboo, is open from 9am to 1am. Restaurant Los Carrizos, with lots of plants and ceiling fans, is open from 7 to 11:30am. La Mariscada, by the water where there's often live entertainment, serves seafood specialties from noon to 11pm. La Cava, the gourmet restaurant, has an extensive wine cellar and is open from 7 to 11:30pm. Aptly named, Las Mojados (meaning "the damp ones") is the poolside bar, open between 10am and dusk.

Services: Laundry and room service, travel agency.

Facilities: The swimming pool, surrounded by palms and lounge chairs, extends under a shady palapa, and this "secret" part of the pool is a favorite with kids; the beach is outfitted with little white Moorish-style tents; the beauty shop also offers massages.

HOTEL HOWARD JOHNSON MARALISA, Calle Alemania s/n, Acapulco, Gro. 39670. Tel. 74/85-6677, or toll free 800/446-4656 in the U.S. Fax 74/85-9228. 90 rms. A/C TV TEL

$ Rates: High season $95–$111 single or double. Low season $80–$90 single or double.

Of the smaller hotels in the row of giants, this, the former Hotel Maralisa, is one of the most congenial. It's got all the things the huge hotels have without the tremendous size: a fine palm-shaded swimming pool, plus a smaller pool, a private stretch of beach, La Mar bar between the beach and the swimming pool, and a dining room overlooking the bay. Lower-priced rooms have two twin beds and higher-priced ones have two double beds and balconies. Whichever accommodation you choose, you'll have a comfortable, modern, air-conditioned room with sliding glass doors (in most cases) opening onto a balcony or walkway. Besides standard rooms there are three handicapped-equipped rooms, a travel agency, and pharmacy/gift shop. It's just off the Costera at Alemania; turn when you see the Baskin-Robbins, and it's on the side street going toward the beach. It's also near the Hotel Acapulco Ritz.

PARAÍSO ACAPULCO RADISSON HOTEL, Costera Miguel Alemán 163, Acapulco, Gro. 39300. Tel. 74/85-5596, or toll free 800/333-3333 in the U.S. Fax 74/85-5543. 422 rms. A/C TV TEL

$ Rates: High season $151–$180 single or double. Low season $115–$125 single or double.

The Paraíso stands right at the eastern end of Papagayo Park on Hornos Beach. Though it's among the resort's older hotels, it has been well maintained. The lofty lobby is an expanse of gleaming black marble leading to large windows overlooking the beach, dotted with little palapas. The hotel's attractive sun deck next to the beach is set with comfy lounge chairs. The guest rooms are spacious, with nice tiled bathrooms, marble vanities, and little balconies. More expensive rooms are those with a sea view. Land-view rooms can be a bit noisy because of the busy traffic along the Costera.

Dining/Entertainment: The rooftop Fragatta Restaurant has a nautical decor and a fabulous view of the bay, and is open 9pm to 3am with a dance floor and live piano music. Beachside is La Pergola, open from noon to 11pm. Las Gaviotas Restaurant is the informal one open from 7am to 11pm.

Services: Laundry and room service, travel agency.

Facilities: Oceanside pool, ice machine on each floor, one handicapped-equipped guest room; floors 2 and 17 are no-smoking.

BUDGET

HOTEL DEL VALLE, Espinoza 150, Acapulco, Gro. 39300. Tel. 74/85-8336
or 85-8388. 18 rms. A/C (6 rms) FAN (13 rms) TEL (6 rms)
$ Rates: $29 single or double, with A/C.

A lackluster greeting is all you'll get here and the desk clerk may try to jack up the price, especially if you call for a reservation. Go in person and insist on the going rate, which is generally posted behind the desk. It's one of several hotels in a row here offering clean, comfortable rooms just steps from the Costera and all the action. Because of its price and location it fills up early. There's a little swimming pool in front. Paraíso Beach is half a block away. Arrive early; simple as it is, this hotel and those around it are in demand. As you drive along the Costera, look for the tiny Hotel Jacqueline and you'll find the Hotel del Valle just behind it.

5. DOWNTOWN: THE ZÓCALO AREA

Numerous budget-quality hotels and *casas de huespedes* (guesthouses) dot the streets fanning out from the zócalo (Acapulco's official and original downtown) and they are among the best buys in Acapulco if you aren't looking for luxury. Be sure to check your room first to see that it has the basic comforts you expect.

HOTEL ASTURIAS, Quebrada 45, Acapulco, Gro. 39300. Tel. 74/83-6548.
15 rms. FAN
$ Rates: $13.50 per person.
This little budget charmer gets high marks for cleanliness and friendly management, plus there's a nice little pool, just big enough to cool off in. Rooms are clean and airy, with tile floors and small tile bathrooms (no toilet seats). Glass louvered windows in each room face the open common walkways of the hotel's interior, letting in light and air (as well as mosquitoes). Rooms have either two double beds or two doubles and a single. To find it from the zócalo, walk up Quebrada three blocks; it's on the left opposite the Secretaria de Finanzas and noticeable for its blue columns on either side of a wide stucco arch over the front porch.

HOTEL ISABEL, La Paz 16 Centro, Acapulco, Gro. 39300. Tel. 74/82-2191 or 83-9816. 36 rms. FAN
$ Rates: $13 single; $21 double; $30 triple.
A short walk from the zócalo, the Hotel Isabel offers four stories of plain, clean rooms with marble-tiled floors and tile bathrooms with pull-string showers and corroded shower heads. Sheets are spiffy clean and pressed. Rooms on the front have small balconies overlooking bustling La Paz. Those on the back have windows on the interior.

HOTEL MISIÓN, Felipe Valle 12, Acapulco, Gro. 39300. Tel. 74/82-3643.
27 rms. FAN
$ Rates: $20 single or double. **Parking:** Free.
Enter the brick, plant-filled courtyard shaded by an enormous mango tree and step back in time to an earlier Acapulco at this tranquil, 19th-century hotel. Old photos of Acapulco show similar hacienda-style architecture, with white stucco walls, red-tiled roofs, and courtyard. And in fact the original L-shaped building is at least 100 years old. The rooms have colonial touches such as colorful tile and wrought iron, and come simply furnished with one or two beds and ceiling fans. Breakfast and lunch are served on the patio. Soft drinks and beer are usually available all day.

6. DOWNTOWN: LA QUEBRADA

Up the hillside west of the zócalo, near the cliff divers' area known as La Quebrada, lie several busy streets dotted with inexpensive hotels. One disadvantage of this area is that every evening until around 11pm, tour buses roar up and down the hill for the high divers' act.

But even so, La Quebrada and neighboring La Paz and Juárez Streets are where to look for the best budget accommodations in the city.

PLAZA LAS GLORIAS/EL MIRADOR, Quebrada 74, Acapulco, Gro. 39300. Tel. 74/83-1221, or toll free 800/342-2644 in the U.S. 91/800-9-0027 in Mexico. Fax 74/82-4564. 100 rms. A/C TV TEL

$ Rates: High season $125 single or double. Low season $90 single or double. **Parking:** On street.

One of the landmarks of "Old Acapulco," the former El Mirador Hotel overlooks the famous cove where the cliff divers perform. Renovated with lush tropical landscaping and lots of handsome Mexican tile, this romantic hotel offers attractively furnished rooms with double or queen-size beds, mini-fridge and wet bar, and large bathrooms with marble counters. Most have a separate living room area and all are accented with handsome Saltillo tile and other Mexican decorative touches. Ask for a room with a balcony (there are 42) and ocean view (95 rooms).

To get there, follow the Costera past the Club de Esquies (on the left), the Pemex station (on the right). Turn right at the Hotel Avenida and follow the street right around the mountain. You'll see the Quebrada and the hotel across the small, deep cove on the left.

Dining/Entertainment: The hotel's La Perla Restaurant has an evening buffet ($35 to $42) and tables with great views of the cliff-diving show. The Don Carlos Coffee Shop offers mediocre food and slow service. The large comfortable and breezy lobby bar is a favorite spot to watch day fade into night on the beautiful cove and bay.

Services: Room service for breakfast and lunch, laundry service, travel agency.

Facilities: There are three pools for lounging and sunning, and a protected area beside a cove with good snorkeling. A mountainside elevator takes you to the saltwater pool.

7. ON PLAYA LA ANGOSTA

If you stand in the zócalo and face the water, to the right the Costera leads to hotels on Playa La Angosta, the hilly peninsula that curves back into the bay, and is just around the bend from La Quebrada and the cliff divers. The hillside location gives these hotels great views of the bay.

Take a Caleta or Caletilla bus along the Costera, which runs along the base of the peninsula, and get off at the Hotel Avenida. Then walk the short block to Playa La Angosta; the hotels are on the left facing the bay; to the right around the mountain is La Quebrada.

MODERATE

HOTEL SINFONIA DEL MAR, Av. López Mateos 183, Fracc. Las Playas, Acapulco, Gro. 39300. Tel. and fax 74/82-5420. 11 rms. A/C
$ Rates: $70–$77 single or double.

Very popular with French Canadians, this is another comfortable inn overlooking Playa La Angosta and the bay. Rooms have white-tile floors, terraces, refrigerators, game-size tables, nice bathrooms, large closets, and black rattan furniture. Two come with large kitchens, two with small kitchens, and two with whirlpools on the terrace. Four have king-size beds and the remainder have one or two double beds. On the fourth floor there's a large pool with a great view of the bay and a small restaurant that is usually open from 8am to 9:30pm.

BUDGET

HOTEL VILLA ROMANA, Av. López Mateos 85, Fracc. Las Playas, Acapulco, Gro. 39300. Tel. 74/82-3995. 10 rms. A/C
$ Rates: High season $40 single; $46–$55 double. Low season $31 single, $47 double.

With terraces facing the sparkling Playa La Angosta, this is one of the most comfortable inns in the area and ideal for a long stay. Some rooms are tiled and others carpeted, and all have a small kitchen with refrigerator. There's a small plant-filled terrace on the second floor with tables and chairs and a fourth-floor pool with a splendid view of the bay. Room 9 is off the pool.

8. NEAR PLAYAS CALETA & CALETILLA

On the southern reaches of the peninsula, a short walk from Caleta and Caletilla beaches, are a number of older budget hotels popular with Mexican couples and families on vacation. Besides budget prices, the advantages here are that most of these hotels are on quiet streets, are near the small beaches, and aren't all that far by bus from the longer stretches of beach on the bay.

The layout of streets in the peninsula that separates the two beaches is confusing, and the disorganization in street names and numbers is enough to drive one to tears. A street will be named Avenida López Mateos, but so will the street meeting at a 90° angle; some streets have two names, while others have none, many buildings have two street numbers.

To get through the confusion, here are explicit directions to the hotel suggestions in this area: Facing Caletilla Beach is a semicircular array of little restaurants, and behind this semicircle and across the street is a large, tree-lined parking lot for the Jai Alai Frontón, a peeling yellowish building at the far end of the parking lot. As you face the parking lot (your back to the water), a street runs along the left side of the lot up the hill. This is supposedly Avenida López Mateos (also marked as Avenida Flamingos) and along it, on the left side of the street, are several good hotels only a few minutes' walk from the beach.

MODERATE

HOTEL BOCA CHICA, Privada de Caletilla s/n (Apdo. Postal 1211), Acapulco, Gro. 39390. Tel. 74/83-6741. Fax 74/83-9513. 45 rms. A/C TEL

$ Rates: High season (including breakfast and dinner) $115 single, $145 double. Low season (no meals) $65 single, $75 double. **Parking:** Free.

This three-story hotel on the headland of the beach offers 180° panoramic views. Lawns, terraces, the pool, the bar, and restaurant are arrayed on different levels, plus there's a private swimming cove and private pier. All rooms have a little veranda, many windows, Venetian tile baths, and plenty of space to unwind. The hotel can also arrange for waterskiing, sailing, scuba diving, deep-sea fishing, surfing, golf, and tennis. Its international restaurant has a sushi bar. It's on a bluff at the end of the Costera, overlooking Caletilla Beach and Roqueta Island.

BUDGET

HOTEL BELMAR, Gran Vía Tropical and Av. de las Cumbres, Acapulco, Gro. 39300. Tel. 74/82-1525 or 83-8098. Fax 74/82-1526. 80 rms. A/C (40 rms) FAN (40 rms)

$ Rates: $35 single; $50 double. **Parking:** Free.

Two small pools and shady patios fill the grassy lawn in front of the hotel. Built in the 1950s, it's among those immaculately kept hotels from that era, with large, well-kept, and breezy rooms, enormous balconies, and relaxing views. Some rooms have two double beds and a single bed, making it perfect for a small family or trio traveling together. It's an ideal place to spread out and unwind. There's a comfortable restaurant/bar.

To get here, face the big Hotel de la Playa between Caleta and Caletilla beaches, take the street to your left, and go about 1½ blocks up the hill.

HOTEL LINDAVISTA, Playa Caleta s/n (Apdo. Postal 3), Acapulco, Gro. 39300. Tel. 74/82-5414. Fax 74/82-2783. 43 rms. A/C (27 rms) FAN (16 rms)

$ Rates: $46 single or double with fan; $53 single or double with A/C. **Parking:** Free.

The old-fashioned Lindavista snuggles into the hillside above Caleta Beach. Older American and Mexican couples are drawn to the well-kept rooms, beautiful views, and slow pace of the area here. There's a small swimming pool and terrace restaurant/bar. To find the hotel from Caleta Beach, head up the hill to the left of the Hotel Caleta.

MOTEL LA JOLLA, Costera Alemán and Av. López Mateos, Acapulco, Gro. 39300. Tel. 74/82-1525 or 83-8098. Fax 74/82-1526. 80 rms. A/C TEL

$ Rates: High season $65 single, $75 double. Low season $53 single, $65 double.

This L-shaped, two-story motel, with bright and modern rooms, surrounds a very pleasant swimming pool handsomely shaded with coconut palms. Although there is no view of the sea whatsoever, you are within a block of the bay and of Caleta and Caletilla beaches here. You'll know you've reached the hotel when you see the flying saucer–shaped restaurant.

CHAPTER 5

WHERE TO DINE IN ACAPULCO

Dining out in Acapulco can be one of the best experiences you'll ever have in Mexico—whether you're clad in a bathing suit and munching a hamburger on the beach, or whether you're seated at a candlelit table with the glittering bay spreading out before you.

Don't be fooled into thinking that fast-food restaurants are necessarily cheap in Mexico. The price of a meal in a deluxe establishment in Acapulco may not be much higher than what you'd pay for something of inferior quality at a mass market restaurant. But the proliferation of U.S. franchise restaurants (McDonald's, Subway, Shakey's Pizza, Baskin-Robbins, Tony Roma's, etc.), has increased competition in Acapulco. To attract their market share, restaurants that were once considered exclusive have lowered prices to compete; the quality of their food is generally much better, often offering more value for the money than supposedly budget restaurants.

The restaurants I've taste-tested below reflect a mixture of both value and good food. And if it's a romantic place you're looking for, you won't have to look far, since Acapulco fairly brims over with such inviting places.

1. SOUTH OF TOWN: LAS BRISAS AREA

VERY EXPENSIVE

RESTAURANT MIRAMAR, Plaza La Vista, Carretera Escénica. Tel. 84-7874.
Cuisine: ITALIAN/FRENCH/MEXICAN. **Reservations:** Required.
$ Prices: Appetizers $10–$15; main courses $22–$31; desserts $3–$12.
Open: Dinner only, daily 6:30pm–midnight.

The Miramar is about as formal as an Acapulco restaurant gets, and with the view of the bay and outstanding food, the dining experience is something not soon forgotten. Waiters wearing black suits and ties are quietly solicitous as you make your selection and ponder the view between courses. The menu, as refined as the service, offers familiar continental classics such as duck in orange sauce, coq

FROMMER'S SMART TRAVELER: RESTAURANTS

1. Some of the best budget meals, including fresh seafood, are to be found around the zócalo in "Old Acapulco." These places are great for breakfast and a leisurely lunch and inexpensive to reach by local bus.
2. Moderately priced restaurants, serving excellent food, line the Costera between the naval base—Icacos Beach area and Papagayo Park. Many are open only in the evening.
3. More expensive restaurants with great views are in the Las Brisas area south of the naval base and before Puerto Marquéz. Expect outstanding service and cuisine. Often prices are quite reasonable.
4. If you're dining at a restaurant with a panoramic bay view, arrive around 6:30pm for the best lighting at day's end.
5. Never eat at a restaurant that's completely empty at prime times.
6. Most restaurants welcome casually dressed patrons—after all, being cool and comfortable is a perk of an Acapulco vacation. However, at the more expensive restaurants, consider wearing something a little spiffy—slacks and a cool short-sleeved shirt for men, and a summer dress or dressy slacks outfit for women.

au vin, and tournedos Rossini, all exquisitely presented. But save room for a dessert, all as memorable as the main courses. Dress up a bit for dining here, but as lightly as possible, since bay breezes are few and the fans aren't quite adequate. When the tab for your wonderful meal comes, check it carefully; I don't know if they get busy and make mistakes or what exactly happens, but sometimes unordered items appear on the bill, or the total is more than the sum of the prices. The Miramar is in the La Vista complex near the Hotel La Brisas.

SPICEY, Carretera Escénica. Tel. 81-1380 or 81-0470.
   Cuisine: INTERNATIONAL. **Reservations:** Recommended on weekends.
$ Prices: Appetizers $7–$15; main courses $16–$40.
   Open: Lunch Mon–Fri 1:30–5pm; dinner daily 7–11:30pm.

For original food with a flair, you can't beat this trendy new restaurant in the Las Brisas area, next to Kookaburas. Diners (in cool attire that's on the dressy side of casual) can enjoy the air conditioning indoors or the completely open rooftop terrace, with its sweeping view of the bay. To begin, try the shrimp Spicey, in a fresh coconut batter with an orange marmalade and mustard sauce. Among the main courses, the grilled veal chop in pineapple and papaya chutney is a good choice, as is the beef tenderloin—prepared with the flavors of Thailand, or Santa Fe style, or blackened á la Louisiana. The chiles rellenos in mango sauce win raves.

EXPENSIVE

GRAZZIEL, Plaza La Vista, Carretera Escénica. Tel. 84-0336 or 84-8143.
   Cuisine: INTERNATIONAL.
$ Prices: Main courses $15–$25.
   Open: Daily 7pm–midnight.

This open-walled hillside restaurant with a vista is on three levels cooled by whirring fans and breezes when the wind is right. At dinner select from such specialties as filet robalo stuffed with huitlacoche in white sauce with strips of salmon, shrimp Grazziel in a crab sauce, or perhaps pasta or steak. At night, soft background piano music entertains while you dine at candlelit tables. It's in the La Vista complex.

MADEIRAS, Carretera Escénica. Tel. 84-4378.
   Cuisine: MEXICAN/CONTINENTAL. **Reservations:** Required.
$ Prices: Fixed-price dinner $40.
   Open: Dinner only, two seatings daily at 7–8:30pm and 9–10:30pm.

Enjoy an elegant meal and a fabulous view of glittering Acapulco Bay at night—all at a reasonable price, considering the excellent and attentive service, outstanding food, and elegant setting. Many frequent visitors think that no trip to Acapulco is complete without dinner at Madeiras. The several small candlelit dining areas have ceiling fans and are open to the evening breezes. Arrive a little early and enjoy a drink in the comfortable lounge. There's also an outlet of Los Castillo Silver from Taxco off the lobby.

Selections might include *tamal al chipotle* (a corn tamale made with tangy chipotle sauce), roasted quail stuffed with tropical fruits, fish cooked in an orange sauce, or old favorites such as filet mignon, beef Stroganoff, and frogs' legs in garlic and white wine. Wines are reasonably priced if you stick to the Mexican labels. It's southeast of town on the scenic highway, and just before the Hotel Las Brisas.

2. THE COSTERA: ICACOS BEACH TO PAPAGAYO PARK

VERY EXPENSIVE

EL OLVIDO, Diana Circle, Centro Marbello. Tel. 81-0203 or 81-0256.
   Cuisine: NOUVELLE MEXICAN.
$ Prices: Appetizers $9–$12; main courses $15–$30.
   Open: Daily 7pm–2am.

You'd never guess this handsome terrace restaurant is tucked back in a shopping mall. Once past the front door, you have the glittering bay views of the posh Las Brisas restaurants without the taxi ride. And the menu is one of the most sophisticated in the city. It's expensive, but each dish is delightful and beautifully presented. Start with one of the 12 house specialty drinks, such as the Olvido (a tequila, rum, Cointreau, and tomato and lime juice concoction) or the Brisas de Coco (made with amaretto creme de coco, rum, and pineapple). You might begin with a delicious cold melon soup or a thick black bean soup with sausage. Among the innovative main courses are ravioli filled with huitlacoche; quail with honey and pasilla chiles; and sea bass with a mild sauce of cilantro and avocado. For dessert, try the chocolate fondue or the guanabana mousse in a rich sapote negro sauce.

El Olvido is in the shopping center fronted by the Aca-Joe clothing store on Diana Circle. Walk into the passage to the left of Aca-Joe and bear left; it's at the far end.

EXPENSIVE

CARLOS 'N' CHARLIE'S, Costera Alemán 999. Tel. 84-1285 or 84-0039.
   Cuisine: INTERNATIONAL.
$ Prices: Appetizers $4–$10; main courses $9–$20.
   Open: Dinner only, daily 6:30pm–midnight.

⭐ For fun, high-decibel music, *and* good food all at the same time, you can't go wrong with this branch of the Carlos Anderson chain. You'll find the usual posters, silly sayings, bric-a-brac, sassy waiters, and menu humor ("splash" for seafood, "moo" for beef). It's always packed, an indication that people like what they get for the price they pay. Come early and get a seat on the terrace overlooking the Costera. It's east of the Diana traffic circle and across the street from the El Presidente Hotel and the Fiesta Americana Condesa.

DA RAFAELLO RISTORANTE, Costera Alemán 1221. Tel. 84-5046 or 84-1000.

Cuisine: ITALIAN.

$ Prices: Appetizers $5–$10; main courses $7–$20; early bird special $14.

Open: Daily 2pm–midnight (early bird special 2–6pm).

Rock-and-brick walls, whirling fans, cool tile floors, a wooden ceiling and large plants, cloth-covered tables and matching chair cushions, plus table flowers, make Da Rafaello an inviting place to dine overlooking the Costera. But best of all the menu has a number of new twists that make the restaurant worth investigating more than once. There's a full range of pastas, plus filet Sicilian-style and blackened steak. Ask about the different daily sauces for either pastas or meat. Crispy salads come in chilled bowls and there's a nice selection of house dressings—I especially enjoyed the unusually tasty Italian one. Desserts include the ever-popular crêpes cajeta (bowing to Mexico) and a full range of coffees including decaffeinated (the latter a rarity in Mexico). The separate bar area has a TV just to bring in special sporting events. It's casual or dressy—however you are will be fine. It's a block from Carlos 'n' Charlie's near the Hotel Fiesta Americana Condesa.

DINO'S, Costera Alemán s/n. Tel. 84-0037.

Cuisine: NORTHERN ITALIAN. **Reservations:** Recommended.

$ Prices: Appetizers $5–$8; main courses $12–$23.

Open: Daily 4pm–midnight.

⭐ A popular dining spot for years, Dino's continues with its combination of good food and service at respectable prices for what you get. Plus from its second story dining room there's a modest bay view between high-rise hotels. The restaurant is famous for its fettuccine Alfredo and waiters prepare it with fanfare, often tableside. Other main courses include broiled seafood and steak, all of which come with baked potato, vegetables, and Dino's special oven-baked bread. It's on the landward side of the Costera beside the Tortuga Hotel and opposite the Langosta Loca.

HARD ROCK CAFE, Costera Alemán 37. Tel. 84-0077.

Cuisine: AMERICAN.

$ Prices: Appetizers $6–$12; main courses $13–$20, sandwiches $8–$13.

Open: Daily noon–2am; live music Wed–Mon 11:30pm–1:30am.

If you like your music loud and your food trendy, dip into this cool and interestingly decorated place. The decor is a combination of nostalgia and museum, all with a modern twist. Elvis memorabilia greets you in the entry area, and elsewhere there's Tyrone Power's matador costume from *Blood and Sand* (1941), Marilyn Monroe's pink satin gloves and shoes from *Gentlemen Prefer Blondes* (1953), Liberace's cowboy boots, the Beatles' gold record for "Can't Buy Me Love," and many others, plus a quote that sets the tone: "God bless Londontown, the Big Apple, and all hard rockers worldwide." Naturally there's a bandstand for the live music and a small dance floor. Now for the food: You can have buffalo wings, nachos, BLTs, hot burger platters with fries, fajitas, and steaks that come with salad and baked potato. And from the soda fountain savor hot–fudge sundaes, cheesecake, banana splits, or milk shakes. It's on the seaward side towards the southern end of the Costera, south of the Convention Center and opposite El Cabrito.

HARD TIMES, Costera Alemán 112 alto. Tel. 84-6447.
   Cuisine: GRILLED MEATS.
   $ Prices: Salad bar $8; main courses $7–$23.
   Open: Dinner only, Mon–Sat 6pm–midnight; bar 6pm–1am.
This popular second-floor restaurant overlooks the Costera. Walls are decorated in a depressions-era theme, with old automobile bumpers and hubcaps, all in keeping with hard times. But it's good times on your plate. The salad bar in high season is one of the best in Mexico, with crispy fresh ingredients like you'd expect at home. They're famous for their barbecued baby pork ribs, sweet-and-sour baked ribs, and spicy Cajun ribs, all brought to your table sizzling on a little grill. No one will think twice if you tuck your napkin into your collar or lick your fingers while working your way through the feast. There's fresh seafood, too, including charbroiled fish and shrimp served five ways. Or try the Tex-Mex chicken with guacamole, beans, rice, and flour tortillas and fajitas. For dessert the strawberry crêpes with ice cream or bananas flambé are excellent, or have something from the extensive coffee list. It's on the landward side of the Costera opposite the Fiesta Americana Condesa and Baskin-Robbins.

SU CASA/LA MARGARITA, Av. Anahuac 110. Tel. 84-4350 or 84-1261.
   Cuisine: INTERNATIONAL. **Reservations:** Recommended.
   $ Prices: Appetizers $6–$10; main courses $12–$25.
   Open: Daily 6pm–midnight.
Su Casa (Your House) is one of the most delightful restaurants for dining with a view while enjoying some of the most creative food in the city.
Owners Shelly and Angel Herrera opened this restaurant on the patio of their hillside home in 1982 at the suggestion of friends who'd tasted their wonderful home-cooked meals. Both are aficionados in the kitchen and both are on hand nightly to greet guests to their patio. They are still adding to the menu, so that each time you go, there's something new to try. But some things are standard, such as the unusual chile con carne, which is served both as a main dish and as an appetizer; shrimp a la patrona in garlic; and marinated and grilled chicken Su Casa, grilled fish and steak, delicious barbecue chicken, and enchiladas in green sauce. The flaming filet al Madrazo, a delightful brochette, is first marinated in tropical juices. Those are just a few of the unusual main courses. Most come with refreshing garnishes of cooked banana or pineapple, often a baked potato or rice, plus there are off-the-menu specials to ask about. The margaritas are big and delicious. Su Casa is on a hillside above the Convention Center. Highly recommended.

SUNTORY, Costera Alemán at Maury. Tel. 84-8088 or 84-8766.
   Cuisine: JAPANESE. **Reservations:** Recommended.
   $ Prices: Suntory course $18; Midori course $28; Imperial course $48; sushi plates $20–$35; á la carte meals $12–$48.
   Open: Daily 2pm–midnight.
For a refreshingly cool and serene respite from Acapulco's heat, sand, and zooming Costera, try this wonderful bit of Japan in Mexico. Dine with air conditioning inside with large windows facing a beautiful Japanese garden or

outside on the patio beside the gardens and peaceful waterfall. Though prices are expensive, the food is outstanding, and appreciated as much by the local upper crust as by tourists who know good Japanese food when they taste it. The extensive menu includes the Suntory course, a teppanyaki with a choice of U.S. ribeye, chicken, or fish, all with vegetables, crisp salad, small bowl of soup, and a heaping main platter (bring a big appetite), most of which is cooked at your table. The more expensive Midori course includes much of the Suntory course plus an appetizer, pickled vegetables, and dessert. The extensive Imperial course, for which you'll need a huge appetite, incorporates those items already mentioned but with shrimp salad, lobster soup, and a teppanyaki that includes lobster, and fresh fruit. The à la carte menu includes grilled and fried main courses, tempuras, and sushi. The delicious sushi platters come with between 16 and 22 beautifully prepared and presented pieces, and include a glass of wine and misoshiro soup; either platter is enough for two or three people to share. Drinks to try besides the traditional hot or cold sake include the jarra Suntory, a mixture of white wine with mango and peach flavorings, and Midori, a melon-based liqueur. There's also a full list of imported and domestic wines and liquors. Highly recommended.

MODERATE

EL CABRITO, Costera Alemán 1480. Tel. 84-7711.
   Cuisine: NORTHERN MEXICAN.
$ Prices: Breakfast $5–$13; appetizers $4–$8; main courses $7–$16.
   Open: Daily 8am–1am.
With its arched adobe decor and waitresses in embroidered dresses and location in the heart of the Costera, this restaurant is aimed at the tourist trade. But its authentic and well-prepared specialties attract Mexicans in the know—a stamp of approval I find comforting. Among its specialties are *cabrito al pastor* (roasted goat), charro beans, northern-style steaks, and burritos de machaca. Those with a liberal palate might venture into tasting broiled goat heads—considered a delicacy by aficionados. Regional specialties from other areas include Jalisco-style birria and mole Oaxaca-style. The great guacamole is slightly spicy, the tortillas fresh and light, plus the enchiladas and quesadillas are excellent. Dine inside or outside on the patio facing the Costera. It's on the ocean side of the Costera opposite the Hard Rock Cafe, and south of the Convention Center.

ITALIANISSIMO, Diana Circle, Costera Alemán. Tel. 84-0052.
   Cuisine: ITALIAN.
$ Prices: Appetizers $4.75–$9; main courses $7.75–$17.50.
   Open: Daily noon–midnight.
This restaurant's new location behind the Aca-Joe clothing store at Diana Circle is easy to miss if you don't know it's there. This location has air conditioning and cool gray marble floors. The restaurant does delicious tableside preparations with pizzazz—such as scampi Stroganoff with vodka sauce. And the pastas are homemade. For appetizers, try the Caesar salad or the heavenly mussels in white wine sauce. Dessert could be Irish coffee and chocolate cake.

MARISCOS PIPO, Costera Alemán and Victoria. Tel. 84-0165.
   Cuisine: MEXICAN/SEAFOOD.
$ Prices: Appetizers $4–$14; main courses $6–$25.
   Open: Daily 1–9:30pm.
This branch of the famous zócalo-area seafood restaurant has a reputation spanning decades. This second branch is larger, brightly decorated, and has slightly higher

FROMMER'S COOL FOR KIDS: RESTAURANTS

Hard Rock Cafe (see p. 100). If the burgers and fries, buffalo wings, and nachos don't keep kids occupied, the walls will—they're decorated with memorabilia from Elvis Presley to Marilyn Monroe.

Da Rafaello Ristorante (see p. 100) This is a good place for kids to order spaghetti prepared just about any way imaginable. It's breezy here, with a balcony overlooking the busy Costera, which kids can watch between courses.

prices, but the same good food. Try the grilled red snapper *(huachinango a la parrilla)* or red or black clams on the half shell. It's on the ocean side of the Costera east of the Convention Center and close to CICI.

RESTAURANT COCULA, Costera Alemán 10. Tel. 84-5079.
   Cuisine: MEXICAN.
$ Prices: Appetizers $3.25–$5; main courses $5–$18.
   Open: Mon–Wed and Fri 6pm–1am, Thurs and Sun 2pm–1am.
You can dine on the patio out front, or on one of the two air-conditioned levels of terraces. Appetizers include guacamole, black-bean soup, and watercress salad. Grilled meats are the specialty and you can choose broiled chicken, quail, spiced pork sausage, ribs, shish kebab, or a mixed grill.
   It's next to Fersato's on the inland side of the east end of the Costera, across from State of Guerrero Cultural Center and the Acapulco Dolphins Hotel.

RESTAURANT FERSATO'S, Costera Alemán 44. Tel. 84-3949.
   Cuisine: MEXICAN.
$ Prices: Breakfast $2.50–$6.50; main courses $4.75–$16.
   Open: Daily 7am–midnight.
The big dining room beneath the tiled roof and stone arches welcomes with colorfully clad tables. There's an extensive menu of seafood, chicken, and steaks. Try the mole, the black beans, or the *mixiotes* with chicken, or lamb wrapped in maguey leaves. Fersato's is on the inland side of the Costera across from the CICI, and the Acapulco Dolphins Hotel.

SERAPHINO, Costera Alemán. Tel. 84-5150.
   Cuisine: FRENCH CANADIAN.
$ Prices: Breakfast $4–$7; appetizers $6.50; main courses $10.50–$18.
   Open: Breakfast and lunch Mon–Sat 8:30am–12:30pm; dinner Mon–Sat 5:30–11pm.
   Closed: May–Oct.
This cute and casual little bistro is a welcome find for French Canadians who want it their way, and anyone else who's curious about it, too. Owners Claudette and Eugéne Therrien say that, among other things on their seven-page menu, the barbecue sauce and salad dressings are unique and the pudding is special, too. The French Canadians find friends here, so if you're dying to speak French, this is the place. While the owners are busy pleasing Canadians, they honor others with a menu in French, Spanish, and English. The breakfast menu, too, bows to tastes from the U.S., French-speaking Canada, and Mexico. On the main menu there are a few

Italian and Mexican appetizers. To find it look for the pink awning on the second story opposite the Hyatt Regency at the southern end of the Costera.

LA TORTUGA, Costera Alemán 5A. Tel. 84-6985.
   Cuisine: MEXICAN.
$ Prices: Appetizers $4–$8; main courses $4.50–$15.
   Open: Daily 10am–1am.

This small, congenial outdoor restaurant with cloth-covered tables occupies two greenery-filled terraces shaded by enormous mango trees. The extensive menu offers a good sampling of food from several Mexican regions such as Oaxaca tamales, chicken mixiotes, and tortilla soup. Specialties to try include shrimp-filled crêpes and the Tortuga combination with grilled meat, tostada, enchilada, stuffed pepper, guacamole, beans, and chips. Or just select from one of the 12 kinds of tortas. To find it, walk a half block inland from the Costera at the corner of Lomas del Mar and across from the Hotel Torre de Acapulco.

BUDGET

ANTOJITOS MAYAB, Costera Alemán 151. No phone.
   Cuisine: YUCATAN.
$ Prices: Main courses $1.60–$7; comida corrida $4.65.
   Open: Daily noon–midnight; comida corrida served noon–5pm.

A cool, clean little eatery, this one fills a formerly empty niche among quick-food places with a few of the most popular specialties from the Yucatán area of Mexico. Nowhere else in town will you find tacos filled with cochinta pibil or escabiche, besides the usual fillings of chicken or shrimp. Antojitos include turkey *panuchos* (small flat corn cakes topped with turkey, onions, beans, and cheese), empanadas, and tostadas. Yucatán tamales are served after 5pm. You'll find this place opposite the new blue La Gran Plaza shopping center, next to McDonald's and half a block from the Ritz Hotel.

100% NATURAL, Costera Alemán 2280. Tel. 84-4562.
   Cuisine: MEXICAN/VEGETARIAN.
$ Prices: Breakfast $4–$6; main courses $5.50–$9; fruit and vegetable drinks $3–$4; sandwiches $3.50–$5.
   Open: Daily 7am–11pm.

You'll see branches of 100% Natural in just about every area of Acapulco, most with green awnings. Menus include soups, salads, sandwiches, fruit, yogurt, shakes, and pasta dishes that please vegetarians and carnivores alike. Although each is part of a franchise, they're individually owned, so the hours vary. This one is on the east end of the Costera, near the Romano Days Inn.

3. DOWNTOWN: THE ZÓCALO AREA

The old downtown area of Acapulco is packed with simple, inexpensive eateries of all types serving up tasty food for very low prices. It's easy to pay more elsewhere in Acapulco and not get such consistently good food as what you'll find at the restaurants in this part of town. To explore this area, start right at the zócalo and stroll west along Juárez. After about three blocks you'll come to Azueta, lined with small seafood cafes and streetside stands.

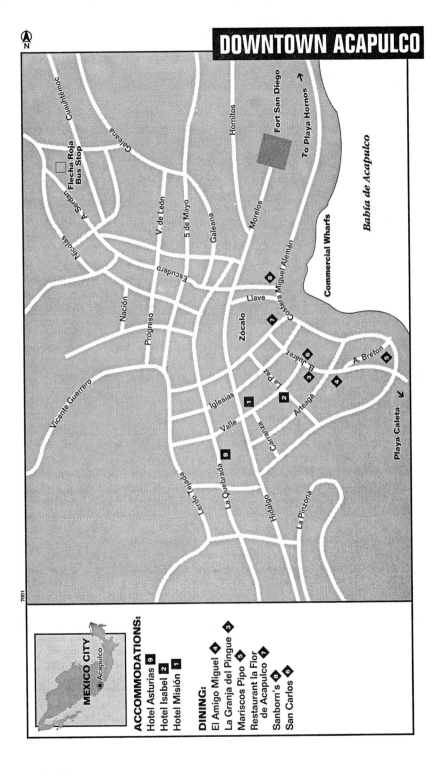

DOWNTOWN ACAPULCO

N

7001

Cuauhtémoc

A. Sedán

Flecha Roja
Bus Stop

Galeana

Nicolás

Hornitos

Fort San Diego

To Playa Hornos

V. de León

5 de Mayo

Galeana

Morelos

Bahía de Acapulco

Escudero

Nación

Progreso

Costera Miguel Alemán

Commercial Wharfs

Llave

Zócalo

8

7

Juárez

6

A. Breton

3

5

Vicente Guerrero

Iglesias

La Paz

4

1

2

Carranza

Arteaga

Playa Caleta

Valle

Lerdo Tejeda

La Quebrada

9

Hidalgo

La Pinzona

MEXICO CITY

Acapulco

ACCOMMODATIONS:

Hotel Asturias **9**
Hotel Isabel **2**
Hotel Misión **1**

DINING:

El Amigo Miguel **4**
La Granja del Pingue **3**
Mariscos Pipo **5**
Restaurant la Flor
de Acapulco **7**
Sanborn's **8**
San Carlos **6**

MODERATE

LA GRANJA DEL PINGUE, Juárez 10. Tel. 83-5339.
  Cuisine: ECLECTIC/PASTRIES/ICE CREAM.
  $ Prices: Breakfast $3; main courses $3–$5; lunch special $4.
  Open: Daily 7am–10pm.

Ⓢ   Specializing in ice cream and French/Viennese pastries, this unusual restaurant in an original Acapulco house is the cooperative effort of alumni and prep-school students of the Acapulco Children's Home. Its eclectic menu includes hamburgers, Tex-Mex chili con carne, and a dinner special after 5pm, usually in the American-home-cooking genre. Coffee refills are free. The dining area is a pretty shaded patio hung with folk-art masks and piñatas. Bring your paperback novels to exchange here. It's two blocks west of the zócalo on Juárez.

MARISCOS PIPO, Almirante Breton 3. Tel. 83-8801 or 82-2237.
  Cuisine: SEAFOOD.
  $ Prices: Main courses $4.75–$29.
  Open: Daily 11am–8pm.

★   This classic place is a local favorite and the original location; there are now three others in Acapulco. Diners can look at photographs of old Acapulco on the walls while sitting in the airy dining room, decorated with hanging nets, fish, glass floats, and shell lanterns. The English-language menu lists a wide array of seafood, including ceviche, octopus, crayfish, and baby-shark quesadillas. To find Mariscos Pipo, walk five blocks west from the zócalo on Juárez past Azueta and bear left at the fork in the road.

RESTAURANT LA FLOR DE ACAPULCO, zócalo s/n. Tel. 82-1073 or 82-5018.
  Cuisine: MEXICAN.
  $ Prices: Main courses $3–$16.
  Open: Daily 8am–11pm; comida corrida served from 1:30pm til it runs out.
The food is mediocre for the price you pay, but this is the best place to people-watch in Acapulco, and a nice place to start the day with a good cup of coffee while the plaza comes to life. With its prime location on the zócalo, it's been a landmark for years, and there's always a good number of foreigners dining among the locals. Umbrella-shaded tables with bright orange cloths are set out on the sunny plaza and in an airy dining room with ceiling fans. The extensive menu includes chicken mole, enchiladas, and carne asada a la tampiqueña, as well as a small selection of seafood, breakfasts, and snacks. La Flor de Acapulco is on the east side of the zócalo.

SANBORN'S, Costera Alemán and Escudero. Tel. 82-6167.
  Cuisine: AMERICAN/MEXICAN.
  $ Prices: Breakfast $4–$7; main courses $5.50–$14.
  Open: Daily 7:30am–11pm.
The best of the American-style restaurants, Sanborn's has a cool dining area with American colonial decor, brass light fixtures, and well-padded booths around the walls. It's especially good for breakfast, though it also has good enchiladas, club sandwiches, burgers, *sincronizadas* (ham and cheese melted between corn tortillas), pastas, and fancier fare such as fish and steaks. Beer, wine, and cocktails are served, too. For an inexpensive snack, buy pastries to go at the store's bakery. Of course, a lot of people just stop in for ice cream or other desserts and to browse through the excellent book and magazine section for which the chain is justly famous. Upstairs

are clean bathrooms. To find it, walk two blocks east of the zócalo on the Costera. The other Sanborn's (tel. 84-4465) is in a high-rise building on the Costera at Condesa Beach near El Presidente Hotel and it has more books and magazines.

BUDGET

EL AMIGO MIGUEL, Juárez 31 and Azueta. Tel. 83-6981.
   Cuisine: SEAFOOD.
$ Prices: Main courses $4–$12; lobster $17.50.
   Open: Daily 10:30am–9:30pm. **Closed:** New Year's Day.
This restaurant is so popular among knowing locals that it's expanded upstairs and across the street while still retaining its reason for being—good food and service. Red tablecloths and fish on the wall decorate this simple restaurant where fresh seafood is king. The open-air dining rooms are usually brimming with seafood lovers. Occasionally wandering musicians entertain—pay by the song. Try the stuffed crab, the snapper, or the baby shark or the fish filet in garlic—all fresh and well prepared. El Amigo Miguel is three blocks west of the zócalo on Juárez at Azueta.

SAN CARLOS, Juárez 5. Tel. 82-6459.
   Cuisine: MEXICAN.
$ Prices: Breakfast special and comida corrida $3.50; main courses $3.50–$8.
   Open: Daily 8am–10:30pm; comida corrida served 1–6pm.
Colorful tablecloths brighten this cheery and clean cafe where western-style food such as charcoal-broiled chicken or fish is served at chuck-wagon prices. Take a table either on the front patio or in the open and fan-cooled dining room. On Sunday the specialty is chicken mole. For the daily comida corrida, besides a choice of soup, there are usually almost a dozen main courses to select from. You'll find the San Carlos just a few steps off the zócalo on Juárez.

4. SPECIALTY DINING

DINING WITH A VIEW Among the pleasures of vacationing in Acapulco is dining with a fabulous view of the city spread out before you. Good places for this include **Madeiras, Grazziel, Miramar, Trebeca,** and **Kookabura,** all in the Las Brisas area; **Su Casa** on a hill above the Convention Center; **La Bahía Restaurant** at the Sheraton Hotel; the **Bella Vista Restaurant** (now open to the public) at the Hotel Las Brisas; the rooftop **Fraggata Restaurant** at the Paraíso Radisson Hotel; and the 18th-floor **Techo del Mar** (Roof of the Sea), the fine-dining restaurant at the Hotel Fiesta Americana Condesa.

BREAKFAST/BRUNCH Among the good places for an economical breakfast and brunch is a strip of competing little restaurants, including **100% Natural** (mentioned above), on the Costera just before the Romano Days Inn and south of the Convention Center. Other options include the breakfast buffet at the **Hotel Continental Plaza** and **Seraphino,** a French-Canadian restaurant opposite the Hyatt Regency and near the naval base.

EATING ON THE BEACH The area around Caleta and Caletilla beaches used to be rather down-at-the-heels, but not long ago the municipal authorities pumped lots of money into public facilities here. Now the beaches have nice shady palapas and beach chairs, clean sand, and fine palm trees. Three buildings have been built to house *vestidores, regarderas* (changing rooms, showers, and lockers), and restaurants. Little dining places line the outer periphery of the buildings, and the kitchen work is done at the center (peek around to the kitchen to see boys cutting up fish for the pot).

To find a good meal, wander along the rows of restaurants, looking for busy spots where people are eating (and not just sipping drinks). Study menus, which will either be displayed or handed to you on request. Although the restaurants may tend to look all the same, you'll be surprised at the difference in prices. *Filete de pescado* (fish filet) might be $4 at one place, and twice as much at another; beer can cost anywhere from $3 to $8.

WHAT TO SEE & DO IN ACAPULCO

Acapulco abounds with great **beaches** and opportunities for **water sports.** But it's also pleasant to take a walk early in the day (before it gets too hot) around the **zócalo,** called Plaza Alvarez. Visit the cathedral—the bulbous blue onion domes make it look more like a Russian Orthodox church, and it was actually designed as a movie theater! From the church, turn east along the side street going off at a right angle (Calle Carranza without a marker), where an arcade offers newsstands and shops.

A fabulous view of Acapulco awaits from the top of the hill behind the cathedral. Take a taxi up the hill from the main plaza, following the signs leading to La Mira.

City tours, day-trips to Taxco, cruises, and other excursions and activities are offered through local travel agencies.

1. THE BEACHES & THE BAY

BEACHES Here's the rundown, from west to east around the bay. **Playa La Angosta** is a small, sheltered, and often deserted cove just around the bend from La Quebrada (where the cliff divers perform).

South of downtown on the Peninsula de las Playas lie **Caleta and Caletilla Beaches,** separated by a small outcropping of land where the new aquarium and water park, **Mágico Mundo Marino,** stands. It is open daily (see "Museums and Special Attractions," below). Here you'll find thatch-roofed restaurants, water-sports equipment to rent, and the brightly painted boats that ferry passengers to Roqueta Island. Mexican families favor these beaches because they're close to several inexpensive hotels. And in the late afternoon fishermen pull their colorful boats up on the sand and sell their catch and sometimes oysters on the half shell. Beach chairs and an umbrella rent for around $6 for the day on almost all beaches.

The pleasure boats dock at **Playa Larga,** also south of the zócalo. Charter fishing trips take off from here. In the old days these downtown beaches—Larga, Caleta, Caletilla—were what Acapulco was all about and where it began. Nowadays the beaches and the resort development stretch the entire four-mile length of the bay's shore.

Going east from the zócalo, the major beaches are **Hornos** (near Papagayo Park), **Hornitos, Condesa,** and **Icacos,** followed by the naval base (La Base) and **Punta del Guitarrón.** After Guitarrón Point the road climbs to the legendary Westin Las Brisas (see Chapter 4, "Where to Stay in Acapulco"). Past Las Brisas, the road continues on to **Puerto Marquéz** and **Punta Diamante,** about 12 miles from the zócalo where the fabulous Acapulco Princess and Pierre Marqués hotels dominate the landscape.

The bay of **Puerto Marquéz** is an attractive area for swimming. The water is calm, the bay sheltered, and waterskiing is available. Past the bay lie **Revolcadero Beach** and a fascinating jungle lagoon.

Note: Each year in Acapulco at least one or two unwary swimmers drown because of deadly riptides and undertow. Swim *only* in Acapulco Bay or Puerto Marquéz Bay, but even there be careful of undertows!

ROQUETA ISLAND The island is a delightful place to snorkel, sunbathe, hike to a lighthouse, visit a small zoo, or eat lunch. Boats leave from Caletilla Beach every half hour from 9:30am until the last one returns at 5pm. The cost is $5.50 round-trip, or $9.75 on a glass-bottom boat (use the same ticket to return on any launch). You may disagree, but I don't think the glass-bottom–boat ride is worth the money. Purchase tickets directly from any boat that is loading or from the information booth on Caletilla Beach (tel. 82-2389). The booth also rents inner tubes, small boats, canoes, pedal boats, and beach chairs; waterskiing and scuba diving can also be arranged there.

BAY CRUISES A wonderful way to see the whole bay is from the deck of a boat, and Acapulco has a variety from which to choose—yachts, huge catamarans, trimarans, single- and double-decker—you name it. Cruises are offered mornings, afternoons, and evenings. Some offer buffets, open bars, and live music and others have snacks, drinks, and taped music. The music, by the way, may be loud enough to preclude talking. Prices range from around $20 to $60. In previous editions of this book, I mentioned the cruise companies by name, but the list and phone numbers change so dramatically from year to year that doing so was futile. To find out what cruises are currently operated, contact any Acapulco travel agency or hotel tour desk. They usually have a scrapbook with pictures and brochures so that you can get a good idea about a potential cruise before booking it.

2. SPORTS & RECREATION

WATER SPORTS An hour of **waterskiing** can cost as little as $30 or as much as $60. Caletilla Beach, Puerto Marquéz Bay, and Coyuca Lagoon have waterskiing facilities.

Scuba diving costs $40 for 1½ hours of instruction, if booked directly with the instructor on Caleta Beach, or $45 to $55 if arranged through a hotel or travel agency. Dive trips start around $50 per person for one dive.

Boat rentals are the least expensive on Caletilla Beach, where an information booth (tel. 82-2389) rents inner tubes, small boats, canoes, pedal boats, and beach chairs; it can also arrange waterskiing and scuba diving.

For **deep-sea fishing** excursions, go to the pale pink building of the Boat Cooperative (tel. 82-1099) opposite the zócalo. Charter fishing trips from here run

$100 to $150 for seven hours. Booked through a travel agent or hotel, fishing trips start at around $150 to $200 for four people.

Parasailing, though it is not without risks (such as landing on a building or palm tree) can be a fantastic thrill. The pleasure of floating high over the bay in a parachute towed by a motorboat is yours for $45. Most of the parasail rides operate on Condesa Beach.

LAND SPORTS A round of 18 holes of **golf** at the Acapulco Princess Hotel (tel. 84-3100) costs $70 for guests and $107 for nonguests. At the Club de Golf Acapulco (tel. 84-0782), off the Costera next to the Convention Center, play nine holes for $36 or 18 for $50.

Horseback-riding tours on the beach are available through the Lienzo Dharro "Mexico Real" (tel. 85-0331) near the Acapulco Princess Hotel. The two-hour rides depart at 9:30am, 11:30am, and 3:30pm daily and cost $40, including two beers or soft drinks.

Tennis at one of the tennis clubs open to the public costs around $11 per hour. Try the Club de Golf Acapulco (tel. 84-4824), open daily from 7am to 6:30pm: singles cost $11 an hour, doubles $16.

BULLFIGHTS Traditionally termed the Fiesta Brava, the bullfights are held during Acapulco's winter season at a ring up the hill from Caletilla Beach. Tickets purchased through travel agencies cost around $40 and usually include transportation to and from your hotel. The festivities begin each Sunday in winter at 5:30pm.

3. MUSEUMS & SPECIAL ATTRACTIONS

CENTRO CULTURAL DE ACAPULCO, Costera Alemán. No phone.
The State of Guerrero's Instituto Guerrerense de la Cultura sponsors this cultural center, located in a complex of small buildings in a shady grove across from the Acapulco Dolphins Hotel and Fersato's Restaurant, near the eastern end of the Costera. Buildings contain crafts exhibits (many for sale), or host classes in painting or guitar, poetry readings, and performances of music and dance.
Admission: Free.
Open: Daily 9am–2pm and 5–8pm. **Directions:** Walk one block east of CICI.

FORT SAN DIEGO, Costera Alemán east of the zócalo. No phone.
The original Fuerte de San Diego was built in 1616 to protect the town from pirate attacks. At that time, the port was wealthy from its trade with the Philippine Islands, which like Mexico were part of Spain's enormous empire. The fort you see was rebuilt after extensive damage by an earthquake in 1776.

IMPRESSIONS

Once you master this simple art (of water skiing) it can do wonders for your self-esteem. You begin to feel years younger, and may even come to look upon yourself as perhaps a pretty fair athlete after all. . . .The boat will hastily pull you by the floating photographers' shack. If you will hold on to the tow rope with one hand for a moment and wave at the camera with the other, you can have a picture of yourself taken and printed on a dozen postal cards. . . .It might change your whole life.
—JOHN WILHELM, *GUIDE TO MEXICO,* 1966

Today it houses the **Museo Histórico de Acapulco** (Acapulco Historical Museum), filled with exhibits that tell the fascinating story of Acapulco as a port for conquest of the Americas, conversion to Catholicism of the natives, and trade with Asia. Though all is in Spanish, most of the exhibits are self-explanatory.

The first room has changing shows. Other rooms chronical Acapulco's pre-Hispanic past, the coming of the conquistadores complete with Spanish armor, the Spanish imperial conquest of the South Seas for which Acapulco was a base, and a 6-foot-tall model of the *Manila Galleon*, one of the famous ships that sailed back laden with treasures from Asia as well as artifacts from the China trade, including fine chests, vases, textiles, and furniture.

Admission: $4.50; free on Sun.

Open: Tues–Sun 10:30am–4:40pm. Best time is in the morning, for the "air conditioning" is minimal. **Directions:** Follow Costera Alemán past old Acapulco and the zócalo; the fort is on a hill on the right. *Note:* You can reach the fort by a road through a military zone; coming from the main plaza, look for the road on the left, landward side of the Costera. If you're in good shape, you can climb a cascade of stairs opposite the cargo docks.

MÁGICO MUNDO MARINO, Caleta and Caletilla beaches. Tel. 83-1215.

It's easy to spend at least a half day at the new water park and aquarium, which offers tanks of sea lions, turtles, and dolphins; exhibits of shells; popular movies (many from the U.S.); a swimming pool with a water slide; and an ocean-swimming area with floating sun deck. Probably the most interesting attraction are a series of large aquariums of tropical fish from around the world, with informational explanations in Spanish and English. There are two bars, and an attractive terrace restaurant overlooking the water. At the umbrella-shaded restaurant you can order breakfast, lunch, snacks, and drinks.

Admission: $7.75 adults, $6 children.

Open: Daily 9am–7pm; restaurant 9am–5pm. **Directions:** Take a Caleta or Caleta Hornos Base bus, which stops in front of the beach and Mágico Mundo.

CICI, Costera Alemán at Colón. Tel. 84-1970.

This sea life and water park offers a variety of swimming pools with waves, water slides, and water toboggans. Dolphin shows at noon, 2:30, and 5pm are in English and Spanish. Amenities include a cafeteria and changing rooms. It's located east of the Convention Center.

Admission: $11.50 adults, $9.75 children (under 2 years old, free).

Open: Daily 10am–6pm.

4. SAVVY SHOPPING

Acapulco is not the best place to buy Mexican crafts, but there are a few interesting shops. The best are at the **Mercado Parazal** (often called the **Mercado de Artensanías**) on Calle Velásquez de León near 5 de Mayo in the downtown zócalo area. When you see Sanborn's, turn right and walk several blocks. Stall after covered stall of curios from all over the country are here, including silver, embroidered cotton clothing, rugs, pottery, and papier-mâché. Artists from Guerrero state paint village folk scenes on ceramics while waiting for patrons. It's a pleasant place to spend a morning or afternoon. Shopkeepers are vigilant but not too pushy, though they'll test your bargaining mettle. The starting price will be astronomical, and getting the

FROMMER'S FAVORITE ACAPULCO EXPERIENCES

Watching the Sun Rise by the Pier In predawn downtown Acapulco it's a memorable experience to watch silhouettes of fishermen against an orange-and-black sky unload fresh catches of seafood while restaurateurs buy the day's quantity fresh from the ocean.

Deep-sea Fishing Start the day gliding over the water with the coastline and fabulous villas in the background and the possibility of catching a sailfish in the offing.

Dining with a View Dining with a panoramic bay view is a fabulous way to end as many days as you have in this resort city.

Enjoying Fresh Seafood Fresh daily catches make their way to restaurants citywide and preparations are as varied as the city's many restaurants.

Sunset Viewing at Pie de la Cuesta When the mountains obscure Acapulco sunsets (and even when they don't), it's still enjoyable watching the last rays of daylight at this laid-back beach village 10 miles north of the zócalo.

Watching the Cliff Divers Anytime, but especially at the flamelit 10:30pm show, it's a thrill watching the famous cliff divers at La Quebrada plunge with torches 130 feet into the inky-black Pacific waters.

Shopping Spend a morning browsing for crafts at the Mercado Parazal near the zócalo. And don't overlook the hotel boutiques and shops along the Costera specializing in resort wear

price down may take more time than you have. But as always, acting disinterested enough to walk away often brings it down in a hurry. Before buying silver here, examine it carefully and be sure it has the .925 stamp on the back. The market is open daily from 9am to 8pm.

For a familiar, brightly lit department store aimed at tourists, with fixed prices, try **Artesanías Finas de Acapulco** (tel. 84-8039), called AFA-ACA for short. To find it, go east on the Costera until you see the Hotel Romano Days Inn on the seaward side and Baby-O disco on the landward side. Take the street between Baby-O and the Hotel El Tropicano. That's Avenida Horacio Nelson. On the right, a half block up, is AFA-ACA, a huge air-conditioned store, popular with tour groups. The merchandise includes clothes, marble-top furniture, saddles, luggage, jewelry, pottery, papier-mâché, and more. The store is open Monday through Saturday from 9am to 7:30pm and Sunday 9am to 2pm. **Sanborn's** is another good department store.

The **Costera Alemán** is crowded with boutiques selling resort wear, and lots of skintight, skimpy, and bangle-laden clothes. Look for a sale. These stores have an abundance of attractive summer clothing for prices that are lower than you might pay in the U.S. When they have a sale, that's the time to stock up on some incredible bargains. Pay close attention to the quality of zippers; sometimes Mexican zippers are not up to the task. One of the nicest air-conditioned shopping centers on the Costera is **Plaza Bahía,** which has two stories of shops as well as small fast-food restaurants. It's located at Costera Alemán 125 (tel. 86-2452), immediately west of the Acapulco Plaza Hotel. The shops in front of the Acapulco Plaza Hotel include a fine silver shop, Tane.

5. EVENING ENTERTAINMENT

SPECIAL ATTRACTIONS

Cliff divers *(clavadistas)* perform at La Quebrada each day at 12:45pm, 7:30pm, 8:30pm, 9:30pm, and 10:30pm for $4 admission. From a spotlit (at night) ledge on the cliffs in view of the lobby bar and restaurant terraces of the Hotel Plaza Las Glorias/El Mirador, each solitary diver (there are five or more) plunges into the roaring surf 130 feet below after praying at a small shrine nearby. To the applause of the crowd that has gathered, they climb up the rocks and accept congratulations and gifts of money from onlookers. The best show is at 10:30pm when they dive with torches.

If you want to watch the diving from the hotel terraces, there's a cover charge of $11.50 in the evening. You can also watch while having dinner ($43 per person) on one of the several terraces overlooking the bay and cliff divers. In a romantic setting with candlelit tables, you can come for the first show and dine through all the shows if you like. Reservations (tel. 83-1155) are recommended during high season. However, if you aren't dining, you might try arriving at the lobby bar 30 minutes before a performance and ordering drinks; the cover charge is not always collected from people who are already there. The hotel coffee shop, Don Carlos, which also has a terrace with good views, serves snacks and drinks but has unbelievably slow service.

The **Gran Noche Mexicana** featuring the **Acapulco Ballet Folklórico** is held in the plaza of the Convention Center every Tuesday, Thursday, and Saturday at 8pm. With dinner and open bar, the show costs $50; general admission (including three drinks) is $20. Call for reservations (tel. 83-1155) or consult a local travel agency.

Another excellent **Mexican Fiesta** and **folkloric dance show** that includes **voladores from Papantla** (flying pole dancers) is held at the Marbella Plaza near the Continental Plaza Hotel on the Costera on Monday, Wednesday, and Friday at 7pm. The $42 fee covers the show, buffet, open bar, taxes, and gratuities. Make reservations through a travel agency. Many major hotels also host Mexican fiestas and other theme nights that include dinner and entertainment. Consult a travel agency for information.

NIGHTCLUBS & DISCOS

Acapulco is as famous for its nightclubs as it is for its beaches. The problem in making specific recommendations is that the clubs open and close with shocking regularity, making it very difficult to give accurate information. Some general tips will help: Every club seems to have a cover charge ranging from $15 to $30; domestic drinks can cost anywhere from $5 to $10; many of them periodically waive the cover charge or offer some other promotion to attract customers. Another trend is a big cover charge but an open bar, and free admission for women. Most cater to a hip, young crowd, with flashing lights moving to the fast beat of mega-decibel music. To find out the current situation, call the disco, or look for promotional material around hotel reception areas, at travel desks or concierge booths, and check local publications.

Several hotels have their own bars, supper clubs, and nightclubs with floor shows. Other good bets are informal lobby or poolside cocktail bars, which often offer live trio, marimba, or rock and roll entertainment.

Acapulco has its own spectacular culture and convention center, the **Centro Acapulco,** on the eastern reaches of the bay between Condesa and Icacos beaches. Designed with extravagant Mexican taste, the Centro has rolling lawns; you enter via a grand promenade framing a central row of pools and high-spouting fountains. Within the modern center are several forms of entertainment: a mariachi bar, a piano bar, a disco, a movie theater, a legitimate theater, a café, a nightclub, several restaurants, and outdoor performance areas.

AFRO ANTILLANOS, Costera Alemán at Cuando la Cosa 32. Tel. 84-7235.

Live tropical and salsa music is the specialty of the house at this relatively new disco, not far from the Continental Plaza Hotel. Open Friday through Sunday 9:30pm to 4am; open bar closes at 3am.

Admission: $15–$20 with open bar.

BABY-O, Costera Alemán s/n. Tel. 84-7474.

Across from the Romano Days Inn, this intimate disco has a small dance floor surrounded by several tiers of tables and sculpted, cavelike walls. Well-heeled locals like to come here to wind down and end the evening—or morning, as it were. It opens at 10:30pm nightly.

Admission: $15–$20.

EXTRAVAGANZZA, Carretera Escénica. Tel. 84-7154 or 84-7164.

If you have something trendy to wear, you might venture up to this snazzy chrome-and-neon extravaganza. It's perched on the side of the mountain, between Los Rancheros Restaurant and La Vista Shopping Center. You can't miss the neon lights. The plush, dimly lighted interior dazzles with a sunken dance floor and panoramic view of Acapulco Bay. The door attendants wear tuxedos, so don't expect to get in wearing shorts, jeans, T-shirts, tennis shoes, or sandals. It opens nightly at 10:30pm; fireworks blast off at 3am. Call to find out if reservations are needed.

Admission: $15–$20.

FANTASY, Carretera Escénica. Tel. 84-6727 or 84-6764.

Recently redecorated, this club has a fantastic bay view and sometimes waives the cover charge or reduces it as a promotion. Periodically during the evening it puts on a good show with green lasers, which it also shoots out across the bay. The

---

IMPRESSIONS

For gaiety and merry-making, you just can't beat Acapulco! Here is the only place I've been where I have seen an entire party of men and women in full evening dress leap into a pool; here is the place to dance in the gently flapping surf as a rhumba band plays coaxingly till dawn. Here also is a big collection of fishing boats, water-skiing equipment galore, and even nightly water follies. All these things make Acapulco one of the really mad places in the world. I love it!
—JOHN WILHELM, *GUIDE TO MEXICO,* 1966

dress code does not permit shorts, jeans, T-shirts, or sandals. Reservations are recommended. Located in the La Vista Shopping Center, it's open nightly from 10:30pm to 4am.
Admission: $15–$20.

MAGIC, Costera Alemán at Yucatán. Tel. 84-8816.
One of the newer discos, Magic draws a youthful crowd to its pyramid-shaped building with a waterfall in front. It lies on the east end of the Costera near the Romano Days Inn. The dress code frowns on shorts, tennis shoes, and sandals. Open nightly at 10:30pm to 3am.
Admission: $15–$20, if open bar $16–$20.

THE NEWS, Costera Alemán s/n. Tel. 84-5904.
The booths and love seats ringing the vast dance floor can seat 1,200, so this disco can double as a concert hall. But while high-tech in style, it's laid-back and user-friendly. It doesn't even have a dress code! Across the street from the Hyatt Regency, it opens at 10:30pm nightly and closes about 3am.
Admission: $15–$20.

6. AN EASY EXCURSION TO PIE DE LA CUESTA

With the completion of the new toll road between Acapulco and Mexico City, day trips to the Chilapa Sunday market or to other towns (see Chapter 7) are easier. However, ten miles north of Acapulco's downtown zócalo is Pie de la Cuesta, a one-street beachfront village that's world famous for its sunsets. Just a half hour from Acapulco, it makes an interesting day-long or sunset-watching experience. For as long as Acapulco has been a tourist destination, visitors have been coming here to lie in a hammock, sip a cool drink, and watch the sun drop below the horizon.

Since the beach faces the open sea, it's too dangerous to swim, but the inexpensive little hotels and restaurants that line the beach make it a great hideaway for the world-weary and not-too-picky traveler. However, deciding this is for you *and* arranging lodging requires a pioneer spirit.

Famous it may be, but it's been neglected in the grand development scheme. Telephone service and city water were finally connected in 1992. There are no street addresses and no door-to-door mail service. Residents go to the casual post office if they are expecting mail, otherwise they don't bother. Generally there are plenty of rooms unless it's a major Mexican holiday. For Christmas, Easter, or New Year's, it's best to arrive days early and stake your territory. If the hotel of your choice doesn't have a restaurant, there are plenty of palapa-topped restaurants on the beach or in other hotels to choose from.

To get to Pie de la Cuesta from the airport, take the airport colectivo transportation to the zócalo in Acapulco. A taxi from there costs between $6 and $15 one-way, depending on how well you bargain and how much luggage you have. Buses leave frequently from the Acapulco zócalo.

If you drive, continue west along the peninsula, passing Coyuca Lagoon on your right, until you have almost reached the small air base at the tip. Along the way, you'll be invited to drive into different sections of beach by various private entrepreneurs, mostly small boys.

There's no charge for sitting under the thatched palapas on the public beach even if boys try to collect a fee.

WHERE TO STAY

CASA BLANCA HOTEL AND RESTAURANT, Pie de la Cuesta, Gro. No phone. 10 rms.
$ Rates: $40 single or double.
Behind a red-brick arched wall draped in bougainvillea, this simple but inviting place is clean and well tended. Rooms all have one double and one single bed, shelves for belongings, a cloth-covered table, and two chairs. Showers in the tile bathrooms spray everything in sight. The restaurant is open daily between 8am and 8pm when there are guests. There's a cozy sitting area in the dining area and shady, palm-lined path to the beach, just steps away. The price is a bit steep for what you get, so ask for a discount.

HOTEL PUESTA DEL SOL, Pie de la Cuesta, Gro. Tel. 74/60-0412.
8 main house rms, 10 beachfront rms, 6 bungalows with kitchens. FAN
$ Rates: $25 in the main house; $30 on the beach; $20 with kitchen.
Old and aging, this is still one of the more inviting inns in the area. It's down an unpaved side street on the left, just after the first *tope* (speed bump). It's more than 50 years old, on a big tree- and palm-filled beachfront property. Like a graceful old hacienda house, shaded by giant palms, its welcoming but aging charms are set off by an arch-lined patio shaded by giant palms. Rooms upstairs in the main house are small and not as colorful as those that front the beach. There's a swimming pool, and family-style dining for all three meals takes place on the pleasant patio. Rooms are clean and well painted with tile floors. Bathroom showers spray everything in sight. A few rooms have refrigerators, and two of the beachfront rooms have enclosed porches. The restaurant is open daily.

CHAPTER 7

EXCURSIONS TO CHILPANCINGO & THE CENTRAL VALLEYS

- **WHAT'S SPECIAL ABOUT CHILPANCINGO & THE CENTRAL VALLEYS**
1. **CHILPANCINGO**
2. **CHILAPA**
3. **OLINALÁ**
4. **TLAPA**

A trip north of Acapulco to Chilpancingo, the Guerrero state capital on Highway 95, and the Central Valleys (the region east of Chilpancingo on Highway 93 to Tlapa), will take you to a part of Mexico that is in some ways preserved in a time capsule. Travelers bent on getting to Acapulco or Taxco and Mexico City often streak past this area and miss entirely the rich festival and folk craft traditions that flourish not far from the new modern toll road that links the capital and the Pacific Coast. Olinalá, Mexico's lacquer artists capital, and the Sunday market at Chilapa are but two of the unusual attractions of this area.

This was once the land of the *arrieros* (mule drivers) whose domain it was from the Conquest almost until 1928, when the first highway linking Acapulco with Mexico City finally opened. For more than 200 years they carried the contents of the Manila galleons from Acapulco across these rugged mountains to Mexico's main commercial cities. Eventually they were put out of business, first when the train reached Iguala and finally when the highway opened. So, for much of its written history, the area was cut off from the rest of the world, and in some ways, part of it still is. A glance at the map shows few roads penetrating this rugged, mountainous part of the Sierra Madres.

As the state's seat of government, Chilpancingo, is, of course, a clean, modern city. Chilapa, Tixtla, and Tlapa, east of the state capital, look like many small Mexican towns or county commercial centers, and are somewhat accustomed to modern business practices and the Sunday influx of outsiders. But in the small villages, the life, customs, and dress you may encounter along the way are tied to traditions going back centuries, where travel even today is often by horse and burro, and roads to not-so-far-off villages resemble creekbeds, which, even if you can manage to drive them, will take hours.

Guerrero is known for its traditional village regional dances, and costumes—especially masks—worn during village celebrations, which have important local significance. This is the route to follow to see some of that tradition as a part of daily life. For foreign travelers, the Central Valleys is one of the most culturally rich and easiest to reach areas in Guerrero, though it is the least traveled by tourists. Along this route saints' days and other important events in the community calendar are celebrated with folk dances and ceremonies often not seen in other parts of Mexico.

WHAT'S SPECIAL ABOUT CHILPANCINGO & THE CENTRAL VALLEYS

Craft Villages
☐ Olinalá, famous for its fabulous lacquer furniture industry, Atzacualoya for fine utilitarian pottery, and Zitlala and Acatlán, known for beautiful skirts and tiger masks.

Colorful Murals
☐ Tixtla's murals of local history in the municipal palace are some of the most beautiful in the country.

An Outstanding Market
☐ Chilapa's Sunday market is loaded with baskets, pottery, masks, and farm produce.

Festivals
☐ Outstanding festivals include Día de la Candelaria in Atzacualoya, Petición de Lluvias in Zitlala, and Día de San Francisco in Olinalá.

Regional Dances
☐ Guerrero's centuries-old, vibrant celebrations showcase traditional costumes and unusual dances during village festivals.

In these villages many of the people speak Nahuatl, the language of the Aztecs, and other indigenous languages. Many women (though fewer now) wear clothing with Spanish elements, adopted after the Conquest, in vivid colors, often of satin material, with a ruffled blouse and tiered skirt that comes just below the knees. A rebozo (shawl) is always about the shoulders, usually with an infant inside. Fewer men than in the past wear the traditional homespun white shirt and pants with huaraches (handmade leather sandals), opting instead for regular pants and shirt, boots, and hat. In Zitlala, though now more rarely, women wear beautiful woven wrap skirts intricately embroidered in silk with birds, animals, and flowers, and embellished with sequins. For everyday use they wear it inside out, reversing it for "good" occasions.

Outside Chilpancingo, accommodations are modest, and travelers here must forgive such lapses as no toilet seats, reluctant or nonexistent hot water, and meager-but-clean quarters; on the other hand the cost isn't high for accommodations or food, which is generally good. The cultural rewards, however, are abundant, and the village people are among the most good-hearted I've met in the country.

Small villages in the Central Valleys, or for that matter almost anywhere off the main highway, are not accustomed to outsiders. Enter their villages respectfully. Before taking a picture of someone, ask permission, or try to establish some kind of rapport. The people in this area are generally very agreeable about having their pictures taken, and are often honored by it, but feel insulted if it's done on the sly. I've taken pictures, then returned a year or so later with copies, which thrills the subjects beyond imagination. At festivals, however, where dancers are anonymous behind masks, they may aggressively ask for money in return for a picture. Before you pay, be sure they hold still for just the picture you want. In general, be cautious about paying for the privilege of photographing someone, because before you know it, you will be surrounded by people pestering for a share. Take along balloons, ballpoint pens, and new pencils to give to children. Candy and gum aren't suggested because villagers don't have access to good dental care. Sometimes it's polite to offer enough money for a round of soft drinks for a dance group, but only if you've taken lots of pictures.

These and other traditions are among those you'll experience in Chilpancingo and the Central Valleys. Books listed under "Folk Art" in Chapter 1, "Getting to Know Mexico and the Triangle of the Sun," are excellent background reading for this region.

1. CHILPANCINGO

80 miles N of Acapulco, 100 miles S of Taxco

GETTING THERE By Bus Chilpancingo has two bus stations. Both are north of town center and you'll need to take a taxi. The main bus station is **Central Camionera,** 21 de Marzo at Juárez, where Flecha Roja has service from Acapulco, Chilapa, Mexico City, and Cuernavaca every half hour; eight buses daily from Taxco (some in the wee hours of the morning); and one bus from Olinalá. Transportes Gracela has hourly buses from Mexico City, Acapulco, Iguala, Chilapa, and Tlapa; from Toluca via Taxco five times daily, and from Zihuatanejo, twice daily. Transportes Cuauhtémoc has 13 daily buses from Mexico City and 17 from Acapulco. At **Estrella de Oro** station (tel. 2-2130), at Avenida Juárez 53 opposite Hotel Posada Melendez, nine buses a day arrive from Mexico City, two from Zihuatanejo, four from Taxco, and five from Iguala.

By Car From the highway, take any street leading into town—because the city is so confusing to enter, it won't make any difference if you have directions or street names. Signs marking streets are spare to nonexistent. Directional signs through town are even worse. Two signs point to Tixtla (the turnoff point for points east—Chilapa, Olinalá, and Tlapa), but once you've turned and followed the sign, you're on your own winding through the streets asking directions to find the highway itself. Other signs point to Acapulco or Mexico City. Nothing says "Centro."

DEPARTING By Bus From Central Camionera, Flecha Roja has 10 daily buses to Tlapa; one to Olinalá at 3pm; seven to Taxco, the first at 1am and the last at 11pm; and to Chilapa, Acapulco, Cuernavaca, and Mexico City buses every half hour. Transportes Gracela has hourly buses to Mexico City, Acapulco, Iguala, Chilapa, and Tlapa; two buses daily to Zihuatanejo; and four to Taxco, at 7:45am, 11:45am, 2pm, and 9:15pm. Transportes Cuauhtémoc has 17 buses to Acapulco and 13 to Mexico City. At Estrella de Oro Station buses go to Taxco at 9:15 and 11:15am and 6:45pm; to Zihuatanejo at 10:15am, 3:30pm, and 6:45pm; to Iguala five times daily; and to Mexico City, 10 times daily with the first departure at 6am and the last at midnight. (See "Olinalá" later in this chapter for the best means of getting there.)

C hilpancingo (alt. 4,462 ft., pop. 150,000) is the capital of the state of Guerrero, and is a busy hub of commerce and government. Except for the regional museum, it does not offer much that is of interest to the tourist. However, it is an excellent and inexpensive base for exploring the region. Chilapa, with its fabulous Sunday market, is only 18 miles away, and many other villages and towns are within easy driving distance.

ORIENTATION

INFORMATION   Hotel desk clerks are the most readily available source of tourist information, though they don't have giveaway maps. Locals are very helpful with directions.

GETTING AROUND   Taxis are the most convenient means of transportation. A ride between the market and the zócalo costs between $1.50 and $2.50. City buses run along main arteries in and out of city center, but there are no printed schedules.

CITY LAYOUT   Chilpancingo spreads up the hillside from the freeway to the mountains leading to Chilapa. Wherever you are, to find downtown, look for the white spires of the Templo de Santa Mariá de la Ascunción, which is on the main square and next to the Palacio del Gobierno and Regional Museum.

WHAT TO SEE & DO

Besides excursions to villages around Chilpancingo, the city's **central plaza** is a beautiful public square, with restaurants, bookstores, and banks.

MUSEO REGIONAL, Plaza Cívica. No phone.
   This repository of regional history, housed in a grand old building with a big open patio in the center, is flanked by walls of rousing murals painted by Roberto Cueva del Río, which are deteriorating. To see the museum, begin on the right with rooms showing the geology and natural history (including a butterfly collection), Indian artifacts, and agriculture. A map shows the Olmec influence in Guerrero with the possible routes of Olmec communications from the Yucatán, Veracruz, and the area around Mexico City based on pottery and other objects on display. Another area shows the Conquest and the meeting of two worlds, followed by the division of labor after the Conquest, and evangelization of the natives primarily by the Augustinian priests in the 16th century. Another room deals solely with rural Guerrero, an important section, since so much of the state is rural. A few of the explanations are in English.
   To the right of the entrance is an excellent bookstore with a good selection of well-researched and -written literature about the state, its dance and cultural traditions, famous people, and history. Most publications are in Spanish. It's open the same hours as the museum.
   The museum is on the main plaza, next to the Templo de Santa María de la Asunción.
   Admission: Free.
   Open: Tues–Sun 11am–6pm.

IMPRESSIONS

The road we were following was the famous "Acapulco Trail," leading from that part of the Pacific to the city of Mexico, and which has been worn by the feet of countless mules and burros for three hundred years and over. It is a twelve-days journey from the capital to Acapulco, and one must procure his entire outfit in the city he leaves, unless he chance to fall in with a conducta on the route, which is of rare occurrence.
—F.A. OBER, TRAVELS IN MEXICO 1884

Some Mexicans believe that the mysterious region from which Montezuma obtained his supplies of gold—which was never revealed to the Spaniards—is situated somewhere in Guerrero.
— W.E. CARSON, MEXICO: THE WONDERLAND OF THE SOUTH, 1909

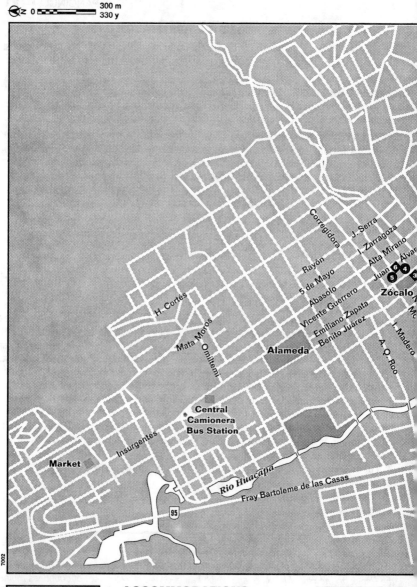

300 m
330 y

Corregidora
J. Serra
I. Zarragoza
Alta Mirano
Rayón
Juan N. Álvar
5 de Mayo
Abasolo
Vicente Guerrero
Emiliano Zapata
Benito Juárez
Zócalo
H. Cortés
Mata Moros
Omiltemi
Alameda
I. Madero
A. O. Roo
**Central
Camionera
Bus Station**
Insurgentes
Market
Rio Huacapa
Fray Bartoleme de las Casas
95

MEXICO CITY
Chilpancingo &
The Central Valleys

ACCOMMODATIONS:
Conjunto Turístico Jacarandas **1**
Hotel Posada Melendez **2**

DINING:
Cafetería y Restaurante
El Portal **3**
Restaurant La Tortuga **6**

ATTRACTIONS:
Museo Regional **4**
Templo de Santa Mar
de la Asunción **5**

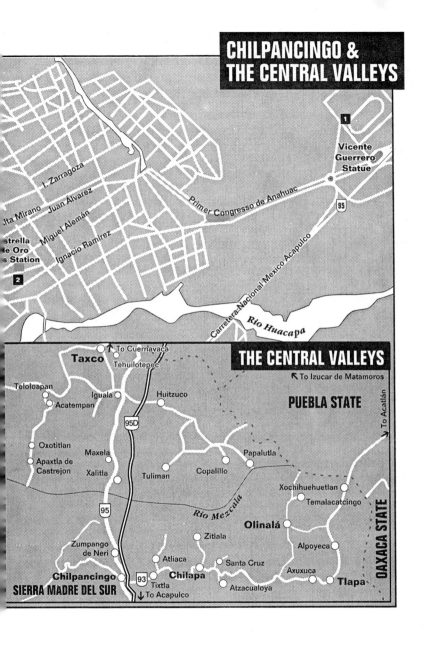

CHILPANCINGO & THE CENTRAL VALLEYS

1

Vicente
Guerrero
Statue

95

I. Zarragoza

Juan Alvarez

lta Mirano

Miguel Alemán

strella
le Oro
s Station

Ignacio Ramirez

Primer Congresso de Anahuac

Carretera Nacional Mexico Acapulco

2

Río Huacapa

THE CENTRAL VALLEYS

To Cuernavaca

Taxco

Tehuilotepec

↖ To Izucar de Matamoros

Teloloapan

Iguala

Huitzuco

PUEBLA STATE

To Acatlán

Acatempan

95D

Oxotitlan

Maxela

Papalutla

Apaxtla de
Castrejon

Xalitla

Tuliman

Copalillo

Xochihuehuetlan

Temalacatcingo

95

Río Mezcala

Olinalá

OAXACA STATE

Zumpango
de Neri

Zitlala

Alpoyeca

Atliaca

Santa Cruz

Axuxuca

Chilpancingo

93

Chilapa

Tlapa

SIERRA MADRE DEL SUR

Tixtla

↓ To Acapulco

Atzacualoya

WHERE TO STAY

CONJUNTO TURÍSTICO JACARANDAS, Av. Ruffo Figueroa s/n, Col. Burócratas, Chilpancingo, Gro. 39060. Tel. 747/2-4444. Fax 747/2-4506. 65 rms. TEL

$ Rates: $41 single; $59 double.

Set in beautiful grounds overlooking the city, this is Chilpancingo's most modern hotel and it's owned and operated by the state. The staff is friendly and helpful. The large rooms are carpeted and have two double beds and worn Formica furniture. Rooms on the second and third floors have balconies overlooking the grounds. There's a restaurant/bar open for all three meals Monday through Saturday, a beautiful swimming pool set in the middle of the grassy lawn, a disco that is open on weekends, and a movie theater open nightly. It's on the southern edge of town, and there are signs pointing the way from the highway.

HOTEL PARADOR MARQUÉS, Blv. V. Guerrero, Km 27, Carretera Acapulco/México, Chilpancingo, Gro. 39060. Tel. 747/2-6773 or 2-9542. Fax 747/2-7885. 40 rms. TV TEL

$ Rates: $58 single or double. **Parking:** Free.

This roadside motel seems like an oasis after a long drive. Located on the highway at the far (Acapulco) end of Chilpancingo, it's a comfortable place to end the day. The two stories of clean rooms offer nothing beyond the ordinary in looks, but the beds are good, the water is hot, and you'll get a good night's rest. Floor fans in each room are all that's needed in this climate. Two restaurants and a bar cover all the meals. For recreation, horseback riding can be arranged, and the hotel has two squash courts.

HOTEL POSADA MELENDEZ, Juárez 50, Chilpancingo, Gro. 39000. Tel. 747/2-2050 or 2-3087. 33 rms. TEL

$ Rates: $31 single; $39 double.

This beautifully kept hacienda-style hotel, which dates from the 1940s, has beautiful tile details throughout and still uses the wonderful old (but handsomely maintained) furniture. Rooms are freshly painted and clean with tile floors and all-tile bathrooms. Some rooms have balconies overlooking the interior yard and these will be quieter. In back there's a large pool in the shady courtyard. The restaurant, which serves excellent economically priced food, is open daily from 7am to 9pm. The hotel offers long-distance service at the reception desk between 7am and 9:30pm.

WHERE TO DINE

CAFETERIA Y RESTAURANTE EL PORTAL, Plaza Central Congreso de Anahuac, Centro Comercio Portales. Tel. 2-4668.
Cuisine: MEXICAN.

$ Prices: Breakfast $2.75–$5; main courses $3.50–$7; comida corrida $5.
Open: Daily 8:30am–11pm.

This restaurant is tucked in among the arcades on one side of Chilpancingo's main plaza. With its view of the passing downtown life, this is a good place to take a break. The pork steak a la mexicana is quite good. For simple refreshment they also have espresso and cappuccino coffee.

RESTAURANT LA TORTUGA, Plaza Cívica, Bravo 1. Tel. 2-2563.
Cuisine: MEXICAN/ITALIAN.

$ Prices: Breakfast $1.75–$4; main courses $5–$6; pizzas $6–$16.
Open: Mon–Sat 8am–10pm, Sun 9am–9pm.

With its green awnings visible on one side of the main plaza, La Tortuga offers a good vantage point for taking in downtown life while enjoying the food. The menu has wide appeal with burgers and fries, sandwiches, pizzas, Mexican platters, and steak. It's a good place to enjoy an espresso or cappuccino, or cool off with a beer.

NEARBY ATTRACTIONS

GRUTAS DE JUXTLAHUACA   The Caves of Juxtlahuaca are something out of the ordinary. They are renowned in these parts for three ancient murals and a few small figures painted by the Olmecs between 1000 and 600 B.C. Part of the cave adventure requires wading or swimming in an underground pool to finish the tour; wear tennis shoes and clothes you don't mind getting wet. Guides using gas lamps lead visitors through some magnificent caverns, all of which take around two hours.

Andrés Ortega (tel. 747/5-1024, ext. 107), who lives just off Colotlipa's main square, is a well-known guide; ask anyone to point you to his house. Other guides are also available at the main square. A cave tour runs around $30 and the cost can be shared by a group. On weekends lots of visitors come to the caves; that's the best time to join a group and share the price.

To reach the caves, drive southwest of Chilpancingo on Highway 95 towards Acapulco. Turn left at Petaquillas and follow the road through Mochitlán and Quechultenango to Colotlipa. From the turnoff it takes 45 minutes to an hour to drive on primarily paved roads with lots of potholes, wandering goats, cows, and burros. The caves are about four miles from Colotlipa and are open daily from 8am to 5pm.

ZUMPANGO DEL RÍO/ZUMPANGO DE NERI   Fifteen miles north of Chilpancingo, this city once known as Zumpango del Río is now Zumpango de Neri, but many people still use the old name. Market day is Sunday; you'll almost always find a supply of the area's local pottery, a fragile reddish clay painted with sienna-colored flowers. Día de Candelaria, February 2, is the town's biggest festival, and celebrations go on for around two weeks. During the celebration, both entrances to the town churchyard are decorated with grand arches decorated with red, white, and black beans, much the way flower arches are done elsewhere in Mexico.

XALITLA [CHALITLA]   Thirty miles north of Chilpancingo (about an hour's drive on the free highway) is the turnoff for Xalitla (sometime spelled Chalitla; either way pronounced Sha-*leet*-lah), which leads to the village of that name and to the **Artisans Cooperative,** on the right side of the highway. It's easy to miss the single row of shops, though the new sign, which reads *Artesanías*, makes it more visible. The cooperative is a good, one-stop place to find crafts from small villages all around this arid valley region. Here you'll find pottery from Ameyaltepec and San Augustín Oapan, colorful carved and painted saints, hundreds of masks from many villages and representing many dances, and unfired clay necklaces, as well as pottery and bark paintings with village scenes. Almost 30 years ago a connection was made between bark-paper makers in a small village in Puebla with the artists of this area. From that connection came all the bark-paper paintings sold widely throughout Mexico. Xalitla (the village more or less behind the cooperative) is full of these artists, as is Ameyaltepec, a few miles by rugged dirt road off Highway 95. You can buy the bark and clay paintings made in Xalitla at the cooperative, or in the village. If you drive through Xalitla (the roads are narrow and sometimes turn into paths) artists will often invite you in to see their inventory. Or if you stop for a soft drink in town, artists will bring their batch of rolled-up paintings to you, one by one, each quietly waiting a turn. Of course, they are disappointed when you don't buy and you can't buy from everyone, so it's sometimes simpler to select something at the cooperative or wait until you get to Taxco, where these and other crafts are sold in the streets by these same villagers.

San Augustín Oapan, about 1½ hours east by dirt road, is a village of potters who make bowls, large water jars, and tall skinny figures decorated in sienna-colored paint. Shopping at the cooperative, however, is often more useful in terms of purchases than a visit to the village where the objects are made. Many of the better pieces are sold at the cooperative. The villages don't have central shops, so you must go from house to house visiting with artisans—not at all uninteresting—but very time-consuming and often not productive. Sometimes they have nothing to sell because it's all at the cooperative or in stores in Acapulco, Taxco, Cuernavaca, or Mexico City.

IGUALA   Sixty-five miles north of Chilpancingo is the historic city of Iguala, 30 miles from Taxco, where Agustín de Iturbide proclaimed Mexico's independence from Spain. Iguala was originally settled by Chontales, but after the Conquest Franciscan priests built churches, and Spaniards settled there soon after.

Head to the **market** here, which is known for gold-filigree jewelry sold outside the market area. Inside the market look for baskets from all over the area as well as pottery, especially the fat jugs with women's faces from Tuliman, a village east of Iguala. During Easter week there are many processions of penitents, and October 4 is the celebration of San Francisco.

---

2. CHILAPA

115 miles NE of Acapulco, 35 miles E of Chilpancingo, 24 miles
E of Tixtla, 75 miles W of Tlapa, 135 miles SE of Taxco

GETTING THERE   By Bus   Five daily buses leave from Acapulco's Estrella Blanca station, going to Chilpancingo where you change to Chilapa buses, which run every half hour. The trip from Acapulco takes around four hours and to Chilapa from Chilpancingo just over an hour.

By Car   The new four-lane toll highway between Acapulco and Mexico City cuts the driving time between the two from 6 hours to around 3½. (It bypasses Taxco.) Driving the two-lane free highway that winds through the villages takes about two hours from Acapulco to Chilpancingo, and another 45 minutes to an hour to Chilapa. Follow signs for the right turn onto the two-lane paved highway from Chilpancingo to Chilapa. From Tixtla to Chilapa takes 35 minutes. Be alert for wandering farm animals grazing beside the highway.

DEPARTING   By Bus   Chilapa has two bus distribution points. In the central village **white minibuses** (holding about 30 people) that go to nearby barrios and villages line up opposite Abarotes Shiela on Calle Revolución, about two long blocks from the plaza in the direction of the highway. Pay as you board; the cost is minimal. One bus goes west and covers the area known as **Cruzero Santa Ana,** stopping at Claveles, Provedencia, Amate Amarillo, Chautla, El Limón, Cruzero de Cuautenango, and finally Santa Ana. The **Nejapa** route goes east stopping at El Terero, El Banco, Amatitlan, La Cruz Verde, Nejapa, and Texcal. Zitlala buses leave from the Central Camionera.

The main bus station, **Central Camionera,** is five blocks west of the cathedral; it has two classes of buses (both of the school-bus variety). The green-and-white

Lineas Unidas del Sur (tel. 5-0032) is the first you see upon arriving at the station. Ignore the sign outside listing departure times that are ancient history, and ask the ticket seller for the correct schedule. When I checked, there were 11 daily buses to Tlapa, the first at 3am and the last at 11pm; six daily buses to the Estrella Blanca station in Acapulco; two daily buses to Mexico City (at 11pm and midnight), and two to Olinalá (at 4:30pm and 1am), both four-hour trips (see "Olinalá" below in this chapter). Buses to Chilpancingo leave every half hour. The **Cerro Azul** line, goes to villages not covered by the white minivans—Acatlán and Zitlala (at 5, 6, and 7am), Tepoztlán, Pantitlán, Ahuihuyuco, and Tlanipatla. These buses, in poor condition and often with missing windows, are used by locals carrying farm produce (including caged chickens or turkeys) to and from market. For Chilapa's Sunday market and on festival days, many more buses run between Chilapa and these villages. Don't hesitate to use them, but remember their main function is local transportation, not tourist comfort.

C hilapa (alt. 4,266 ft., pop. 40,000) is famous for its Sunday market (*tianguis*), which brings village craftsmakers and farmers from miles around to spread their wares around the village square.

Among various interpretations, the name *Chilapa* comes from a Nahuatl word meaning "in the red river," "place of colored water," or "chili water"—all meanings having to do with red-hot chili peppers. Evidence of the first humans crossing the area appears between 500 and 700 B.C., with the Olmecs, the Cohuixcas, and later the Mixtecs. Around 1458, Emperor Moctezuma Illhuicamina put Chilapa and the surrounding region under Aztec rule. Today, Chilapa is largely composed of residents of mixed Spanish and Indian heritage with surrounding communities of indigenous groups speaking Nahuatl, the language of the Aztecs.

Entering the pleasant village of Chilapa with its traffic flowing easily around a large tree-shaded plaza, one would not suspect its past as a center of fierce political opposition, at least since post-Conquest times. As early as 1531 Cortés sent Spaniards to quell an uprising of the indigenous population who were rebelling against Spanish rule; that encounter brought them officially under Spanish domination by 1532, and the first Augustinian friars arrived the following year.

During the movement for independence, Chilapa was widely known for its support of the movement, and José María Morelos y Pavón came more than once to recruit troops in the plaza; there's a statue of him in Chilapa's central square. At least 5,000 locals held off the forces of Maximilian for 15 days in 1864, during the French intervention. Considering that peasants in this area suffered under the dictatorship-presidency of Porfirio Díaz and participated forcefully in the revolution (1910–17) to oust him, it's an odd footnote in the city's history that in 1871 Chilapa was named "Chilapa de Porfirio Diáz," a name now fallen from use.

ORIENTATION

INFORMATION Ask at your hotel for local directions and general information. The **Centro Cultural.** at the crossroads from the highway to Chilapa, will have information on local cultural events and regional festivals.

CITY LAYOUT Highway 93 from Chilpancingo leads east into Chilapa. After passing the population sign you'll see a Pemex **gas station** on the right, and several repair shops and restaurants. A short distance on is the **crossroads** left to Acatlán and Zitlala and right immediately into Chilapa on its main street, Revolución, which leads past the **Centro Cultural** immediately on your left as you turn, and five long blocks to the **central plaza.** Visible on the left side of the crossroads is the **Hotel Las Brisas,** the best Chilapa offers. If you continue on the highway, in a minute you'll encounter two murderous *topes.* On the right after the first set of topes, is FidePal, the **Sala de Exposición de Artesanías,** a large complex where palm-leaf crafts from the region are assembled and distributed. About a half mile farther is the turn off to the right onto Municipio Libre, a wide busy street, which leads to the **bus station,** which is about a mile farther on the left. The highway also leads to Olinalá and Tlapa, two other villages mentioned later in this chapter, and to Atzacualoya, mentioned under Chilapa's "Special Events" (see below). The **town plaza** is bounded by **Insurgentes,** which fronts the cathedral, **Revolución** (the main street leading in from the highway), opposite it, **Avenida José María Andraca** with the supermarket, and at the far end of the plaza opposite the cathedral is a pedestrians-only street that fronts the **Municipal Palace** and city jail.

GETTING AROUND   There isn't much need for transportation within the city, since everything is within walking distance of the main plaza, the bus station, or the highway crossroads. However, taxis can be found around the bus station and plaza and near the crossroads. For going to outlying villages by local colectivo minivans or buses, see "Departing by Bus," above.

FAST FACTS

Area Code   The telephone area code is 747.

Bank   A branch of Bancomer is on the east side of the main plaza, open Monday through Friday from 9:30am to 1:30pm.

Business Hours   Most restaurants and businesses are closed on Thursday.

Climate   Generally speaking, the climate is warm except December through February when mornings and evenings can be fairly nippy, and there are often unseasonal rains that add to the chill. Hotels have no heat. Be prepared for rain anytime. If it's really rainy and you find you're knee-deep in muddy streets, rubber boots are sold at the supermarket on the plaza.

Supermarket   There's a supermarket on the east side of the main square where you can stock up on bottled water and other essentials.

WHAT TO SEE & DO

SUNDAY MARKET

Chilapa's main attraction is its wonderful, clean Sunday market, which spreads out from the central plaza and spills onto adjacent streets. It's worth a detour here just to experience this market.

Local vendors begin arriving the night before and continue to arrive with their salable goods even after the market is in full swing. Park several blocks away,

---

IMPRESSIONS

Stop an Indian on a mountain trail, market-bound with a load of pottery on his back, and offer to buy the lot at his own price. Nine times out of ten he will refuse to sell at any figure. To part with his pots would deprive him of excuse to go to market. Money is but heavy metal; the plaza is colour and news and life.
—STUART CHASE, *MEXICO: A STUDY OF TWO AMERICAS,* 1931

beyond the arteries clogged with loaded trucks headed for the plaza. The selling banter is low-key, but bargaining is part of the custom. The market is neatly divided between the various products: Cooked food stalls and fresh baked goods are left of the plaza; regionally made, colorful handwoven and machine-stitched baskets and bright woven straw flowers are in front of and to the left of the cathedral; mask vendors selling the delightful tiger masks and other Guerrero masks, are generally in the middle of the street to the left of the cathedral. A sea of locally produced low-fired pottery unfolds beside the parklike plaza in a large open part of the square fronting the city jail. In the center of the open plaza are rows of fresh produce, neatly piled on the ground on squares of cloth or plastic—chilis, radishes, onions, peppers, beans, corn, bunches of huge garlic, cones of brown sugar, and salt. Brightly colored painted chairs with rush straw seats, made by jail inmates, are sometimes sold at the jail door or to the right of the church. Only one or two vendors sell lacquerware from Olinalá (see "Olinalá," below). Just about the only regional craft you won't find at the market are Acatlán skirts and leather tiger dance masks, both made by villagers north of Chilapa (see "Nearby Attractions," below). Few of the rebozos, for which this village was once famous, are made here.

The market vendors are gentle, friendly people, unspoiled by too much contact with the outside (although very brusque craft-shop owners from Mexico City and Acapulco jab their way through the crowds and demand low prices for volume purchases). Sellers smile and chat with strangers in Spanish, and among themselves in Nahuatl, and are personally pleased when you buy from them. During the bargaining process you'll notice that if you offer a price in Spanish, they discuss it in Nahuatl, then come up with an answer in Spanish. If you offer dollars, the process and discussion lengthen, because they must decide the last-known exchange rate, then decide if your offer is a good one—all in good humor.

THE CATHEDRAL

At the far end of the plaza, you can't miss the cathedral with its two towers and statue of St. Gabriel the Archangel attacking Satan over the building's principal portico. A crowd gathers just before noon each Sunday, and again at 8pm, when doors in the right tower open, and out come life-size mechanical figures of Juan Diego and Father Zumarraga, the priest who finally listened to Juan's description of the miraculous apparition of the Virgin Mary. The figures signify the moment that Juan Diego showed Father Zumarraga the image of the Virgin in his cloak, which became the widely revered Virgin of Guadalupe. Inside the church, notice the enormous stained-glass windows, each one commemorating the different patron saints of nearby cities and villages such as Acapulco, Taxco, Tixtla, and Chilpancingo.

IMPRESSIONS

In some regions of Mexico, the cutting of trees to be used in making masks is undertaken only at specific times. In some parts of Guerrero, for example, trees have traditionally been cut during the luna menguante (waning of the moon), preferably at sunrise during the month of January.
—DONALD CORDRY, *MEXICAN MASKS*, 1980

In . . . Guerrero, it is believed that masks assume the spirit of the animals they represent and protect the wearer against evil during religious ceremonies.
—MARION OETTINGER, *FOLK TREASURES OF MEXICO*, 1990

SPECIAL EVENTS

One of the reasons for spending time in this area is to experience some of the unusual village festivals and the special dances during the festivities.

Regional Dances

Knowing something about the regional dances and how to recognize them will enhance a visit to any village festival. Here are a few of those for which Guerrero is famous and which you will likely see in this area and other parts of Guerrero.

MAROMEROS Literally, *maromeros* means "somersaulters." But these masked dancers in shiny costumes bounce and leap on a tightrope wearing anything on their feet from tennis shoes to sandals. The dance is said to date from pre-Hispanic times and is often seen at religious festivals around Tixtla and Atzacualoya.

LOS DIABLOS The dance of the devils grew up as a result of evangelization by Catholic friars. It symbolizes good and evil, with the devil wearing a red costume and red mask, wielding a sword, and fighting other masked and costumed dancers representing either Christians or death, dressed as a skeleton. As many as 20 men take part accompanied by musicians.

MOROS Y CRISTIANOS The dance of the Moors and Christians is seen at village festivals all over Mexico danced by groups of men as well as groups of women. Moors, of course, represent non-Christians battling Christians; the performers are attired in shiny soldier helmets and flowing satin capes and carry swords. Dancers go around the church atrium in pairs or single file, again and again—one dance group can perform for hours.

DANZA DE LOS TLACOLOLEROS The "dance of the slash-and-burners" is a pre-Conquest dance. All over Mexico peasants are accustomed to clearing forests (by cutting the trees and burning the wood) in order to farm new fields when their old ones give out. This dance represents this farming ritual and is accompanied by two or three musicians playing a violin and drum or guitar. The central character may wear a long taillike belt of cut-up woven tires or some other shiplike object, which he snaps and whips at his opponents (the other masked and costumed dancers). The sound of the whip is symbolic of the crackling fire during the burning of the forests. The object is to kill a tiger (dressed in costume, of course), which represents a bad god or evil. The dance has several parts: looking for the tiger, hitting with the whip in the process of looking, then finding the tiger and killing it.

Besides this one, tiger dancers with a wide variety of masks and costumes appear in many dances, including *Danza de los Tejorones, Danza de los Xochimilcos, Danza de los Tecuanes*, and *Danza de los Maizos*.

LA CHILENA The Chilena is a variation of a dance probably brought from Chile and it's seen almost exclusively in Guerrero, especially along the coast and in Tixtla. It's a flirtatious kind of dance and very lively, with both men and women taking part, accompanied by guitars and singing.

LOS PESCADORES The "fishermen's dance" is symbolic of a day in the life of a fisherman with man against the elements. Dancers wear black masks and colorful wooden fish attached at the waist. At the end, the fish symbolically thrash in the water, and the dancers break the fish with machetes.

Festivals

Below are some of the best village festivals around Chilapa:

ATZACUALOYA Día de Candelaria, on February 2, is this village's best festival. Sometime between noon and 3pm dancers begin to perform in the churchyard. As the afternoon wears on as many as six groups at once may be performing—Moors and Christians, maromeros, tlacololeros, doce pares de Francia, and more. It's quite something to see and there's a big local market on that day.

CHILAPA   Chilapa's patron saint is the Virgin of Guadalupe and celebrations on **December 12** and **August 15** honor her with towers of fireworks (*toritos*), regional dances, and a running of the bulls. On December 12, a torch lighted in Mexico City and passed along the route by runners arrives in Chilapa.

TIXTLA   Tixtla is known for its lively dancing and gay festivals. On **January 17** is the **Día de San Antonio Abad,** patron saint of animals, in which village animals are brought to the church for a blessing. **May 15** is the **Fiesta de San Isidro Labrador.** Both men and women participate in the regional dances, with the men wearing the typical homespun white shirts and pants and straw hats and the women wearing ruffled skirts and blouses. Fireworks are a big part of the festival. **August 9** commemorates the **birthday of Vincente Guerrero,** second president of Mexico, who was born here. On **October 18** is the **Fiesta of Santa Lucía,** with dances and fireworks similar to those during the San Isidro celebration.

ZITLALA   One of the most unusual festivals in Mexico occurs in Zitlala each **May 1 and 2.** Called **La Peticíon para las Lluvias** (Petititon for Rains), the purpose is to petition the gods for sufficient rains to produce good crops. On the evening of May 1 the whole town forms a procession of candle-carrying penitents climbing to nearby sacred mountains (Cerro de Zitlaltepec and Cerro El Cruzco, the highest). El Cruzco is topped with three crosses, representing three neighborhoods in Zitlala. The cave there is considered sacred, and those who enter say they have heard the wails of the dead. During these two days costumed dancers from the different neighborhoods (*barrios*) dance as tigers symbolically fighting each other in the streets. Years ago these fights became quite vicious, but have toned down in recent years. The origin of the neighborhood hostility dates back to the Conquest when rival Spaniards occupied the town. During **Carnaval,** the three days before the beginning of Lent, the same kind of symbolic fighting goes on in the atrium of the Zitlala church, except that this time the dancers are dressed as women. On **September 10,** the town honors the patron saint San Nicolás Tolentino. Men dressed as women dance in the church courtyard and that night, men dressed as tigers climb to the church tower playing the teponaxtle, a pre-Conquest wooden instrument made from hollowed logs. Tuesday, the last of Carnaval begins with the Danza de los Xochimilcos, a collective penitence in which almost the whole town takes part, followed by or simultaneous with symbolic battles by men in women's clothing.

NEARBY ATTRACTIONS

Using Chilapa as a launching point, you can delve into the fascinating customs and crafts of this area, many of which date from pre-Conquest times.

As you walk through the villages you may be asked to enter someone's home, especially if they have something to sell. Always you'll be offered a chair, or stool, usually a small one low to the ground, even if a family member has to be left standing. Accept their hospitality, for it's honestly offered. It is their way of honoring guests and the custom exists in the most humble of huts. Even if you don't buy something, it's courteous to shake hands, and acknowledge everybody, and say *gracias* profusely before leaving. Your reward for showing every courtesy and respect to these people, even if you can't communicate by language, will often be a flow of love and a warming experience you'll remember for a lifetime.

The road north, a distance of 6½ miles between Chilapa through Acatlán to Zitlala, is paved now but ends where the village begins. Other roads mentioned are unpaved and rough, but passable by ordinary car. After a rain, be careful of muddy roads which can be as slippery and as dangerous as snow.

ACATLÁN

To get to Acatlán from Chilapa's main plaza, take the main street (Revolución) to the highway, cross the highway (with the Las Brisas Hotel on your left), and Acatlán is three miles straight ahead.

This village with rough, rutted dirt and rock streets lined with adobe-brick homes, is famous for its makers of leather and papier-mâché masks, and for its weavers and embroiderers of some of Mexico's most beautiful regional skirts. A few people make small figures and whistles of brightly painted clay. The women of Acatlán once wore the skirts themselves, but now are devoted only to making them for the women of neighboring Zitlala (where even they are wearing them less and less often). The skirts, made of hand-loomed panels from five to eight feet long, are black cotton, with thin white stripes. On these basic panels silk-like thread is used to embroider elaborate moving figures of birds, deer, rabbits, and other animals, embellished with sequins. The more expensive skirts (upwards of $200) have many tiny figures and muted tones and a masterful placement of sequins. The less expensive ones ($50 to $75) have larger embroidered figures, brighter colors, and no sequins.

If you want to the see the local crafts, park anywhere that looks convenient and ask around for local craftsmen who will invite you into their homes and bring out what they've made. The vocabulary here is *faldas* (skirts), *blusas* (blouses), *mascaras* (masks), and *figuras de barro* (figures made of clay).

ATZACUALOYA

It's about 1½ miles from the edge of Chilapa to the turnoff (right) to Atzacualoya, and the battered sign is easy to miss. Then it's a few miles farther on a dirt road to the town. This is a village of potters whose finely made broad, deep bowls are finished off around the rim with a smooth sienna color made from rusty water. Thump one and listen to the fine ring of well-made pottery. Potters put samples of their wares in front of their homes, and if you're interested in seeing more, just knock. Often they are firing pieces under piles of wood in the open courtyards of their homes. They also bring these to the Sunday market in Chilapa. The best time to visit Atzacualoya is on February 2, during the **Día de Candelaria,** when the churchyard rocks with native dancing (see "Special Events," above).

ZITLALA

Three and a half miles north of Acatlán (using the same road from Chilapa to Acatlán) is Zitlala, another thatched-roofed, adobe-walled Nahua village with dirt

---

IMPRESSIONS

During the festival held (in Zitlala) in early May, there is a battle between two types of Tigres, green ones and yellow ones, which I believe have some reference to green and yellow corn. The entire fiesta is a petition for rain. There is great competition and resentment between the three districts of the village. Whether this resentment is artificially produced in order to cause bloodshed I do not know. However, even at the present time, it is necessary to bring policemen from the larger village of Chilapa to see that people are not badly hurt. The Tigres carry long ropes containing huge knots, and with these they beat each other over the head and body. The head is protected by extremely heavy painted leather Tigre masks. . . . In former times people were killed during the fiestas, and blood is still shed each year.
—DONALD CORDRY, *MEXICAN MASKS*, 1980

and cobblestoned streets. Children riding burros burdened with water cans fetch water from the communal well in the afternoons, and cowherds lead cows in for milking. In this village some women still wear the traditional embroidered skirt by the women of Acatlán (see description under "Acatlán," above). Unless it's a special occasion, however, such as a church or a festival day, they wear them inside-out to protect the embroidery from pulling and becoming soiled. One major industry here is broom making, so you see brooms stacked in the street, and inside homes, the preparation of straw for the brooms. Another is palm weaving. They weave it in long strands and sell it to the cooperative in Chilapa, where it's machine-stitched into hats, baskets, and purses, which are then sent to markets throughout the area. Here, too, there are maskmakers, who especially make the leather tiger masks used during the Rain Festival (*Petición para las Lluvias*) in May (see "Special Events," above). Stroll the streets, go to the food market, and climb the stony street to the hilltop church of San Nicolás, founded by Augustinian friars in the 1600s.

TIXTLA

From Chilpancingo, 18 miles away, most people barrel on past this village in a mad dash for Chilapa or Olinalá. But Tixtla is the most physically charming of all the villages along this route. The name Tixtla comes from a Nahuatl word meaning "corn masa," probably because the area once was devoted completely to raising corn. Any of the main turnoffs from the highway will eventually lead to the grand, tree-shaded main square flanked on one side by the Parroquia de San Martín (the village church) and the Municipal Palace and the market. Two of Mexico's famous sons were born here, Ignacio Manuel Altamirano, father of Mexican literature, and Vincente Guerrero, independence leader and second president of the republic, each with a fine statue on the plaza.

Absolutely don't miss the wonderful murals in the **Municipal Palace.** Begun in 1987 and finished in 1991 under the direction of artist Jaime Gómez del Payón, they are some of the most beautifully painted in the country. Even if you aren't a mural fan, see these—local history almost dances off the walls and the lively facial expressions are actually those of locals. The palace is open weekdays from 8am to 6pm and occasionally on Saturday or Sunday. Visit the **market,** where you may find the colorful and finely woven palm hats used in dances here, the carved wooden black-and-white bulls used in the dance of Santa Lucía, and marigold and pink *flor de malancita* used to decorate graves. The **Altamirano Museum** is in the Barrio Santiago, a few blocks west of the plaza, but it's seldom open.

See "Special Events," above, for details on village festivals.

WHERE TO STAY

HOTEL BELLA VISTA, Calle 3 Norte 106, Chilapa, Gro. 41000. Tel. 747/ 5-0287 or 5-0088. 13 rms (12 with bath).

$ Rates: $18 single; $22 double. **Parking:** Free in interior of hotel.

This hotel is my second choice after the Hotel Las Brisas. The name means beautiful view, but there are no views except of the opposite three stories of rooms. Rooms are clean enough and serviceable, but definitely no-frills. Some have both a double and single bed, others only one double bed. One room has three beds, and its bathroom is across the hall. Fresh paint is rapidly replaced by mold. The shower sprays the entire bathroom.

To find it, with your back to the cathedral, walk one block to the left and turn right; the hotel is a half block down on the left. Cars enter via large doors on Calle 5 Sur.

HOTEL LAS BRISAS, Prolongación Av. Revolución 2, Chilapa, Gro. 41000. Tel. 747/5-0769. 20 rms (all with bath).
$ Rates: $21 single, $31 double.

This is by far the best hotel in Chilapa, but you'll need to get here by late morning to get a room, especially on Saturday, the day before the big Sunday market. Or call ahead for a reservation. Rooms have tile floors, comfortable beds, small but clean tile bathrooms, and windows opening either to the outside walkway, or interior corridor. It's on the left side of the highway at the crossroads entering Chilapa (right) or to Acatlán (left).

HOTEL SEÑORIAL, Revolución 409, Chilapa, Gro. 41000. Tel. 747/5-0036. 44 rms.
$ Rates: $9.50 single; $14.50 double.

As you drive toward Chilapa's main plaza from the highway you'll see the aged Hotel Señorial on the left, just before you reach the plaza. Once-fine Puebla tile on the lobby floor and wall borders lies beneath layers of grime. That's the best of the Señorial. The lobby is overcome by plants and tattered furniture. Rooms are only serviceable, with freshly painted walls, worn beds, thin sheets, and lumpy pillows. Ventilation is achieved only by leaving the hall door open. The doorless, tiny, moldy bathrooms have no toilet seats and the sink may be clinging to the wall by a single bolt. Your plumbing skills will be handy in getting the toilet to work. Towels are small, thin, and stiff. A special events room in the back of the lobby may attract the loudest band in the world, which will play until the last patron can pay no more. Stay here as a last resort and bring earplugs. However, do stop in to see the mural in the lobby showing the women of Acatlán weaving and embroidering their elaborately decorated regional skirts.

WHERE TO DINE

Chilapa's restaurant situation is unpredictable. Because it's hard to find a good restaurant, try these listed below, and then ask around for anything new. Several **bakeries** have storefronts on or within a block or two of the central plaza. The **market,** where you can find fresh fruits and vegetables, extends from the plaza back several blocks toward the main highway. Many restaurants close early or only open through midday, and may be closed on Thursday.

COCINA ECONÓMICA, Revolución 417. Tel. 5-0884.
Cuisine: MEXICAN.
$ Prices: Breakfast $3; comida corrida $3.50.
Open: Fri–Wed 8am–5pm.

This sparkling clean little restaurant, with quick and courteous service, is the best the village has to offer. Each day's different menu of soup and plate lunch is posted on the wall. The pollo cassera, a sort of chicken stew with side helpings of beans, rice, and tortillas, was especially good. The drink menu includes wine and beer. The clean cooking kettles are lined up within view on one side of the room and the front has windows facing the street. It's next to Pizzas Bandido, about four blocks from the main square as you come from the highway.

PIZZAS BANDIDO, Revolución 419. No phone.
Cuisine: PIZZA/SANDWICHES.
$ Prices: Pizza $4.75– $11.50; sandwiches $1–$4.
Open: Tues–Sun 1pm–midnight.

This new eatery on the main street four blocks from the square offers good food and lousy service. Mexico has a tough time getting a pizza right, but this little restaurant makes a good attempt with a thin, just-crunchy-enough crust and tasty toppings. Thirteen pizza variations are on the menu; the sausage and mushroom is a good choice. This is one of the few places that's open on Thursday.

TORTAS Y TACOS EL FOGÓN, Revolución 209. Tel. 5-0106.
   Cuisine: MEXICAN.
$ Prices: Tortas $1; tacos $1.25–$2; soft drinks 50¢; beer $1.60–$2.
   Open: Daily 9am–6pm; tacos served 7pm–midnight.
Opposite the main plaza, you can watch what's happening while you decide between tortas or tacos. The menu is limited, but food is good and the service swift and friendly. Tacos five ways come three to the order, or you can buy them one at a time; be sure to specify.

EN ROUTE TO OLINALÁ & TLAPA

If you're driving, fill up the tank in Chilapa; there may be no more gas until Tlapa. A gas station recently opened in Atlixtac about halfway between Chilapa and the Olinalá turnoff, but don't count on it being open when you pass. And there are no banks in Olinalá, so bring plenty of pesos.

Though it's only 80 miles from Chilapa to Olinalá (most of it paved), the gradual climb of the highway gently winds through the mountains and the trip takes around three hours by car—longer by bus because of frequent stops. You leave the region known as the Central Valleys and enter the region called *La Montaña* (The Mountain), which becomes more arid towards Tlapa. Distant mountains reach close to 10,000 feet but the portion of the winding highway you're driving rises scarcely more than 5,000 feet, dropping as you reach Olinalá, in a valley, and Tlapa. The road is generally in good condition, but be alert to untended animals, portions of missing roadbed, and signs showing areas known for falling rocks. The scenery changes from low forested mountains to pines and palms. You'll pass adobe-walled mountain homes, almost all of which have mud-walled corncribs on the grounds near the house.

After you have gone approximately 56 miles you'll round a bend and the turnoff (left) to Olinalá will be there without warning. The sign that reads TRES CAMINOS is at the turnoff, and another sign later reads OLINALÁ 38 KM, but there's no arrow to indicate that you should turn left there. If you miss it you can always turn around. From there it's 23 miles to Olinalá on an unpaved mountain road, which takes about an hour. The road is wide enough in most places for two cars to pass and will be in better condition in the dry season (November through April) than just after a rain (May through October). As on all Mexican highways, there are no guardrails. It's a pleasant enough drive with grand mountain vistas similar to those you saw on the paved road. There's little vehicular traffic, but a lot of farm animals are herded here, and people walk or ride pack animals along the route. Take your time and enjoy it. You'll see Olinalá in the valley long before you reach it. The Pemex gas station, on the right as you enter town, was inaugurated with great fanfare but never opened.

Tlapa, on the paved highway 41 miles beyond the turnoff to Olinalá, is a good place to overnight if you can't make it to Olinalá over its winding unpaved road before dark.

3. OLINALÁ

80 miles E of Chilapa, 195 miles NE of Acapulco, 41 miles W of Tlapa

GETTING THERE   By Bus   The easiest way to get to Olinalá from Acapulco is via Tlapa, through Chilpancingo or Chilapa. From Tlapa minibuses leave for Olinalá almost hourly between 6am and 6pm. From Acapulco, start out early in the day and go as far as Chilpancingo; change there to one of the 10 Flecha Roja buses to Tlapa. From Chilapa take one of the frequent buses to Tlapa that leave at 6am, 7:30am, 10am, 11am, noon, 1:30pm, and 3pm; change there to an Olinalá bus. The trip between Chilapa and Tlapa is at least three hours—more with stops; allow at least two more hours for the trip between Tlapa and Olinalá. Other buses travel at night from Chilapa to Tlapa, but I don't recommend being on the mountainous highway after dark. (See "By Car," below.) If you don't go via Tlapa there are one or two scheduled buses from Chilpancingo or Chilapa that go directly to Olinalá, but which may not go as scheduled. Flecha Roja has a 3pm bus daily direct to Olinalá from Chilpancingo. In Chilapa Lineas Unidas del Sur schedules two daily trips to Olinalá at 4:30pm and 1am.

By Car   The new four-lane toll road (which goes from Acapulco to Mexico City) is finished. The hour's trip to Chilpancingo costs $30 on the toll road; the old road, still in good condition, takes 2½ hours. From Chilpancingo, take Highway 93 east to Chilapa (one hour), and get gas. From there it's three hours to Olinalá. See also "En Route to Olinalá and Tlapa," above.

O linalá (alt. 4,594 ft., pop. 2,000) is a one-industry town—just about all of the inhabitants are involved one way or another in the making of lacquerware, a craft that is native to Mexico. The name Olinalá comes from a Nahuatl word meaning "next to the earthquakes." Augustinian friars brought the Catholic religion in 1535, and for a long time Olinalá was part of Tlaxcala and Puebla.

Before traveling to Olinalá try to read about it in Carlos Espejel's *Olinalá*, published in Spanish in 1976, which explains the town and craft, or his *Mexican Folk Crafts*, published in English in 1978.

ORIENTATION

After winding through the mountains on the dirt road, you enter Olinalá after crossing a short bridge. At the top of the next hill turn left and follow the street a few blocks to the central square and town basketball court, which will be on your right. At the plaza, immediately on your right, is the Motel Corral. The Hotel Sánchez and the Restaurant Olinalatzin are across the plaza opposite the basketball court. All the shops are within walking distance of the plaza.

FAST FACTS

Area Code   The telephone area code is 747.

Climate   Generally speaking it's warm but pleasant in Olinalá, with chilly mornings and evenings. December through January can be chilly, but at any time it could be cold enough for a jacket. Bring rain gear too, as rains, seasonal or unseasonal, can turn the dirt streets into a mess and increase the chill factor. The rainy season, June through September, brings mosquitoes. Bring insect repellent since hotels don't have screened windows, and the pesky insects like to nip at your legs while you eat.

Currency Exchange   There are no banks or exchange houses in Olinalá. It's best to arrive with enough pesos to cover your purchases and expenses; avoid depending on traveler's checks or dollars that aren't readily accepted or exchanged because it's difficult for merchants to get to a bank.

Gas   Since there's no gasoline station in Olinalá, villagers keep gasoline in large metal containers in their homes. If you're running short, the Hotel Sanchéz usually has enough on hand to sell.

Information   Locals can give directions and information on road conditions to neighboring villages.

Packing and Shipping   If you're planning to purchase anything that you want packed carefully, it's a good idea to bring your own packing material; at the very least bring a large roll of sturdy tape and twine, and plenty of newspapers. Boxes can usually be found here. Wood shavings as packing material are not acceptable at U.S. Customs. You'll also want to supervise the packing, since local merchants and artisans don't understand how boxes are tossed during shipping back to your home.

Telephone   Access to all telephones in town is through the town's *caseta de larga distancia*, on Ybarra a block from the square. It's open between 8am and 8pm and has three lines (tel. 747/2-6458, 2-6517, or 2-6534). Families with phones are reached by first dialing one of the numbers above and asking for the extension or the family by name. But, remember, many families have the same names; be sure to have on hand the exact first and last name you are calling.

When to Come   Olinalá's lacquerwork may be picked over from November through mid-February when Christmas demand has depleted supply.

WHAT TO SEE & DO

SHOPPING   The reason for coming to Olinalá is to find the primary source and widest selection of Mexico's best lacquerware. Wood used in the boxes is the fragrant linaloé, or often pine with linaloé oil brushed on.

Among the many items you'll find are trunks *(baul,* pronounced bah-*ooh*-l) or flat-topped boxes *(caja plano)* usually a separate, detached base with legs. Standard large sizes are 60, 80, and 100 centimeters (24, 32, and 40 in., respectively). Small boxes and trunks range from pencil size to boxes large enough for 24 cassette tapes or writing paper and envelopes. Tables come in square coffee-table size and as nests of three end tables. Headboards are in all standard bed sizes. There are dressers and

---

IMPRESSIONS

To secure a hot bath in a country hotel is a major operation, shaking the whole establishment to its foundations. Porters, firemen, chambermaids, waiters, all join in the process, converting it into a small fiesta. It is akin to getting up steam on an ocean liner. It takes time, it takes approximately half a day, but ah, what triumph when the tap is finally turned and water, choked with steam, rushes out. Everybody must see the triumph; indeed it is only with the greatest difficulty that the bathroom is cleared. One gets into the tub, one bathes luxuriously enough, one pulls the stopper, hears an alarming sound, and springs for the door. The bathtub is draining directly on the floor, a wild freset headed for one's shoes. Just as one is about to recall the staff regardless, the freset dodges the shoes and drops down a drain in the far end of the room.
—Stuart Chase, *Mexico: A Study of Two Americas*, 1931

armoires too, but generally these are made to order as a complete set. It's handy to bring along a measuring tape and to know measurements if you're looking for something particular. You'll also find serving trays (*charola*) of all sizes, and wall shelves with a small drawer (*repiza*), mirror and picture frames (*marco*), and lidded gourds (*jicara* or *polvera*) in many sizes.

There's quite a division of labor in the making of each piece. Carpenters cut the fragrant trees, and make the boxes or headboards, etc., to order. Women usually prepare the colors, apply them, and do the burnishing, using burnishing stones handed down through generations. Men and boys generally are the painters. Farmers collect turkey quills and sell them to the artists who make brushes from domestic cat hair. Gourds are either grown by the artisans in their family garden in the nearby countryside or sold to them by other farmers. Chia seeds, ground and made into an oil that's mixed with the paint, come from Tepalcingo; the powdered paint pigment comes from Mexico City; and local hunters provide deer tails used to brush on the powdered color layers.

Pieces are decorated three ways: *rayado* (incised), with each layer planned and showing (you can feel and see the layers); *dorado* (painted); and a combination of the two. Purists collect the rayado, but personally I think the dorado and the combination are wonderful. Subjects painted on the surface of any object include a very stylized version of a Mexico City street; owls, swans, geese, and other birds; cats; deer; and a multitude of flowers and leaves in many color combinations. Pieces can be made to order or any color you choose.

For a basis for comparison before you set out to discover your own favorite artisans, I'm suggesting a few lacquer workers whose designs are finely done. Ask anyone where they live. Siriaco Escudero is known for full bedroom sets and mirror and picture frames in a variety of styles. Adolfo Franco and his family do fine dorado work. Justino Rodríguez Romano, who lives in the hills above town on the road to Temalacatzingo, creates beautifully etched and painted bedroom sets to order, but may have boxes, trunks, and polveras on hand to sell. Jesús Rendón makes fine paneled room dividers and trunks with intricate designs.

In general, however, to find the lacquer artisans, stroll the streets and look in doorways. If you see evidence of lacquerware in the front room, or smell the fragrant linaloé wood, just stick your head in the door and say *¿Se vende laca?* (Do you sell lacquer?). If they do, they'll readily invite you in and immediately bring out chairs, telling you to *descansa* (rest yourself). Usually what they have to sell will be on display, or if not, they'll bring it out or take you through the house to where it's kept. If they are working, they'll usually continue and talk to you as they work. If you want a price or have a question, just ask. These artist/merchants are incredibly patient, gracious, and hospitable with visitors.

SPECIAL EVENTS San Francisco, Olinalá's patron saint, is honored October 3 and 4 with a street fair, regional dancing in the plaza and streets, and special religious celebrations. Expect to see the dance of the tiger (*tecuanes*). Tiger masks from Olinalá are decorated differently from those in Zitlala and Acatlán.

WHERE TO STAY

To be assured of a room in Olinalá it's good to arrive early in the afternoon or write ahead and send a check for the first and last nights of your stay. It's especially necessary to reserve well in advance for the village's festivals October 2 to 4, Easter week, and Christmas, when all available rooms in town will be full. If all rooms are taken, ask around if someone is willing to rent a bedroom in their home. If there's time before dark, head for Tlapa where there are a few more hotels. To get there, head out of town, drive back to the highway, and turn left.

HOTEL SÁNCHEZ, Guerrero 5, Olinalá, Gro. Tel. 747/3-0007. 6 rms.
$ Rates: $9.50 single or double with one bed and bath; $15.50 single or double with two beds and bath; $5.75 single without bath; $8 double without bath and with one bed, $11.50 double without bath with two beds.

Frumpy and basic, this inn facing the plaza is looked after by eagle-eyed Señora Sánchez. She can make you feel like a naughty child when you sign the register, but after a few visits she may even hug you good-bye. She wants to be paid in advance and to know how many nights you'll be a guest when you check in. And always leave your key on the lobby hook when you leave—house rule. The lobby is the Sánchez living room, which you walk through to reach rooms in a two-story compound behind. Be prepared to carry your own luggage. Rooms are basic, each with screenless windows facing the outdoor walkway, a bed, a crude table and chair, and a bathroom without a door and no toilet seat. Nails high on the wall are for clothes. But everything is clean and in good repair, with new toilets and sinks. Room 13 has an awful mattress, but other rooms have good beds. Room 12 has windows on two sides—great in summer when rooms can get stuffy, not so great in winter when it's cold.

HOTEL Y RESTAURANT/ZINDY, Calle Guerrero 44, Olinalá, Gro. Tel. 747/3-0114. 10 rms (9 with bath).
$ Rates: $12 single with bath; $15.50 double with bath; $7.75 single or double without bath. **Parking:** Free.

Cecilia Jiménez opened this clean inn (the best in town) in 1992, and runs it from her equally clean little deli below the hotel. Rooms, on two levels behind the store, are large and modern, though sparsely furnished, and come with tile floors. Most rooms have two double beds consisting of a mattress on an oddly high cement slab. A shower curtain makes a door on the small bathrooms. Wall hooks hold clothes. Rooms, all with screenless windows, look onto an arched open-air walkway and the grassy car park in the unkempt grounds. To find it from the plaza turn right in front of the Hotel Sánchez and go 2½ blocks; it's on the left.

WHERE TO DINE

Besides the restaurant mentioned below, there is one upstairs on the opposite side of the plaza, but its hours and service are erratic. A couple of restaurants on side streets function as pozolerías on weekends, and a few vendors sell fruit and vegetables around the square. Several variety stores (*abarotes*) sell packaged soft drinks and snacks. Just in case the restaurant situation worsens, it's a good idea to bring a few provisions of your own, such as bottled water and cheese or peanut butter and maybe some fresh bread from one of the *panaderías* in Chilapa.

RESTAURANT OLINALATZIN, Guerrero 3. Tel. 104.
    Cuisine: MEXICAN.
$ Prices: Breakfast $2.50; main courses $3.25–$4.50; sandwiches and tacos $1–$1.75.
    Open: Daily 9am–9pm.

It's a good thing the food is tasty here because this restaurant is about all Olinalá has to offer. Two to four señoritas whip up a smattering of traditional Mexican dishes such as cheese or chicken enchiladas in green or red (hot) sauce, great tostadas, good tortas, and tasty pork or beef with Mexican sauce as well as tacos. If there are no young men for the señoritas to flirt with, service might be good, otherwise you'll have to concoct extensive gyrations to draw their attention. It's upstairs facing the main plaza a few doors to the right of the Hotel Sánchez.

AN EXCURSION TO TEMALACATCINGO

Temalacatcingo (sometimes spelled without the second "t") is another village of lacquer artisans, who make different pieces from those seen in Olinalá. You'll need a car or to hire a taxi to reach this village, since there's no public transportation to it. Though only 18 miles from Olinalá, it takes an hour to get there on the dirt road. The dirt road isn't particularly bad if it hasn't rained, but it's narrow and rough in places, and winds through several villages. The village is so quiet that when you arrive, you may wonder if it's inhabited. Park the car and walk. Soon people will shyly ask if you'd like to see some lacquer and begin inviting you into their homes. Here they don't use the incised method, but only paint designs on lacquered pieces. They are known for their wall shelves, gourds of all sizes, circus carousels (*caroselas*), small cars and buses, airplanes, two people on a swing (*columpios*) and armadillos with moving heads, among other small objects. The church here, the Templo de Santiago Asóstol, dates from the 16th century and unfortunately is in poor condition.

The best festivals here are on May 7 and 8, September 14 for Santa Cruz, and September 28 and 29, which celebrate San Miguel Archangel. October 18 honors San Lucas, and October 24 is for San Rafael. The tiger dance and the turtle dance figure heavily in the festivities.

4. TLAPA

160 miles E of Chilpancingo, 41 miles E of Olinalá, 120 miles E of Chilapa

GETTING THERE By Bus There are 10 Flecha Roja buses to Tlapa from Chilpancingo. From Chilapa, buses leave for Tlapa at 6am, 7:30am, 10am, 11am, noon, 1:30pm, and 3pm. Buses also travel at night from Chilapa to Tlapa, but these are not recommended because of the mountainous highway. From Olinalá, there are frequent buses between 6am and 6pm.

By Car Tlapa is on the highway, 41 miles beyond the turn off for Olinalá. From Chilpancingo the trip takes about 4½ hours. The trip from Olinalá takes just over an hour.

Tlapa (alt. 3,609 ft., pop. 55,000) is the commercial center of this area, with a good market on Saturday and Sunday. Depending on the reference you consult, the name means "place where they wash," perhaps owing to the shallow, wide river that runs through town, or "place where dyers live," or "burned-down town." Anyway, it exists, like an oasis at the end of what can seem like unoccupied territory, especially if you've driven straight from Chilpancingo.

The town, centered around a pretty, shady plaza, was founded in the 1500s, and is the birthplace of the independence hero Ignacio Comonfort. Though its primarily a *meztizo* town, people in surrounding villages belong to Nahua, Mixtec, and Tlapaneco indigenous groups.

WHAT TO SEE & DO

It's a bustling little town, especially for the **Saturday market** that fans out from the central square and fills adjacent streets. On those days, pottery and other crafts are found more readily among the vendors under the bridge and in the dry riverbed area just as you enter town. If you arrive on any other day and want to see crafts, try the **Artesanías Jiménez,** at Hidalgo 148 just off the main square. Mrs. Jiménez sells a few pieces of regional clothing, and a good supply of lacquerware at prices often below those in Olinalá. There's a **hardware store** with no name at Comonfort 10, also one block from the plaza but in the opposite direction from Artesanías Jiménez. If it's open (the hours are supposedly 8am to 9pm daily) you'll notice it by all the cooking pots and other household objects hanging on the front wall and stacks of pottery around the entry. There are also unique animal-shaped water jugs inside, stacked to the gills on an upper shelf inside.

WHERE TO STAY

HOTEL DULCE MARÍA, Hidalgo 88, Tlapa, Gro. 41300. Tel. 747/6-0054. 44 rms.
$ Rates: $11.50 single with one bed; $13 double with one bed; $20 double with two beds. **Parking:** Free in courtyard.
A second choice to the Posada del Sol, this three-story (no elevator) hotel is a bit rough around the edges. Rooms have peeling painted walls, bathrooms that could use a good scrubbing, no toilet seats, and showers that spray everything in the bathroom. Rough towels and a bar of soap are set out on the bright cotton bedspreads that bring a little cheer to the place, and each room has a table and two chairs. There's good cross ventilation, but no fans.

POSADA DEL SOL, Morelos 63, Tlapa, Gro. 41300. Tel. 747/6-0344. 50 rms.
$ Rates: $16 single with one bed; $29 double with two beds.
One block off the main square, the Posada del Sol is centrally located and has a restaurant that's popular with locals. The three stories of rooms (no elevator) all with doors to the outdoor interior courtyard, are clean, with tile floors, peeling painted walls, and old-timey furniture. There's a swimming pool in the shady courtyard. The restaurant is open Monday through Saturday from 8am to 10pm.

WHERE TO DINE

Besides the restaurant at Posada del Sol, mentioned above, you can pick up snacks and fruit at the market by the main plaza.

SHERRIFF'S RESTAURANT/BAR, Morelos 26. Tel. 6-0496.
Cuisine: MEXICAN.
$ Prices: Breakfast $3; main courses $2–$4.
Open: Daily 8am–10pm.
This modern eatery, with big wood-framed paned windows on the street, offers a lengthy assortment of good food. There's everything from steaks to tacos and enchiladas. Roast chicken is the specialty. They'll make sandwiches to go, handy if you're planning a trip in these parts where there's a dearth of restaurants. It's two blocks off the plaza and two blocks from Artesanías Jiménez. Ask anyone for directions.

CHAPTER 8

GETTING TO KNOW IXTAPA & ZIHUATANEJO

1. ORIENTATION
- **WHAT'S SPECIAL ABOUT IXTAPA & ZIHUATANEJO**

2. GETTING AROUND
- **FAST FACTS: IXTAPA & ZIHUATANEJO**

As Mexico develops, the secluded hideaways that made the Pacific coast an intrepid tourist's dream are being discovered en masse. Such is the fate of Ixtapa and Zihuatanejo.

Not so long ago Zihuatanejo (which in Nahuatl means "water of the yellow hill"), shut off its electricity at 11pm. Now the lights are on 24 hours, and the primitive airstrip has been turned into a jetport welcoming daily flights from Mexico City and the U.S. Before the 1972 opening of Ixtapa, the government-planned resort four miles away, Zihuatanejo had a population of about 4,000; now, together with Ixtapa, its population is more than 50,000.

Within driving distance of Acapulco, which is 158 miles southeast, and a day's drive away from Manzanillo, 353 miles southeast, Ixtapa and Zihuatanejo offer some of the best of both Manzanillo and Acapulco. The two towns are a complementary duo—Zihuatanejo, the growing, bustling seaside town, and Ixtapa, the tranquil sophisticated Mexico-style resort. The pair has developed some of the vibrancy of Puerto Vallarta—some excellent restaurants and shopping and a growing nightlife—while retaining a feeling of the tranquillity found in Manzanillo.

Of all Mexico's planned resorts, Ixtapa is my favorite, primarily because it's peaceful and it offers the visitor a taste of both village life and modern Mexico. Many of the employees now working in hotels are descendants of the original village's fishermen, or grew up in farming communities nearby. If you listen carefully you'll hear these locals call each other "sanca," a term which means something like a true-blue friend, one who'll never lie to you or let you down. A sanca, I'm told, would never sell time-share property.

1. ORIENTATION

ARRIVING

BY PLANE **Aeromexico** flies from Mexico City; **Delta** flies from Los Angeles; **Mexicana** has flights from Dallas, Los Angeles, San Francisco, Guadalajara, Mexico

City, and Puerto Vallarta. Check with a travel agent on the latest charter flights from the U.S. and Canada.

The Ixtapa/Zihuatanejo airport is 20 minutes (about 6½ miles) southeast of Zihuatanejo and 10½ miles (30 minutes) southeast of Ixtapa. Minivans, or *colectivos*, offer transport to hotels in Zihuatanejo and Ixtapa for $15 per person; colectivo tickets are sold just outside the baggage-claim area. A taxi for up to three people will cost $16 to either town.

BY BUS   The bus lines **Estrella Blanca** and **Estrella de Oro** (first class) and **Blanco Frontera** and **Flecha Roja** (second class) serve Ixtapa/Zihuatanejo daily with numerous buses from Acapulco, Mexico City, and nearby cities and towns. The trip from Mexico City takes 6 to 10 hours; from Acapulco it is four to five hours. From Mexico City, Estrellas de Oro buses to Zihuatanejo depart from the Terminal Central de Autobuses del Sur (South Bus Station) near the Tasqueno Metro line.

In Zihuatanejo, the **Estrella de Oro bus station** (Marina Nacional at Morelos) is a few blocks beyond the market and within walking distance of some suggested downtown hotels. The clean, new **Central de Autobuses,** the main terminal where all other buses converge, is a mile or so farther, opposite the Pemex station and IMSS Hospital on Paseo Zihuatanejo at Paseo la Boquita. A taxi from either bus station to most Zihuatanejo hotels costs $2 to $3; going on to Ixtapa would add another $5 or so to the fare.

BY CAR   From Mexico City the shortest route is Highway 15 to Toluca, then Highway 130/134 the rest of the way, though on the latter gas stations are few and far between. The other route is Highway 95D (four lanes) to Iguala, then Highway 51 west to Highway 134. From Acapulco or Manzanillo, the only choice is the coastal Highway 200. The ocean views along the winding, mountain-edged drive from Manzanillo can be spectacular. Between Acapulco and Ixtapa the road is potholed in places, and you should be on guard for a couple of surprise *topes*. The highway parallels the ocean with miles of deserted beaches and dangerously heavy surf, and coconut and mango plantations. Youngsters and adults hold up lobsters for sale by the road, as well as bags of salt (near Las Salinas). At San Luís de la Loma you'll find emergency lodging, but if you can wait until Papanoa there's a nice hotel (see Chapter 10, "An Excursion to Papanoa").

DEPARTING

BY PLANE   Airline offices: **Aeromexico,** Juan Alvarez 34 and 5 de Mayo, near the Banco Banamex (tel. 4-2018 or 4-2019), open daily 9am to 6:30pm; **Delta,** at the airport (tel. 4-3386, 4-3387, or toll free 91/800-9-0221 in Mexico); **Mexicana,** Vicente Guerrero and Nicolás Bravo (tel. 3-2208, 3-2209, or at the airport 4-2227), open daily 9am to 5:30pm.

Taxis are the only option for returning to the airport and charge around $16 for one to three people.

BY BUS   **Estrella de Oro** (tel. 4-3802 or 4-2175) runs five buses to Acapulco daily between 8am and 6pm; the trip takes four to five hours. The 8am bus is local and the rest are de paso but they usually have seats. In Acapulco, the Estrella de Oro station is near many budget hotels. To Mexico City, one direct bus makes the trip in 10 hours.

At the **Central de Autobuses** several companies offer service to Acapulco and other cities: first-class **Estrella Blanca** (tel. 4-3478), and the second-class lines **Flecha Roja** (tel. 4-3477 or 4-3483) and **Blanco Frontera.** If possible, buy your

WHAT'S SPECIAL ABOUT IXTAPA & ZIHUATANEJO

Resorts
☐ Some of Mexico's top exclusive resorts are here, including the Westin, Villa del Sol, and La Casa Que Canta.

Sports
☐ At least 30 nearby dive sites.
☐ Fishing is splendid all year for marlin, sailfish, tuna, and mahi mahi.
☐ Challenging golf is available at Ixtapa's Club de Golf. A portion of the new Marina Ixtapa Golf Course may be open in 1995.

Beaches
☐ From Zihuatanejo to Ixtapa, nine beaches offer plenty of variety.

Marinas
☐ Ixtapa boasts a 600-slip yacht marina.

Fine Dining
☐ Seafood is fresh and abundant, plus there's fine dining at a number of restaurants.

---

ticket the day before and get a reserved seat on one of Estrella Blanca's hourly non-stop buses that originate in Zihuatanejo and depart daily between 6am and 4pm. Estrella Blanca's buses are air-conditioned—when it works. Keep in mind, however, that the Estrella Blanca station in Acapulco is far from suggested hotels and means at least a $7 taxi ride upon arrival. Blanco Frontera has "Plus" service to Acapulco three times a day.

BY CAR Motorists planning to follow Highway 200 from Ixtapa/Zihuatanejo north toward Lázaro Cárdenas and Manzanillo should be aware of recent reports of random car and motorist hijackings on that route, especially around Playa Azul. Before heading in that direction, ask locals and the tourism office about the current situation.

If you're driving from Ixtapa to Acapulco, the road can be very potholed, especially during and just after the May to October rainy season. It normally takes me four hours to drive it, even slowing for potholes, but other readers have written to say it's taken them as long as five or six hours.

TOURIST INFORMATION

The **Zihuatanejo Tourism Office** is on the main square on Alvarez (tel. 4-2000 or 4-2001), open Monday to Friday 10:30am to 3pm and 6 to 9pm. In Ixtapa the **State Office** in La Puerta shopping center (tel. 3-1967 or 3-1968) can answer questions. It's across from the Presidente Hotel, open Monday to Friday 9am to 2pm and 4 to 7pm.

CITY LAYOUT

The fishing village and resort of Zihuatanejo spreads out around the beautiful Bay of Zihuatanejo, framed by the downtown to the north and a beautiful long beach and Sierras foothills to the east. Beaches line the perimeter and boats bob at anchor. A new **Puerto Zihuatanejo Maris** will be constructed adjacent to the village center; yacht slips, condos, and shopping areas are all a part of the plan. The heart of Zihuatanejo is the waterfront walkway Paseo del Pescador (also called the *malecón*), bordering the Municipal Beach. The main thoroughfare for cars, however, is Juan Alvarez, a block behind the malecón.

A good highway connects "Zihua" to Ixtapa, four miles to the northwest. Eight tall hotels line Ixtapa's wide beach, Playa Palmar, against a backdrop of lush palm groves and mountains. It's accessed by the main street, Bulevar Ixtapa. On the opposite side of its main boulevard lies a huge area of shopping malls (most of them air-conditioned), restaurants, and discos. This resort also has a fine golf course. At the far end of Bulevar Ixtapa the new 600-slip **Marine Ixtapa** has opened with private yacht slips. Condominiums, shopping malls, and a Plaza Las Glorias Condo Hotel are under construction, and an 18-hole golf course is being created.

NEIGHBORHOODS IN BRIEF

Ixtapa The resort area, lined with high-rise hotels fronting the beach, also has shopping centers, restaurants, private homes, and condominiums on the landward side.

Marina Ixtapa At the far end of Ixtapa an estuary has been turned into a 430-acre, $500 million luxury-class marina, with an 18-hole golf course, housing, and hotel and condominium development. The golf course is scheduled to be partially open by the end of 1995. Colorful Mediterranean-style, stucco-walled condos with their own yacht slips, and shops are already springing up around the newly finished marina. Slips will accommodate yachts up to 100 feet long. The Golf Club should be operational before the course is finished, offering tennis, swimming, a fully equipped gym with sauna and whirlpool, and a restaurant.

Zihuatanejo The fishing village that started it all is only four miles from Ixtapa. It has small hotels, numerous restaurants and shops, and fronts a beautiful bay.

Puerto Zihuatanejo Maris Zihuatanejo's new yacht basin, adjacent to the town, was etched out in 1991. Developers are selling lots and condominiums and it too will have a shopping complex, but so far no building has begun.

Playa Majahua An isolated beach just northwest of Zihuatanejo, reached by a scenic, paved road, Majahua is slated for development. Until then it's for picnicking only—its big surf makes swimming dangerous (people have drowned here).

Playa Madera and Playa La Ropa Southeast of the town center and separated from each other only by a craggy shoreline are Playa Madera and Playa La Ropa, both accessible by road. Town is just 5 to 20 minutes away, depending on whether you walk or take a taxi.

IMPRESSIONS

The town's principal attraction is its idyllic isolation, its fine swimming and fishing. It folds up early at night. Electric power comes from a small diesel plant that operates from sunset to about 11pm. Telegraph and telephone service (there are no local phones) is available at odd hours of the day at the government building three blocks from the plaza.
—JAMES NORMAN, *TERRY'S GUIDE TO MEXICO,* 1972

For those in the mood for some real exploring, and for those who want to get away from the Americans, you can find a fascinating native village . . . . Zihuatenejo . . . . which has beautiful beaches, unexcelled seafood including oysters fresh off the boat each morning. . . . There are four or five waterfront cafés, too. They turn the lights off each night at 10 P.M., but you can see a primitive rural Indian society (the girls have recently taken to wearing shirtwaists). You can take a bus in . . . . from Acapulco, or you can fly from Acapulco or Mexico City at a round-trip fare of $30.
— JOHN WILHELM, *GUIDE TO MEXICO,* 1966

2. GETTING AROUND

BY BUS A shuttle bus goes back and forth between Zihuatanejo and Ixtapa every 15 to 20 minutes from 6am to 10pm daily, charging about 35¢ one-way. In Zihuatanejo it stops near the corner of Morelos/Paseo Zihuatanejo and Juárez, about three blocks north of the market. In Ixtapa it makes numerous stops along Bulevar Ixtapa. A taxi from one town to the other costs about $5 to $6 one-way; after 10pm rates increase, sometimes as much as 50% (agree on a price before getting in).

BY CAR *Special note:* The highway leading from Zihuatanejo to Ixtapa widens and narrows in an odd way, so if you're driving keep your eyes on the white line, otherwise you'll end up in a parking lot or on a side street paralleling the highway. Surprise speed-control bumps (*topes*) dot the thoroughfare and appear on other streets as well—keep your eyes peeled. And oddly enough, a number of streets have manholes rising above the level of the street—look out!

Street signs are hard to find in Zihuatanejo and Ixtapa, but good signage leads you in and out of both locations. However, both locations have an area called *Zona Hotelera* (Hotel Zone) so if you are trying to reach Ixtapa's hotel zone, you may be confused by signs in Zihuatanejo that also point to that village's hotel zone.

 IXTAPA & ZIHUATANEJO

American Express The American Express office (tel. 753/3-1206; fax 3-0853) is in the Westin Ixtapa and is open Monday through Saturday from 9am to 2pm and 4 to 6:30pm.

Area Code The area code is 753.

Climate Summer is hot and humid, though tempered by the sea breezes and occasional brief showers that usually occur in late afternoon or at night; September is the wettest month.

Currency Exchange It is usually easy to find and convenient to use the currency exchange booths rather than the few banks in Ixtapa/Zihuatanejo. Both banks and currency booths usually give better exchange rates than hotels.

Eyeglasses If you need replacement eyeglasses try Óptica El Anteojo on Bravo near Guerrero and opposite the Casa Aurora. It's open Monday through Saturday from 10am to 2pm and 4 to 8pm.

Gasoline Of the two Pemex stations in Ixtapa, the one on the highway leading to Acapulco and the airport is open all day and into the evening. It's always crowded, but less so in the early morning and evening. The one on the road to Lázaro Cárdenas is usually open during the day.

Laundry Lavandería Super Clean, Gonzalez at Galeana in Zihuatanejo (tel. 4-2347), will wash and iron your clothes.

Pharmacy The Farmacia Coyuca, Bravo at Guerrero (tel. 4-5390), in Zihuatanejo, is part grocery and part pharmacy and carries everything from crackers to toothpaste. It's open daily from 9am to 11pm.

Safety   Generally speaking there is little crime in these two vacation centers. Just be normally alert. Several walkways in the commercial zone of Ixtapa are paved with unmortared tiles that can easily cause a twisted ankle or fall. Cobblestone driveways offer similar perils.

CHAPTER 9

WHERE TO STAY & DINE IN IXTAPA & ZIHUATANEJO

Ixtapa and Zihuatanejo have a growing number of excellent accommodations and outstanding restaurants. However, more than in Acapulco or Puerto Vallarta, food and lodging are still reasonably priced—if you know where to look. In both places, there are many comfortable and affordable hotels. Lodgings and moderately priced restaurants can also be found on Playa Madera and Playa La Ropa, nearby.

1. WHERE TO STAY

IXTAPA

VERY EXPENSIVE

WESTIN BRISAS RESORT, Bulevar Ixtapa, Ixtapa, Gro. 40880. Tel. 753/ 3-2121, or toll free 800/228-3000 in the U.S. Fax 753/3-0751. 428 rms, 19 suites. A/C TV TEL MINIBAR

$ Rates: High season $235 single or double, $272 Royal Beach Club, $481–$1,250 suite. Low season $162 single or double, $200 Royal Beach Club, $375–$1,138 suite.

Parking: Free

Sitting above the high-rise hotels of Ixtapa on its own rocky promontory, the Westin is both literally and figuratively a cut above the others. The austere yet luxurious public areas, all in stone and stucco, are bathed in sweeping breezes and announce that this is a special hotel. The spare luxury carries into the rooms with Mexican tile floors, and grand-but-private, half-shaded and plant-decorated patios with hammocks and lounges. All rooms face the hotel's cove and private beach. The six master suites come with private pools. Water is purified in your tap and there's an ice machine on each floor. The 16th floor is reserved as a no-smoking floor and three rooms on the 18th floor are equipped for disabled travelers.

Dining/Entertainment: Portofino is the elegant and intimate fine-dining restaurant serving Italian cuisine and open from 6 to 11pm. The Bella Vista, a casual airy restaurant, is open from 7am to noon and 7 to 11pm. The Solarium, by the pool, is open from noon to 5pm. Las Fuentes, another pool area eatery, serves snacks and is open from 10am to 5pm. El Mexicano specializes in Mexican food, and serves from 6 to 11pm. The airy lobby bar is one of the most popular places to enjoy sunset cocktails while a soothing trio croons romantic songs of Mexico.

Services: Laundry and room service, travel agency, car rental, massage, babysitting.

Facilities: Shopping arcade with a branch of Tane silversmiths, barber and beauty shop, four swimming pools (one for children), four lighted tennis courts with pro on request, elevator to secluded beach.

EXPENSIVE

DORADO PACÍFICO, Bulevar Ixtapa s/n (Apdo. Postal 15) Ixtapa, Gro. 40880. Tel. 753/3-2025, or toll free 91-800/9-0185 in Mexico. Fax 753/3-0126. 262 rms, 23 suites. A/C TV TEL MINIBAR

$ Rates: $160 single; $170 double; $250–$475 suite. **Parking:** Free.

Built around a 16-story atrium, glass elevators hum up and down overlooking the bustling lobby. Rooms, all with balconies and ocean views, have royal-blue carpet, coordinating plaid bedspreads, and rattan furniture. Junior suites have two balconies plus a sitting area, game table, and swivel TV.

Dining/Entertainment: La Brasserie is the formal European restaurant serving Monday through Saturday from 7pm to midnight. The informal Café La Cascada is open from 7am to 11pm. By the ocean you can enjoy seafood and grilled meat at the Cebolla Roja from 6pm to 11pm. Italian food is served on the front lawn at La Guissepe in the evenings. The pool bar is open during pool hours and the lobby bar serves from 3pm to midnight.

Services: Room and laundry service, travel agency, car rental.

Facilities: One pool, two tennis courts, ice machine on each floor.

KRYSTAL, Bulevar Ixtapa s/n, Ixtapa, Gro. 40880. Tel. 753/3-0333, or toll free 800/231-9860 in the U.S. Fax 753/3-0216. 245 rms, 19 suites. A/C TV TEL MINIBAR

$ Rates: High season $212–$312 single or double, $412–$745 suite. Low season $145 single or double, $238–$380 suite. **Parking:** Free.

Krystal hotels are known in Mexico for the high quality of service and well-maintained rooms. This one is no exception. The multistoried V-shaped building encloses the grounds and pool area. Each spacious, nicely furnished and carpeted room has a balcony with an ocean view, game table, tile bathrooms, and either two double beds or a king-size bed. Master suites have large, furnished triangular-shaped balconies.

Dining/Entertainment: Bogart's (see "Where to Dine" below) serves international cuisine in a Casablanca setting with two seatings between 7:30 and 9:30pm. Rarotonga, the seafood restaurant, has an ocean view and swim-up bar and is open from 7:30 to ll:30am, 1 to 5pm, and 7 to 10:30pm. For something quick and informal there's the Aquamarina Café open from 7am to 11pm. Just off the lobby, the Pasta Nostra offers Italian cuisine including pizza from 6 to 11pm. The Beach Club is the pool and beachside bar. There's live music nightly in the lobby bar, which is open from 8pm to 1:30am. The Krystal's famous Cristine Club, born in Cancún, is reincarnated here with the best disco flash around—open from 10:30pm to 4am.

Services: Laundry and room service, travel agency, auto rental, beauty and barber shop.

Facilities: One swimming pool, two tennis courts, a racquetball court, gym with sauna and masseuse on call. The eighth floor is no-smoking, and there's one handicapped-equipped room. Ice machines are on floors 2, 5, 8, and 11. Boutiques are off the lobby, as are the beauty and barber shops.

OMNI, Bulevar Ixtapa 5A, Ixtapa, Gro. 40880. Tel. 753/3-0003, or toll free 800/843-6664 in the U.S. Fax 753/3-1555. 255 luxury rms, 26 suites. A/C TV TEL MINIBAR

$ Rates: High season $219 single or double, $270–$440 suite. Low season $190 single or double, $270–$440 suite. **Parking:** Free.

The wide, breezy lobby and the sound of fountains are welcoming on arrival at this very spacious resort. Rooms are beautifully furnished, as you might expect of a quality chain hotel, and all come with purified tap water. Junior suites are all on corners with triangular patios and 90-degree views. Studio rooms come with two double beds or a king-size. Master suites have a separate living area, nice-size balcony, whirlpool tub large enough for two people, and a separate shower. The presidential suite has its own private pool. It's toward the far end of Ixtapa Bay between the Krystal Hotel and the Posada Real.

Dining/Entertainment: The open-air La Palapa restaurant, on the beach, has a sea view and specializes in grilled meat. La Gran Tapa, a dinner-only cantina and café, offers Spanish food. The lobby bar, which is open to the breezes, often has live music in the evenings.

Services: Laundry and room service, travel agency, boutiques, beauty and barber shop.

Facilities: One beachside pool, fitness center, massage.

SHERATON IXTAPA, Bulevar Ixtapa, Ixtapa, Gro. 40880. Tel. 753/3-1858 or 3-4858, or toll free 800/325-3535 in the U.S. and Canada, 91-800/90-325-MEX in Mexico. Fax 753/3-2438. 322 rms, 12 suites. A/C TV TEL MINIBAR

$ Rates: High season $165–$265 single or double. Low season $125–$225 single or double. **Parking:** Free.

This grand, resort-style hotel has large, handsomely furnished and open public areas facing the beach; it's a very inviting place to come for a drink and to people-watch. Rooms are as nice as the public areas. Most have balconies with views of either the ocean or the mountains.

Dining/Entertainment: The Veranda restaurant serves a breakfast buffet and is open from 7am to 11pm. La Fonda specializes in Mexican food and is open from 6pm to midnight. El Caracol, the outdoor seafood restaurant, is open from 7am to 6pm. La Gondola, an outdoor casual place, serves pizzas and hamburgers during pool hours. Sanca, the nightclub, is open from 9:30pm to 2am. On Wednesday nights there's a Mexican fiesta with a Mexican buffet and live entertainment outdoors.

Services: Room and laundry service, travel agency, concierge, car rental.

Facilities: There's one beachside pool, four tennis courts, a fitness room, ice machine on each floor, beauty and barber shop, boutiques, pharmacy/gift shop. Thirty-six rooms on the fifth floor are no-smoking. Rooms equipped for the disabled are available.

MODERATE

BEST WESTERN POSADA REAL, Bulevar Ixtapa, Ixtapa, Gro. 40380. Tel. 753/3-1625 or 3-1745, or toll free 800/528-1234 in the U.S. Fax 753/3-1805. 110 rms. A/C TV TEL

$ Rates: $80 single or double. **Parking:** Free.

Each of the plain, motel-type rooms here has two comfortable double beds, a wall-desk/counter and mini-couch, and a small window (some with sea view but no

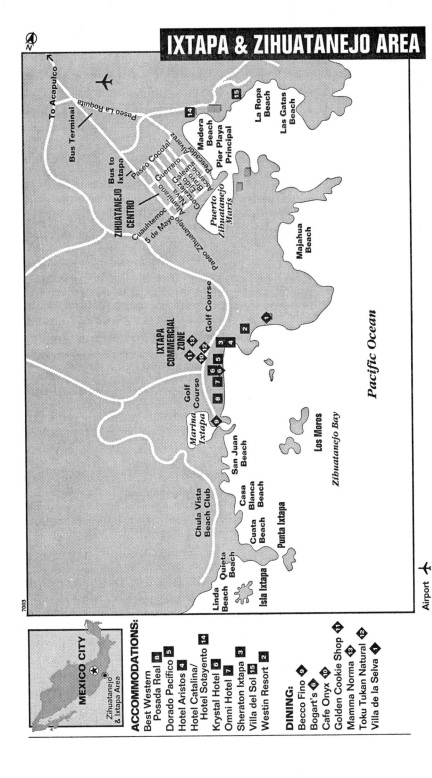

IXTAPA & ZIHUATANEJO AREA

To Acapulco

Bus Terminal

Paseo La Roquita

Bus to Ixtapa

Paseo Cocotal

ZIHUATANEJO CENTRO

Cuauhtemoc

5 de Mayo

Paseo Zihuatanejo

Galeana
Guerrero
Vicente Guerrero
González
Nava
Ejido
Alemán
Ascensio Alvarez
Pescador

Madera Beach

Pier Playa Principal

Puerto Zihuatanejo Maris

La Ropa Beach

Las Gatas Beach

Majahua Beach

Golf Course

IXTAPA COMMERCIAL ZONE

Golf Course

Marina Ixtapa

San Juan Beach

Casa Blanca Beach

Cuata Beach

Chula Vista Beach Club

Punta Ixtapa

Quieta Beach

Linda Beach

Isla Ixtapa

Los Moros

Zihuatanejo Bay

Pacific Ocean

Airport

MEXICO CITY

Zihuatanejo & Ixtapa Area

ACCOMMODATIONS:

Best Western Posada Real **8**
Dorado Pacifico **5**
Hotel Aristos **4**
Hotel Catalina/ Hotel Sotayento **14**
Krystal Hotel **6**
Omni Hotel **7**
Sheraton Ixtapa **3**
Villa del Sol **15**
Westin Resort **2**

DINING:

Becco Fino **9**
Bogart's **6**
Cafe Onyx **10**
Golden Cookie Shop **11**
Mamma Norma **13**
Toku Tukan Natural **12**
Villa de la Selva **1**

7003

FROMMER'S SMART TRAVELER: HOTELS

1. Don't plan a trip to Ixtapa without first asking a travel agent to scour package rates that include both hotel and air travel. Generally these packages will save you considerably on the cost of a trip. Use the hotel listings in this book to help select which hotel's price, location, and amenities will bring you the most satisfaction during your stay.
2. The public rates used in this guide are those anyone would pay if they arrived without a package deal.
3. The most economical hotels are in Zihuatanejo, where you'll find some of the best low-budget accommodations on the Pacific coast; few Zihuatanejo hotels offer package rates, but they may discount rooms during times of low occupancy. The Aristos Hotel in Ixtapa often has super deals.
4. Prices on Playa Madera and Playa La Ropa tend to be higher than those in town, but some people find that the cliffside setting is worth it.
5. If you arrive without reservations during the busiest times of the year, Christmas holidays and Easter week (when hotel prices are higher and vacancies rare), take the first room available. Then, with more time, search for what suits you best.
6. Some of the more expensive hotels raise their rates during the Christmas holidays, then lower them again until the beginning of Easter week.

balcony) with an air conditioner beneath it. The TV brings in U.S. channels. Among the facilities are two pools, two outdoor restaurants, gift shop, and travel desk. Coco's is the pirate-theme restaurant/bar on the beach with hanging basket chairs and music. Request a room on the lower floors; there are no elevators in this four-story hotel. The Lighthouse Restaurant and Euphoria Disco are set apart on the front part of the property, just off Bulevar Ixtapa. Booking directly with the hotel or buying a package may be cheaper than reserving through Best Western. Parking is in an open lot off Bulevar Ixtapa.

It's at the far/northern end of Ixtapa's hotel zone on the beach next to Carlos 'n' Charlie's restaurant.

HOTEL ARISTOS, Bulevar Ixtapa, Ixtapa, Gro. 40380. Tel. 753/3-0011, or toll free 800/527-4786 in the U.S. Fax 753/3-2031. 225 rms. A/C TV TEL

$ Rates: High season $113 single or double. Low season $85 single or double. **Parking:** Free.

The decor at the Aristos might be called "Moorish modern," mixing pointed arches with contemporary lines. The pleasant standard rooms are medium-sized with a sea view (some have balconies) and come with two double beds, marble-trimmed bath, slick contemporary furniture, and TV with U.S. channels. Facilities include three restaurants, piano bar, nightclub, swimming pool, travel agency, shops, two tennis courts, and exercise and water-sports equipment. Laundry, babysitting, and secretarial and business services are also available. Parking is in an open lot off Bulevar Ixtapa. This hotel often offers cut-rate deals, and since it's on the same beach as other more expensive hotels, you can enjoy the setting at a fraction of the price.

ZIHUATANEJO

The term "bungalow" is used loosely in Zihuatanejo as elsewhere in Mexico. A bungalow may be an individual unit with kitchen and bedroom, or with bedroom only. Or it may be a two-story unit or building with multiple units, some of which have kitchens. It may be cozy and nice or rather rustic, and there may or may not be a patio or balcony.

MODERATE

APARTAMENTOS AMUEBLADOS VALLE, Vincente Guerrero 14, **Zihuatanejo, Gro. 40880. Tel. 753/4-2084.** Fax 753/4-3220. 8 apts. FAN
$ Rates: High season $40 one-bedroom apt, $65 two-bedroom apt. Low season $31 one-bedroom apt, $50 two-bedroom apt.

You can rent a well-furnished apartment for a little more than the price of a hotel room. The five one-bedroom apartments accommodate up to three people; the three two-bedroom apartments can fit four comfortably. Each apartment is different, but all are clean and airy, with ceiling fans, private balconies, and kitchenettes. Maid service is provided daily. There's a paperback-book exchange in the office. Luís Valle, the owner, can often find cheaper apartments elsewhere for guests who want to stay several months. Reserve well in advance during high season. It's on Guerrero about two blocks in from the waterfront between Ejido and N. Bravo.

HOTEL ÁVILA, Juan Álvarez 8, Zihuatanejo, Gro. 40880. Tel. 753/4-2010. 27 rms. A/C or FAN TV
$ Rates: High season $63–$70 single, $70–$78 double. Low season $46–$54 single, $54–$61 double. **Parking:** Free.

This hotel offers pricey rooms conveniently located on the beach. Eighteen rooms have private balconies facing town, but no ocean view. The rest share a terrace facing the sea. Rooms with ceiling fan or air conditioning cost the same. Ocean-view rooms are the highest priced in each category. There's a travel agency and restaurant bar off the lobby. The Ávila is near the town plaza basketball court that's on the beach. Prices are too high—ask for a discount.

BUDGET

CASA AURORA, Nicolás Bravo 27, Zihuatanejo, Gro. 40880. Tel. 753/4-3046. 14 rms (all with bath). FAN
$ Rates: High season $14 single, $24 double. Low season $10 single, $20 double.

Located a few minutes from the beach, this hotel offers small rooms and a comfortable second-story porch. The best rooms are no. 12 (a double) and no. 13 (triple), with windows facing the street. To find it, walk inland on Guerrero to Nicolás Bravo.

CASA BRAVO, Nicolás Bravo 11, Zihuatanejo, Gro. 40880. Tel. 753/4-2548. 6 rms (all with bath). FAN
$ Rates: $16 single; $24 double.

A good value for its budget price, this two-story hotel offers clean, plain rooms with mismatched furniture and bare bulbs above the beds. Three second-story rooms at the front of the building have balconies, though this means a bit of street noise. Guests can lounge in the two hammocks in the open-ceilinged lobby. To find it, walk inland on Guerrero to Bravo and turn right.

HOTEL IMELDA, González 11, Zihuatanejo, Gro. 40880. Tel. and fax 753/4-3199. 40 rms (all with bath). A/C (20 rms) FAN (20 rms)
$ Rates: High season $42 single, $54 double. Low season $30 single, $38 double.

Spiffy clean and newly refurbished, this hotel offers value and convenience. All rooms have tile floors and tile bathrooms and come with either two or three double beds. Next door is the hotel's cheerful restaurant, Rancho Grande, which offers an inexpensive comida corrida. It's between Cuauhtémoc and V. Guerrero, one block from the market and four blocks from the beach.

HOTEL SUSY, Juan Álvarez 3 at Guerrero, Zihuatanejo, Gro. 40880. Tel. 753/4-2339. 17 rms (all with bath). A/C (4 rms) FAN (13 rms)

$ Rates: High season $23 single, $29 double. Low season $20 single, $27 double.

Shiny and clean with lots of plants along a shaded walkway set back from the street, this two-story hotel offers small rooms with ceiling fans and louvered-glass windows. Rooms on the upper floor have balconies overlooking the street. Late sleepers and nap-takers should keep in mind that the schoolyard across the way can be noisy. The posada is at the east end of the main street, half a block in from the town beach.

POSADA CITLALI, Vicente Guerrero 3, Zihuatanejo, Gro. 40880. Tel. 753/4-2043. 17 rms (all with bath). FAN

$ Rates: High season $30 single, $35 double. Low season $23 single, $27 double.

The small rooms in this pleasant three-story hotel are arranged around a shady plant-filled little courtyard decked out with comfortable rockers and leather *equipal* furniture. Caged birds complete the restful and tropical scene. Bottled water is in help-yourself containers on the patio. Furnishings in the rooms include ceiling fans, chenille bedspreads, and large wall mirrors with shelves beneath them. The Citlali is at the corner of Álvarez and Guerrero.

PLAYA MADERA

Madera Beach is a 15-minute walk or a $3 taxi ride from town. Most of the accommodations are on the road, Calle Eva S. de López Mateos, that overlooks Madera Beach. If you walk 15 minutes east of town beside the canal, crossing a footbridge and following the road running uphill, you will intersect Mateos.

EXPENSIVE

VILLAS MIRAMAR, Calle Adelita, Playa Madera (Apdo. Postal 211), Zihuatanejo, Gro. 40880. Tel. 753/4-2106 or 4-2616. Fax 753/4-2149. 18 suites. A/C FAN TEL

$ Rates: High season $79 suite for one or two, $89 with ocean view; $115 two-bedroom suite. Low season $50 suite for one or two, $55 with ocean view. **Parking:** Free.

Some of these elegant suites are built around a beautiful shady patio that doubles as a restaurant. Those across the street center around a lovely pool and have private balconies and sea views. Parking is enclosed. To find Villas Miramar, follow the road leading south out of town towards Playa La Ropa, then take the first right after the traffic circle, then left on Adelita.

MODERATE

BUNGALOWS PACÍFICOS, Playa Madera (Apdo. Postal 12), Zihuatanejo, Gro. 40880. Tel. and fax 753/4-2112. 6 bungalows. FAN

$ Rates: High season $60 single or double. Low season $45 single or double.

Providing tranquillity and ample, though simple, comfort, these bungalows come with two bedrooms and fully equipped but rather humble kitchens. The best part of each room is the large terrace, which doubles as a living area with table and chairs, hammock, flowering plants, and magnificent views. The hostess, Anita Hahner, will gladly answer all your questions in four languages, including English. The three-story building is arranged in tiers down the steep hillside, and the beach is just a

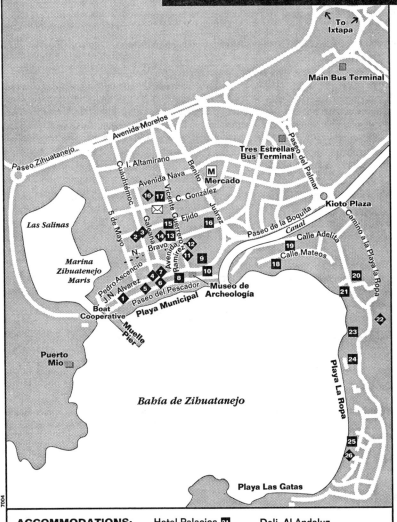

DOWNTOWN ZIHUATANEJO

To Ixtapa

Main Bus Terminal

Avenida Morelos

Paseo Zihuatanejo

I. Altamirano

Cuauhtémoc

Avenida Nava

Benito Juárez

Tres Estrellas Bus Terminal

Paseo del Palmar

M Mercado

C. González

16 17

5 de Mayo

Galeana

Vicente Guerrero

Ejido

15

16

Las Salinas

Paseo de la Boquita Canal

Kioto Plaza

Calle Adelita

2 3

14 13

Bravo

12

19

Calle Mateos

Camino a la Playa la Ropa

Marina Zihuatanejo Maris

N.

11

9

18

Pedro Ascencio

Avenida Ramírez

10

20

J.N. Álvarez

4 7

8

21

5 6

Paseo del Pescador

Museo de Archeología

22

Boat Cooperative

Playa Municipal

23

Muelle Pier

24

Puerto Mío

Bahía de Zihuatanejo

Playa La Ropa

25

26

Playa Las Gatas

7004

ACCOMMODATIONS:
Arco de Noa **19**
Apartamentos
  Amueblados Valle **15**
Bungalows Pacíficos **18**
Casa Aurora **13**
Casa Bravo **16**
La Casa Que Canta **23**
Hotel Ávila **8**
Hotel Catalina **24**
Hotel Imelda **17**

Hotel Palacios **21**
Hotel Susy **10**
Posada Citlali **9**
Villa del Sol **25**
Villas Miramar **20**

DINING:
La Bocana **7**
Cafe La Marina **6**
Casa Elvira **4**
Coconuts **11**

Deli Al Andaluz
  Expresso **2**
Garrobos **1**
Kon-Tiki **22**
La Mesa del Capitan **12**
Nueva Zelandia **3**
La Perla **26**
Panadería Francesa
  (bakery) **16**
La Serena Gorda **5**
Tamales y Atole Any **14**

five-minute walk away. Facing Bungalows Allec, which you see first on Mateos, take the road to the right until you reach its terminus overlooking town. The hotel is on the left.

HOTEL PALACIOS, Calle Adelita, Playa Madera (Apdo. Postal 57), Zihuatanejo, Gro. 40880. Tel. 753/4-2055. 28 rms. A/C (5 rms) FAN
$ Rates: High season $51–$68 single or double. Low season $27–$35 single or double.

This is one of the older hotels on the beach, and it shows. Its good points include separate children's and adults' pools on a beachside terrace, and the ceiling fans and sea breezes. Few rooms have ocean views, although no. 10 and nos. 17 through 21 all have windows on two sides, good vistas, and shared balconies. The highest rates in each category are for rooms with air conditioning.

BUDGET

ARCO DE NOA, Calle Eva S. de López Mateos, Playa Madera, Zihuatanejo, Gro. 40880. Tel. 753/4-2272. 10 rms (all with bath). FAN
$ Rates: High season $28 single, $39 double. Low season $24–$28 single or double.

An excellent value, Arco de Noa is actually a two-story house set back from a front patio landscaped with flowers and a shaded sitting area. The neat, pleasant rooms have large windows with glass louvers, white walls, bright-colored bedspreads, and ceiling fans. Guests are free to use the kitchen and dining room on the premises. Four rooms have sea views. It's on the inland side of Mateos (see directions above).

PLAYA LA ROPA

Some travelers consider Playa La Ropa the most beautiful of Zihuatanejo's beaches. It's a 20- to 25-minute walk south of town on the east side of the bay, or a $2 taxi ride.

VERY EXPENSIVE

LA CASA QUE CANTA, Camino Escénico a la Playa La Ropa, Zihuatanejo, Gro. 40880. Tel. 753/4-2722 or 4-2782, or toll free 800/432-6075 or 800/448-8355 in the U.S. 18 suites. A/C
$ Rates: High season $260–$400 single or double. Low season $215–$315 single or double.

La Casa Que Canta (The House that Sings) opened in 1992, and in looks alone it's one of those very special hotels. Meandering down a mountainside overlooking Zihuatanejo Bay, it was designed with striking molded-adobe architecture. Rooms, all with handsome natural-tile floors, are individually decorated in unusual painted Michoacán furniture, antiques, and stretched-leather equipales. Hand-loomed fabrics are used throughout. All units have large, beautifully furnished terraces with bay views. Hammocks under the thatched roof terraces, supported by rough-hewn vigas, are perfectly placed for watching yachts sail in and out of the harbor. The four categories of rooms, all spacious, get larger as you go up the price scale. Beginning with the smallest, there are three terrace suites, four deluxe suites, nine grand suites, and two private pool suites. Rooms meander up and down the hillside and while no stairs are extensive, there are no elevators. La Casa Que Canta is a member of the Small Luxury Hotels of Mexico organization. Technically it's not on Playa La Ropa; it's on the road leading there. The closest stretch of beach (still not yet Playa La Ropa) is down a steep hill. Children under 18 aren't allowed.

Dining/Entertainment: There's a small restaurant/bar on a shaded terrace over-looking the bay.

Services: Laundry and room service.

Facilities: One freshwater pool on the main terrace and one saltwater pool on the bottom level.

VILLA DEL SOL, Playa La Ropa (Apdo. Postal Box 84), Ixtapa/Zihuatanejo, Gro. 40880. Tel. 753/4-2239, or toll free 800/223-6510 in the U.S., 800/422-5500 in Canada. Fax 753/4-2758. 22 standard mini-suites, 8 deluxe suites, 6 master suites, 11 condominiums. A/C

$ Rates: High season $275–$580 single or double. Low season $150–$365 single or double. Breakfast and either lunch or dinner, $50 per person, is mandatory in high season. 10% gratuity added to everything.

Owner Helmut Leins came from Germany to Zihuatanejo in 1969 and fell in love with gorgeous La Ropa Beach. Within 10 years he'd sold his German engineering company and returned to open a six-room, beachfront hotel that from the beginning won acclaim as a superexclusive, luxurious hideaway. Few inns in Mexico compare to this one for luxury, attention to quality, service, and tranquillity. The hotel is one of two in Mexico to meet the tough standards of the French Relais & Châteaux. It's also a member of Small Luxury Hotels of Mexico. Now the inn has 36 units, following an architectural blend of Mexican and southwestern U.S. pueblo style. Units lie along the beachfront in a U-shape anchored by immaculately kept grounds and the oceanside restaurant and bar. Each spacious, split-level suite (with either one or two bedrooms) comes with a living room facing a private patio and is tastefully furnished with tile floors, Mexican decorative objects, and a king-size bed draped in white netting. Standard rooms don't have TV or telephone. All have fans in addition to air conditioning, plus hairdryers and luxurious bathrobes in the rooms. Some suites have TV, telephone, minibar, in-room safety-deposit boxes, and a small pool on the patio. Eleven of the 18 condominiums are included in the rental pool and all have full kitchens. Most guests are regular clients and make their return reservations a year in advance; however, June and September are slow months and last-minute reservations have a better chance then. Children under 14 aren't allowed during high season.

Dining and Entertainment: There's an open-air restaurant by the beach with classical music. Friday night there's a Mexican fiesta for $30 at the beachside restaurant. Orlando's Bar at beachside is open from 9am to 11pm. Nonguests pay $25 each to use the beach and restaurant and $15 of the cost goes toward the purchase of a meal in the hotel's restaurant. For a small fee, guests can paint ceramics at beachside provided by local Nahuatl-speaking Indians who also sell their painted wares there. Guests use the bar area for table games in the afternoon.

Services: Room service, laundry, beauty shop, travel agency, Tane jewelry store.

Facilities: Two pools, two tennis courts (reserve courts in advance), beauty shop, massage service, paperback lending library.

MODERATE

HOTEL CATALINA and HOTEL SOTAVENTO, Playa La Ropa, Zihuatanejo, Gro. 40880. Tel. 753/4-2032; 604/652-0456 in Canada. Fax 753/4-2975; 604/652-3571 in Canada. 85 rms, 24 bungalows.

$ Rates: $40–$75 standard room; $82–$87 bungalow or terrace room.

Perched high on the hill close to each other and managed together by the same owners, these two attractive hotels were among the first in the area and retain the slow-paced, gracious mood of Zihuatanejo in its early days as a little-known hideaway. The spectacular panoramic views of Playa La Ropa below alone are worth the price of staying here. The terrace rooms of the Sotavento are quite large and decorated with wood furniture that evokes the 1950s and 1960s, including one double and one single bed. Best of all is the large, shared ocean-view terrace, equipped with hammocks and a chaise longue for each room—great for sunning and sunset-watching. The Catalina has recently remodeled many of its rooms with Mexican tile, wrought iron, and other handcrafted touches; these also have lovely terraces with ocean views and come with two queen-size beds. Between them the two hotels cover eight stories climbing the slope and two restaurants and bars. Do ask to see at least a couple of rooms first, as they can vary quite a bit in furnishings and price. Also keep in mind the hike down many steps to the beach (depending on the room level) and the lack of air conditioning, compensated for by the ceiling fans and sea breezes. Nor is there a swimming pool. To get here, take the highway south of Zihuatanejo about a mile, turn right at the hotels' sign, and follow the road to the hotels.

---

2. WHERE TO DINE

IXTAPA

VERY EXPENSIVE

BOGART'S, in the Krystal Hotel, Bulevar Ixtapa. Tel. 3-0333, ext. 3728.
Cuisine: INTERNATIONAL. **Reservations:** Recommended.
$ Prices: Appetizers $6.75–$12; main courses $18–$45; dessert $5–$15.
Open: Dinner daily, first seating 7:30–9pm, second seating 9:30–11:30pm.
This ultra-elegant restaurant carries out the Casablanca theme with Moorish arches and turbaned waiters. Fountains, ferns, glass, crystal, and silver on candlelit tables and soft background piano music speak romance. On the menu you'll find "Los favoritos de Humphrey" (referring to Humphrey Bogart's favorite foods) such as chicken suprême, New Zealand rack of lamb, and broiled rib eye. For a twist there's a Bogie and Ingrid filet of beef and Caribbean lobster. Dress your casual-and-cool best, but no shorts, T-shirts, or sandals are allowed. It faces the boulevard in front of the Krystal Hotel.

VILLA DE LA SELVA, Paseo de la Roca. Tel. 3-0362.
Cuisine: MEXICAN/CONTINENTAL. **Reservations:** Recommended during high season.
$ Prices: Appetizers $6.50–$12; main courses $15–$31.
Open: Daily 6–11pm.
Set on the edge of a cliff overlooking the sea, this elegant restaurant enjoys the most spectacular sea and sunset view in Ixtapa. The elegant candlelit tables are arranged on three terraces; try to come early in hopes of getting one of the best vistas, especially on the lower terrace. The cuisine is delicious and classically rich: Filet Villa de la Selva is red snapper topped with shrimp and hollandaise sauce. The cold avocado soup or hot lobster bisque makes a good beginning; finish with chocolate mousse or bananas Singapore.

FROMMER'S SMART TRAVELER: RESTAURANTS

1. Less expensive restaurants are found in Zihuatanejo.
2. Since this resort is growing, don't be afraid to try new restaurants not listed in this book that look interesting or offer good meals for the money.
3. For an inexpensive meal, shop in the public market for fresh peelable fruits and visit a bakery for fresh bread. Have a picnic on the beach or on the veranda of your room.
4. Fine dining here is usually less expensive than a comparable restaurant meal at home.

EXPENSIVE

BECCO FINO, Marina Ixtapa. Tel. 3-1770.
   Cuisine: NORTHERN ITALIAN.
$ Prices: Breakfast $5.50–$8; appetizers $5.50–$13; pastas $9–$12.50; chicken and beef dishes $12.50–$19.
   Open: Daily 9:30am–midnight.

If you like Italian food, try this casual but classy restaurant early in your stay, since you'll probably want to return again and again. Experienced owner Angelo Rolly Pavia lays before his guests the northern Italian specialties he grew up knowing and loving—all packed with flavor. Sitting at the breezy marina, diners peruse the menu, which includes dishes with pasta shapes you may never have heard of. Following the pasta list there's a full offering of items from the bay or barnyard. Ravioli, a house specialty, comes stuffed with whatever seafood is in season. I tried the *gameri ariagliati al pepe rosa* (shrimp in pink pepper), which was just snappy enough to mix well with the oregano, garlic, and olive oil. Of course, order the delicious garlic bread. And for a white Italian wine (Angelo has a wide selection), try the Crovo Duca de Salapauta. Service is attentive and friendly. Highly recommended.

MODERATE

CAFE ONYX, Bulevar Ixtapa, opposite the Hotel Plaza Ixtapa. Tel. 3-0346.
   Cuisine: INTERNATIONAL.
$ Prices: Breakfast $3.50–$6.25; appetizers $4.50–$12; main courses $9.75–$20.
   Open: Daily 8am–midnight.
Owing to its appealing breezy location and good service, you'll see diners enjoying their meals here at all hours. The menu runs the gamut from fajitas and sandwiches to spaghetti, pizza, steaks, and seafood. Main courses come with vegetables. Bread and butter are extra. Many people come just for mid-afternoon or late-evening coffee and dessert—they serve espresso and cappuccino and banana splits, to name a few offerings.

GOLDEN COOKIE SHOP, Los Patios Center. Tel. 3-0310.
   Cuisine: PASTRIES/SANDWICHES/INTERNATIONAL.
$ Prices: Breakfast $2.50–$5.75; sandwiches $5.50–$7; main courses $5–$9.75.
   Open: Mon–Fri 9am–9pm, Sat 9am–5pm.

Although the name is misleading—there's more than cookies here—the freshly baked cookies and pastries are worthy of a detour and the coffee menu is the most extensive in town. Breakfast can be simple—yogurt, toast, and jam, or a danish roll—or an elaborate full American or Mexican breakfast. You're in for another treat if you have one of the large sandwiches made with fresh soft bread and deli sliced fillings of ham, turkey, cheese, salami, tuna, and knockwurst. The house sandwich contains the works—ask for a description. Main courses include barbecue chicken, taco and pasta salads, and chicken curry. There's no sign, so look up on the second level next to Mac's Prime Rib and you'll see the eatery with tables set out on the veranda.

MAMMA NORMA, La Puerta Center, Bulevar Ixtapa. Tel. 3-0274.
   Cuisine: ITALIAN/AMERICAN.
$ Prices: Breakfast $3.50–$6.50; main courses $6.50–$14; pizza $10–$12.
   Open: Daily 8am–11pm; deliveries 3–11pm.
This small cafe with red-checked tablecloths offers 17 kinds of pizza as well as soups, pasta salads, hamburgers and other sandwiches, enchiladas, tacos, and breakfast for reasonable prices. It will also deliver pizza to Ixtapa hotels. It's in the mall opposite the hotel zone.

BUDGET

TOKO TUKAN NATURAL, Los Patios Center. Tel. 3-0717.
   Cuisine: SANDWICHES/FRUIT/VEGETARIAN.
$ Prices: Breakfast $2.75–$5; tacos and sandwiches $4.50–$10.
   Open: Daily 8am–10pm.
Outdoors and umbrella-shaded, this casual restaurant is popular for breakfast and brunch. Ample fruit plates come loaded, plus they serve fresh fruit and vegetable drinks as well as salads. Hotcakes come in combinations with bananas, raisins, and apples. There's a good selection of tacos and sandwiches, all of which come with meat. It faces the boulevard beside Aca Joe.

ZIHUATANEJO

EXPENSIVE

COCONUTS, Guerrero 4. Tel. 4-2518.
   Cuisine: MEXICAN. **Reservations:** Recommended during high season.
$ Prices: Appetizers $5–$7.50; main courses $15.50–$23.
   Open: Daily 6pm–2am. **Closed:** Nov–Mar.
Dinner can be romantic here on the lush tropical patio, while tiny lights twinkle in the trees and mariachis stroll in now and then to play. For a seafood mood, try the Filet Coconuts—red snapper in a delicious light sauce. For dessert, splurge on the crêpes Suzette and Irish coffee. It's about half a block on Guerrero, between Álvarez and Bravo and near the Hotel Zihuatanejo.

EL PATIO, 5 de Mayo 3 at Álvarez. Tel. 4-3019.
   Cuisine: SEAFOOD/MEXICAN.
$ Prices: Breakfast $4–$7; Mexican platters $7.50–$30; seafood $12–$25.
   Open: Daily 9am–2pm and 3–11pm.
Casually elegant, this patio restaurant is decorated with baskets and at night flickering candles create a romantic atmosphere. Whatever you're a fan of it's likely you'll find it here. There are fajitas and steak, chicken, chiles rellenos, green or red enchiladas, and lobster in garlic sauce. The breakfast menu is typical, but you can also order hamburgers and salads. In the evenings musicians often play Latin American favorites. It's one block inland from Álvarez and next to the church.

MODERATE

LA BOCANA, Álvarez 13. Tel. 4-3545.
Cuisine: MEXICAN/SEAFOOD.
$ Prices: Breakfast $4–$6.75; main courses $7.75–$23.
Open: Daily 8am–11pm.

One of Zihuatanejo's finest seafood restaurants, La Bocana is known for its huge *plato de mariscos*—a seafood platter that feeds two to four people. It comes heaped with lobster, crayfish, shrimp, fish filet, rice, and salad. Mariachis and marimba bands come and go on Sunday. It's on the main street near the town plaza.

CASA ELVIRA, Paseo del Pescador s/n. Tel. 4-2061.
Cuisine: MEXICAN/SEAFOOD.
$ Prices: Appetizers $3.50–$6; main courses $8.50–$23.
Open: Daily 8am–10pm.

Casa Elvira almost always has a crowd drawn by its neat, clean atmosphere and by the wide selection of low-cost lunches and dinners on its bilingual menu. House specialties are snapper and lobster; it also serves meat dishes and chicken mole. The most expensive seafood platter includes lobster, red snapper, and jumbo butterfly shrimp. Although you can't see the ocean from the tables, you're close enough to hear the waves. It's on the west end of the waterfront near the town pier.

EL DELI, Cuauhtémoc 12. Tel. 4-3850.
Cuisine: DELI/AMERICAN.
$ Prices: Breakfast $3.75–$7; main courses $7.50–$11; sandwiches $5–$9.
Open: Daily 8am–11pm.

American home cooking and deli fare are the specialties at this tiny eatery with wall booths and three sidewalk tables. Stock up on picnic supplies or get sandwiches with salami, prosciutto, ham—or a bagel and lox. Or have something heartier such as steak, barbecued ribs, and Caesar salad. The extensive breakfast menu includes just about any breakfast concoction you've ever heard of and some you haven't. It's two blocks inland on Cuauhtémoc near Bravo.

GARROBOS, Álvarez 52. Tel. 4-2977.
Cuisine: MEXICAN/SEAFOOD.
$ Prices: Appetizers $4.75–$7; main courses $6–$18.
Open: Daily 2–10pm.

This roomy and very popular restaurant presents large meat and seafood main dishes attractively with rice and two vegetables. It also serves the Spanish dish paella and the local specialty *tiritas de pescado*, little strips of marinated fish (as with ceviche, the fish is "cooked" by the lemon or lime juice). In the evening trios often serenade diners. You'll find it towards the west end of Álvarez beneath the Hotel Raul Tres Marías Centro.

BUDGET

Zihuatanejo's **central market,** located on Avenida Benito Juárez (about five blocks inland on Guerrero and right on Nava to Juárez), offers cheap, tasty food. Local señoras set up rough-and-ready cook stalls to serve the villagers who come to market daily. The food is best at breakfast and lunch because most marketing is finished by afternoon. Be sure to choose what is hot and freshly cooked.

For more cheap eats in Zihuatanejo, try Calle Ejido between Cuauhtémoc and Guerrero, where rows of inexpensive **taco shops** line the street. Also here are the Expendio de Pan "El Buen Gusto," a **bakery shop,** and a *juguería*, or **juice stand**—in short, all you need for a low-budget feast.

CAFE LA MARINA, Paseo del Pescador 9. Tel. 4-2373.
   Cuisine: PIZZA/SANDWICHES.
$ **Prices:** Pizzas $5.75–$8; sandwiches $2.50.
   Open: Mon–Sat 9am–9pm.
This popular, beachfront hangout has only a handful of tables on the front porch and lackadaisical service. But it dishes out pizza with toppings that range from pineapple to ham and seafood. Patrons also consume large *tortas* (sandwiches) that come with bean sprouts and avocado. While you wait, browse through the English paperbacks for sale or for trade here. It's on the waterfront by the Casa Marina shops.

EL BUEN GUSTO, Guerrero 4. Tel. 4-3231.
   Cuisine: BAKED GOODS.
$ **Prices:** Most items 25¢–$5.
   Open: Mon–Sat 7:30am–10pm.
Small but packed with goodies, this pastry shop offers what's usually found in a Mexican bakery, and then goes beyond it by offering banana bread, French bread, doughnuts, and cakes. It's between Paseo del Pescador and Bravo.

NUEVA ZELANDA, Cuauhtémoc 23 and Ejido. Tel. 4-2340.
   Cuisine: MEXICAN.
$ **Prices:** Tortas $3.25–$5.50; enchiladas $5–$6.25; fruit-and-milk licuados $1.50; cappuccino $2.
   Open: Daily 8am–10pm.
One of the most popular places in town, this clean, open-air snack shop welcomes diners with nice touches like shiny wood tables and sparkling mirrors on the walls. Favorites include the rich cappuccino sprinkled with cinnamon, and the pancakes with real maple syrup. But the mainstays of tortas and enchiladas make up the bulk of the menu. For only 5¢ more order cappuccino-to-go (say "para llevar") and get twice as much coffee. Close by is the Panadería Francesa (French Bakery) with delicious pastries. You'll find it three blocks inland from the waterfront.

PANADERÍA FRANCESA, Gonzalez 15 between Cuauhtémoc and Guerrero. Tel. 4-4520.
   Cuisine: BAKERY.
$ **Prices:** Bread 40¢–$2.50; baguettes 50¢; wheat bread $2.
   Open: Daily 7am–9pm.
To go with your cappuccino-to-go from nearby Nueva Zelanda (see above), buy sweet pastries here. Or grab a long baguette or loaf of whole-wheat bread for picnic supplies. It's two long blocks west of Juárez and the market area.

LA SIRENA GORDA, Paseo del Pescador s/n. Tel. 4-2687.
   Cuisine: MEXICAN.
$ **Prices:** Breakfast $3.50–$8; main courses $6.25–$9.75.
   Open: Thurs–Tues 6am–10pm.
For the best inexpensive breakfast in town, head to La Sirena Gorda for a variety of eggs and omelets, or hotcakes with bacon as well as fruit with granola and yogurt. For lunch or dinner try the house specialty, seafood tacos. There's always a short list of daily specials such as blackened red snapper, steak, or fish kebab. Patrons enjoy the imaginative wall painting of the fat mermaid (la sirena gorda) and the casual sidewalk-cafe atmosphere under ceiling fans. It's on the west end of the waterfront near the town pier.

TAMALES Y ATOLE ANY, Bravo 33. No phone.
   Cuisine: MEXICAN.
$ **Prices:** Tamales $1.25; tortas $3.
   Open: Mon–Wed and Fri 5–11pm, Thurs and Sat 1–11pm.

Brightly lit and with lots of tables and chairs festooned in colorful loomed cloths and serapes, this is the place to try one of the 13 different tamales or eight flavors of atole. The tamales come wrapped in either corn or banana leaves with a sweet flavor or with meat, squash, or cheese inside. Some come with green or red sauce and others with mole. There's a choice of tortas too, including the oaxaqueño special with chicken in mole sauce and another with pork vinaigrette in red sauce. It's a few doors from the Hotel Aurora.

PLAYA MADERA & PLAYA LA ROPA
MODERATE

KON-TIKI, Camino a Playa La Ropa. Tel. 4-2471.
   Cuisine: PIZZA.
$ Prices: Pizza $9–$25.
   Open: Daily 1pm–midnight; happy hour 6–7pm.
In the air-conditioned dining room on a cliff overlooking the bay, enjoy 13 types of pizzas in three different sizes. The vegetarian is topped with beans, peanuts, onion, mushroom, bell pepper, garlic, pineapple, and avocado. There's also a big-screen sports-video bar, open the same hours.

LA PERLA, Playa La Ropa. Tel. 4-2700.
   Cuisine: SEAFOOD.
$ Prices: Breakfast $2.50–$6.50; appetizers $3.25–$18; main courses $8–$16.
   Open: Daily 10am–10pm; breakfast served 10am–noon.
There are many palapa-style restaurants on Playa La Ropa, but La Perla is one of the best. Cloth-covered tables under the trees and thatched roof make for pleasant dining. Plus the long swath of pale sand stretching out in either direction and an array of wooden chairs under palapas combine with good food to make La Perla a favorite with visitors. The "filet of fish La Perla" is cooked deliciously, wrapped in foil with tomatoes, onions, and cheese. Around sunset, visitors gather in the bar to watch the news on the TV, which shows American channels. It's near the southern end of La Ropa Beach. Take the right fork in the road; there's a sign in the parking lot.

ROSSY, Playa La Ropa. No phone.
   Cuisine: SEAFOOD/SANDWICHES/TACOS.
$ Prices: Breakfast $3.25–$4; tacos $2.50–$4; seafood $2.50–$16; beer $1.50; margarita $3.50.
   Open: Daily 9am–10pm.
Another locally favorite beachside restaurant, this one too is casual with orange and yellow cloth-covered tables and peach and orange chairs and lounges near the water. The menu emphasizes seafood with a short beef and taco section. Seafood includes ceviche, breaded lobster, and river crawfish during the rainy season. It's at the far end of La Ropa Beach. Take the left fork in the road and follow it to the end.

CHAPTER 10

WHAT TO SEE & DO IN IXTAPA & ZIHUATANEJO

The major attraction in the area is, of course, the beaches, which stretch for miles along the coast. Fishing, water sports such as sailing and scuba diving, and sunset cruises attract tourists.

Ixtapa has a wide beach lined with high-rise hotels against a backdrop of lush palm groves and mountains. The resort also has a fine golf course. Zihuatanejo's beach curves around a small, natural bay in which fishing boats and sailboats bob at anchor.

1. SPORTS & ATTRACTIONS

The Archeology Museum of Zihuatanejo Petatlán, at the east end of Paseo del Pescador near Guerrero, tracks the Costa Grande from its pre-Hispanic times (when it was known as Cihuatlán) through the colonial era. Most of the ancient artifacts of pottery and stone demonstrate extensive trade with other cultures and far-off regions—with Toltec and Teotihuacán cultures near Mexico City, with the Olmecs on the Gulf of Mexico, and with areas known today as the states of Nayarit, Michoacán, and San Luis Potosí. Indigenous groups from this area paid tribute to the Aztecs with cotton *tilmas* (capes) and chocolate (*cacao*). Some of the archeological finds are from a site found several years ago near the airport. The museum is nicely done and worth the half hour or less it takes to stroll and read; information is in Spanish. Admission is 75¢ and it's open Tuesday through Sunday from 10am to 5pm.

THE BEACHES

ZIHUATANEJO

Besides the peaceful Playa Municipal, Zihuatanejo has three other beaches: Madera, La Ropa, and Las Gatas. At Zihuatanejo's town beach, **Playa Municipal,** the local fisherman pull up their colorful boats on the sand. Small shops and restaurants line the waterfront, making this a great spot for people-watching and absorbing the flavor of daily village life. This beach is protected from the main surge of the Pacific.

Madera Beach, just east of the Municipal Beach, is open to the surf but generally tranquil. Many attractive budget lodgings overlook this area from the hillside.

South of Playa Madera is Zihuatanejo's largest and most beautiful beach, **Playa La Ropa,** a long sweep of sand with a great view of the sunset. Some lovely small hotels and restaurants nestle into the hills and palm groves edging this shoreline. Although it's also open to the Pacific surge, the waves are usually gentle. A taxi from town costs $1.75.

Along a rocky seaside path that leads south from La Ropa is **Playa Las Gatas,** which is protected by a coral reef and is popular with snorkelers. The open-air seafood restaurants on this beach also make it an appealing lunch spot for a splurge. Although you can hike here, it's much easier to take the "ferry" (a small motorboat with a sunshade) from the boat cooperative (tel. 4-2056) at the Zihuatanejo town pier, which runs every 10 minutes from 8am to 4pm (a 10-minute trip; round-trip fare about $2.75). Usually the last ferry back leaves Las Gatas at 4:30pm; be sure to double-check! Snorkeling gear can be rented at the beach.

IXTAPA

Ixtapa's main beach, **Playa Palmar,** is a lovely arc of white sand edging the hotel zone, with dramatic rock formations silhouetted in the sea. The surf here can be rough; use caution and never swim when a red flag is posted.

Playa Quieta is a tranquil beach on the mainland across from Isla Ixtapa, about seven miles north of Ixtapa. Water-taxis here ferry passengers to Isla Ixtapa for about $3.50 round-trip.

Playa Las Cuatas is a pretty beach and cove a few miles north of Ixtapa.

Playa Vista Hermosa is a pretty beach framed by striking rock formations and bordered by Camino Real Ixtapa Hotel high on the hill.

Playa Majahua is an isolated beach, where development is planned, just west of Zihuatanejo, reached by a scenic, paved road. Majahua is for picnicking only—its big surf makes swimming dangerous (people have drowned here).

WATER SPORTS & BOAT TRIPS

Probably the most popular boat trip is to **Isla Ixtapa** for snorkeling and lunch at El Marlin restaurant. Though available as a tour through local travel agencies, you can go on your own from Zihuatanejo by catching the boat that leaves the boat cooperative at the town pier at 11am, returning at 4:30pm. The cooperative (tel. 4-2056) is open daily from 8am to 5pm. Boats leave around 11am for Isla Ixtapa and return by 4pm, charging about $18 for the round-trip (lunch not included). Along the way you'll pass dramatic rock formations and the **Los Moros de Los Péricos Islands,** known for the great variety of birds that nest on its rocky points jutting out into the blue Pacific. On Ixtapa Island you'll find good snorkeling and a nature trail through an unfenced wildlife area with a few exotic birds and animals. Oliverio rents snorkeling gear on the island. Be sure to catch the last water-taxi back at 4pm.

Fishing trips can be arranged with the boat cooperative at the Zihuatanejo town pier (tel. 4-2056) and cost from $120 to $180, depending on the size of boat, length of time, etc. (though most trips are six hours). The cost usually includes bait and tackle and soft drinks. The cost is higher through a local travel agency ($180 to $360). Both small game and deep-sea fishing are offered. Sailfish are plentiful and there's abundant marlin, yellowfin tuna, and dorado (mahi-mahi). Tell the skipper if

FROMMER'S FAVORITE
IXTAPA/ZIHUATANEJO EXPERIENCES

Sunset Watching As in other places along Mexico's Pacific coast, finding a perfect place to watch the sun set is an obligatory part of any vacation.

Deep Sea Fishing Spend a morning on the water reeling them in, then have your skipper take you to Ixtapa Island to cook your fish and eat it there.

Lazing This resort is so relaxing that lying on the beach, beside a pool, or stretched out on a hammock on your private patio becomes an easy daily ritual.

Dining Around In both Ixtapa and Zihuatanejo there are excellent restaurants, enough to explore something new every day, with an emphasis on fresh seafood.

Scuba Diving Exploring the fascinating underwater caves and abundant sea life offshore becomes a whole new reason for returning to Ixtapa annually.

Lounging on La Ropa Beach Relaxing for a day at La Ropa Beach in front of La Perla Restaurant is a wonderful way to make your cares disappear.

you want to "catch and release," something most people do. If you want to eat the fish you catch, ask the captain to filet it, then take it to a restaurant in Zihuatanejo such as Casa Elvira or La Mesa del Capitán, where they'll prepare it for your dinner. The Annual Sailfish Tournament takes place in late October or early November (the winning sailfish in 1991 weighed 116.8 lbs). Trips that combine fishing with a visit to near deserted ocean beaches that extend for miles along the coast from Zihuatanejo can also be arranged as can trips starting at the new Marina Ixtapa, a bit north of the Ixtapa hotel zone.

Sunset cruises on the trimaran *Tri Star* (tel. 4-3589) depart from the Puerto Mio pier daily, 5 to 8pm. They include live music and open bar. Tickets purchased at the town pier cost about $35. Sometimes night and moonlight cruises are available.

WATER SPORTS Rentals for sailboats, Windsurfers, and other water sports equipment are usually available at Club de Playa Omar, La Ropa Beach in Zihuatanejo (tel. 4-3873), and at the main beach, Playa Palmar, in Ixtapa. **Parasailing** is also available at both beaches. Arrange **waterskiing** for $25 an hour at the town pier in Zihuatanejo and on the main beach in Ixtapa.

Scuba diving trips are arranged through the **Zihuatanejo Scuba Center** on Paseo del Pescador 4 (tel. 4-2147; fax 4-4468). Fees start around $70 for two dives, including all equipment and lunch. Marine biologist and dive instructor Juan Barnard speaks excellent English and is extremely helpful and knowledgeable about the area, which has nearly 30 different dive sites including walls and caves. Diving is done year-round, though the water is clearest May through December with 100-foot visibility or better. **Surfing** is good at Petacalco Beach north of Ixtapa.

LAND SPORTS & ACTIVITIES

Bullfights are held on Sunday or Wednesday afternoons during the winter season at the Plaza de Toros (bullring) in Zihuatanejo. Most hotel travel agencies can arrange tickets.

In Ixtapa the **Club de Golf Ixtapa** has an 18-hole course designed by Robert Trent Jones, Jr. Bring your own clubs or rent them here. The greens fee is $35. Caddies are $20 or electric carts cost $35 for one or two people. Throughout the course you'll see trees bearing mangos, avocados, limes, oranges, almonds, and even plants drooping with coffee beans. Regular golfers are accustomed to seeing exotic birds such as cranes, parrots, and macaws. Alligators live in the water hazards, so naturally it's unwise to retrieve balls that land there. The course is open daily from 7am to 7pm. Call for reservations (tel. 3-1062 or 3-1163). The new 18-hole course in Ixtapa may be playable by 1995. Designed by Robert Von Hagge of Texas, almost two miles of canals flow through the course, adding to the golfing challenge.

For **horseback riding,** guided trail rides from the Playa Linda Ranch (about seven miles north of Ixtapa) to Posquelite in the countryside can be arranged through the travel agency Turismo Caleta (tel. 3-1062 or 3-1163) for $35.

To polish your **tennis** serve in Zihuatanejo, try the La Ceiba Tennis Club near Playa Madera, or the Hotel Villa del Sol at Playa La Ropa (tel. 4-2239 or 4-3239). In Ixtapa, the Club de Golf Ixtapa has five tennis courts, lighted at night; it also rents equipment. Fees are $10 an hour; $12 an hour at night. Call for reservations (tel. 3-1062 or 3-1163). In addition, the Sheraton, Westin, and many hotels on the main beach of Ixtapa have courts.

The **Chula Vista Beach Club** (no phone) on Playa Las Cuatas north of Ixtapa offers free miniature golf, volleyball, and Ping-Pong, but bring your own water-sports equipment. The attractive restaurant/bar on the beach is open daily from 11am to 6pm; no admission fee. Taxi fare is about $8 to $10 round-trip from Ixtapa; $15 from Zihuatanejo.

TOURS & NEARBY ACTIVITIES

A **countryside tour** of fishing villages, coconut and mango plantations, and the **Barra de Potosí Lagoon** (known for its tropical birds) 14 miles south of Zihuatanejo is available through Turismo Caleta (tel. 4-2491 or 4-2493) and other local travel agencies for $35.

Excursions to **Los Moros de Los Péricos islands** for birdwatching can usually be arranged through local travel agencies, though it would probably be less expensive to rent a boat with a guide at the town pier in Zihuatanejo. The islands are offshore from Ixtapa's main beach.

CASA DE LA TORTUGA, 6 miles north of Ixtapa on Highway 200. Tel. 3-1659.
A young American couple invites guests to the patio of their modest beachfront bungalow for a home-cooked lunch of lobster, shrimp, or fish. Owner Dewey McMillan picks up guests in town daily around 1pm, arriving at the beach house in time for swimming, sunning, and exploring the unpopulated beach before settling in for a memorable feast. Afterward there's still time for relaxation before returning

around 5pm. It's very casual and comfortable and the meal is one of the best I've ever eaten. The whole thing, including transportation from Ixtapa to the beach home, is $25. For reservations call Dewey McMillan between 8:30am and 1pm. Or you can make arrangements in advance by fax (753/4-2790). If you have difficulty reaching McMillan, call Anita Hayner at Bungalows Pacíficos (see Chapter 9, "Where to Stay and Dine in Ixtapa and Zihuatanejo," above) on Playa La Ropa in Zihuatanejo and she may be able to help.

SAVVY SHOPPING

ZIHUATANEJO

Like other resorts in Mexico, Zihuatanejo has its quota of T-shirt and souvenir shops. But it's becoming a better place to buy Mexican crafts, folk art, and jewelry. Spreading inland from the waterfront for three or four blocks are numerous small shops worth exploring as well as impromptu street markets from time to time. Besides the places listed below, check out **Alberto's,** Cuauhtémoc 15, and **Ruby's,** Cuauhtémoc 7, for jewelry. Three stores stand out from the rest.

COCO CABANA COLLECTIBLES, Guerrero and Álvarez. Tel. 4-2518.

Next to Coconuts Restaurant, this shop is crammed with carefully selected crafts and folk art from all over the country, including fine Oaxaca wood carvings. Owner Pat Cummings once ran a gallery in New York, and the inventory reveals her discriminating eye. With a purchase, they'll cash your dollars at the going rate. It's opposite the Hotel Citalli. Store hours are Monday through Saturday, 10am to 2pm and 4 to 10pm.

GALERÍA MAYA, Bravo 31. Tel. 4-3606.

Small but packed, this folk art store offers Guatemalan jackets, santos, silver, painted wooden fish from Guerrero, tin mirror frames, masks, lacquer gourds, rain sticks, and embroidered T-shirts. It's open Monday through Saturday, 10am to 2pm and 5 to 9pm.

CASA MARINA, Paseo del Pescador 9. Tel. 4-2373.

Extending from the waterfront to Álvarez near 5 de Mayo, this building houses four shops, each one specializing in handcrafted wares. El Embarcadero sells casual cotton clothing that's embroidered or made of hand-loomed fabric, both from Mexico and other Latin American countries. La Tzotzil specializes in "Maya" crafts, offering a fine assortment of textiles, tunics, and folk art from Guatemala and southern Mexico. At El Jumil, nearly every inch of wall space is covered with grinning or leering masks of all kinds—carved, painted, papier-mâché, and more. The shop also sells silver jewelry. And La Zapoteca carries serapes, hammocks, and handsome wool weavings and rugs from Oaxaca. Open daily, 9am to 9pm during high season; 10am to 2pm and 4 to 8pm the rest of the year.

IXTAPA

Zealous shoppers shouldn't overlook Ixtapa, which has several malls of air-conditioned shops with a variety of goods from fashionable resort wear to contemporary art, from T-shirts to folk art. But there's nothing like the sophistication or variety you might find in Cancún (on Mexico's Yucatán peninsula). All the shops are within the same area on Bulevar Ixtapa, across from the beachside hotels. Formerly I noted a few special ones, but shops change with such rapidity that my attempt proved futile from edition to edition. So now I suggest that you enjoy the pleasure of browsing and discovery on your own. Among the shops are many places to cool off with a drink or renew vigor with a meal. Shop hours are the same as Zihuatanejo's.

2. EVENING ENTERTAINMENT

With an exception or two, Zihuatanejo nightlife dies down around 11pm or midnight. For a good selection of discos, hotel fiestas and special events, and fun watering holes with live music and dancing, head for Ixtapa. But keep in mind that the shuttle bus stops at 10pm, and a taxi ride back to Zihuatanejo after that hour costs $5 to $8 (though the fare could be shared). Many discos and dance places stay open until the last customers leave, so closing hours vary. During the off season (after Easter to before Christmas) hours vary; some places open only on weekends.

THE BAY CLUB AND SAMBA CAFÉ, Camino a Playa La Ropa, Zihuatanejo. Tel. 4-4844.

It's fun to dance under the stars on the beautifully lit patio surrounded by tropical plants. The restaurant/bar is perched on a hillside, with a splendid view of the town lights and bay. Live music ranges from jazz and tropical to soft rock. The mesquite-grilled dinners are expensive, but you can come after dinner hours and enjoy the music, ordering an appetizer or dessert. Drinks cost between $3 and $6 and snacks $6 to $10. A full dinner would run $25 and up. Open daily during high season 9:30pm to midnight; happy hour 5 to 7pm. Closed in summer.

Admission: Free.

CARLOS 'N' CHARLIE'S, Bulevar Ixtapa (just north of the Hotel Posada Real), Ixtapa. Tel. 3-0085.

Decorated with all sorts of nostalgia, bric-a-brac, silly sayings, and photos from the Mexican Revolution, this restaurant/nightclub offers party ambience plus good food. The eclectic menu humorously includes iguana in season, with Alka Seltzer and aspirin on the house. Out back by the beach is an open-air section (part of it shaded) with a raised wooden platform called the "pier" for "pier-dancing" at night, thus mixing the sound of the surf with recorded rock and roll. Restaurant open daily from noon to midnight; pier dancing 9pm to 3pm.

Admission: After 9pm for dancing, $5 women, $10 men (includes drink tokens).

CHRISTINE, in the Hotel Krystal, Bulevar Ixtapa, Ixtapa. Tel. 3-2318 or 3-0333.

This flashy streetside disco is famous for its opening light show, which includes classical music played on a mega-sound system. A half-circle of tables on tiers overlooks the dance floor. No tennis shoes, sandals, shorts, or jeans are allowed, and reservations are advised during high season. Drinks cost from $4 to $7. It's open daily during high season from 10:30pm to the wee hours, light show at midnight.

Admission: $14.

EUFORIA DISCO, Bulevar Ixtapa, Ixtapa. Tel. 3-1190 or 3-1250.

At the turnoff to Carlos 'n' Charlie's you can't miss the Euforia Disco, next to the Lighthouse Restaurant and in front of the Hotel Posada Real. Tiers of tables rise on one side of the circular dance floor, behind which is a landscape setting with a volcano that actually erupts. Go early in time to see the sound and light show. No shorts are allowed. Drinks cost between $4 and $6. Ask about seasonal discounts on the admission. It's open daily during high season from 10:30pm to the wee hours.

Admission: $16.

SANCA BAR, in the Ixtapa Sheraton Hotel, Bulevar Ixtapa, Ixtapa. Tel. 3-3184 ext 2112.

Sanca is slang for "pal," and visitors seem to enjoy the easy camaraderie of this rancho-rustic bar where live salsa and other tropical music are played. Drinks cost around $4.50 to $5. It's open nightly from 10:30pm to 1:30am. Some nights "yards" of beer (a special long glass) are two-for-one.

Admission: $5.

HOTEL FIESTAS & THEME NIGHTS

Many hotels hold Mexican fiestas and other special events that usually include dinner, drinks, live music, and entertainment for a fixed price ($20 to $30). The **Sheraton Ixtapa** (tel. 3-1858) is famous for its Wednesday-night fiesta; good Mexican fiestas are also held by the **Krystal Hotel** (tel. 3-0333) and **Dorado Pacífico** (tel. 3-2025) in Ixtapa, and the **Villa del Sol** (tel. 4-2239) on Playa La Ropa in Zihuatanejo. The **Westin Ixtapa** (tel. 3-2121) and the **Sheraton Ixtapa** also put on theme nights featuring the cuisine and music of different countries. Call to make reservations (travel agencies also sell the tickets) and be sure you understand what the fixed price covers (drinks, tax and tip are not always included). These fiestas and theme nights may not be offered in low season.

3. AN EXCURSION TO PAPANOA

Less than 50 miles from Ixtapa on Highway 200 towards Acapulco is Papanoa. This hamlet of 5,000 folks is primarily involved in agriculture but there's one cliffside hotel catering to vacationers who are content with simple pleasures. This will appeal to travelers who like a touch of bygone Mexico or who enjoy discovering off-beat and secluded places without the service or frills of more expensive inns. From the patio of the hotel you can see (and walk to) an uninhabited beach stretching for miles with nothing but waves making glassy scallops in the sand. If you make this drive on a Sunday, most of the villages along here have a special market on that day. On the roadside vendors hold up lobsters and salt for sale. The highway skirts the ocean where powerful waves break on lonely beaches. The undertow is too powerful for safe swimming. Look out for surprise *topes* and slow down for iguanas crossing the road.

HOTEL PAPANOA, Carretera 200, Papanoa, Gro. Tel. 742/2-0150. 30 rms. FAN

$ Rates: $40 single, $60 double.

This old roadside inn has an air of the 1950s when people piled out of the cities in search of a weekend getaway. The large dining room with enormous round dining tables still caters to big families who find this the ideal place for a holiday. During the week it's almost deserted. With arches over the veranda and hacienda-style architecture, guest rooms are in one wing off the dining room. Most of the well-used rooms are small and have black tile floors, two twin beds, and couches doubling as beds. Sinks are outside the bathroom in each room. Four large units have two bedrooms and come with a single bed and a double bed. All have either a patio or balcony facing the highway. There's a nice-sized clean and shaded pool one level below the dining room, with a grand vista of the beach below. The restaurant is open daily from 7am to 8pm. Christmas and Easter the hotel is always full. Any other holiday and on weekends get there early in the day to be assured of a room. Other times the room selection is yours and it never hurts to ask for a discount if they aren't full. Reservations may also be made by calling 5/560-1571 or 5/654-0641 in Mexico City.

CHAPTER 11

GETTING TO KNOW
TAXCO & THE
REGION

- **WHAT'S SPECIAL ABOUT TAXCO & THE REGION**
- **1. ORIENTATION**
- **2. GETTING AROUND**
- **FAST FACTS: TAXCO**

This is the land of the Aztecs and Cortés. The Taxco and Cuernavaca region, composed of both the states of Guerrero and Morelos, paid tribute to the Aztecs in pre-Hispanic times, and was later included in the land apportioned to Hernán Cortés after the Conquest of Mexico, at the time he was made marqués of the Valley of Oaxaca. His domain stretched, in sections, from Mexico City south to Oaxaca, but he spent his time primarily in this area—both near and far from Mexico City, the capital he had conquered, destroyed, and rebuilt.

Taxco de Alarcón sits on a hill among hills, and almost everywhere you walk in the city there are fantastic views. The name "Taxco" (pronounced "*tahs*-ko"; alt. 5,850 ft.; pop. 87,000) is derived from the Nahuatl word *tlachco*, meaning "place of the ball game." "Alarcón" honors a favorite son, Juan Ruiz de Alarcón, a famed 16th-century dramatist, whose birthplace it is believed to have been.

Renowned for its silver mines, first worked in the time of Cortés, Taxco is the oldest mining center in the Americas. Cortés first sent Spaniards to the area in search of tin, needed in the manufacture of cannons. The founding of the four-century old silver mine, Cantarranas, is attributed to Cortés, though it is more likely that his son, Martín, actually started the mine. In its silver boom days in the 1700s, Taxco was ranked as one of the top silver-producing areas, equal to the fabulous mining center of Pachuca, northeast of Mexico City.

In the 1930s, the silver mines were revived, for all practical purposes, by an American, William Spratling. Taxco now ranks fourth in mining in Mexico, but its fame today rests more on the artistry of its silversmiths. Almost 200 silver shops, many of them one-man factories, line the cobbled streets all the way up into the hills. The Cantarranas outbuildings (the name means "singing frogs") now house Taxco's tourism office and convention center. Taxco is busy, crowded, and commercial all day, with hundreds of taxis and minivan buses vying with tourists for space in the narrow streets. In the evenings, after the tourists on day-trips depart, uniformed students wearing knee socks and carrying satchels replace them in the passageways, shopkeepers take a breath, restaurants thin out, and Taxco becomes like any other Mexican town.

WHAT'S SPECIAL ABOUT TAXCO & THE REGION

An Outstanding Church
- [ ] The opulent Santa Prisca y San Sebastián in Taxco, among the country's four outstanding baroque churches.

Festivals
- [ ] Taxco's Easter week pageantry and Tepoztlán's pre-Lenten Carnaval, among the country's most picturesque.
- [ ] The bizarre festival celebrating the jumil insect in November on the Huixteco Mountain outside Taxco.
- [ ] Jornadas Alarconianas, a festival of drama, music, and literary events.

Language Schools
- [ ] Cuernavaca's well-known language schools that cater to foreigners learning Spanish.
- [ ] UNAM's art and language school in Taxco.

Museums
- [ ] The Museo Spratling and Silver Museum in Taxco.
- [ ] The Museo de Cuauhnahuac and Museo Casa de Robert Brady in Cuernavaca.

Special Cities and Villages
- [ ] Taxco, a city on a hill.
- [ ] Ixcateopan, with its marble streets.
- [ ] Tepoztlán, with its village life, markets, and festivals.

Resorts
- [ ] Cuernavaca's springlike weather and resort hotels make it a mecca for vacationers pursuing relaxation.

Silver
- [ ] With more than 200 silver shops, Taxco is Mexico's "Silver Capital."

1. ORIENTATION

ARRIVING

Taxco is 185 miles north of Acapulco, 50 miles south of Cuernavaca, and 111 miles south of Mexico City.

BY BUS Taxco has two bus stations. **Estrella de Oro** buses arrive at their own station on the southern edge of town. If you have only a small suitcase, take one of the white minivans marked "Santa Prisca" or "Zócalo" that stop in front of the station and go to town center. Otherwise take a taxi since the hills from the station to town are steep. **Flecha Roja** buses arrive at the new station on Avenida Kennedy at the eastern edge of town.

From Mexico City, Estrella de Oro, Calzada de Tlalpan 2205, at the Central de Autobuses del Sur (Metro: Tasqueño), has five buses a day to Taxco and the trip takes three hours. Lineas Unidas del Sur/Flecha Roja also has several buses a day, but is a second choice to Estrella de Oro. **From Iguala** there are Flecha Roja buses every 15 minutes and hourly buses from the Cacahuamilpa Caves. **From Chilpancingo** seven Flecha Roja buses go to Taxco. **From Cuernavaca** you can catch an Estrella de Oro bus as it passes through, if there are seats available from Mexico City via Cuernavaca. There are several buses daily from both **Acapulco and Zihuatanejo.**

BY CAR From Mexico City, take Paseo de la Reforma to Chapultepec Park and merge with the Periférico that will take you to Highway 95D on the south end of town. From the Periférico take the Insurgentes exit and merge until you come to the Cuernavaca-Tlalpan sign. Choose either Cuernavaca Cuota (toll) or Cuernavaca Libre (free). Continue south around Cuernavaca to the Amacuzac interchange and proceed straight ahead for Taxco. The drive from Mexico City takes about 3½ hours. Fill up with gas at Cuernavaca. From Cuernavaca, the exit for Taxco on the toll road is about 11 miles from Taxco. A new portion of the toll road is planned to lead directly into Taxco.

From Acapulco take Highway 95 through Iguala to Taxco. Portions of the new toll road may be open when you travel; the old two-lane road winds through villages and is slower but in good condition.

If you come from either Cuernavaca or Mexico City, you'll arrive above the town and see it sprawling in the valley and up the hillsides below. If you come from Acapulco you'll be on the southern edge of town and won't get a good view until you're almost there. The road from both Acapulco and Cuernavaca becomes Avenida John F. Kennedy and runs along the outer edges of town center. To get to town center, follow the traffic heading toward the bell towers of the Santa Prisca Church, which you can't miss. Taxco's streets are extremely narrow and many are one way, the traffic is extremely congested, and there's very little street parking.

DEPARTING

Estrella Blanca/Flecha Roja lines (tel. 2-0131) have "Plus" service to Mexico City at 5 and 7am, and 2 and 4pm, and service to Cuernavaca every 30 minutes from 5am to 8pm. **Estrella de Oro** (tel. 2-0648) has direct service to Mexico City at 7am and noon, and service with one stop in Cuernavaca at 9am and 4 and 6pm. Estrella de Oro also services Chilpancingo and Acapulco at 7 and 9am and 3:30pm.

TOURIST INFORMATION

The **Dirección de Turismo** (tel. and fax 762/2-2274), run by the state of Guerrero, has offices at the arches on the main highway at the north end of town, useful if you're driving into town. The office is open daily from 9am to 3pm and 6 to 9pm. To get there from the Plaza Borda, take a combi ("Zócalo Arcos") and get off at the arch over the highway. When you see the arches, you're at the tourism office. This building and the grounds and buildings that descend the hillside in back are Taxco's convention center. Formerly these buildings were part of Cantarranas, the silver mine belonging to Martín Cortés, son of Hernán Cortés.

IMPRESSIONS

I called this town the absolute equal of any hill town in France or Italy and that statement I have never desired to take back. Knowing all the chief European hill towns, I am in a position to do my personal comparing and I still feel that this treasure of Mexico is as good as the very best in the Old World.
—SYDNEY A. CLARK, *MEXICO: MAGNETIC SOUTHLAND*, 1944

The cobblestones of the streets (in Taxco) were smoothed to a slippery surface by generations of bare feet. At one point I stood above the roof-tops and looked down at the descending slopes of the red-tiled roofs, built in a style special to the place. The whole town was roofed in this way during the eighteenth century by the silver-king, José de la Borda, who wished to see from the balcony of his own palace a sight that would remind him of his native Seville.
— JONATHAN CAPE, *TEMPLES OF THE SUN AND MOON: A MEXICAN JOURNEY*, 1954

CITY LAYOUT
The center of town is the tiny Plaza Borda shaded by perfectly manicured Indian laurel trees. On one side is the imposing, pink-stone, twin-towered church of **Santa Prisca y San Sebastián;** the other sides are lined with whitewashed, red-tile-roofed buildings housing the famous **silver shops,** restaurants, and several **museums.** Beside the church, deep in a crevice of the mountain, is the **city market.** Brick-paved streets stretch out from here in a helter-skelter fashion up and down the hillsides. Besides the silver shops the plaza swirls with tourists and walking vendors with arms loaded with everything from hammocks, lace tablecloths, and colorful blankets to cotton candy, bark paintings, watercolors, baskets, and balloons. Very few streets have street signs.

Avenida John F. Kennedy is the main thoroughfare around the city; it links the highways from Mexico City and Acapulco. For a few blocks, as you enter from Mexico City under the arches, it is known as Calle Florida.

Taxco Viejo, or Old Taxco, is a few miles south of town. It is the site of the original Taxco, where there is still a small town. Near it are **workshops** of two of Taxco's famed silversmiths, Los Castillo and Spratling (see "Attractions" in Chapter 13). **Tehuilotepec,** north of town on the road to Cuernavaca, is the site of Borda's first mine, and his home, which is the new Museo Mineria.

2. GETTING AROUND

The Plaza Borda and the Plazuela San Juan are the two main locations for finding empty taxis and minivans. However, talk of prohibiting traffic around the zócalo continues because of the street congestion and the damage dust and vehicular fumes are doing to the church. So there may be changes in traffic patterns when you travel.

BY BUS White minivans, called combi or *burrito* (little burro), go in and out of town center from the arches, "Los Arcos" by the tourist information office to the zócalo/Plaza Borda in town center and to the southern outskirts on Avenida Kennedy and to nearby Tehuilotepec or "Tehui" as it's known for short. A ride costs around 35¢; just pass the money to the driver when you board. When you want to get off say *baja* (down) so that the driver knows you want off at the next stop. Villagers are very helpful, so if you're unsure of how to get somewhere or where to get off, just ask the driver or one of the other passengers.

BY TAXI Volkswagen Beetle taxis, with the passenger seat missing, are everywhere and charge $2 to $3 for trips in town. Empty ones are difficult to find around dusk when people are leaving work and school.

BY CAR Unless you are using your car for an excursion out of town, it's best to park it and leave it when you first arrive. Narrow, congested, steep, and unmarked streets make for very difficult driving around town.

 TAXCO

Area Code The area code is 762 (formerly it was 732).
Bookstore The Casa Dominguez, Calle Arco 7 (tel. 2-0133), has a small

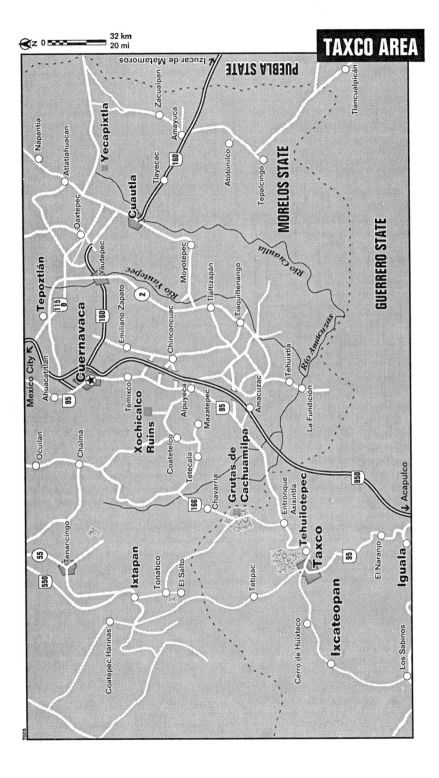

TAXCO AREA

assortment of English-language magazines, newspapers, and books. It's on the narrow street on the right side of the Santa Prisca Church and open Monday through Saturday from 10am to 2pm and 4 to 8pm and on Sunday from 10am to 2pm. Another bookstore, Agencia de Publicaciones (tel. 2-0794), is a couple of doors down and open daily from 9am to 8pm.

Climate Generally Taxco is warm during the day, usually in the 80s, but is cool enough for a sweater in the mornings and from sunset on. Though I've never seen a drop of rain on my many trips to Taxco, it has a reputation for having torrential downpours. Thus Santa Prisca, for whom the church is named, is the patron saint of storms.

Footwear Because Taxco's stone-paved streets are steep and slick, wear only sturdy, rubber-soled shoes.

Post Office The post office has moved to the outskirts of Taxco on the highway heading toward Acapulco. It's in a row of shops with a black-and-white sign reading "Correo."

Safety Generally speaking, Taxco has little crime. However, recently there have been robberies of people walking along the dark narrow passageways in the central village. So keep that in mind; don't flash money around, and secure your valuables.

Scams Upon arrival in Taxco, some taxi drivers at the bus stations and tour guides who greet you receive a payoff to take you to certain hotels in Taxco. They'll even go so far as to tell you the hotel where you have reservations is closed in order to take you to a hotel where they get a kickback. Proceed with your plans, and leave these guys to their dirty tricks.

Spanish and Art Classes In 1993, the Universidad Anónima de Mexico (UNAM) opened its doors in the buildings and grounds of the Hacienda del Chorillo, formerly part of the Cortés land grant. Here students can study silversmithing, Spanish, drawing, composition, and history under supervision of UNAM instructors. Classes have between 10 and 15 students and courses generally run for three months. The school will provide a list of prospective accommodations in town, which consists primarily of hotels. As an alternative, I suggest you select an inexpensive hotel for the first several nights, then search for something more reasonable for a lengthy stay. At locations all over town there are notices of furnished apartments or rooms for rent at reasonable prices. For information about the school, contact the Dirección de Turismo (tourist office) in Taxco (see above under "Tourist Information") or write the school directly: UNAM, Hacienda del Chorillo, Taxco, Gro. 40200 (tel. 762/2-3690).

Telephone Farmacia Oscarin, Av. Kennedy 47 (tel. 2-1847), opposite the Flecha Roja bus station, serves as the community long-distance telephone center. For a small service fee (around $4) they'll dial the number you want, then you step into a private booth to take your call. If you call collect, the service fee is the only charge. Otherwise you pay both the service fee and the cost of the call. It's open Monday through Saturday from 8:30am to 9pm and on Saturday from 8:30am to 2pm.

Tour Guides Self-appointed guides wearing navy blue shirts will probably flag you down on the highway into town, or approach you on the zócalo (Plaza Borda) and offer their services. Ask to see their **Dirección de Turismo** credentials. Those with credentials are government-licensed guides who usually speak very good English, are reliable, and have been serving tourists all their lives. If you've never been to Taxco and have limited time for sightseeing, these guides can save the day. They'll offer to drive your car, which makes sightseeing easier, but it's up to you. Before you start, agree on the price for the guide's service. Be aware that these men receive a commission on your purchases (as does any other person offering to lead you around). The Tourism Department (see "Tourist Information," above) can also arrange for a guide—usually one of these in the blue shirts. Cost for a half day of sightseeing is around $50.

Used Clothing   The Casa Hogar de Taxco (Children's Home of Taxco) needs donations of good used clothing of any size, and for any climate, for men, women, or children. What they don't use in the home they give away to needy families or sell to support the home. Donations are badly needed and are accepted at the reception desk of the Hotel Melendez, just off the Plaza Borda. For more information on the home, write Casa Hogar de Taxco, Apdo. Postal 155, Taxco, Gro. 40200.

CHAPTER 12

WHERE TO STAY & DINE IN TAXCO

1. WHERE TO STAY
2. WHERE TO DINE

Taxco is a visitor's dream—charming and picturesque, with a vibrant cultural life and boasting a respectable selection of well-kept and delightful hotels. Prices tend to "bulge" at holiday times (especially Easter week), and although it is no longer the bargain it once was, prices are reasonable compared to coastal resorts. One suggestion: Light sleepers may want to bring along earplugs, for Taxco's stony streets resound with car traffic, and animal sounds echo through the canyons all night.

1. WHERE TO STAY

EXPENSIVE

HACIENDA DEL SOLAR, Apdo. Postal 96, Taxco, Gro. 40200. Tel. 762/2-0323. Fax 762/2-0587. 22 rms.

$ Rates: $85–$135 single; $118–$170 double; $185 single junior suite; $219 double junior suite. Holiday rates are approximately double these and may include some meals.

Located on a hilltop with magnificent views of the surrounding valleys and the town are several Mexican-style cottages. Decor is slightly different in each one, but most include bathrooms done in handmade tiles, lots of beautiful handcraft works as accents, colonial-style construction, hand-painted folk murals, and red-tile floors. Beds have bright, cheerful colored spreads to match the warm sunlight that enters each room. Several rooms have Gothic-vaulted tile ceilings, and fine private terraces with panoramic views.

Accommodations are rented as doubles only, in three grades. Standard rooms have no terraces and only showers in the baths; deluxe rooms have sunken tubs with showers and terraces. The largest and most luxurious accommodations are the junior suites. The prices I quote here are those given me by the management right at the hotel. If you make a reservation through a travel agent back home, you may be quoted a significantly higher price.

Besides the marvelous hilltop setting, guests at the Hacienda del Solar enjoy a nice big heated swimming pool surrounded by lots of green grass for sunning, beautifully planted grounds with rough stone walks, flowering shrubs, shade trees, a tennis court, and a cocktail lounge named the Salón Colibri. Meals are served in the hacienda's own restaurant, La Ventana de Taxco. (See "Where to Dine," below, for details).

It's 2½ miles south of town center, off Highway 95 to Acapulco; look for signs on the left.

HOTEL MONTETAXCO, Fracc. Lomas de Taxco (Apdo. Postal 84), Taxco, Gro 40200. Tel. 762/2-1300 or 2-1301, or toll free 91-800/9-8000 in Mexico. Fax 762/2-1428. 160 rms. TV TEL

$ Rates: Sun–Thurs $108 single or double; Fri–Sat $120 single or double.

You can't miss this hotel on a mountaintop near the north entrance of town. Views of Taxco from here surpass any in town. You enter via a winding cobbled lane up the mountain that seems never to end. From the lobby, past the beautiful pool and Toni's, the palapa-topped gourmet restaurant, Taxco unfolds below—magnificent. Rooms are stylishly furnished, some with balconies, some with views, some with both. Besides Toni's, the evening-only restaurant with a panoramic view, there's another restaurant serving all three meals. Windows, is the town's best disco (see "Evening Entertainment" in Chapter 13). Off the lobby are several very good silver shops and boutiques. On the grounds is a nine-hole golf course, three tennis courts, and more shops; horseback riding can be arranged.

POSADA DE LA MISIÓN, Av. Kennedy 32 (Apdo. Postal 88), Taxco, Gro. 40200. Tel. 762/2-0063. Fax 762/2-2198. 80 rms, 70 suites. TV TEL

$ Rates: Standard single or double $92 with twin beds in old section; small suite $115 single or double; large suite $153 single or double.

Completely renovated and updated in recent years, this is fast becoming the best hotel near the central village. Rooms, all with colonial decor and using Mexican tiles, textiles, and crafts, exude the charm visitors enjoy in Mexico. Some have fireplaces. A new, three-story, all-suite section was added several years ago. Most of what the management calls suites are just nice-sized rooms with balconies facing great Taxco views. The Acapulco and Ixtapa suites are the largest in this section, and come with handsome large living rooms and large bedrooms with king-size beds with a long balcony overlooking Taxco stretching the length of both rooms. However, the multiflight of stairs (no elevator) required to reach these two rooms may leave you breathless. The least expensive rooms are those in the older section, which come with two twin-size beds and a common walkway that doubles as a patio. The latter admit the nightly sounds of Taxco's dogs, roosters, donkeys, and fireworks more than the more expensive rooms facing the interior. The panoramic restaurant here, while very expensive and not necessarily memorable for its food, affords a fabulous view of the village. There's a comfortable lobby bar as well. The outdoor pool is framed by the famed Juan O'Gorman mural. You might want to have a look at the mural even if you are not staying at the hotel. The hotel is conveniently reached by minibuses headed for the zócalo.

MODERATE

HOTEL LOMA LINDA, Av. Kennedy 52, Taxco, Gro. 40230. Tel. 762/2-0206. Fax 762/2-5125. 62 rms.

$ Rates: $65 single; $75 double.

Rates at this hotel are too high for the quality of the rooms. You're paying for convenience and parking at this motel-like inn. Nevertheless, it fills up by early afternoon. The single-story rooms surround the large interior grounds where there's a pool, children's play area, and plenty of parking space. Some rooms face the town (and thus Taxco's nightly barking dogs) while others face the mostly unoccupied mountains toward the Cuernavaca/Mexico City entry side of town. Rooms are large, sunny, and comfortable with tile floors and a balcony, but otherwise sparsely furnished. Though it's on the outskirts of the central village, combis marked "Zócalo" are frequent and stop at the entrance and will drop you in the central village in minutes. There's a nice hotel restaurant opposite the office that is open daily from 7:30am to 9:30pm. There's also a convenient Ladatel phone in the lobby, and desk clerks sell plastic Ladatel cards to use it; it's good for long distance since the operators answer quickly. However, for local calls ask to use their phone; it's cheaper than Ladatel. Arriving from Mexico City or Cuernavaca, the hotel is on the left before you reach town center.

HOTEL SANTA PRISCA, Plazuela de San Juan 7, Taxco, Gro. 40200. Tel. 762/2-0080 or 2-0980. Fax 762/2-2938. 34 rms.

$ Rates: $31 single standard room, $45 double standard room; $40 single suite, $57 double suite; suites nos. 25 and 26 $100 single or double.

One of the older and nicer hotels in town offers rooms that are small but comfortable, with older bathrooms (showers only), tile floors, wood beams, and a colonial atmosphere. There's a reading area in an upstairs salon overlooking Taxco, a lush patio with fountains, and a lovely dining room done in mustard and blue. To find it from the Plaza Borda, walk down the street left of Paco's Bar to the next plaza, San Juan, and the hotel is up a ramp on the left.

HOTEL TAXCO VICTORIA, Apdo. Postal 83, Taxco, Gro. 40200. Tel. 762/ 2-1014 or 2-0010. Fax 762/2-0617. 100 rms.

$ Rates: Standard room $38 single, $40 double; deluxe suite $47 single, $54 double; junior suite $66 single or double.

The Taxco Victoria clings to the hillside above the town, with breathtaking views from its flower-covered verandas. It's a personal favorite partly for the views and partly because it has all the charm of Old Mexico. Furnishings, as beautifully kept as if they were purchased yesterday, whisper of the hotel's heyday in the 1940s. In the guest rooms, nestled into nooks and crannies of the rambling hillside buildings, are vanities constructed with handmade tiles, local tin-craft reading lamps, old prints of Mexico and Taxco, beamed ceilings, craftwork bedspreads and throw rugs, a plant or two, bathrooms with tubs, and, in many cases, a small private terrace. In front of each standard room there's a table and chairs set out on the tiled common walkway linking the rooms. Deluxe rooms have private terraces; each junior suite has a bedroom, a large nicely furnished living room, and a spacious private terrace overlooking the city. There's a lovely pool and an overpriced restaurant, both with great views of Taxco. Even if you don't stay here, come for a drink in the comfortable bar/living room, then stroll on the terrace and drink in the fabulous view. From Plazuela de San Juan go up a narrow cobbled, winding street named Carlos J. Nibbi to no. 57 on the hilltop.

BUDGET

HOTEL CASA GRANDE, Plazuela de San Juan 7, Taxco, Gro. 40200. Tel. and fax 762/2-1108. 12 rms (all with bath).

$ Rates: $15 single; $24 double; $28 triple.

One of Taxco's most basic hotels is housed in one of its oldest buildings, ideally located on Plazuela de San Juan. Rooms are dark and small but nicely kept with tile baths but no toilet seats. Some rooms have one or two double beds, others have twin beds, and all have overbed lights. Mattresses are soft so test yours before signing in. There's a small restaurant/bar, La Concha Nostra, in the front that overlooks the plazuela and is open for breakfast only.

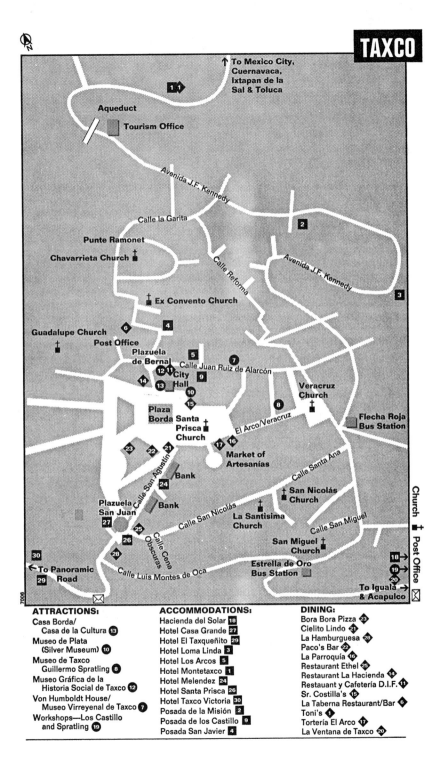

TAXCO

To Mexico City,
Cuernavaca,
Ixtapan de la
Sal & Toluca

Aqueduct

Tourism Office

Avenida J.F. Kennedy

Calle la Garita

Punte Ramonet

Chavarrieta Church

Calle Reforma

Avenida J.F. Kennedy

Ex Convento Church

Guadalupe Church

Post Office

Plazuela
de Bernal

Calle Juan Ruiz de Alarcón

City
Hall

Veracruz
Church

Plaza
Borda

Santa
Prisca
Church

El Arco/Veracruz

Flecha Roja
Bus Station

Market of
Artesanías

Calle Santa Ana

Bank

Calle San Agustín

San Nicolás
Church

Plazuela
San Juan

Bank

Calle San Nicolás

La Santísima
Church

Calle San Miguel

Calle Cana
Obscuras

San Miguel
Church

To Panoramic
Road

Calle Luis Montes de Oca

Estrella de Oro
Bus Station

To Iguala
& Acapulco

Church ✝ Post Office

7006

ATTRACTIONS:
Casa Borda/
  Casa de la Cultura 13
Museo de Plata
  (Silver Museum) 10
Museo de Taxco
  Guillermo Spratling 8
Museo Gráfica de la
  Historia Social de Taxco 12
Von Humboldt House/
  Museo Virreyenal de Taxco 7
Workshops—Los Castillo
  and Spratling 19

ACCOMMODATIONS:
Hacienda del Solar 18
Hotel Casa Grande 27
Hotel El Taxqueñito 29
Hotel Loma Linda 3
Hotel Los Arcos 5
Hotel Montetaxco 1
Hotel Melendez 24
Hotel Santa Prisca 26
Hotel Taxco Victoria 30
Posada de la Misión 2
Posada de los Castillo 9
Posada San Javier 4

DINING:
Bora Bora Pizza 23
Cielito Lindo 21
La Hamburguesa 28
Paco's Bar 22
La Parroquía 16
Restaurant Ethel 25
Restaurant La Hacienda 13
Restauant y Cafetería D.I.F. 11
Sr. Costilla's 15
La Taberna Restaurant/Bar 6
Toni's 1
Tortería El Arco 17
La Ventana de Taxco 20

HOTEL LOS ARCOS, Juan Ruíz de Alarcón 12, Taxco, Gro. 40200. Tel. 762/2-1836. 21 rms (all with bath).

$ Rates: $25 single; $35 double.

Los Arcos is a converted monastery (1620). The handsome inner patio, bedecked with Puebla pottery, and the gaily dressed restaurant area are centered around a fountain. The rooms are nicely but sparsely furnished, with natural tile floors and colonial-style furniture. You'll be immersed in colonial charm and blissful quiet, though you're only a couple of minutes from the Plaza Borda. To find it from the Plaza Borda, follow the hill down (with the Hotel Agua Escondida on your left), and make an immediate right at the bottom of the hill; the hotel is a block down on the left, opposite the Posada Los Castillo.

HOTEL MELENDEZ, Cuauhtémoc 6, Taxco, Gro. 40200. Tel. 762/2-0006. 33 rms (all with bath).

$ Rates: $25 single; $37 double.

The old-timey Hotel Melendez has overpriced, simply furnished rooms. Some are airy and have blue-tile walls and ornate glass and metalwork doors on the bathrooms. Several have terrific views. However, don't take Rooms 5, 6, 7, or 8 unless you're desperate—they're oddly located and sort of claustrophobic. And avoid any room next to the stairwell where noise echoes through tile corridors straight into your room. The hotel's restaurant, with windows overlooking Taxco, is on the ground floor. To find it from the Plaza Borda, go left of Paco's Bar and it's a half a block on the left.

POSADA DE LOS CASTILLO, Juan Ruíz de Alarcón 3, Taxco, Gro. 40200. Tel. 762/2-1396. Fax 762/2-2935. 14 rms (all with bath).

$ Rates: $25 single; $30 double.

The small rooms at Posada de los Castillo surround a courtyard on four levels. Each is simply but beautifully furnished with handsomely carved doors and furniture. Bathrooms have either tubs or showers. Just off the lobby, there's a branch of Los Castillo silver store. (The Castillo family also owns the hotel.) To find the hotel from the Plaza Borda, follow the hill down (the Hotel Escondida will be on your left), make an immediate right at the bottom of the hill, and the hotel is a block farther on the right, opposite the Hotel Los Arcos.

POSADA SAN JAVIER, Ex Rastro 4, Taxco, Gro. 40200. Tel. 762/2-3177. 18 rms (all with bath).

$ Rates: $25 single; $30 double.

If you follow the directions below, you'll discover the office of this hotel and several of the simple but pleasant rooms. The rest of the rooms are across a large, verdant lawn (with swimming pool). Finding them is like meandering up and down the halls of a rock-walled castle. Here and there are sitting areas with magazines. Rooms A through D are easiest to reach from the front door. There is no elevator, but the hotel rates make it worth the effort.

To get here, find the post office on Juárez Street and Restaurante Los Reyes. Estacas is the pedestrian-only, stepped-cobblestone street beside the restaurant. Walk down it to the first level and take the high level (left) to the second door. A faded sign announces the hotel, but just in case you have trouble, it's the door on the right. Enter it and go down, down, down. For entering by the parking lot, ask the manager for directions.

2. WHERE TO DINE

Taxco gets a lot of day-trippers from the capital and visitors passing through on their way to Acapulco. There are not enough restaurants to fill the demand, so prices are high for what you get.

VERY EXPENSIVE

TONI'S, in the Hotel Montetaxco. Tel. 2-1300.
   Cuisine: STEAKS/SEAFOOD. **Reservations:** Recommended.
$ Prices: Appetizers $6; main courses $25–$40.
   Open: Tues–Sat 7:30–1am.
Toni's is an intimate and classy restaurant high on a mountaintop, enclosed in a huge, cone-shaped thatched palapa with a panoramic view of the city below. Eleven candlelit tables sparkle with crystal and crisp linen. For the best views, try to get a booth by the panoramic windows. The limited menu of shrimp or beef won't keep guests returning night after night, but what they serve is superior. Try the house salad and the tender, juicy prime roast beef, which comes with Yorkshire pudding, creamed spinach, and baked potato.
   Lobster is also available. To get there take a combi to the convention center/tourist office, then hail a cab from there for around $3.50.

LA VENTANA DE TAXCO, in the Hacienda del Solar, Highway 95 South. Tel. 2-0587.
   Cuisine: ITALIAN/INTERNATIONAL. **Reservations:** Recommended.
   Open: Daily 1–10:30pm.
On my last visit service and food flavor were slipping at this beautiful, once highly recommended restaurant. Still it's a gracious place to linger if just for drinks and dessert. During the day the floor-to-ceiling windows (*ventanas*) reveal Taxco in all its hillside splendor; at night flickering candles on each table make this one of the most romantic places in Mexico. Come early for drinks in the comfortable *sala* (living room). Time between courses is pleasantly measured, so this is a place to dine leisurely or enjoy drinks and dessert—don't rush. It's south of Taxco on the highway to Acapulco. Look for signs on the left for the Hotel Hacienda del Solar.

MODERATE

BORA BORA PIZZA, Plaza Borda, Callejón de las Delicias 4. Tel. 1-1721.
   Cuisine: ITALIAN.
$ Prices: Pizza $5–$20; spaghetti $4.75–$8.50; beer $1.75; wine $2.50.
   Open: Daily 1pm–midnight.
For the best pizza in town, go to Bora Bora Pizza overlooking the Plaza Borda. Without any fanfare a pair of quiet youths here serve up mouthwateringly delicious pizza. The crusts are light and chewy and the ingredients are sparkling fresh—quite an unexpected treat. Tables are festooned in hot pink and purple, and pots of purple petunias decorate the tiny balconies overlooking the plaza.

CIELITO LINDO, Plaza Borda 14. Tel. 2-0603.
   Cuisine: MEXICAN/INTERNATIONAL.

$ Prices: Appetizers $4–$6.25; main courses $10–$14.
Open: Daily 9am–10pm.

The Cielito Lindo is probably the most popular place for lunch on the plaza, perhaps more for its visibility and colorful decor than for the food—which is fine, not great. The tables covered in white and laid with blue-and-white local crockery are usually packed, and plates of food disappear as fast as the waiters can bring them. You can get anything from soup to roast chicken, enchiladas, tacos, steak, dessert, and a frosty margarita.

PACO'S BAR, Plaza Borda, upstairs. No phone.
  Cuisine: MEXICAN.
$ Prices: Main courses $7–$20.
  Open: Daily noon–10:30pm.

After a hard day of climbing Taxco's hills while shopping, and museum hopping, Paco's, overlooking the Plaza Borda, is a great place to pause. Drinks are anywhere from $1.25 for soft drinks, through beer at about $1.50, with more sophisticated concoctions costing up to $3.75. They've augmented the menu here, hoping to attract diners as well as drinkers. There's a full menu from oysters to lobster, chicken, steak, and Mexican plates.

RESTAURANT LA HACIENDA, Calle Bailar, off Plaza Borda. Tel. 2-0663.
  Cuisine: MEXICAN/AMERICAN.
$ Prices: Appetizers $2–$4; main courses $2–$14.
  Open: Daily 7:30am–9pm.

The Restaurant La Hacienda boasts white linen, colorful table settings, a simple colonial decor, and an extensive menu—everything from enchiladas to steak and pasta to hamburgers. Despite its trappings, it's a small family-run operation, so the service is friendly if a little slow. Entrance is either through the Hotel Agua Escondida lobby or side street off the Plaza Borda.

RESTAURANT Y CAFETERÍA D.I.F., Juárez 3, Plazuela del Bernal. Tel. 2-0588.
  Cuisine: MEXICAN/INTERNATIONAL.
$ Prices: Breakfast $3.50–$4; main courses $3.25–$13.50; comida corrida $6.25.
  Open: Daily 8:30am–7:30pm; comida corrida served noon–closing.

On a corner just behind the Casa Borda, this small, charming restaurant attracts a lot of diners. Proceeds go to support a government agency that helps families and homeless or neglected children. The cheery walls are full of regional masks. Woven straw covered chairs are pulled up to cloth-covered tables. The menu includes steaks, seafood, and Mexican specialties. The two-course comida corrida serves more than its competitors do for about the same price. Look for the restaurant opposite Los Castillo silver shop.

SR. COSTILLA'S ("Mr. Ribs"), Plaza Borda 1. Tel. 2-3215.
  Cuisine: INTERNATIONAL.
$ Prices: Appetizers $4.75–$10; main courses $9.75–$20.
  Open: Daily 1pm–midnight.

The offbeat decor here includes a marvelous antique jukebox, a fake skeleton, and a ceiling festooned with the usual assortment of cultural flotsam and jetsam. A few tiny balconies hold a few minuscule tables that afford a view of the plaza and church, and these fill up long before the large dining room does. The menu is typical Andersonese (like the Carlos Anderson restaurants you may have encountered in your Mexican travels), with Spanglish jive and a large selection of everything from soup through steaks, sandwiches, and the eponymous spareribs to desserts and coffee. Wine, beer, and drinks are served. It's next to the Santa Prisca Church above Patio de las Artesanías.

LA TABERNA RESTAURANT/BAR, Juárez 8. Tel. 2-5226.
Cuisine: ITALIAN/INTERNATIONAL.
$ Prices: Appetizers $3.50–$11; main courses $6.50–$22.
Open: Daily 1pm–midnight.

⭐ La Taberna is the best eatery in town, and looks as though it should be more expensive than it is. It beckons from the porch all decked out in turquoise-and-white napkins and cloths. Climb the stairs and enter the old stone house with its front sala-turned-bar and pass to the interior plant-filled patio for a welcome respite and al fresco dining. The owners are the same as Bora Bora Pizza's and the food is consistently good. Try the fettuccine La Taberna, which comes with ham, bacon, tomatoes, and mushrooms. There are six kinds of crêpes, and 14 selections of either beef, chicken, or fish. Among them you'll discover chicken Kiev and chicken and beef brochettes.

To find it from the Plaza Borda, go down the hill beside the Hotel Agua Escondida bearing leftish, then right to the next bend. Taberna is a few steps farther on your left as you turn the corner.

BUDGET

LA HAMBURGUESA, Plazuela de San Juan 5. Tel. 2-0941.
Cuisine: TACOS/HAMBURGERS/MEXICAN.
$ Prices: Breakfast $3.25–$4.75; tacos and burgers $3.25–$7; main courses $3–$8; comida corrida $5.75.
Open: Daily 8am–midnight; comida corrida served 1–5pm.

The tables are always full at this small restaurant a few steps off the Plazuela de San Juan. A few cloth-covered tables are set outside on the porch and others inside, but both have a view of the busy plaza. The menu is small but offers soup, yogurt and fruit, Mexican plate meals, burgers and fries, and tacos—all filling and cheap.

RESTAURANT ETHEL, Plazuela de San Juan 14. Tel. 2-0788.
Cuisine: MEXICAN.
$ Prices: Soups $2.50; main courses $5.50–$10; comida corrida $7.75.
Open: Daily 9am–10pm; comida corrida served 1–5pm.

A family-run place, Restaurant Ethel is kept clean and tidy, with a homey atmosphere, white throws, and colorful crumb cloths on the tables. The hearty daily comida corrida consists of soup or pasta, meat (perhaps a small steak), dessert, and coffee. It's opposite the Hotel Santa Prisca on the Plazuela de San Juan, one block from the Plaza Borda.

TORTERÍA EL ARCO, Calle del Arco 11. No phone.
Cuisine: TORTAS/MEXICAN.
$ Prices: Tortas $1.75–$3.25; tacos $1.75; pozole $2.50–$3.
Open: Daily 9am–6pm.

Though small, with only five stools, this place is popular and the prices are right for a budget meal. Tortas come five ways plus there are enchiladas, tacos, and hamburgers as well as green, white, or red pozole on Thursday. You'll find it on the narrow street on the right side of the Santa Prisca Church.

CHAPTER 13

WHAT TO SEE & DO IN TAXCO

1. ATTRACTIONS
- **DID YOU KNOW . . . ?**
- **FROMMER'S FAVORITE TAXCO EXPERIENCES**
2. SAVVY SHOPPING
3. EVENING ENTERTAINMENT

With more than 200 shops selling silver, shopping for the brilliant metal is *the* major pastime, the main reason most tourists come to Taxco. But Taxco's cultural show is on an upward move. Besides the opulent, world-renowned Santa Prisca y San Sebastián Church, the Spratling archeology museum, and the Silver Museum, three new museums have been added—the Museo Virreynal de Taxco, Museo Mineria, and Museo Gráfica de la Historia Social de Taxco en el Siglo XX (Taxco's 20th-Century History in Prints and Photographs). Several more museums are planned, including a Museum of 19th-Century Customs, the Taxco City Museum, and the Jewish Museum. Throngs of spectators come for Easter week commemorations and the Jornadas Alarconianas in May, as well as the National Silver Fair in November that attracts foreign entrants as well. Besides being the silver capital of Mexico, Taxco has been dubbed the City of Festivals and Museums. (See "Special Events," below.)

1. ATTRACTIONS

IGLESIA SANTA PRISCA Y SAN SEBASTIÁN, Plaza Borda.

⭐ No visitor to Taxco should miss seeing Santa Prisca y San Sebastián Church. Named after two 12th-century Roman martyrs, it's one of Mexico's top four baroque churches. (Tepozotlán north of Mexico City, the Valenciana Church in Guanajuato, and the Zacatecas Cathedral are the other three).

This is Taxco's centerpiece parish church, around which village life takes place. Located facing the Plaza Borda, it was built with funds provided by José de la Borda, the French miner who struck it rich in Taxco's silver mines. Begun in 1751 and finished in 1759, the church was dedicated by the Archbishop of Manila (the Philippines), and Borda's son, Manuel, became the first parish priest. Every gilded, ornate inch is a study in religious symbolism, which was important for teaching Christianity to the native populations who couldn't read. The architectural conception is attributed to Cayteano de Sigüenza, from Mexico City, who drafted plans for the church.

The ultra-carved rose-colored stone facade is flanked by two elaborately embellished steeples, considered to be the finest examples of baroque architecture in the New World.

Those figures you see on the steeples are the apostles. The colorful domes are covered in tile from Puebla with yellow and green, signifying St. Joseph, and blue and white, the colors of Mary, mother of Christ.

Inside, the intricacy of the gold-leafed saints and cherubic angels is positively breathtaking. There are so many cherubic figures that they seem almost in motion. Several of the altars, the cherubs, scrolls, and other architectural elements are believed to be the work of two brothers, Isidoro Vicente and Luis de Balbas, sons of Gerónimo de Balbas who sculpted the altarpieces in the Metropolitan Cathedral in Mexico City.

The paintings by Miguel Cabrera, Mexico's most famous 18th-century artist, are the pride of Taxco. Santa Prisca is depicted in a Cabrera painting on the left as you enter, over the arched entry to the Chapel of Jesus of Nazareth, and San Sebastián appears in a painting on the opposite wall over a side door to the outside. Notice how the elaborate frames are coordinated with the interior architecture.

At the top of the unbelievably ornate gilded main altar is a representation of the Eternal Father, flanked by numerous winged cherubs, and by San Sebastián, Santa Prisca, Michael the Archangel, the Sacred Heart of Jesus, St. Peter, St. Ambrose, St. Gregory the Great, St. Jerome, and St. Augustine, finished off by the twelve apostles. Isidoro Vicente de Balbas is believed to be master creator of the main altar.

During restoration of the church, which started in 1988, a hidden room, containing several Cabrera paintings and funerary pieces was discovered below the main altar. Among them was a sculpture of a phoenix, thought to be a remembrance used during the funeral of José de la Borda. The discoveries are displayed at Taxco's new Museo Virreynal. The room behind the altar is also now open and contains even more Cabrera paintings.

Guides, both small boys and adults, will approach you outside the church offering to give a tour. The adults, of course, are more likely to speak English, and it's worth the small price to get a full rendition of what you are seeing. Make sure the guide's English is good, however, and establish whether the price is per person or per tour. It's customary to tip 50¢ or so if the tour is a good one.

Admission: Free.

Open: Daily 8am–11pm.

SILVER MUSEUM [Museo de Plata], Plaza Borda. Tel. 2-0558.

The Silver Museum, operated by a local silversmith, is not a traditional public-sponsored museum, but it's well worth a visit. After entering the building, left of the Santa Prisca (in the same building as Sr. Costilla's restaurant), look for a sign on the left. The museum is downstairs. Though small, it does a much-needed job of describing the history of silver in Mexico and Taxco, as well as displaying some historic and contemporary award-winning pieces. Time spent here seeing quality silver work will make you a more discerning shopper in Taxco's dazzling silver shops.

Admission: $1.25.

Open: Daily 10am–5pm.

MUSEO DE TAXCO GUILLERMO SPRATLING, Calle Porfirio Delgado. Tel. 2-1660.

⭐ A plaque (in Spanish) explains that most of the collection of pre-Columbian art displayed here, and the funds for creating this museum, came from William Spratling, an American born in 1900 who studied architecture in the U.S., later settled in Taxco, and organized the first workshops that turned out high-quality silver jewelry. From this first effort in 1931 the town's reputation as a center of artistic silver work grew to what it is today. In a real sense, Spratling put Taxco on the map. He died in 1967 in a car accident. Having said that, you'd expect this to be a silver museum, but it's not; for Spratling silver, go to the Spratling Ranch. The entrance floor of this museum displays a fine collection of pre-Columbian statues and implements in clay, stone, and jade. The lower floor has changing exhibits. Signs are in English and Spanish.

To find it, turn left out the Santa Prisca Church and left again at the corner; the museum is on the left at the end of the street. Or if you're at the Humboldt house, go left out the front door and up the stone ramp you'll see on the right side of the street. The museum is on the left.

Admission: $3.50; free Sun and holidays.

Open: Tues–Sat 10am–5pm, Sun 9am–3pm.

VON HUMBOLDT/MUSEO VIRREYNAL DE TAXCO, Calle Juan Ruiz de Alarcón. Tel. 2-5501.

⭐ Stroll along Ruiz de Alarcón (the street behind the Casa Borda), looking for the richly decorated facade of the von Humboldt House, where the renowned German scientist and explorer Baron Alexander von Humboldt (1769–1859) visited Taxco and stayed one night in 1803. The Humboldt house has known many uses, including that of guesthouse, run for 40 years until the mid-1970s by the von Wuthenau family. The museum that now occupies the building houses 18th-century memorabilia pertinent to Taxco, most of which came from a secret room discovered during the recent restoration of the Santa Prisca y San Sebastián church in Taxco. It's a fascinating museum, especially if you take a guided tour. However, signs with detailed information are in both Spanish and English.

To the right as you enter are two huge "tumelos," rare three-tiered funerary paintings. The bottom two were painted in honor of the death of King Carlos III of Spain. The top one, with a carved phoenix on top, is believed to have been painted for the funeral of José de la Borda. The three stories of the museum are divided by eras and persons famous in Taxco's history. In the *sala* (room) dedicated to José de la Borda is a copy of a painting (which hangs in the church) showing him dressed in the finery of his times, with samples of such garments in other cases. In a room of photographs are pictures of Taxco's 10 principal churches. Another room shows paintings of what workshops must have been like during the construction of the Santa Prisca y San Sebastián Church. Another section is devoted to historical information about Don Miguel Cabrera, Mexico's foremost 18th-century artist. Fine examples of clerical garments decorated with gold and silver thread hang in glass cases for close-up viewing. More well-restored Cabrera paintings are hung throughout the museum; some were found in the frames you see, others were haphazardly rolled up. And, of course, a small room devoted to von Humboldt shows what this young explorer looked like and gives a short history of his sojourn through South America and Mexico.

FROMMER'S FAVORITE
TAXCO EXPERIENCES

Experiencing Easter Week [Semana Santa] The pageantry of this serious and uncommercialized celebration is an unforgettable experience.

Discovering the Iglesia Santa Prisca y San Sebastián Take time to gaze at length and in detail at the church's wonderful interior.

People Watching Sitting on a park bench under the shady Indian laurels of the Plaza Borda, you can observe the daily swirl of tourists, street vendors, and taxis.

Shopping Visit the workshops of the silversmiths and shop for silver. Also look for vendors on the street, selling colorful baskets and bark-paper folk paintings.

Relaxing in Paco's Bar From Paco's lofty perch you can unwind, have some refreshment, and watch plaza life.

Dining at La Taberna With its comfortable ambience and consistently excellent food and service, it's a cool, serene respite from Taxco's crowded streets.

Drinks at the Hotel Taxco Victoria Enjoy drinks in the cozy "living room" of this beautiful 1940s-era hotel overlooking Taxco.

Taking Photographs From every possible angle, the village offers wonderful photo opportunities.

Admission: $3.50.
Open: Tues–Sat 10am–5pm, Sun 9am–3pm.

MUSEO GRÁFICA DE LA HISTORIA SOCIAL DE TAXCO EN EL SIGLO XX, Plaza Bernal.

Using great photographs and engravings produced over the last 90 years, this small, interesting new museum shows Taxco's metamorphosis into a major touristic center. You'll recognize many existing streets and buildings and their changing uses over the years. It faces the Plaza Bernal, behind the Casa Borda, and opposite Los Castillo silver shop.
Admission: Free.
Open: Tues–Fri 9am–3pm and 6–8pm, Sat–Sun 10am–2pm and 4–6pm.

CASA BORDA/CASA DE LA CULTURA, Plaza Borda.

Catercorner from the Santa Prisca Church and facing the Plaza Borda, this was José de la Borda's home. It's being converted from governmental office use to a city cultural center with performing arts and changing exhibits. Check to see the progress when you travel.

MERCADO CENTRAL, Plaza Borda.

To the right of the Santa Prisca Church, behind and below Berta's, Taxco's central market meanders deep inside the mountain. Among the curio stores you'll find the food stalls and cook shops, always the best place for a cheap meal. Jumils are also sold here in leafy basket containers (see "Special Events," below).
Open: Daily 7am–8pm.

NEARBY ATTRACTIONS

SPRATLING RANCH WORKSHOP, 6 miles south of town, on the Acapulco highway. No phone.

Spratling's hacienda-style home/workshop on the outskirts of Taxco once again hums with busy hands reproducing his unique designs. A trip here will show you what distinctive Spratling work was all about. Spratling designs crafted today show the same fine work because even Spratling's workshop foreman is employed again overseeing the development of a new generation of Spratling silversmiths. Prices are high, but the designs are unusual and considered collectable. There's no store in Taxco, and unfortunately, most of the display cases hold only samples. With the exception of a few jewelry pieces, most items are by order only. To get there, hire a taxi and ask the driver to wait.

Admission: Free.

Open: Mon–Sat 9am–5pm.

LOS CASTILLO WORKSHOP, 5 miles south of town on the Acapulco highway. No phone.

Antonio Castillo was one of hundreds of young men to whom William Spratling taught the silversmithing trade in the 1930s. And he was among the first to branch out with his own shops and line of designs, which over the years have earned him a fine name. Now his daughter, Emilia, creates her own noteworthy designs, among which are stunning pieces with silver fused into porcelain. Drawings of Emilia's small daughter, Alejandra Romo Castillo, have been used to create whimsical silver jewelry. You can visit the Castillo workshop five miles south of town, but there's no sales outlet at the workshop. His store, Los Castillo, is just off the Plaza Borda, reached by walking down the hill beside city hall—the store, with a big sign, is just ahead. Customers can watch silversmiths at work here as well. Besides Taxco, Castillo has shops in Mexico City and Cancún, and an outlet at Madeiras restaurant in Acapulco.

Open: Shop, daily 9am–7pm; workshop, Mon–Fri 9am–5pm.

TEHUILOTEPEC

Only 3½ miles from Taxco, on the road to Cuernavaca, is the cobblestoned village of Tehuilotepec, where José de la Borda worked his first mine and built his home. The house, a tall but small stone-and-stucco building opposite the town square and church, has been restored and converted into the **Museo Mineria.** To see it, make arrangements with the tourism office in Taxco. It houses artifacts relating to Taxco's mining history. Though small, the well-done displays show diagrams of the earth and interior workings of a mine, Baron von Humboldt's mine map, the route silver took when it left Taxco, and methods of colonial-era silver extraction. Donated mining equipment is on display. The town church, with its gilded retablo, was built by Borda and the paintings are attributed to Cabrera. From the vantage point of the museum you can also see San Ignacio, the mine that funded the building of the Santa Prisca y San Sebastián Church.

Tehuilotepec is also the village where Taxco's Easter week commemoration begins. Early on Good Friday the town gathers for mass at the church and afterward reverently takes its figure of Christ on a donkey through the streets and continues on the highway to Taxco. There they are joined by men dressed as Roman soldiers, Pharisees, and other biblical characters; when the procession reaches the Santa Prisca church, another mass is held. Flecha Roja buses and combis marked "Tehui" go here frequently from Taxco.

CACAHUAMILPA CAVES

The Grutas de Cacahuamilpa are about 20 miles northwest of Taxco, off the free portion of Highway 95. It makes a nice detour if you're on your way to Cuernavaca. You can join a group tour (every hour on the hour) of these mammoth caverns, said to stretch some 43 miles within the earth (don't worry—you don't get to see the entire 43 miles!). Flecha Roja buses go frequently from Taxco. When you get off at the caves, be sure to ask when buses return.

The caves are truly awesome, worth a visit even if you're not generally a cave fancier. Judging by the graffiti in the caves, everyone important, from Empress Carlota to Mexican presidents, has come to admire them. Hours are 10am to 3pm daily; admission costs $3.50. Tours are in Spanish only, but you'll pick up the salient points—the geologic grandeur and beauty speak for themselves.

SPECIAL EVENTS

From January 18 to 20, the town commemorates the **feast days of Santa Prisca and San Sebastián.**

Holy Week in Taxco is one of the most compelling events in the country, beginning the Friday a week before Easter with evening processions every night and several during the day. Parish elders lovingly decorate church altars with beautiful fresh fruit and branches. The most riveting procession, on Thursday evening, lasts almost four hours and includes villagers from the surrounding area carrying statues of saints, followed by hooded members of a society of self-flagellating penitents chained at the ankles and carrying huge wooden crosses and bundles of thorns. On the Saturday morning before Easter the Plaza Borda fills with people watching the procession that reenacts the three times Christ stumbled and fell while carrying his cross. Despite the visiting throngs who crowd the city during that week, especially the last Thursday and Friday, it is an uncommercialized, reverent week of biblical ceremony involving Taxco and nearby small mountain communities.

In the middle of May the **Jornadas Alarconianas** features plays, music, and literary events in honor of Juan Ruiz de Alarcón (1581–1639), a world-famous dramatist from Taxco.

But most unusual of all is the **Jumil Festival,** held the first Monday after the Day of the Dead, which is celebrated on November 1 and 2. Practically the whole town goes to the Huixteco mountain south of town to picnic and eat jumils. An insect that to me resembles a stink bug, jumils are especially abundant in that area from October through February. This energetic insect, which seems constantly in motion, is considered (by some) to be a delicacy when toasted and eaten with salsa,

---

IMPRESSIONS

The cave of Cacahuamilpa, whose actual wonders equal the fabled descriptions of the palaces of Genii, was until lately known to the Indians alone—or, if the Spaniards formerly knew anything about it, its existence was forgotten amongst them. But, although in former days it may have been used as a place of worship, a superstitious fear prevented the more modern Indians from exploring its shining recesses—for here, it was firmly believed, the evil spirit had his dwelling and, in the form of a goat with long beard and horns, guarded the entrance of the cavern. The few who ventured there and beheld this apparition brought back strange tales to their credulous companions, and even the neighbourhood of the enchanted cave was avoided, especially at nightfall.
—FANNY CALDERÓN DE LA BARCA, LIFE IN MEXICO, 1841.

chiles, and tortillas. Most outsiders abhor the thought of dining on jumils. Knowing this, locals playfully relate how delicious live jumils are, assuming you get them in your mouth before they crawl out the end of the tortilla onto your cheek. Even those who don't plan to eat the critters go for the outing since it's a day of relaxation in the country and away from the hubbub of Taxco.

Taxco's **Silver Fair** takes place from mid-November through mid-December and includes competition for silver sculptures from among the top silversmiths from Taxco, elsewhere in Mexico, and the world. Besides silver competition, this festival brings lots of fireworks, parades through the already congested streets, and the crowning of a silver queen.

Other festivals that are being established include **The Popular Band Festival** probably each October, and the **Organ Music Festival** tentatively scheduled for each August.

2. SAVVY SHOPPING

With so many shops, it's almost impossible to suggest where you might find the piece that will suit your taste. However some of the workshops with longtime names in Taxco's silver business are those of **Spratling, Castillo, Pineda,** and **Ballesteros.** Los Castillo's dazzling shop is on the Plaza Bernal just off the Plaza Borda in the central village. It's open daily from 9am to 7pm. Spratling's handsome designs are made and sold from the Spratling ranch on the highway to Acapulco. (See "Nearby Attractions," above, about the Castillo Workshop.) Both Elena Ballesteros and Antonio Pineda have showrooms on or just off the Plaza Borda and on Kennedy Avenue. Besides these, I have found good buys in jewelry shops at the Hotel Montetaxco and Hotel de la Borda. Sterling silver objects are stamped *.925*—be sure to check if you buy. Shopkeepers will usually point out which cases hold silver pieces (*plata*) and which hold *alpaca*, or imitation silver. Silver plate is *plata plateada*. Whether or not you'll find bargains depends on how much you know about quality and the price of silver. Nowhere in the country will you find the quantity and variety of silver that exists in Taxco. Besides the sleek, modern pieces of jewelry, more ornate classic Mexican jewelry reproductions from early in this century are reappearing. Try on jewelry, and test the hooks, hinges, and latches. Pierced-earring stems are sometimes too long or not long enough. And examine the

IMPRESSIONS

Taxco would be quite another place without William Spratling. Nowadays, everyone who talks about Mexico is sure to mention him. . . . Perhaps this evening he has brought in (to Bertha's) a beautiful serving spoon, with a graceful rosewood handle, and ask everyone what he thinks of it. Only a few heretics ever object. He hangs his beaver-colored Texan sombrero on a hook and lights his stubby Acapulco cigar.

Doña Bertha's is the best place to gather, the best place to meet new arrivals, to see old friends who are busy all day. . . . At the cantina hour, there are always hors d'oeuvres, such as Mexico offers: fried pig fat which is crisp and delicious—particularly if you eat some before you are told its origin—or there are shrimps and anchovies. . . . Eaten while you listen to stories, which seem to grow funnier as Doña Bertha keeps filling the copitas—Bill Spratling's little silver cups.
—HEATH BOWMAN, MEXICAN ODYSSEY, 1936

piece carefully to make sure designs match up. Even though prices are marked on each piece, most shopkeepers will bargain for a lower price, especially if you don't come with a tour guide and if you buy more than one piece.

3. EVENING ENTERTAINMENT

Taxco's nighttime action is centered in the luxury hotels. The **Montetaxco** (tel. 2-1300), and **Posada de la Misión** (tel. 2-0063), have their clubs or lounges. **La Taberna** (see Chapter 12, "Where to Dine") stays open until midnight. **Paco's Bar** (also mentioned in Chapter 12) is very popular anytime. And finally there's Taxco's dazzling disco, **Windows,** high up at the Hotel Montetaxco. The whole city is on view from there and music runs the gamut from the hit parade to hard rock. For a cover of $8 you can boogie from 10pm to 3am on Saturday.

Completely different in tone is **Berta's,** right next to the Santa Prisca church. Opened in 1930 by Berta, who made her fame on a drink of the same name (tequila, soda, lime, and honey), Berta's is traditionally the gathering place of the local gentry. Spurs and old swords decorate the walls, and a saddle is casually slung over the banister of the stairs leading to the second-floor room, where tin masks leer from the walls. A Berta costs about $3.50; rum, the same. It's open daily from 10am to around 10pm.

CHAPTER 14

EXCURSIONS TO IXCATEOPAN & CUERNAVACA

1. IXCATEOPAN
2. CUERNAVACA

Two interesting excursions can be made from Taxco, south to the picturesque mountain village of Ixcateopan, or north to Cuernavaca, a busy city, for a complete change of pace.

1. IXCATEOPAN

40 miles S of Taxco

GETTING THERE   By Bus and Taxi   There is no bus service. Local buses from Taxco go only as far as Chichila, so hiring a taxi is the only option.

By Car   The turnoff off the Acapulco highway is near the edge of Taxco, and clearly marked. The two-lane highway is paved, but potholed; the trip takes an average of 90 minutes.

On the way to the interesting mountain village of Ixcateopan, from Taxco, you pass the Cerro Huizteco (of jumil-festival fame); La Cascada, a waterfall; and several villages devoted to making cedar furniture, the scent of which fills the air. You see marble outcroppings, for which the area is known. This accounts for the marble-chip pavement of Ixcateopan's streets. Colonial buildings in this placid town have an Andean look, with low-slung red-tile roofs and covered walkways fronting the whitewashed buildings around the large, shady main square with its small bandstand. Everywhere you hear the sound of saws whirring. Finished pieces of furniture sit outside workshops, waiting to be loaded into trucks for the trip down the mountain.

Ixcateopan, which means "in the temple of cotton" or "here is the church" in Nahuatl, has been the center of controversy for more than 50 years. Local inhabitants and many indigenous groups in Mexico believe that the remains of Cuauhtémoc, the last Aztec emperor, are buried here. Cuauhtémoc's stoic leadership during the Spanish Conquest has earned him the highest admiration among Mexicans. Numerous statues (there are two here) and streets named for him honor his memory countrywide. The story is told that after he had been tortured to death by the conquistadores, loyal followers carried his body over the mountains to Ixcateopan and secretly buried him under the altar of the parish church, which was then under construction. In 1949, when a villager told the parish priest that he, a descendant of Moctezuma and Cuauhtémoc, possessed secret ancient family documents relating to Cuauhtémoc's burial place, the village became the center of a frenzy of media attention. However, scholars who studied the hitherto unknown remains excavated from under the altar say that the bone fragments are not all human, and that there is no certainty that the human fragments belonged to Cuauhtémoc. Villagers believe that the ruins of Aztec houses and ceremonial platforms at the edge of the village were the home of Cuauhtémoc's grandparents, but scholars point out that there is no evidence to show who once occupied the ruins. Descendants of Cuauhtémoc, who still live in Ixcateopan, feel betrayed, and have again hidden their documents.

Over the years the church and town have become known as "Altar of the Fatherland and Center of Mexicanness."

WHAT TO SEE & DO

The pilgrimage site is the **original parish church** that contains the altar and Cuauhtémoc's remains. One room to the right of the altar is the **Museum Altar de la Petria Maria de la Ascención;** it has a few historic documents and artifacts under glass. The **Museo de la Resistancia Indigenista (Museum of Indian Resistance)** on the main square is in a restored one-story colonial home with a large interior patio. Displays chronicle the history of Mexico's native groups. Both the church and museum are open daily from 9am to 5pm, and there's no admission.

SPECIAL EVENTS   The town church is in a building near the town square. The festival of its patron saint, **Santo Niño de Atocha,** is celebrated from January 1 to January 6, accompanied by processions, Indian dancing, and a fair. On October 18, the **Feast of St. Lucas,** there are fireworks, music, and local regional dances. These include dances of Moors and Christians, tecuanes, the dance of the eight crazy ones, and the dance of twelve pairs from France. Market day is Sunday.

Every year, on **February 28,** groups from all over the Americas come to pay homage to the bones that they believe to be Cuauhtémoc's, displayed under glass in front of the altar in the church. During this pilgrimage time, various indigenous groups perform religious dances in the courtyard of the church; speechmaking politicians come too.

WHERE TO STAY & DINE

CASA DE HUESPEDES SARA HERNÁNDEZ, Calle Guerrero s/n, Ixcateopan, Gro. 40430. Tel. 733/2-9715. 8 rms (5 with bath).
$ Rates: $11 single or double without bath; $15–$22 single or double with bath.
This newly opened inn is the Hernández home made from a colonial-era building centered around an interior patio. The neatly kept rooms have pine and cedar furniture and one has a king-size bed. Rooms with shared bath are downstairs. Two new rooms are upstairs and more rooms are planned. Several small restaurants around the village square will do for meals, but you might bring along bottled water.

2. CUERNAVACA

50 miles S of Mexico City, 50 miles N of Taxco

GETTING THERE   By Bus   Buses leave Taxco's **Estrella de Oro** (tel. 12-3055) station at 9am, 4pm, and 6pm. **Flecha Roja** (tel. 12-5797) has more frequent service from Taxco.

By Car From Taxco, go north on Kennedy for about 11 miles, which will take you to the new toll road, the quickest and most efficient way to get to Cuernavaca. The toll one-way is about $6. You can also choose the old Cuernavaca Libre (free) road, which takes longer because it passes through several villages and through farming country.

DEPARTING By Bus Your best bet is to return to Taxco on **Flecha Roja,** which has the more frequent service. **Estrella de Oro** has six de paso buses to Taxco and Acapulco, but to reserve a seat you must pay the price of the ticket to Mexico City. On weekdays and nonholiday times, you can generally get a seat without reserving ahead. In both stations, check departure times when you arrive.

L eaving village life behind for a day-trip to the busy city of Cuernavaca (alt. 5,058 ft.; pop. 800,000), capital of the state of Morelos, is easy to do from Taxco. The drive by bus or car takes just over an hour. Visiting the city's museums, restaurants, and surrounding villages will easily consume a day or more, depending on your interests and time.

Cuernavaca has been popular as a resort ever since the time of Moctezuma. José de la Borda of Taxco built gardens here that Emperor Maximilian used as a retreat over a century ago. Mexicans say the town has a climate of "eternal spring," and on weekends the city is crowded with day-trippers from surrounding cities, which on weekends results in jammed roads especially between Mexico City and Cuernavaca and restaurants and hotels may be full as well.

The Indian name for this town was Cuauhnahuac, which means "at the edge of the forest." The city's symbol today is an Indian pictogram of a tree speaking. People have lived here, next to the whispering trees, since about A.D. 1200, but only in the early 1400s did the area come under the sway of the Aztecs, who established huge hunting parks for themselves, beginning a tradition of Cuauhnahuac as a resort for the wealthy and powerful.

The conquistadores, when they arrived, heard "Cuauhnahuac" but said "Cuernavaca," so the whispering tree become a cow's horn.

Emperor Charles V gave Cuernavaca to Cortés as a fief, and the conquistador built a palace here in 1532 (now the Museo de Cuauhnahuac) and lived there on and off for half a dozen years before returning to Spain. Cortés introduced sugarcane cultivation to the area, and Caribbean slaves came to work in the cane fields. His sugar hacienda at the edge of town is now the luxurious Hotel de Cortés. The economics of large sugarcane growers failed to serve the interests of the indigenous farmers and there were numerous uprisings in colonial times.

After independence, mighty landowners from Mexico City gradually dispossessed the remaining small landholders, converting them to virtual serfdom. It was this condition that led to the rise of Emiliano Zapata, the great champion of agrarian reform, who battled the forces of wealth and power during the Mexican Revolution following 1910.

ORIENTATION

ARRIVING By Bus The **Estrella de Oro station** is about 14 blocks from the town center, to the left as you go out the front door. "Centro" buses or taxis will take you into town.

The **Flecha Roja station** is about eight blocks north of the town center. For a "Centro" bus, walk over one street. If you want to walk to town, turn right from the front door, walk about seven blocks, and turn left.

INFORMATION   Cuernavaca's **State Tourist Office** is at Av. Morelos Sur 802, between Jalisco and Veracruz (tel. 73/14-3860 or 14-3920), half a block north of the Estrella de Oro bus station, and about a 10- or 15-minute walk south of the cathedral. Hours are Monday through Friday from 9am to 8pm, on Saturday and Sunday till 5pm.

CITY LAYOUT   In the center of the city are two contiguous plazas. The smaller and more formal of the two is square, with a Victorian gazebo (designed by Monsieur Eiffel of Tour Eiffel fame) at its center. This is the **Jardín Juárez.** The larger, rectangular plaza planted with trees, shrubs, and benches is the **Jardín de los Héroes,** also sometimes called the **Plaza de Armas** or the **Alameda.** These two tree-filled plazas are the hub for strolling vendors selling balloons, baskets, bracelets, and other crafts from surrounding villages. It's all easy going, and one of the best pleasures is grabbing a park bench or table in a nearby restaurant just to watch. On Sunday afternoon and Sunday and Thursday evenings, orchestras often play in the gazebo of the Jardín Juárez. At the eastern end of the Alameda is the Cortés Palace, the conquistador's residence, which now serves as the Museo de Cuauhnahuac.

This city's street numbering system—or, rather, systems—are extremely confusing. City fathers have become dissatisfied with the street numbers every 10 or 20 years, and have imposed a new numbering system each time. Thus you may find an address given as "no. 5" only to find that the building itself bears the number "506."

GETTING AROUND   Frequent buses go from downtown to all the outlying centers. Just tell a local where you want to go and usually they will go out of their way to help you. Taxis are relatively inexpensive in Cuernavaca; $3 should get you from downtown to the outlying Herb Museum, for example. Determine the fare before taking off.

WHAT TO SEE & DO

If you plan to visit Cuernavaca on a day-trip, the best days are Tuesday, Wednesday, or Thursday (and perhaps Friday). On weekends the roads, the city, its hotels and restaurants are filled with people from Mexico City, and prices jump dramatically. On Monday, the museum—which you definitely must see—is closed.

You can spend one or two days sightseeing in Cuernavaca pleasantly enough. If you've come on a day-trip, you may not have time to make all of the excursions listed below, but you'll have enough time to see the sights in town.

The most important place to visit is the former home of the conquistador Hernán Cortés.

ATTRACTIONS

CORTÉS PALACE AND THE MUSEO DE CUAUHNAHUAC, at the eastern end of the Jardín de los Héroes. No phone.

The museum is housed in the Cortés Palace, the former home of Hernán Cortés, who led the Conquest of Mexico. Begun by Cortés in 1530, it was finished by the conquistador's son, Martín, and later served as the legislative headquarters for the state of Morelos. It's in the town center, at the eastern end of the Jardín de los Héroes.

Inside the main door, go to the right. If you've recently visited the National Museum of Anthropology in Mexico City, these displays of humanity's early times will be familiar. Passing through these exhibits, you come to a little court in which are the ruins of a Tlahuica temple. In keeping with conquistador policy, Cortés had his mansion built right on top of an older structure.

The northern wing of the palace, on the ground floor, houses exhibits from the colonial era: suits of armor juxtaposed with the arrows, spears, and maces used by the Indians. Upstairs in the northern wing are costumes, domestic furnishings, carriages, and farm implements from Mexico of the 1800s, mostly from *haciendas azucareras* (sugar plantations). There are also mementos of the great revolutionaries Francisco Madero and Emiliano Zapata.

Through the door on the right are more exhibits from colonial times, including several fascinating pages from "painted books," or Indian codices, that survived the book burnings of the Spaniards. There's also a clock mechanism (*reloj*) from Cuernavaca's cathedral, thought to be the first public clock on the American continent.

When you get to the east portico on the upper floor, you're in for a treat. A large mural commissioned from Diego Rivera by Dwight Morrow, U.S. ambassador to Mexico in the 1920s, depicts the history of Cuernavaca from the coming of the Spaniards to the rise of Zapata (1910). It's fascinating to examine the mural in detail. Above the north door, the Spaniards and their Indian allies, armed with firearms, crossbows, and cannon battle the Aztecs, who have clubs, spears, slings, and bows and arrows. Above the door is a scene of Aztec human sacrifice (remember this).

Moving southward along the wall, men struggle with a huge tree, perhaps symbolizing the Aztec "universe." Next, the inhabitants of Mexico are enslaved, branded, and made to yield their gold. The figure in a white headscarf is José María Morelos, one of the leaders in Mexico's fight for independence from Spain.

Moving along, malevolent priests, backed by lancers, subjugate the Indians spiritually; dressed in white, they stand peaceably and respectfully, at the orders of the priests. The Spaniards build a new society using the Indians as slave labor.

The scenes on the sugar plantations are from the time after independence when the wealthy and powerful dispossessed the native population of their land in order to create the huge sugar haciendas. While the Indians slave away, the blancos recline in hammocks. Nearby, priests and friars direct the building of churches and monasteries by native labor; the churchmen accept gold from the Indians' and only one poor friar sits with the women and children, teaching them the doctrines of the church.

Above the south door is an auto-da-fé, or burning of heretics, from the Spanish Inquisition. The scene is chronologically out of place, but Rivera obviously meant to contrast it to the Aztec sacrifice over the north door, opposite. He's saying, "Aztecs or Catholics—the more it changes, the more it stays the same." Rivera firmly believed that Communism would break the cycle of man's inhumanity to man, but the Stalinist purges of the 1930s were yet in the future when Rivera painted this superb mural. It's ironic that his "religion" (Communist ideology) led to the same excesses of ideological fanaticism as did Aztec cosmology and the Catholic Inquisition.

In the upper-left corner of the southern door, Indian revolutionaries are hanged by slave drivers. In the lower left, Zapata leads a group of revolutionary campesinos brandishing their farming tools as weapons.

The frieze beneath the mural is interesting as well, done in a chunky 1930s style that is very art deco, but also very Rivera. It looks to me as though he was inspired by the many Aztec friezes.

Admission: Tues–Sat $4.50; Sun free.
Open: Tues–Sun 10am–5pm.

CATEDRAL DE LA ASUNCIÓN, corner of Hidalgo and Morelos.

As you enter the church precincts and pass down the walk, try to imagine what life in Mexico was like in the old days. Construction on the church was begun in 1533, a mere 12 years after Cortés conquered Tenochtitlán (Mexico City) from the

Aztecs. The churchmen could hardly trust their safety to the tenuous allegiance of their new converts, so they built a fortress as a church. The skull and crossbones above the main door is not a comment on their feelings about the future, however, but rather a symbol for the Franciscan order, which had its monastery here in the church precincts.

Inside, the church is stark, even severe, having been refurbished in the 1960s. The most curious aspect of the interior is the mystery of the frescoes. Discovered during the refurbishing, they depict Christian missionary activity and persecution in Japan, and are painted in Japanese style. No one is certain who painted them, or why. The cathedral is three blocks southwest of the Jardín de los Héroes.

Admission: Free.

Open: Daily 8am–10pm.

MUSEO CASA ROBERT BRADY, Calle Netzahualcoyotl 4. Tel. 12-1136.

This museum in a private home created from the Franciscan cloister of the Cuernavaca Cathedral contains a private art collection. Among them are pre-Hispanic and colonial pieces; oil paintings by Frida Kahlo and Rufino Tamayo; handcrafts from America, Africa, Asia, and India. It's small and so perhaps not worth the price of admission, which includes a guide in Spanish. English- and French-speaking guides are available if requested at the time of your reservation. The museum is located behind the cathedral between Calles 20 de Noviembre and Hidalgo.

Admission: $4.50.

Open: Thurs–Fri 10am–2pm and 4–6pm, Sat 10am–2pm. *Call ahead for reservations.* Special visits can be arranged during other days at a special price.

PALACIO MUNICIPAL, corner of Av. Morelos and Callejón Borda. Tel. 18-5719.

On Cuernavaca's Palacio Municipal, or Town Hall, there's a ceramic tile plaque to the right of the door that reads "Honorable Ayuntamiento de Cuernavaca" (town council); to the left, "Cuauhnahuac," with the city's tree symbol. Walk into the brick, stone, and stucco courtyard anytime the building is open. Besides the unusual and attractive building, you should tour the large old oil paintings hung in the arcades on the first and second floors. On the north wall, ground floor, paintings explain the making of "feathered mosaics." In the north arcade, on the upper floor, are scenes from Cuernavaca's pre-Hispanic culture: Tlahuicans making pottery, storing corn (maize), being shaken down by an Aztec tax collector, and harvesting cotton. On the east wall, the scenes continue: the Indians gather maguey leaves, pound them to release the fibers, and weave cloth; a priest offers a chicken to the god Tepuztecatl. The Aztec goldsmiths' craft is explained in a canvas with 17 smaller panels. In the southeast corner are two murals, done by R. Cueva in 1962, with scenes from the revolution. The Palacio Municipal stands directly west of the cathedral, across Avenida Morelos at the corner of Callejón Borda.

Admission: Free.

Open: Mon–Fri 9am–2pm and 4–6pm (often at other times as well).

JARDÍN BORDA, Av. Morelos 103, at Hidalgo. Tel. 12-0086.

A half a block from the cathedral is the Jardín Borda, or Borda Gardens. One of the many wealthy builders to choose Cuernavaca was José de la Borda, the Taxco silver magnate, who ordered a vacation house built here in the late 1700s. The large enclosed garden next to the house was actually a huge private park, laid out in Andalusian style with little kiosks and an artificial pond. Maximilian found it worthy of an emperor, and took it over as his private preserve in the mid-1800s. But after that, the Borda Gardens fell on hard times. Decades of neglect followed.

IMPRESSIONS

I spent many a restful hour in the old Borda Gardens and derived a good deal of amusement from the walls of the shady arbors, which bore hundreds of inscriptions by enthusiastic visitors, chiefly American tourists from such romantic places as "Union City, Neb.," "Grimesville O.," and "Tin Can. Wash." But such comments as "Hey fellows, Cuernavaca's all right, and don't you forget it," or "Say, why can't we annex Cuernavaca to Grand Rapids?," however well-meaning, scarcely harmonize with the antique.
—W. E. CARSON, MEXICO: THE WONDERLAND OF THE SOUTH, 1909

The paintings from the history of the French intervention enhance a stroll through the gardens. Here are the scenes you'll see: First, Emperor Maximilian and Empress Carlota arrive in Cuernavaca for the first time; then, Maximilian, while out for a ride, gets his first glimpse of La India Bonita, who was to become his lover. The next scene is of court festivities in the Borda Gardens, with courtiers taking turns rowing little boats. Finally, Maximilian's niece pleads with President Benito Juárez, after the siege of Querétaro, to spare the emperor's life. (At the time, Carlota was off in Europe, trying to round up support for her husband's cause, without result.) Juárez refused her request, and Maximilian, along with two of his generals, was executed by firing squad on the Hill of Bells in Querétaro a few days thereafter.

On your stroll through the gardens you'll see that same little artificial lake on which Austrian, French, and Mexican nobility rowed in little boats beneath the moonlight. Ducks have taken the place of dukes, however, but there are rowboats for rent. The lake is now artfully adapted to be an outdoor theater, with seats for the audience on one side, and the stage on the other. The Borda Gardens have been completely restored, and were reopened in October of 1987 as the Jardín Borda Centro de Artes. In the gateway building are several galleries for changing exhibits, a cafe for refreshments and light meals, and several large paintings showing scenes from the life of Maximilian and from the history of the Borda Gardens.

Admission: 80¢.
Open: Tues–Sun 10am–6:30pm.

MUSEO DE LA HERBOLARIA, 200 Matamoros.

This museum of traditional herbal medicine, in the southern suburb of Acapantzingo, has been set up in a former resort residence built by Maximilian, the Casa del Olindo, or Casa del Olvido. It was here, during his brief reign, that the Austrian-born emperor would come for trysts with La India Bonita, his Cuernavacan lover. Restored in 1960, the house and gardens now preserve the local wisdom in folk medicine. Take a taxi, or if driving ask directions.

Admission: Free.
Open: Daily 10am–5pm.

PIRÁMIDE DE TEOPANZOLCO, northeast of town center. No phone.

You'll need a taxi to reach the curious Teopanzolco pyramid, northeast of the center of town. Now set in a park, the pyramid was excavated beginning in 1921. As with most Mesoamerican cultures, the local Tlahuicans reconstructed their principal religious monuments at the end of a major calendar cycle by building a new, larger structure right on top of the older one. Here you can clearly see the two different structures of the older and newer.

Admission: $3.50
Open: Daily 9am–5pm.

IMPRESSIONS

If you ask a Tepoztecan, shortly after high noon, what time a given fiesta dance will start, he is likely to reply: "It will take place right now at about three or five o'clock." This is as definite to him as it is infuriating to one who, like the author, was reared in sight of the Waltham Watch factory. Mexicans, even as Russians, have no mechanical time sense. "Mañana," tomorrow, stretches from 12:01 A.M. through the weeks and months to infinity. It is far more difficult and painful for a Westerner to rid himself of his clock habits than of his appendix. But once the operation is over and wound healed, there is much to be said for right now at three or five o'clock. There is much to be said for consigning unpleasant business to an endless mañana.
—STUART CHASE, MEXICO: A STUDY OF TWO AMERICAS, 1931

NEARBY ATTRACTIONS

If you have enough time, there are some interesting side trips around Cuernavaca. To the north you'll find pine trees and an alpine setting; to the east, lush hills and valleys.

TEPOZTLÁN

Less than 20 miles northeast of Cuernavaca, this **Tlahuica** village (not to be confused with Tepozotlán north of Mexico City), almost surrounded by mountains, predates the Conquest. Because it remained isolated and relatively unchanged from Aztec times until well into the 20th century, it became the subject of numerous anthropological studies earlier this century. The ruins of an Aztec temple, Tepozteco, honoring the god of pulque (a fermented drink) are on a sheer rock outcropping 1,200 feet above the town. The town itself is built around a 16th-century **Dominican monastery.** After scholars brought attention to Tepoztlán it became for a time a popular tourist destination (it is the Martínez family village, called "Azteca," in Oscar Lewis's *Five Families*). But today, it's relatively little visited by foreigners, though throngs of visitors from Mexico City swarm it on weekends.

On the street behind the monastery (actually the back of the monastery) is the **Museo Arqueología Carlos Pellicer,** with a fine collection of pre-Hispanic artifacts. It's open Tuesday through Sunday from 9am to 5pm. Admission is $1.25.

The best times to come are Sunday and holidays when there's generally a very good street market around the central square with lots of crafts from neighboring states. Tepoztlán's folk healers (*curanderos*), for which the village is well known, are often there selling medicinal herbs and other magical cures. The market is especially good during Carnaval (three days before Ash Wednesday), a movable date usually in February; and around Day of the Dead, November 1 and 2.

During **Carnaval** colorful costumed and masked dancers perform, a very popular time for outsiders to come. If you plan to go at that time, arrive early in the day to stake out a good observation point before things get too congested. **September 8** is the festival honoring the god of pulque, another occasion when dancers appear, and the market will be especially large.

There are several restaurants around the square as well as a couple of good inns. To get here take one of the frequent buses or minivans by the Cuernavaca market. Tourists don't use these much and other passengers generally go out of their way to be helpful and will let you know when to get off.

CUAUTLA

Almost 30 miles southeast of Cuernavaca, a 20-minute drive from Tepoztlán, is Cuautla, a city of thermal springs. Many buses or minivans leave for Cuautla from the Mercado Central. Estrella Roja, at Galeana and Cuauhtemotzin, about eight blocks south of Cuernavaca's town center serves Cuautla, Yautepec, Oaxtepec, all in this area.

In Cuautla's downtown area, there is park after park with picnic areas, and public pools, often filled with thermal spring water. Probably the most famous one is Agua Hedionda, a gigantic swimming pool a few miles east of town. The name means "stinking water' because of the water's odorous sulfur content, which you smell long before you get there. Cuautla is the center for the area's sugar industry and during cane season, trucks loaded with cane stalks clog highways, and chimneys belch smoke and ashes into the sky. Cuautla was a center of resistance during the War of Independence, and during the Revolution in 1910, Emiliano Zapata made it his headquarters.

XOCHICALCO RUINS

About 16 miles southwest of Cuernavaca along Highway 95 (the "Libre"—no-toll—road to Taxco) is the town of Alpuyeca; 9½ miles northeast of **Alpuyeca** are the ruins of Xochicalco, the "House of Flowers," a walled city high on a mountaintop. Xochicalco boasts a magnificent situation, and a complex of buildings dating from about A.D. 600 through 900. Most interesting is the **Temple of the Feathered Serpents,** with beautiful bas-reliefs depicting a Maya chieftain. There's also a ball court, underground passages, and other temples. Xochicalco is of interest to archeologists because it seems to have been the point at which the Teotihuacán, Toltec, Zapotec, and Maya cultures met and interacted as seen in the mixture of the temple carvings. Archeoastronomists have studied it for its relation to the stars and sun, which seem to have been a pivotal reason for laying the city out as they did. You can visit the ruins from 8am to 5pm daily, but you'll need a car to get there. Admission is $3.50.

LANGUAGE SCHOOLS

As much as for its springlike weather, Cuernavaca is known for its Spanish-language schools, aimed at the foreigner. Generally the schools will help students find lodging with a family, or provide a list of potential places to stay. Rather than make a long-term commitment with a family-living situation, try it for a week, then decide. Below are the names and addresses of some of the schools. The whole experience, from classes to lodging, can be quite inexpensive, and the school may accept credit cards for the class portion.

Mexican Lyceum of Languages is located at Isla Mujeres 14, Colonía Quintana Roo, Cuernavaca, Mor. 62060.

Instituto Teopanzolco is also well known and it is located at Calle Teopanzolco 102-BIS, Colonía Vista Hermosa, Cuernavaca, Mor. 62290. Or write Apdo. Postal 103-A, Cuernavaca, Mor. 62280. Or contact **John Díaz,** a representative of the school in the U.S. at 410 Escobar St., Fremont, CA 94539 (tel. 408/732-0807).

There's also **Universal, Centro de Lengua y Comunicación Social A.C.,** Apdo. Postal 1-826, Cuernavaca, Mor. 62000.

WHERE TO STAY

Chances are good that you are only visiting Cuernavaca for the day, but in case you plan to spend the night, here are some tips on finding a good room at a reasonable price. Because so many visitors use Cuernavaca for a retreat, hotels may be full on weekends and holidays, but empty at other times. A few local hoteliers adapt their policies and prices to these weird shifts. Inns seldom have air conditioning or even fans because of the refreshing climate.

VERY EXPENSIVE

CAMINO REAL SUMIYA, Interior Fracc. Sumiya s/n, Col. José Parres, Jiutepec, Mor. Tel. 73/20-9199, or toll free 800/7-CAMINO. Fax 73/20-9155. 163 rms, 6 suites. A/C MINIBAR TV TEL

$ Rates: High season $185–$255. Low season $180–$250. Ask about low season packages and discounts.

About seven miles south of Cuernavaca, this unusual resort (whose name means "the house on the corner") was once the home of Woolworth heiress Barbara Hutton. Using materials and craftsmen from Japan, she constructed her $3.2 million estate in 1959 on 30 beautifully wooded acres as an exact replica of a house in Kyoto. Out of financial necessity, Hutton sold Sumiya (one of her many homes throughout the world) and its rare Asian antiques for $500,000 nearly 20 years later. The main house, a series of large interconnected rooms and decks, overlooks the grounds and today houses the resort's lobby and restaurants. Nearby on the grounds is an authentic Kabuki-style theater where Hutton brought Japanese entertainers to perform for her guests; it is used now for special events. Beyond it lies a Japanese garden with stones placed in position as the Japanese islands.

The exterior of the three stories of guest rooms, which are clustered in buildings flanking manicured lawns, seems plain in comparison with the striking architecture of the main house. But the interiors evoke Japan with austere but comfortable furnishings and scrolled wooden doors. Three types of sliding doors in each room face the gardens: one is screened to let in Cuernavaca's cool springlike weather; another is glass; and another completely darkens the room. Rooms have direct-dial long-distance phones, fax connections, three-prong electrical outlets, in-room wall safes, hairdryers, and robes. Guests on the Camino Real Club floors enjoy a separate venue for continental breakfast, afternoon snacks, and evening appetizers and drinks.

Sumiya's charm is its relaxing atmosphere, which is best enjoyed mid-week, since escapees from Mexico City may fill the place on weekends. To find it from the freeway, take the Atlacomulco exit and follow the Sumiya signs. If Cuernavaca is your point or origination, ask for directions, since the route is complicated (Cuernavaca is a $5 taxi ride away). It's not far from the Hacienda de Cortés, mentioned below.

Dining/Entertainment: La Arboleda, the outdoor restaurant shaded by enormous Indian laurel trees, serves all three meals from 7am to 11pm. Sumiya, the fine-dining restaurant, has both terrace and indoor dining overlooking the grounds and is open in the evenings. The menu is international with several Japanese specialties. A snack bar by the pool is open daily from 10am to 6pm.

Services: Room service.

Facilities: Business center, pool, 10 tennis courts.

EXPENSIVE

HOTEL CLARION CUERNAVACA RACQUET CLUB, Francisco Villa 100, **Col. Rancho Cortés, Cuernavaca, Mor. 62120. Tel. 73/11-2067,** or toll free 800/228-5151 in the U.S. Fax 73/17-5483. 33 suites. MINIBAR TV TEL
$ Rates: Weekdays $110 single or double. Weekends and high season (Dec 15–Easter week), reserve at least 3 weeks in advance if your stay includes a weekend. **Parking:** Free.

One of the city's most exclusive inns, the Hotel Clarion Cuernavaca Racquet Club is set among secluded grounds in a hilly northern Cuernavaca suburb in a lovely residential neighborhood. Five of the suites are in the original mansion and built around a central patio. Others are on two levels reached by twisty garden-lined pathways. Each of the spacious quarters is beautifully furnished with tasteful use of Mexican pottery and textiles; all have fireplaces and furnished balconies.

If you are staying here without a car you can avoid high taxi costs by using the system of neighborhood minivans up and down the mountain to the Emiliano Zapata Monument. From there frequent buses go to and from town. The savings will be substantial.

Dining/Entertainment: La Terraza on the terrace facing the lawns and tennis courts is open from 7:30am to 7pm. El Patio, set back a bit, but with the same view, is open evenings from 7 to 11pm. Both have international menus.

Services: Room and laundry service. Guide service available.

Facilities: There are a heated pool, nine tennis courts, and a men-only sauna. A tennis pro is on staff to give lessons by the hour at a small charge.

HOTEL HACIENDA DE CORTÉS, 90 Plaza Kennedy (Apdo. Postal 430), **Cuernavaca, Mor. 62240. Tel. 73/15-8844** or 16-0867. Fax 73/15-0035. 22 suites. TEL
$ Rates: $75 single; $101 double; $120 single or double suite; $231 imperial suite for six people. **Parking:** Free.

In the suburb of Atlacomulco, just off the Cuernavaca/Acapulco highway, lies the Hacienda de Cortés, a true legacy of the conqueror of Mexico built as the Hacienda de San Antonio Atlacomulco to process sugarcane during the 1600s. Through uprisings and the Mexican Revolution, it remained in the conqueror's family, and was abandoned, restored, and abandoned until it was finally converted to one of the country's most splendid hacienda hotels in the 1970s. Little of the hacienda's architecture has changed since the days of the conquistadores. Towering chimneys from the sugar-processing era still loom above the beautiful suites, all in original hacienda rooms edging the immaculate interior gardens. Each room is furnished with carefully chosen antiques, area rugs, and Mexican textiles. This is a true getaway, the only drawback being its distance from town.

Dining/Entertainment: The vine-covered, stone-walled grinding room is the dining room today, where trios strum romantic tunes during mealtime. Umbrella-covered tables are also set out in front of the restaurant with a view of the large flower-filled interior lawn, gardens, and hacienda compound. It's open from 7am to 10:30pm.

Services: Room and laundry service.

Facilities: There's a small secluded pool.

LAS MAÑANITAS, Ricardo Linares 107, Cuernavaca, Mor. 62000. Tel. 73/14-1466 or 12-4646. Fax 73/18-3672. 22 rms. TEL **Bus:** Buses going north on Morelos stop within a half a block of the hotel.

$ Rates: $80–$92 double; $130–$280 suite. **Parking:** Free.

Las Mañanitas, near the city center, is among Cuernavaca's best-known luxury lodgings. Antique headboards, heavy brass candlesticks, authentic period furniture and decorations, and large bathrooms make each room a charmer. Many have verdant, vine-encumbered balconies big enough for sitting and sipping while overlooking the emerald lawns where peacocks and other exotic birds strut and preen, and fountains tinkle musically. Thirteen rooms have fireplaces, and the hotel also has a heated swimming pool and valet parking.

Accommodations come in four types, all doubles. The less expensive rooms are simple but charming and allow you to splurge and live the good life when others, staying in the terrace suites, patio suites, and luxurious garden suites, are paying a great deal more.

MODERATE

HOSTERÍA LAS QUINTAS, Av. Las Quintas 107 (Apdo. Postal 427), Cuernavaca, Mor. 62440. Tel. 73/18-3949. Fax 73/18-3895. 8 rms, 52 suites. TV TEL

$ Rates: $80 single; $96 double; $122 single terrace suite; $140 double terrace suite; $146–$165 suite with Jacuzzi. **Parking:** Free.

Long established as an island of tranquillity in this bustling city, the Hostería Las Quintas is east of the city center, set among grassy lawns and meandering pathways edged by cascading purple bougainvillea, bonsai, palms, banana and flame trees, yellow day lilies, red amaryllis, and exotic bird-of-paradise plants. Each room is furnished in the colonial style and has deep-red-tiled floors, and either a balcony or terrace. Some have fireplaces. Section four, with Rooms 31 to 40, is the most secluded and tranquil.

Dining/Entertainment: The restaurant-bar is open from 7am to 11pm, with lunch served between 1 and 5pm.

Services: Room and laundry service, concierge.

Facilities: There's one pool set out on the beautiful lawn. Golf arrangements can be made at Tabachines Golf Club and, a distance from town on the way to Cuautla, at the Hacienda San Gaspar. Both have 18-hole courses. Tennis can be arranged at The Tennis Palace or, a bit farther out near Atlacomulco, at Club Sumiya (Barbara Hutton's former home).

LA POSADA DE XOCHIQUETZAL, Leyva 200 (Apdo. Postal 203), Cuernavaca, Mor. 62000. Tel. 73/18-5767. 14 rms. TV TEL

$ Rates: $60–$70 single or double; $95 suite. **Parking:** Free.

At La Posada de Xochiquetzal (pronounced "So-chee-*ket*-zahl") you get your money's worth in beauty, for the posada's high walls conceal many delights: a small swimming pool, lush gardens with fountains, tasteful colonial-style furnishings, a good restaurant, patios, and large and small guest rooms. Even if you don't come to stay, come for a meal in the Allegro Café (see "Where to Dine," below). Walk three long blocks to the right of the Cortés Palace; or walk two blocks east (right) of Pullman Morelos bus station.

BUDGET

HOTEL CÁDIZ, Alvaro Obregón 329, Cuernavaca, Mor. 62000. Tel. 73/18-9204. 17 rms (all with bath). FAN

$ Rates: $32 single; $40 double. **Parking:** Free.

Every now and then I discover a hotel with the kind of homey charm that makes me want to return. Such is the Hotel Cádiz, run by the gracious Aguilar family. You may have known it as the Hotel María Cristina, and long before that it was a diet sanatorium. Each of the fresh, simple rooms is furnished differently and there's lots of nostalgic tile and big old sinks. The grounds, set back from the street, make a pleasant respite, plus there's a pool and small inexpensive restaurant open for all three meals. It's north of town center near Avenida Ricardo Linares and the ISSTE Hospital.

HOTEL LAS HORTENSIAS, Hidalgo 22, Cuernavaca, Mor. 62000. Tel. and fax 73/18-5265. 23 rms.

$ Rates: $25 single; $27–$32 double.

The Hotel Las Hortensias, two blocks south of Jardín Juárez, is another convenient downtown hotel converted from an old house on an odd hillside site. Rooms are small, simple, and modern with colonial accents. Look at your prospective room first—some are dark and some have windows that only look onto the walkways. The nice, quiet little garden with a fountain and green grass provides an oasis in the midst of the city.

A NEARBY PLACE TO STAY IN CUAUTLA

HOTEL HACIENDA COCOYOC, Cuautla, Mor. Tel. 735/6-2331, or toll free 800/878-4484 in the U.S. and Canada. Fax 735/6-1212. 300 rms and suites. FAN TEL

$ Rates: Standard room $75 single, $90 double; $165–$170 single or double suite with a pool.

Cocoyoc, an exclusive hacienda hotel set on 166 acres, lies off Highway 115, to your right before you enter Cuautla proper, less than an hour east of Cuernavaca. Beyond the main gate and guarded entry, the original hacienda building, the one you see first, houses the reception area and several original hacienda rooms. The rest of the colonial-style rooms and suites are located throughout the manicured grounds, gardens, and plazas. Twenty-four of the rooms have private pools.

The Nahuatl word Cocoyoc means "the place of coyotes," but nothing of its present or past suggests coyotes lived here. Instead, the region surrounding the hacienda became a haven for generations of Moctezuma's family before the Conquest of Mexico. Moctezuma established royal gardens and orchards here. After the Conquest, dominion passed to Hernán Cortés as part of the land granted him as Marqués of the Valley of Oaxaca. Later, as a result of Cortés's romantic liaison with one of Moctezuma's daughters, it passed back to the descendants of Moctezuma. Cortés' agricultural contribution was the establishment of the sugarcane industry in the region, where it thrives today. The hacienda that eventually became a hotel in 1968 began in 1614 as a sugarcane processing plant. The original hacienda chapel is used for weddings, and the Trapiche Disco, with its vaulted stone ceilings, was once a cane-grinding room. The main swimming pool meanders around the ancient aqueduct that carried water to power the mill.

Side trips from Cocoyoc would include Tepoztlán (best on Saturday), Cuautla (with its many thermal-water public pools), and the convent route within a 25-mile radius, all of which can be arranged through the hotel for a reasonable price.

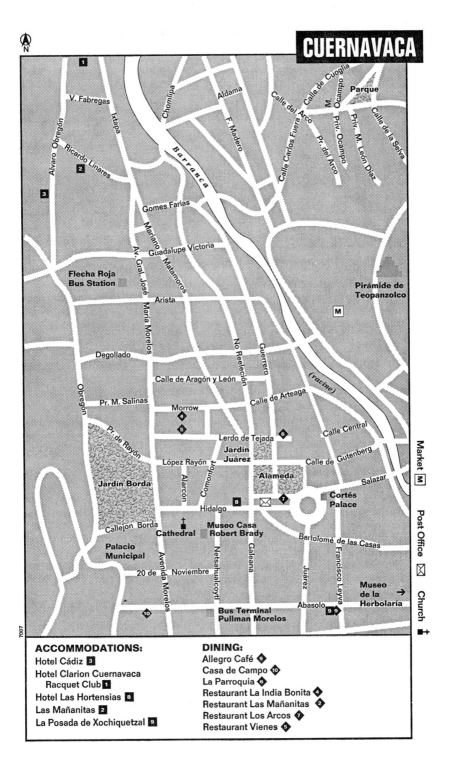

CUERNAVACA

ACCOMMODATIONS:

Hotel Cádiz **3**
Hotel Clarion Cuernavaca
    Racquet Club **1**
Hotel Las Hortensias **8**
Las Mañanitas **2**
La Posada de Xochiquetzal **9**

DINING:

Allegro Café **9**
Casa de Campo **10**
La Parroquia **6**
Restaurant La India Bonita **4**
Restaurant Las Mañanitas **2**
Restaurant Los Arcos **7**
Restaurant Vienes **5**

Market **M**

Post Office ⊠

Church ■✝

Weekends the hacienda is packed with citizens from the capital and their families, but on weekdays the atmosphere is tranquil—the best time to go. If there's any drawback to Cocoyoc, it is that some of the brick walkways connecting the rooms carry sound like a megaphone. Room numbers in the 600s and 700s are relatively quiet. The spacious Casco Suite 317 in the original hacienda building, with its antique furnishings and four-poster bed, would be an ideal choice for a honeymoon.

If you want to come for lunch and a look around from Cuernavaca, grab one of the frequent buses or minivans by the market in Cuernavaca. Tell the driver to let you off at Cocoyoc.

Dining/Entertainment: There are three restaurants and as many bars, all of which are open when there is high occupancy. Midweek there may be only one restaurant and a bar open for service. But you'll always have a choice of eating indoors or outdoors with a view of the grounds and pools. The Trapiche Disco is usually open on weekends.

Services: The hotel will arrange transportation from Mexico City if notified in advance. A bar with live music is open weekdays. The hotel also offers facials, massage, and a sauna.

Facilities: There are a nine-hole golf course, riding trails, three tennis courts, two swimming pools, and 24 guest rooms with private pools. There's access to an 18-hole golf course and 11 additional tennis courts nearby. Ask about special golf packages and special activities at Christmas.

WHERE TO DINE

VERY EXPENSIVE

CASA DE CAMPO, Abasolo 101. Tel. 12-4947 or 18-2635.
  Cuisine: INTERNATIONAL. **Reservations:** Recommended.
$ Prices: Breakfast buffet $12; appetizers $9–$25; main courses $23–$31; Sun brunch $38.
  Open: Mon–Sat 8am–11:30pm; bar until 1am; champagne brunch Sun 9am–12:30pm (closed after brunch).

The elegant Casa de Campo has become a fine-dining rival to the longtime favorite, Las Mañanitas. It, too, comes complete with strolling peacocks and blue-and-red parrots. Housed in a converted one-story town home, built in a U shape around beautiful, spacious grounds, Casa de Campo has spared no expense in the furnishings or the continued attention to the food. Main courses include red snapper in créole sauce, fresh salmon, chateaubriand, and daily specials. Every exquisite detail is coordinated, from the pastel apricot, blue, and white table coverings with matching chair cushions and china. Dining rooms open to the terrace and grounds, and throughout the serving hours there's some kind of live entertainment, be it a crooning trio or marimbas in the garden or soft piano in the bar.

RESTAURANT LAS MAÑANITAS, Ricardo Linares 107. Tel. 14-1466 or 12-4646.
  Cuisine: MEXICAN/INTERNATIONAL. **Reservations:** Recommended.
$ Prices: Appetizers $7–$18; main courses $14–$25.
  Open: Lunch daily 1–5pm; dinner daily 7–10:30pm; bar noon–midnight.

The Restaurant Las Mañanitas set the standard for lush and sumptuous in Cuernavaca. Dining tables are set out on an airy, shaded terrace with a view of the gardens. The decor and ambience are lightly colonial and the service is extremely friendly and attentive. When you arrive, you can enjoy cocktails in the cozy sala and when you're ready to dine a waiter will present a large blackboard menu of at least a half-dozen daily specials. The specialty is Mexican with an international flair using whatever fruits and vegetables are in season and offering a full selection of fresh seafood, beef, pork, veal, and fowl.

To find it from the Jardín Borda, walk 5½ long blocks north; buses going north on Morelos stop within a half a block of the hotel.

MODERATE

ALLEGRO CAFE, Leyva 200, at Abasolo. Tel. 18-5767.

Cuisine: MEXICAN/INTERNATIONAL.
$ Prices: Main courses $5–$11.
Open: Tues–Thurs 8am–5pm, Fri–Sat 8am–11pm; Sun noon–5pm.

You'll see the dining room as you enter the inn's unimpressive doorway. This quiet haven offers colonial arches shading inviting sitting areas and open-air or glass-enclosed dining, all with a view of the lush gardens. The popular hostelry is also well known for its good food. Specialties include carneasada tampiqueña, beef brochette, and chicken fajitas. To find it, walk two blocks south of the Cortés Palace, and it's at the corner of Abasolo and Juárez.

RESTAURANT LA INDIA BONITA, Morrow 1066B. Tel. 18-6967.

Cuisine: MEXICAN.
$ Prices: Breakfast $3–$10.75; main courses $4–$11.
Open: Tues–Sat 8:30am–8pm, Sun 8:30am–6pm.

This new location of La India Bonita may well be its best. Housed among the interior patios and portals of the restored home of former U.S. Ambassador Dwight Morrow (1920s), it's gracious and sophisticated. And it's definitely one of Cuernavaca's restaurant havens, where you come to relax and enjoy the setting as well as the food. Specialties include *mole poblano* (chicken with a sauce of bitter chocolate and fiery chiles), and *filet a la parrilla* (charcoal-grilled steak). Plus there are several off-the-menu daily specials. A breakfast mainstay is the gigantic desayuno Maximiliano, a huge platter based on enchiladas. It's two blocks north of the Jardín Juárez between Matamoros and Morelos.

RESTAURANT LOS ARCOS, Jardín de los Héroes 4. Tel. 12-4486.

Cuisine: MEXICAN.
$ Prices: Breakfast $3.25–$5.50; main courses $4.75–$12; fixed-price lunch $7.
Open: Daily 7am–11pm.

Cuernavaca's best-located sidewalk cafe is the Restaurant Los Arcos, right next to the post office and on the Alameda. Wrought-iron tables and chairs, shaded by umbrellas, are set out within view of the Cortés Palace, and all three meals are served every day. The menu runs the gamut from sandwiches and enchiladas to chicken and steaks. There's even a set-price lunch, called the *menu del día*. Recommended.

BUDGET

LA PARROQUIA, Guerrero 102. Tel. 18-5820.

Cuisine: MEXICAN/PASTRIES.
$ Prices: Breakfast $2.50–$6; main courses $6–$13; comida corrida $8.75.
Open: Daily 8am–12:30am.

This place does a teeming business, partly because of its great location right off the jardín and partly because it has fairly reasonable prices for Cuernavaca. It's open to the street with a few outdoor cafe tables and perfect for watching the changing parade of street vendors and park life.

It's opposite the Parque Juárez and almost next to Viena Pastelería.

RESTAURANT VIENES, Lerdo de Tejada 4, corner of Comonfort. Tel. 14-3404.

Cuisine: VIENNESE/PASTRIES.

$ Prices: Breakfast $1.25–$5; appetizers $5–$16; main courses $7–$16.

Open: Daily 8am–10pm.

The Restaurant Vienes is next to the pastry shop Los Pasteles del Vienes. It's an authentic European-style cafe. Brass trim and cafe curtains make for an elegant atmosphere in which you can enjoy a full selection of soups, salads, sandwiches, and also more substantial fare such as wienerschnitzel, chicken dishes, and cheese fondue. Pastries and succulent cakes and tarts fill several huge refrigerated cases, so don't fill up before dessert time. It's two blocks northwest of the Jardín Juárez between Lerdo de Tejada and Morrow, corner of Comonfort.

APPENDIX

FOR YOUR INFORMATION

A. VOCABULARY
B. MENU SAVVY
C. CONVERSION TABLES

A. VOCABULARY

Traveling on or off the beaten track, you will encounter many people in service positions who do not speak English. Many Mexicans who can understand English are embarrassed to speak it. But most Mexicans are very patient with foreigners who try to speak their language; it helps a lot to know a few basic phrases.

For convenience, I've included a list of simple phrases for expressing basic needs, followed by some menu and food items.

BASIC VOCABULARY

English	Spanish	Pronunciation
Good day	**Buenos días**	*bway*-nohss *dee*-ahss
How are you?	**¿Cómo está usted?**	*koh*-moh ess-*tah* oos-*ted*
Very well	**Muy bien**	mwee byen
Thank you	**Gracias**	*grah*-see-ahss
You're welcome	**De nada**	day *nah*-dah
Good-bye	**Adiós**	ah-*dyohss*
Please	**Por favor**	pohr *fah*-bohr
Yes	**Sí**	see
No	**No**	noh
Excuse me	**Perdóneme**	pehr-*doh*-ney-may
Give me	**Déme**	*day*-may
Where is . . . ?	**¿Dónde está . . . ?**	*dohn*-day ess-*tah*
the station	**la estación**	a ess-tah-see-*own*
a hotel	**un hotel**	oon *oh*-tel
a gas station	**una gasolinera**	oon-nuh gah-so-lee-*nah*-rah
a restaurant	**un restaurante**	oon res-tow-*rahn*-tay
the toilet	**el baño**	el *bahn*-yoh
a good doctor	**un buen médico**	oon bwayn *may*-dee-co
the road to . . .	**el camino a . . .**	El cah-*mee*-noh ah
To the right	**A la derecha**	ah lah day-*ray*-chuh
To the left	**A la izquierda**	ah lah ees-ky-*ehr*-dah
Straight ahead	**Derecho**	day-*ray*-cho
I would like	**Quisiera**	keyh-see-*air*-ah
I want . . .	**Quiero . . .**	kyer-oh
to eat	**comer**	*ko*-mayr
a room	**una habitación**	*oon*-nuh ha-bee-tah-see-*own*
Do you have?	**¿Tiene usted?**	*tyah*-nay oos-*ted*
How much is it?	**¿Cuánto cuesta?**	*kwahn*-to *kwess*-tah
When?	**¿Cuándo?**	kwahn-doh

What?	**¿Qué?**	kay
There is (Is there?)	**¿Hay . . .**	eye
Yesterday	**Ayer**	ah-*yer*
Today	**Hoy**	oy
Tomorrow	**Mañana**	mahn-*yawn*-ah
Good	**Bueno**	*bway*-no
Bad	**Malo**	*mah*-lo
Better (best)	**(Lo) Mejor**	(loh) meh-*hor*
More	**Más**	mahs
Less	**Menos**	*may*-noss
No Smoking	**Se prohibe fumar**	seh pro-*hee*-beh foo-*mahr*
Postcard	**Tarjeta postal**	tahr-*hay*-ta pohs-*tahl*
Insect repellent	**Rapellante contra insectos**	rah-pey-*yahn*-te *cohn*-trah een-*sehk*-tos

1	**uno** (*ooh*-noh)	15	**quince** (*keen*-say)	60	**sesenta** (say-*sen*-tah)
2	**dos** (dohs)	16	**dieciseis** (de-ess-ee-*sayss*)	70	**setenta** (say-*ten*-tah)
3	**tres** (trayss)	17	**diecisiete** (de-ess-ee-see-*ay*-tay)	80	**ochenta** (oh-*chen*-tah)
4	**cuatro** (*kwah*-troh)	18	**dieciocho** (dee-ess-ee-*oh*-choh)	90	**noventa** (noh-*ben*-tah)
5	**cinco** (*seen*-koh)	19	**diecinueve** (dee-ess-ee-*nway*-bay)	100	**cien** (see-*en*)
6	**seis** (sayss)	20	**viente** (*bayn*-tay)	200	**doscientos** (dos-se-*en*-tos)
7	**siete** (*syeh*-tay)	30	**treinta** (*trayn*-tah)	500	**quinientos** (keen-ee-*ehn*-tos)
8	**ocho** (*oh*-choh)	40	**cuarenta** (kwah-*ren*-tah)	1,000	**mil** (meal)
9	**nueve** (*nway*-bay)	50	**cincuenta** (seen-*kwen*-tah)		
10	**diez** (dee-*ess*)				
11	**once** (*ohn*-say)				
12	**doce** (*doh*-say)				
13	**trece** (*tray*-say)				
14	**catorce** (kah-*tor*-say)				

USEFUL PHRASES

Do you speak English? **¿Habla usted inglés?**

Is there anyone here who speaks English? **¿Hay alguien aquí qué hable inglés?**

I don't understand Spanish very well. **No lo entiendo muy bien el español.**

What time is it? **¿Qué hora es?**

May I see your menu? **¿Puedo ver su menú?**

The check, please. **La cuenta, por favor.**

Do you accept traveler's checks? **¿Acepta usted cheques de viajero?**

What did you say? **¿Mande?** (colloquial expression for American "Eh?")

I want (to see) a room. **Quiero (ver) un cuarto (una habitación).**

for two persons **para dos personas**

with (without) bath **con (sin) baño**

We are staying here only one night (one week). **Nos quedaremos aqui solamente una noche (una semana).**

We are leaving tomorrow. **Partimos mañana.**

What do I owe you? **¿Cuanto lo debo?**

BUS TERMS

Autobús Bus
Camión Bus or truck
Carril Lane
Directo Nonstop
Equipajes Baggage (claim area)
Foraneo Intercity
Guarda equipaje Luggage storage area
Llegadas Gates
Local Originates at this station

De Paso Originates elsewhere; stops if seats available
Primera First (class)
Recibo de Equipajes Baggage-claim area
Sala de Espera Waiting room
Sanitarios Toilets
Segunda Second (class)
Sin Escala Nonstop
Taquilla Ticket window

POSTAL TERMS

Aduana Customs
Apdo. Postal Post office box (abbreviation)
Buzón Mailbox
Correo Aéreo Airmail
Correos Postal service
Entrega Inmediata Special Delivery, Express

Estampilla or Timbre Stamp
Giro Postal Money order
Lista de Correos General Delivery
Oficina de Correos Post office
Paquete Parcel
Registrado Registered mail
Seguros Insurance (insured mail)
Sello Rubber stamp

B. MENU SAVVY

BREAKFAST [DESAYUNO]

Jugo de naranja Orange juice
Café con crema Coffee with cream
Pan tostada Toast
Mermelada Jam
Leche Milk
Té Tea
Huevos Eggs
Huevos cocidos Hard-boiled eggs

Huevos poches Poached eggs
Huevos fritos Fried eggs
Huevos pasados al agua Soft-boiled eggs
Huevos revueltos Scrambled eggs
Tocino Bacon
Jamón Ham

LUNCH, SUPPER & DINNER [ALMUERZO, COMIDA & CENA]

SOUP [SOPA]

Caldo Broth
Caldo de pollo Chicken broth
Menudo Tripe soup
Sopa clara Consommé

Sopa de lentejas Lentil soup
Sopa de chicharos Pea soup
Sopa de medula Bone-marrow soup

SEAFOOD [MARISCOS]

Almejas Clams
Anchoas Anchovies
Arenques Herring
Atún Tuna
Bagre Catfish
Cabrilla Black sea bass
Calamares Squid
Camarones Shrimp
Caracoles Snails
Corvina Bass
Dorado Dolphinfish
Huachinango Red snapper
Jaiba Crab
Jurel Yellowtail
Langosta Lobster
Lenguado Sole
Lobina Black bass

Macabi Bonefish
Marlin azul Blue marlin
Marlin blanco White marlin
Marlin rayado Striped marlin
Mero Grouper
Mojarra Perch
Ostiones Oysters
Pescado Fish
Pez espada Swordfish
Pez vela Sailfish
Robalo Sea bass/snook
Sabalo Tarpon
Salmón Salmon
Salmón ahumado Smoked salmon
Sardinas Sardines
Solo Pike
Trucha arco iris Rainbow trout

MEATS [CARNES]

Ahumado Smoked
Alambre Shish kebab
Albóndigas Meatballs
Aves Poultry
Bistec Steak
Cabrito Kid (goat)
Callos Tripe
Carne Meat
Carne fría Cold cuts
Cerdo Pork
Chiles rellenos Stuffed peppers
Chicharrones Pig's skin cracklings
Chorizo Spicy sausage
Chuleta Chop
Chuleta de carnero Mutton chop
Chuletas de cordero Lamb chops
Chuletas de puerco Pork chops
Conejo Rabbit
Cordero Lamb
Costillas de cerdo Spareribs

Faisán Pheasant
Filete de ternera Filet of veal
Filete milanesa Breaded veal chops
Ganso Goose
Hígado Liver
Jamón Ham
Lengua Tongue
Lomo Loin
Paloma Pigeon
Pato Duck
Pavo Turkey
Pechuga Chicken breast
Perdiz Partridge
Pierna Leg
Pollo Chicken
Res Beef
Salchichas Sausages
Ternera Veal
Tocino Bacon
Venado Venison

VEGETABLES [LEGUMBRES]

Aguacate Avocado
Aceitunas Olives
Betabeles Beets
Cebolla Onions
Champinones Mushrooms
Chicharos Peas
Col Cabbage
Coliflor Cauliflower
Ejotes String beans

Elote Corn (maize)
Esparragos Asparagus
Espinaca Spinach
Frijoles Beans
Hongos Mushroom
Jícama Potato/turnip-like vegetable
Lechuga Lettuce
Lentejas Lentils
Papas Potatoes

Pepino Cucumber
Rabanos Radishes
Tomate Tomato

Verduras Greens, vegetables
Zanahorias Carrots

SALADS [ENSALADAS]

Ensalada de apio Celery salad
Ensalada de frutas Fruit salad
Ensalada mixta Mixed salad
Ensalada de pepinos Cucumber
    salad

Guacamole Avacado salad
Lechuga Lettuce salad

FRUITS [FRUTAS]

Chavacano Apricot
Ciruela Prune
Coco Coconut
Durazno Peach
Frambuesa Raspberry
Fresas con crema Strawberries with
    cream
Fruta cocida Stewed fruit
Granada Pomegranate
Guanabana Green pearlike fruit
Guayaba Guava
Higos Figs

Lima Lime
Limón Lemon
Mamey Sweet orange fruit
Mango Mango
Manzana Apple
Naranja Orange
Pera Pear
Piña Pineapple
Platano Banana
Tuna Prickly pear fruit
Uva Grape
Zapote Sweet brown fruit

DESSERTS [POSTRES]

Arroz con leche Rice pudding
Brunelos de fruta Fruit tart
Coctel de aguacate Avocado
    cocktail
Coctel de frutas Fruit cocktail
Compota Stewed fruit
Fruta Fruit
Flan Custard

Galletas Crackers or cookies
Helado Ice cream
Nieve Sherbet
Pastel Cake or pastry
Queso Cheese
Torta Cake
Yogurt Yogurt

BEVERAGES [BEBIDAS]

Agua Water
Brandy Brandy
Café Coffee
Café con crema Coffee with cream
Café de olla Coffee with cinnamon
    and sugar
Café negro Black coffee
Cerveza Beer
Ginebra Gin
Hielo Ice
Jerez Sherry
Jugo de naranja Orange juice
Jugo de tomate Tomato juice
Jugo de toronja Grapefruit juice
Leche Milk

Licores Liqueurs
Manzanita Apple juice
Refrescos Soft drinks
Ron Rum
Sidra Cider
Sifón Soda
Té Tea
Vaso de leche Glass of milk
Vino blanco White wine
Vino tinto Red wine

CONDIMENTS & CUTLERY

Aceite Oil
Ajo Garli
Azúcar Sugar
Bolillo Roll
Copa Goblet
Cilantro Coriander
Cuchara Spoon
Cuchillo Knife
Manteca Lard
Mantequilla Butter

Mostaza Mustard
Pan Bread
Pimienta Pepper
Sal Salt
Sopa de arroz Plain rice
Taza Cup
Tenedor Fork
Tostada Toast
Vinagre Vinegar
Vaso Glass

PREPARATIONS

A la parrilla Grilled
Al horno Baked
Asado Roasted
Bien cocido Well done
Cocido Cooked
Cocina casera Home cooking
Empanado Breaded

Frito Fried
Milanesa Italian breaded
Poco cocido Rare
Tampiqueño Long strip of thinly sliced meat
Veracruzana Tomato, garlic, and onion-topped

MENU ITEMS

Agua fresca Fruit-flavored water, usually watermelon, cantaloupe, chia seed with lemon, hibiscus flower, or ground melon-seed mixture

Antojito A Mexican snack, usually masa based with a variety of toppings such as sausage, cheese, beans, onions; also refers to tostadas, sopes, and garnachas

Atole A thick, lightly sweet, warm drink made with finely ground rice or corn and flavored usually with vanilla; often found mornings and evenings at markets

Botana A light Mexican snack—an antojito

Buñelos Round, thin, deep-fried crispy fritters dipped in sugar or dribbled with honey

Burrito A large flour tortilla stuffed with beans or sometimes potatoes and onions

Cajeta Caramelized cow or goat milk often used in dessert crêpes

Carnitas Pork that's been deep-cooked (not fried) in lard, then steamed and served with corn tortillas for tacos

Caviar de Chapala Carp eggs, usually seasoned and fried and made into tacos or soup

Ceviche Fresh raw seafood marinated in fresh lime juice and garnished with chopped tomatoes, onions, chiles, and sometimes cilantro and served with crispy, fried whole corn tortillas

Chayote Vegetable pear or mirliton, a type of spiny squash boiled and served as an accompaniment to meat dishes

Chiles rellenos Poblano peppers usually stuffed with cheese, rolled in a batter and baked; but other stuffings may include ground beef spiced with raisins

Chorizo A spicy red pork sausage, flavored with different chiles and sometimes with achiote, or cumin and other spices

Churro Tube-shaped bread fritter, dipped in sugar and sometimes filled with cajeta or chocolate

Cilantro An herb grown from the coriander seed, chopped and used in salsas and soups

Enchilada Tortilla dipped in a sauce and usually filled with chicken or white cheese and sometimes topped with tomato sauce and sour cream (enchiladas suizas—Swiss enchiladas) or covered in a green sauce (enchiladas verdes) or topped with onions, sour cream, and guacamole (enchiladas potosiños)

Frijoles refritos Pinto beans mashed and cooked with lard

Gorditas Thickish fried corn tortillas, slit and stuffed with choice of cheese, beans, beef, chicken, with or without lettuce, tomato, and onion garnish

Guacamole Mashed avocado, plain or mixed with onions and other spices

Horchata Refreshing drink made of ground rice or melon seeds, ground almonds, and lightly sweetened

Huevos mexicanos Scrambled eggs with onions, hot peppers, and tomatoes

Huevos rancheros Fried egg on top of a fried corn tortilla covered in a tomato sauce

Manchamantel Translated means "tablecloth stainer," a stew of chicken or pork with chiles, tomatoes, pineapple, bananas, and jícama

Masa Ground corn soaked in lime used as basis for tamales, corn tortillas, and soups

Mixiote Lamb or chicken baked with carrots, potatoes, and sauce in parchment paper from a maguey leaf

Mole Pronounced "*moh*-lay," a sauce made with 20 ingredients including chocolate, peppers, ground tortillas, sesame seeds, cinnamon, tomatoes, onion, garlic, peanuts, pumpkin seeds, cloves, and tomatillos; developed by colonial nuns in Puebla, usually served over chicken or turkey

Molletes A bolillo cut in half and topped with refried beans and cheese, then broiled; popular at breakfast

Pan de muerto Sweet or plain bread made around the Days of the Dead (November 1–2), in the form of mummies, dolls, or round with bone designs

Pan dulce Lightly sweetened bread in many configurations, usually served at breakfast or bought at any bakery

Papadzules Tortillas stuffed with hard-boiled eggs and seeds (cucumber or sunflower) in a tomato sauce

Pibil Pit-baked pork or chicken in a sauce of tomato, onion, mild red pepper, cilantro, and vinegar

Pipian Sauce made with ground pumpkin seeds, nuts, and mild peppers

Pozole A soup made with hominy and pork or chicken, in green chile sauce and topped with choice of chopped white onion, lettuce or cabbage, radishes, oregano, red pepper, and cilantro

Pulque Drink made of fermented sap of the maguey plant

Quesadilla Flour tortilla stuffed with melted white cheese and lightly fried or warmed

Salsa mexicana Sauce of fresh chopped tomatoes, white onions, and cilantro with a bit of oil; on tables all over Mexico

Salsa verde A cooked sauce using the green tomatillo and puréed with mildly hot peppers, onions, garlic, and cilantro; on tables countrywide

Sopa de calabaza Soup made of chopped squash or pumpkin blossoms

Sopa seca Not a soup at all, but a seasoned rice, which translated means "dry soup"

Sopa Tlalpeña A hearty soup made with chunks of chicken, chopped carrots, zucchini, corn, onions, garlic, and cilantro

Sopa tortilla A traditional chicken broth–based soup, seasoned with chiles, tomatoes, onion, and garlic, bobbing with crisp fried strips of corn tortillas

Sope Pronounced "*soh*-pay," a botana similar to a garnacha, except spread with refried beans and topped with crumbled cheese and onions

Tacos al pastor Thin slices of flavored pork roasted on a revolving cylinder dripping with onion slices and juice of fresh pineapple slice

Tamal Incorrectly called tamale (*tamal* singular, *tamales* plural), meat or sweet filling rolled with fresh masa then wrapped in a corn husk, a corn or banana leaf and steamed; many varieties and sizes throughout the country

Tikin xic Also seen on menus as "tikin chick," charbroiled fish brushed with achiote sauce

Torta Sandwich, usually on bolillo bread, usually with sliced avocado, onions, tomatoes, with a choice of meat and often cheese

Tostadas Crispy fried corn tortillas topped with meat, onions, lettuce, tomatoes, cheese, avocados, and sometimes sour cream

C. CONVERSION TABLES

METRIC MEASURES

Length

1 millimeter	=	0.04 inches (or less than ¹⁄₁₆ in)
1 centimeter	=	0.39 inches (or just under ½ in)
1 meter	=	1.09 yards (or about 39 inches)
1 kilometer	=	0.62 miles (or about ⅔ of a mile)

To convert kilometers to miles, multiply the number of kilometers by .62 (for example, 25 km × .62 = 15.5 mi).

To convert miles to kilometers, multiply the number of miles by 1.61 (for example, 50 mi × 1.61 = 80.5 km).

Capacity

1 liter   =   33.92 fluid ounces or 1.06 quarts or 0.26 gallons

To convert liters to gallons, multiply the number of liters by 0.26 (for example, 50 liters × .26 = 13 gallons).

To convert gallons to liters, multiply the number of gallons by 3.79 (for example, 10 gal × 3.79 = 37.9 liters).

Weight

1 gram	=	0.04 ounces (or about a paperclip's weight)
1 kilogram	=	2.2 pounds

To convert kilograms to pounds, multiply the number of kilograms by 2.2 (for example, 75kg × 2.2 = 165 pounds).

To convert pounds to kilograms, multiply the number of pounds by .045 (for example, 90 lb × .45 = 40.5 kg).

Temperature

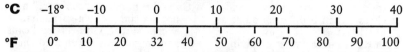

To convert degrees C to degrees F, multiply degrees C by 9, divide by 5, and add 32 (for example, ⅑ × 20°C + 32 = 68°F).

To convert degrees F to degrees C, subtract 32 from degrees F, then multiply by 5, and divide by 9 (for example, 85°F − 32 × ⅑ = 29°C).

CLOTHING SIZE EQUIVALENTS

You'll want to try on clothing you intend to buy, but here are some equivalents in case you're buying gifts for friends. Note that women's blouse sizes are the same in the U.S. and Mexico.

WOMEN'S DRESS

U.S.	6	8	10	12	14	16	18	20	22
Mex.	36	38	40	42	44	46	48	50	52

WOMEN'S SHOES

U.S.	5	5.5	6	6.5	7	7.5	8	8.5	9
Mex.	35	35.5	36	36.5	37	37.5	38	38.5	39

MEN'S COLLAR

U.S.	14	14.5	15	15.5	16	16.5	17	17.5	18
Mex.	36	37	38	39	40	41	42	43	44

MEN'S JACKET

U.S.	38	40	42	44	46	48	50	52	54
Mex.	48	50	52	54	56	58	60	62	64

MEN'S SHOES

U.S.	8	8.5	9	9.5	10	10.5	11	11.5	12
Mex.	41	41.5	42	42.5	43	43.5	44	44.5	45

INDEX

Moctezuma, 9, 17, 25, 196, 206
Money, 34–38. *See also* Currency and exchange
wiring funds, 72
Morelos y Pavón, José María, 11, 17, 127, 198
Moros y Cristianos (regional dance), 130
Mosquitoes, 43, 44
Municipal Palace (Tixtla), 133
Murals and muralists
Chilpancingo: Museo Regional (Robert
Cueva), 121
Cuernavaca
Cortés Palace (Diego Rivera), 198
Palacio Municipal (Robert Cueva), 199
history of, 20, 21–22
Tixtla: Municipal Palace (Jaime Gómez del
Payón), 133
Museo Arqueología Carlos Pellicer (Tepoztlán),
201
Museo Casa Robert Brady (Cuernavaca), 199
Museo de Cuauhnahuac (Cuernavaca),
197–98
Museo de la Herbolaria (Cuernavaca), 200
Museo de la Resistencia Indigenista
(Ixcateopan), 195
Museo de Plata (Taxco), 187–88
Museo de Taxco Guillermo Spratling (Taxco),
188
Museo Gráfico de la Historia Social de Taxco en
el Siglo XX (Taxco), 189
Museo Histórico de Acapulco, 112
Museo Minería (Tehuilotepec), 190
Museo Regional (Chilpancingo), 121
Museo Virreynal de Taxco (Taxco), 21,
188–89
Music, 25–26
recordings, 31
Mythology, 3, 23–24

Nahua Indians, 8, 24–25
Napoléon III, 11
Newsletters, 33, 46
Newspapers, 69

OLINALÁ, 118, 136–40
accommodations, 138–39
climate, 136–37
currency exchange, 137
lacquerware of, 129, 136, 137–38
restaurants, 139–40
shopping in, 137–38
sightseeing, 137–38
telephone, 137
traveling to, 136
Olmecs, 3, 6–7, 19, 121, 125
Ometeotl, 24
Onyx, 65

Package tours, 53
Packing for your trip, 45
Pancho Villa (Doroteo Arango), 12, 18
PAPANOA, 170

Parasailing
Acapulco, 111
Ixtapa/Zihuatanejo, 166
Paz, Octavio, 23
Pedro, San, 39
Peoples, 24–25. *See also specific peoples*
books about, 29
Petrol, 58–59, 138, 146
Pets, 69
Photography
cameras and film, 66
restrictions on, 69, 119
PIE DE LA CUESTA, 116–17
accommodations, 117
Planning and preparing for your trip, 32–72
Playa Caleta (Acapulco), 109
Playa Caletilla (Acapulco), 109
Playa Larga (Acapulco), 109–10
PLAYA LA ROPA, 145, 156–58, 163, 165, 166
PLAYA MADERA, 145, 154, 156, 163, 165
Police, 38, 69
Politics, 13–14
Postclassic Period (A.D. 900-1500), 8–9. *See also*
Aztecs
Pottery, 65
Acatlán, 132
Atzacualoya, 132
Chilapa, 129
history of, 20
San Augustín Oapan, 125, 126
Tlapa, 141
Xalitla (Chalitla), 125
Preclassic Period (1500 B.C.-A.D. 300), 3,
6–7. *See also* Olmecs
Prices, 69
Puerto Marquéz Bay (Acapulco), 110

Quetzalcoatl, 9, 23, 24

Rebozos, 65, 119
Recordings, 31
Religion, 3, 23
Restaurants. *See list of individual establishments
at end of Index*
menu terms, 213–18
Restrooms, 69
Retirees, 46
RÍO BALSAS, 2
riverboat race, 2
Rivera, Diego, 17, 21
Cortés Palace (Cuernavaca), murals in, 198
ROQUETA ISLAND, 110
RVs (recreational vehicles), 61

Safety, 69–70, 77–78, 147, 176
SAN AUGUSTÍN OAPAN, 126
Santa Anna, Antonio López de, 18
Santa Prisca y San Sebastián (Taxco), 15, 21,
186–87
books about, 29, 30
Scams, 37–38, 70, 176

ACCOMMODATIONS

ACAPULCO

Acapulco Dolphins Hotel (Icacos Beach area, M), 87
Acapulco Princess (south of town, VE), 79, 82
Acapulco Ritz Hotel (Papagayo Park area, M), 90, 92
Acapulco Sheraton Resort (south of town, E), 83–84
Calinda Acapulco Quality Inn (Condesa Beach area, E), 88
Camino Real Diamante (south of town, VE), 82–83
Continental Plaza Acapulco (Condesa Beach area, E), 88–89
Fiesta Americana Condesa Acapulco (Condesa Beach area, E), 89–90

Hotel Acapulco Tortuga (Condesa Beach area, M), 90
Hotel Asturias (Zócalo area, B), 93
Hotel Belmar (near Playas Caleta & Caletilla, B), 96
Hotel Boca Chica (near Playas Caleta & Caletilla, M), 95–96
Hotel del Valle (Papagayo Park area, B), 93
Hotel el Cano (Icacos Beach area, E), 86–87
Hotel Howard Johnson Maralisa (Papagayo Park area, M), 92
Hotel Isabel (Zócalo area, B), 93
Hotel la Palapa (Icacos Beach area, M), 87–88
Hotel Lindavista (near Playas Caleta & Caletilla, B), 96

Key to abbreviations B = Budget; E = Expensive; M = Moderately priced; VE = Very expensive.

RESTAURANTS

Now Save Money on All Your Travels by Joining
FROMMER'S ™ TRAVEL BOOK CLUB
The World's Best Travel Guides at Membership Prices

FROMMER'S TRAVEL BOOK CLUB is your ticket to successful travel! Open up a world of travel information and simplify your travel planning when you join ranks with thousands of value-conscious travelers who are members of the FROMMER'S TRAVEL BOOK CLUB. Join today and you'll be entitled to all the privileges that come from belonging to the club that offers you travel guides for less to more than 100 destinations worldwide. Annual membership is only $25 (U.S.) or $35 (Canada and foreign).

The Advantages of Membership

1. Your choice of *three* free FROMMER'S TRAVEL GUIDES (any *two* FROM-MER'S COMPREHENSIVE GUIDES, FROMMER'S $-A-DAY GUIDES, FROMMER'S WALKING TOURS *or* FROMMER'S FAMILY GUIDES—plus *one* FROMMER'S CITY GUIDE, FROMMER'S CITY $-A-DAY GUIDE *or* FROMMER'S TOURING GUIDE).
2. Your own subscription to **TRIPS AND TRAVEL** quarterly newsletter.
3. You're entitled to a **30% discount** on your order of any additional books offered by FROMMER'S TRAVEL BOOK CLUB.
4. You're offered (at a small additional fee) our **Domestic Trip-Routing Kits.**

Our quarterly newsletter **TRIPS AND TRAVEL** offers practical information on the best buys in travel, the "hottest" vacation spots, the latest travel trends, world-class events and much, much more.
Our **Domestic Trip-Routing Kits** are available for any North American destination. We'll send you a detailed map highlighting the best route to take to your destination—you can request direct or scenic routes.

Here's all you have to do to join:

Send in your membership fee of $25 ($35 Canada and foreign) with your name and address on the form below along with your selections as part of your membership package to **FROMMER'S TRAVEL BOOK CLUB, P.O. Box 473, Mt. Morris, IL 61054-0473.** Remember to check off your *three* free books.
If you would like to order additional books, please select the books you would like and send a check for the total amount (please add sales tax in the states noted below), plus $2 per book for shipping and handling ($3 per book for foreign orders) to:

FROMMER'S TRAVEL BOOK CLUB
P.O. Box 473
Mt. Morris, IL 61054-0473
(815) 734-1104

[ ] **YES.** I want to take advantage of this opportunity to join FROMMER'S TRAVEL BOOK CLUB.
[ ] **My check is enclosed.** Dollar amount enclosed_____*
(all payments in U.S. funds only)

Name_____
Address_____
City_____ State_____ Zip_____
All orders must be prepaid.

To ensure that all orders are processed efficiently, please apply sales tax in the following areas: CA, CT, FL, IL, NJ, NY, TN, WA and CANADA.

*With membership, shipping and handling will be paid by FROMMER'S TRAVEL BOOK CLUB for the three free books you select as part of your membership. Please add $2 per book for shipping and handling for any additional books purchased ($3 per book for foreign orders).

Allow 4–6 weeks for delivery. Prices of books, membership fee, and publication dates are subject to change without notice. Prices are subject to acceptance and availability.

AC1

Please Send Me the Books Checked Below:

FROMMER'S COMPREHENSIVE GUIDES
(Guides listing facilities from budget to deluxe,
with emphasis on the medium-priced)

	Retail Price	Code		Retail Price	Code
☐ Acapulco/Ixtapa/Taxco 1993–94	$15.00	C120	☐ Japan 1994–95 (Avail. 3/94)	$19.00	C144
☐ Alaska 1994–95	$17.00	C131	☐ Morocco 1992–93	$18.00	C021
☐ Arizona 1993–94	$18.00	C101	☐ Nepal 1994–95	$18.00	C126
☐ Australia 1992–93	$18.00	C002	☐ New England 1994 (Avail. 1/94)	$16.00	C137
☐ Austria 1993–94	$19.00	C119	☐ New Mexico 1993–94	$15.00	C117
☐ Bahamas 1994–95	$17.00	C121	☐ New York State 1994–95	$19.00	C133
☐ Belgium/Holland/ Luxembourg 1993–94	$18.00	C106	☐ Northwest 1994–95 (Avail. 2/94)	$17.00	C140
☐ Bermuda 1994–95	$15.00	C122	☐ Portugal 1994–95 (Avail. 2/94)	$17.00	C141
☐ Brazil 1993–94	$20.00	C111	☐ Puerto Rico 1993–94	$15.00	C103
☐ California 1994	$15.00	C134	☐ Puerto Vallarta/Manzanillo/ Guadalajara 1994–95 (Avail. 1/94)	$14.00	C028
☐ Canada 1994–95 (Avail. 4/94)	$19.00	C145	☐ Scandinavia 1993–94	$19.00	C135
☐ Caribbean 1994	$18.00	C123	☐ Scotland 1994–95 (Avail. 4/94)	$17.00	C146
☐ Carolinas/Georgia 1994–95	$17.00	C128	☐ South Pacific 1994–95 (Avail. 1/94)	$20.00	C138
☐ Colorado 1994–95 (Avail. 3/94)	$16.00	C143	☐ Spain 1993–94	$19.00	C115
☐ Cruises 1993–94	$19.00	C107	☐ Switzerland/Liechtenstein 1994–95 (Avail. 1/94)	$19.00	C139
☐ Delaware/Maryland 1994–95 (Avail. 1/94)	$15.00	C136	☐ Thailand 1992–93	$20.00	C033
☐ England 1994	$18.00	C129	☐ U.S.A. 1993–94	$19.00	C116
☐ Florida 1994	$18.00	C124	☐ Virgin Islands 1994–95	$13.00	C127
☐ France 1994–95	$20.00	C132	☐ Virginia 1994–95 (Avail. 2/94)	$14.00	C142
☐ Germany 1994	$19.00	C125	☐ Yucatán 1993–94	$18.00	C110
☐ Italy 1994	$19.00	C130			
☐ Jamaica/Barbados 1993–94	$15.00	C105			

FROMMER'S $-A-DAY GUIDES
(Guides to low-cost tourist accommodations and facilities)

	Retail Price	Code		Retail Price	Code
☐ Australia on $45 1993–94	$18.00	D102	☐ Israel on $45 1993–94	$18.00	D101
☐ Costa Rica/Guatemala/ Belize on $35 1993–94	$17.00	D108	☐ Mexico on $45 1994	$19.00	D116
☐ Eastern Europe on $30 1993–94	$18.00	D110	☐ New York on $70 1994–95 (Avail. 4/94)	$16.00	D120
☐ England on $60 1994	$18.00	D112	☐ New Zealand on $45 1993–94	$18.00	D103
☐ Europe on $50 1994	$19.00	D115	☐ Scotland/Wales on $50 1992–93	$18.00	D019
☐ Greece on $45 1993–94	$19.00	D100	☐ South America on $40 1993–94	$19.00	D109
☐ Hawaii on $75 1994	$19.00	D113	☐ Turkey on $40 1992–93	$22.00	D023
☐ India on $40 1992–93	$20.00	D010	☐ Washington, D.C. on $40 1994–95 (Avail. 2/94)	$17.00	D119
☐ Ireland on $45 1994–95 (Avail. 1/94)	$17.00	D117			

FROMMER'S CITY $-A-DAY GUIDES
(Pocket-size guides to low-cost tourist accommodations
and facilities)

	Retail Price	Code		Retail Price	Code
☐ Berlin on $40 1994–95	$12.00	D111	☐ Madrid on $50 1994–95 (Avail. 1/94)	$13.00	D118
☐ Copenhagen on $50 1992–93	$12.00	D003	☐ Paris on $50 1994–95	$12.00	D117
☐ London on $45 1994–95	$12.00	D114	☐ Stockholm on $50 1992–93	$13.00	D022

FROMMER'S WALKING TOURS

(With routes and detailed maps, these companion guides point out the places and pleasures that make a city unique)

	Retail Price	Code		Retail Price	Code
☐ Berlin	$12.00	W100	☐ Paris	$12.00	W103
☐ London	$12.00	W101	☐ San Francisco	$12.00	W104
☐ New York	$12.00	W102	☐ Washington, D.C.	$12.00	W105

FROMMER'S TOURING GUIDES

(Color-illustrated guides that include walking tours, cultural and historic sights, and practical information)

	Retail Price	Code		Retail Price	Code
☐ Amsterdam	$11.00	T001	☐ New York	$11.00	T008
☐ Barcelona	$14.00	T015	☐ Rome	$11.00	T010
☐ Brazil	$11.00	T003	☐ Scotland	$10.00	T011
☐ Florence	$ 9.00	T005	☐ Sicily	$15.00	T017
☐ Hong Kong/Singapore/			☐ Tokyo	$15.00	T016
Macau	$11.00	T006	☐ Turkey	$11.00	T013
☐ Kenya	$14.00	T018	☐ Venice	$ 9.00	T014
☐ London	$13.00	T007			

FROMMER'S FAMILY GUIDES

	Retail Price	Code		Retail Price	Code
☐ California with Kids	$18.00	F100	☐ San Francisco with Kids (Avail. 4/94)	$17.00	F104
☐ Los Angeles with Kids (Avail. 4/94)	$17.00	F103	☐ Washington, D.C. with Kids (Avail. 2/94)	$17.00	F102
☐ New York City with Kids (Avail. 2/94)	$18.00	F101			

FROMMER'S CITY GUIDES

(Pocket-size guides to sightseeing and tourist accommodations and facilities in all price ranges)

	Retail Price	Code		Retail Price	Code
☐ Amsterdam 1993–94	$13.00	S110	☐ Montréal/Québec City 1993–94	$13.00	S125
☐ Athens 1993–94	$13.00	S114	☐ Nashville/Memphis 1994–95 (Avail. 4/94)	$13.00	S141
☐ Atlanta 1993–94	$13.00	S112	☐ New Orleans 1993–94	$13.00	S103
☐ Atlantic City/Cape May 1993–94	$13.00	S130	☐ New York 1994 (Avail. 1/94)	$13.00	S138
☐ Bangkok 1992–93	$13.00	S005	☐ Orlando 1994	$13.00	S135
☐ Barcelona/Majorca/Minorca/ Ibiza 1993–94	$13.00	S115	☐ Paris 1993–94	$13.00	S109
☐ Berlin 1993–94	$13.00	S116	☐ Philadelphia 1993–94	$13.00	S113
☐ Boston 1993–94	$13.00	S117	☐ San Diego 1993–94	$13.00	S107
☐ Budapest 1994–95 (Avail. 2/94)	$13.00	S139	☐ San Francisco 1994	$13.00	S133
☐ Chicago 1993–94	$13.00	S122	☐ Santa Fe/Taos/ Albuquerque 1993–94	$13.00	S108
☐ Denver/Boulder/Colorado Springs 1993–94	$13.00	S131	☐ Seattle/Portland 1994–95	$13.00	S137
☐ Dublin 1993–94	$13.00	S128	☐ St. Louis/Kansas City 1993–94	$13.00	S127
☐ Hong Kong 1994–95 (Avail. 4/94)	$13.00	S140	☐ Sydney 1993–94	$13.00	S129
☐ Honolulu/Oahu 1994	$13.00	S134	☐ Tampa/St. Petersburg 1993–94	$13.00	S105
☐ Las Vegas 1993–94	$13.00	S121	☐ Tokyo 1992–93	$13.00	S039
☐ London 1994	$13.00	S132	☐ Toronto 1993–94	$13.00	S126
☐ Los Angeles 1993–94	$13.00	S123	☐ Vancouver/Victoria 1994–95 (Avail. 1/94)	$13.00	S142
☐ Madrid/Costa del Sol 1993–94	$13.00	S124	☐ Washington, D.C. 1994 (Avail. 1/94)	$13.00	S136
☐ Miami 1993–94	$13.00	S118			
☐ Minneapolis/St. Paul 1993–94	$13.00	S119			

SPECIAL EDITIONS

	Retail Price	Code		Retail Price	Code
☐ Bed & Breakfast Southwest	$16.00	P100	☐ Caribbean Hideaways	$16.00	P103
☐ Bed & Breakfast Great American Cities (Avail. 1/94)	$16.00	P104	☐ National Park Guide 1994 (avail. 3/94)	$16.00	P105
			☐ Where to Stay U.S.A.	$15.00	P102

Please note: if the availability of a book is several months away, we may have back issues of guides to that particular destination. Call customer service at (815) 734-1104.